Books by Brendan Gill

The Trouble of One House
The Day the Money Stopped
Cole:
   A Book of Cole Porter Lyrics and Memorabilia
Tallulah
Happy Times
Ways of Loving:
   Two Novellas and Eighteen Short Stories
Here at *The New Yorker*
Lindbergh Alone
Summer Places
Many Masks:
   The Life of Frank Lloyd Wright

A New York Life

Of Friends and Others

Brendan Gill

POSEIDON PRESS
New York · London · Toronto · Sydney · Tokyo · Singapore

POSEIDON PRESS
Simon & Schuster Building
Rockefeller Center
1230 Avenue of the Americas
New York, New York 10020

Designed by Edith Fowler
Manufactured in the United States of America

10 9 8 7 6 5 4 3 2 1

Library of Congress Cataloging in Publication Data

Gill, Brendan, date.
  A New York Life : of friends and others / Brendan
    Gill. p. cm.
  1. Celebrities—New York (N.Y.)—Biography.
2. New York (N.Y.)—Biography. 3. Gill, Brendan,
date.—Friends and associates.
I. Title.
F128.25.G55 1990
920.0747—dc20
[B]
                                        90-41129
                                          CIP
ISBN 0-671-69523-1

For Donald Oresman

"Our shelter from the stormy blast."
—ISAAC WATTS (1674–1748)

Contents

FOREWORD   11

Joseph Alsop   15
Ben Sonnenberg   23
Harry Mali   39
Joseph Campbell   46
Louise Nevelson   58
George Plimpton   64
John Betjeman   69
Eleanor Roosevelt   74
Henry-Russell Hitchcock   83
William Adams Delano   88
Yale Kneeland   94
Jay Rousuck   98
Edgar Kaufmann, Jr.   109
Mary and Ben Bodne   114
Padraic Colum   120
André Kertész   123
Brendan Behan   131
Simon Verity   140
Dorothy Parker   144
Wallace K. Harrison   151

The Irish: Barry, O'Neill, Fitzgerald, O'Hara 159
Ellen Stewart 182
Jerome Zerbe 187
Maxwell Anderson 197
Offenbach and Ives 205
Arnold Whitridge 214
Alec Waugh 220
Emma Jane Bowen 224
Georges Simenon 231
Bernard Rudofsky 253
Nigel Nicolson 257
William H. Whyte, Jr. 265
Al Hirschfeld 272
Harold Lloyd 279
Buster Keaton 283
Virgil Thomson 287
Theodore Besterman 292
Ter Fuller 297
Walker Evans 302
Man Ray 306
Gerald and Sara Murphy 312

AFTERWORD 335

Foreword

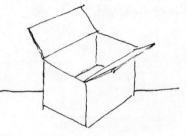

WHEN I WAS five or six years old, my choice of a future career teetered back and forth between architecture and writing. I began to lose interest in the practice of architecture when it turned out that it had much to do with numbers, which I felt alien to. Especially distasteful to me was the discovery, encountered in the course of learning how to add and subtract, that when I subtracted a number in a row of figures from what appeared to be a smaller number in the row above it, I could always "borrow" from an adjacent number in that upper row. Being New England–born and bred, I knew in my bones that borrowing was a sin. No mathematics, no architecture for me!

There remained the bewitching temptation of literature, especially as it was made manifest in the form of metaphors. My mother died when I was seven, but long before that sad event she had introduced me to the magical nature of words, which permits them to stand for several things at once. At a tea party, she served ladyfingers, and I remember asking her, "Are they *really* ladies' fingers?" No, nor did they need to be; they resembled ladies' fingers and so were and were not ladies' fingers. How wonderful! Next came the day when at a dinner party she served chicken à la king. Kings existed in fairy tales; what had a king to do with that speckled red, green, and ivory dish upon our table? As for the merrily lilting "à la"—what on earth could that be? A la *façon du roi?* Words in a

11

different language altogether? Mother, mother, tell me more! And then my father and mother went to the theatre and sat in a box. A box? Why on earth would grown-ups sit in a box, which was something that I kept my toys in? No, no, my darling, not *that* kind of a box. And so my eyes became saucers—yes, saucers—and my heart began to hammer—yes, hammer—and I perceived then and there and once and for all what my Hartford neighbor Wallace Stevens was soon to be setting down as the truth that all writers should live by, to wit: "Words of the world are the life of the world."

A New York Life

Joseph Alsop

THE ALSOPS OF AVON! To many of us who were growing up in Hartford in the early decades of this century, the words had a ring of literary romance about them, for the Alsops were a family that seemed to us fortunate in being settled—rooted forever, or so it seemed—in a given place made sacred to them by the reinforcements of time. In our eyes, they resembled one of those sturdy British dynasties that we were accustomed to encountering in novels, which possessed over many generations a family seat, tucked away among rooky elms, in a water-meadow in some green countryside. It happened that thousands of miles to the west of England, the Alsop farm did indeed lie in a green countryside and did indeed boast elms and a water-meadow running down to the banks of the Farmington River, in a Connecticut township that by chance bore a celebrated English name. From a literary point of view, only the rooks were missing, and in their absence our common American crows would certainly suffice.

Driving out of Hartford along Route 44, one climbed the long eastern slope of Talcott Mountain, then dropped abruptly, by a serpentine, high-crowned, black-tarred road, into the valley of the Farmington River, where, at the junction with Route 10, one glanced to the right to catch sight of the immense cattle barns of the Alsop farm. Beyond the barns lay the big white house that had become in my imagination the

15

Alsops' hereditary "seat." In those days, I knew of the Alsops only by repute. I would hear the name mentioned in conversation among the parents of my school companions—Bill Bulkeley, Pete Carey, Bill Cole—and I would read of them from time to time in the newspapers, for Joseph Alsop, the father of the family, wasn't merely a bluff country squire of the old stripe; he was also, along with his wife, Corinne Robinson Alsop, a member of the state legislature and he was for many years chairman of the state Public Utilities Commission.

Mrs. Alsop was a first cousin of Eleanor Roosevelt and, more significantly, her friend. Because there were so many Roosevelts scattered up and down the Eastern seaboard, it wasn't a rarity to be related to one or another of them (I am reminded of Sacheverell Sitwell's witticism about social life in England: "Sooner or later, almost everyone marries a Guinness"), but to be a friend of Eleanor's was an authentic distinction, at first because she was a niece of a president of the United States and then because she was the wife of the governor of New York and finally because she was the wife of still another president of the United States. Like most proper upper-class folk in Connecticut in those days, the Alsops were Republicans; their Roosevelt cousins were Democrats, but blood was thicker than the mere murky water of politics, and one gathered that the Alsops were prepared to forgive their cousins for having joined the party of the great unwashed outsiders—Irish, Italians, Poles, and the like.

There were four Alsop children: Joseph, Jr., Stewart, John, and Corinne. Stewart was a classmate of mine at Yale and John was a class behind me. Stewart was gentle and John was funny (he and I were members of an informal undergraduate society known as the Pundits, whose purpose, not often achieved, was simply to *be* funny). As for Joe, all I knew of him at the time that Stew and I were graduating from Yale and each in his own way venturing for the first time into the world of journalism, was that he had already successfully entered that world, after having graduated from Groton and Harvard; that he was short and very fat, with a broad, thick-nosed, Netherlandish face and heavy-lidded eyes; that he was extremely snobbish; and that he was thought to be a homosexual.

Of the last of these attributes of Joe Alsop, although it was often hinted at, no direct word was ever spoken in my presence; as far as I am concerned, it remains an hypothesis to this day. (When Joe died, in

1989, even the old-fashioned euphemism that used to serve as a convenience to obituary writers—that the deceased had been a lifelong bachelor—didn't apply; it was a charming story told about Joe that, his closest friend having died at an unexpectedly early age, Joe at fifty chivalrously made haste to marry the widow and become a stepfather to the children, who adored him. Such as it may have been, the marriage lasted a number of years.) In the Hartford of the 1920s, the very word "homosexual" was almost unknown. Playing back the home movie of memory, I realize that when my father, a distinguished physician and surgeon, would say of such-and-such a person that he was "effeminate," he meant to convey to me that that person was a homosexual, but the word itself never crossed his lips. He had spent a couple of years studying medicine in Vienna at the turn of the century, among doctors of whom at least one or two were friends of Freud and who surely discussed with my father the sexual Pandora's box that Freud was then engaged in prising open, but when it came to sex, my father remained as primly inhibited in speech as any Yankee spinster.

I remember the astonishment I felt when, just before the outbreak of the Second World War, the aristocratic Joe consented to write a piece for the *Saturday Evening Post*, then the most popular weekly magazine in America—the magazine of the middle-class American heartland— about how fat he was and how strenuously he had been dieting in order to lose weight. The article was accompanied by photographs: fat Joe and somewhat-less-fat Joe, both taken in profile at full-length in a dark blue suit, before and after. Was it permissible for aristocrats to write about such matters—expose themselves in such photographs—before an audience of bourgeois, gum-chewing rubberneckers? Or was I missing the point? Was it the case that *only* aristocrats could afford to stoop to such practices and not feel in the least embarrassed by them?

Though he remained plump, Joe took care never to regain the "unwieldy corpulency"—Donne's phrase—that he had unluckily achieved in youth. Dark-rimmed spectacles became a sort of trademark of his, and when Art Buchwald wrote a humorous play called *Sheep on the Runway* about a pompous newspaper correspondent making a nuisance of himself in an emergent African nation, the actor who played the role, Martin Gabel, being appropriately short and stocky, had only to put on a pair of spectacles and adopt a certain rasping, hesitant, interrogatory tone of voice to make the likeness to Joe an utterly convincing one. There is no outwitting an aristocrat: Joe affected to be pleased to find himself being caricatured on Broadway.

With a fellow reporter, Robert E. Kintner, Joe launched a syndicated newspaper column that achieved an immediate success. When Kintner moved on to become an executive of the National Broadcasting Company, his place was taken by Stew Alsop. In the long years of "liberal" ascendancy in Washington, the Alsop brothers, true to their heritage, were among the few voices available to the Republican party, but so convincingly had Joe transformed himself into a sharp-tongued, world-weary character in a novel by Evelyn Waugh that one tended to think of him not as an American Republican but as a British Tory. I suspect that his distant cousin Franklin Delano Roosevelt thought of Joe in those terms, and not without amusement—the president had been encountering Tories of Joe's type up and down the Hudson River valley all his life, as well as at Groton and Harvard. The truth was that FDR liked the type, in part because he perceived that politically he had nothing to fear from them. Moreover, he was bent on saving them from themselves, though they would have hotly denied that any such manifestation of his benevolence was called for. Least of all would they care to be saved by him, an antagonist of all that they believed Groton and Harvard and the Hudson valley stood for. To them he remained a second-rate Mamma's boy, whom they would not have trusted with their money or (before he came down with polio) their women.

Tragically, in his late fifties, Stew Alsop was found to be suffering from an incurable cancer. In a book called *A Stay of Execution*, he wrote about the disease with a candor and an absence of resentment over his imminent demise that an ancient Roman stoic might well have envied. Some years earlier, the brothers had given up their joint proprietorship of the column, with Stew accepting a position on *Newsweek* magazine. After Stew's death, Joe lost interest in the hurly-burly of topical journalism; he was not only middle-aged but content to be middle-aged, wearing the mask—convincing in his case—of a sage in a city of yahoos; his mind was respected, though his opinions were not. (Joe remained a champion of the war in Vietnam to the very end.) He had a snug and pleasing town house in Georgetown, in which he gave dinner parties that one could imagine the ghosts of Adams and Royce and James (William, not Henry) longing to attend; too bad that among the living the standard of a sour aptness of utterance had fallen so low, but Joe was doing his best to uphold that standard. He became a scholarly amateur in the field of art history. Like Edmund Wilson's speculations about the Dead Sea Scrolls, Joe's speculations about the rise and sudden end of the ancient Minoan culture were published in *The New Yorker* and gave him a reputation as a popularizer—a species of writer that the popularizer Roger Kennedy calls, with tongue in cheek, "that noblest of creatures." As he grew older, Joe turned, as most writers do, inward; he began to recount telltale anecdotes about his own kind, which he defined as the "Wasp Ascendancy."

Reading a portion of these memoirs in the *New York Review of Books* brought me round on the Great Circle route of memory to my last glimpse of Joe, a few summers ago, at the Knickerbocker Club in New York. By chance, Joe and I, returning from Europe by plane, had encountered each other in the vexing chaos of the customs shed at Kennedy airport. It was a Sunday night in August, and we agreed to share a taxi into New York and enjoy a nightcap together at his club, the "Knick." When we got to the clubhouse, it proved to be locked. Ringing the front-door bell, we roused a night porter, who admitted us with much under-his-breath grumbling. The bar was closed, the lights had been turned off in most of the rooms, and there were no other members in the clubhouse. Joe was every bit as practiced at grumbling as the night porter was and had a more extensive vocabulary for the purpose; nevertheless, he had offered to play host and he did his best not to lose his temper. He had a locker in the bowels of the club, from which, fumbling with a key in the gloom, he extracted a bottle of Scotch, which we carried upstairs. Not without difficulty, two glasses were located in a pantry, and we settled ourselves in the depths of comfortable chairs in the library. Beyond the big Georgian windows of the clubhouse, Fifth Avenue was brilliantly lighted and deserted, and beyond the avenue lay the sumptuous darkness of Central Park.

Fatigued by the flight and irritated by the lack of service at the club, what would we be bound to talk about if not the decline and fall of civilization? Which is to say, of course (for we were not totally out of touch with reality), the decline and fall of the tiny portion of twentieth-century civilization that we had both been in a position to observe. Why had the Wasp Ascendancy lost its grip? What had become of that sense of continuity by means of which, in the Connecticut in which we had both grown up, a certain class had maintained its firm hold on the reins of governance, both financial and political? When Governor Morgan Bulkeley, grandfather of my Yale classmates Morgan and Bill Bulkeley, had disapproved of a measure about to be voted on by the state legislature, he had simply locked the members of the legislature out of the state capitol building. Somewhat less high-handedly but with the same self-assurance, when a U.S. senator from Connecticut, Frank Brandegee, committed suicide, Governor Hiram Bingham (father of still another Yale classmate of mine, the late Jonathan Bingham) had promptly appointed himself senator to take the dead man's place. Responsibilities were accepted, carried out, and handed on. My father was a member of the board of directors of a couple of Hartford banks; when he died, my elder brother was elected in his place. Critics called such boards "self-perpetuating"; they frowned on family "legacies" of this nature, but Joe and I, on that gloomy Sunday evening at the Knick, were sure that much good had resulted from the process and that its disappearance was to be deplored. We groaned and growled and griped and drank our Scotch, feeling all the better for having made ourselves feel worse than we had any true reason to feel. Two aging Jeremiahs, we stumped out onto the avenue and said our goodbyes. Behind us, the night porter slammed the clubhouse door hard, thus gaining, in his fashion, the last word.

Recently, and for the first time in many years, I drove from Hartford out over Talcott Mountain and down the great curve of Route 44—multilaned concrete now, instead of the old narrow high-crowned black asphalt—into the valley of the Farmington River. In Avon, at the foot of the mountain, I glanced to the right to catch sight of the Alsop cattle barns; they had vanished without a trace. As for the broad pastures beside the river, on which the Alsop cattle had grazed, they had been transformed into a public golf course, called the Bel Campo. (As I was afterward to learn, it bears an Italian name because among the members of the syndicate that bought the property and built the golf course are several descendants of Italian immigrants who had been laborers on the Alsop farm.)

In Avon, I stopped at the house of a friend, one who had long been intimate with the Alsops, and in the course of my visit discovered that much that I had assumed to be true about the family had been a product

of my youthful imagination. It was the case, for example, that Joseph
Alsop, Sr., had purchased the farm only in 1902 and had brought
Corinne Robinson to it as his bride in 1909. What I had perceived in the
1920s as an ancient rootedness was now revealed to me to have existed
for less than two decades. Moreover, and to me shockingly, when by the
1970s both the Alsop parents were dead, it was Joe Alsop who had
precipitated the sale of the farm. Joe, the embodiment of the Wasp
Ascendancy, the champion of tradition, of continuity—how was it
possible for him to have been the agent of rupture, of discontinuity? The
family friend was blunt. He said that as one of the heirs to the property,
Joe had insisted upon its sale because of his "insatiable desire for cash."
Joe had also insisted on selling property in Middletown, Connecticut,
that had been in the possession of the family since 1690, and for the
same reason: to gain cash.

His surviving brother and sister aside, Joe had many nieces,
nephews, grandnieces, and grandnephews, but he was himself, after all,
by his own choice without direct descendants; by his own choice, he was
also a person who wished to live well. This led to his pursuing two
contradictory intentions at the same time: one was to keep the family
name going and the other was to deny himself nothing. In drawing up
his will, this childless bachelor acted upon the first intention so
vigorously that he felt obliged to add a memorandum of explanation. It
is a charmingly idiosyncratic document, which one can tell Joe took a
great deal of pleasure in composing; his grumbly voice is in every word,
and so is his wit:

> The favoritism shown my male relations in this my will and
> testament is bound to cause storms among my female kin. They are
> a brilliant and formidable lot. I wish to put on record in advance,
> therefore, my deep sympathies for my trustees and others charged
> with executing my will and testament.
>
> The explanation for the features of this will that my female
> relations may find repugnant is in fact very simple, indeed. I care
> greatly, perhaps foolishly, about my name. As my father used to say,
> "Our branch of the Alsop tribe has survived ten generations on this
> side of the Atlantic, always keeping their noses just above water."
>
> This is now a vastly more difficult feat. First of all, for a reason
> which fills me with deep pride in the United States. To be specific,
> the very great advantages that were accorded certain groups of

Americans have now quite properly been caused to vanish. And we are all, with some tragic exceptions, "citizens with an equal share."

Secondly, the very best education available, which it could be taken for granted in the old days would be provided as a matter of right for all male members of my family, has now grown so inordinately expensive that anyone who still takes this for granted is not living in the real world.

Consequently, I have shaped my will, perhaps unfairly, to give the next generation of male Alsops, who will pass on the Alsop name, the best chance of getting the kind of education that will permit them, in my father's phrase, to keep their noses above water.

With this task, in fact, I charge the male members of the Alsop name to whom I have shown preferential treatment.

As for this childless bachelor's second intention—to deny himself nothing—plainly it collided head-on with the first intention, and in practice made it more difficult to carry out successfully. The more money Joe spent, the less money there would be for his preferred male heirs. Surely he perceived the irony of a situation in which, when it suited his convenience, he found himself simultaneously upholding an old WASP tradition and betraying it. If so, he took care to ignore the irony. One has to say this for the aristocrats: they keep their doubts to themselves.

Ben Sonnenberg

FOR A QUARTER of a century or more, Ben Sonnenberg was surely the most famous public-relations man in the country. In my middle years, he was to become one of my best friends, but as a young journalist I would have nothing to do with him, feeling that he and his colleagues were my natural adversaries. Their professional function was to create a favorable public image for the individuals and corporations that hired them—in Sonnenberg's words, "to build plinths for little men to stand on." This odious labor depended upon a ruthless, continuous exploitation of the press, and I was determined not to help the exploiters achieve their goals.

Sonnenberg and I would encounter each other at parties and nod and smile; nothing more. Invitations to his grand house on Gramercy Park were civilly regretted. Some of my colleagues on *The New Yorker*— Geoffrey Hellman, John Bainbridge—would regale me with stories of the wonders the house contained and the variety of the guests (many of them personally unknown to Sonnenberg) who were entertained there. Ordinary press agents and public-relations men used to be pleased when, as the first fruits of their skill, they succeeded in getting their clients listed in *Who's Who*. This was a trifling feat for Sonnenberg; it was his boast that he could procure for any businessman-client of his what was then the apogee of fame in this country—a cover story in *Time*.

To my astonishment, he often made good on this boast. With little or no editing, the *New York Times* would publish press releases composed by underlings in Sonnenberg's office, and thanks to his close friend Hellman, he also placed many a story in the "Talk of the Town" department of *The New Yorker*. Eventually, he managed to have a Profile of himself published in *The New Yorker*. As one might expect, it was written by Hellman, who was amused by Sonnenberg's professional and social audacities and who, being rich and wellborn, had no fear of being thought to have been taken advantage of by an aggressive outsider.

Over the years, although he earned what he described as a "torrential" income, Sonnenberg had accumulated little capital—indeed, in pursuing his desire to live like a millionaire, in an exquisite house filled with exquisite things, he had often found himself heavily in debt. Quite late in life, he became in fact what he had long boldly affected to be. When a little company that he had helped to found, had accepted stock in, and had professionally touted—a manufacturer of bread and other bakery products called the Pepperidge Farm Company—was sold to the Campbell Soup Corporation, Sonnenberg found himself in possession of several million dollars. Shortly thereafter, he gave up the unworthy occupation of building plinths; instead, he became a consultant, working at home on an informal basis, in slippered ease, among his pipes, books, and pictures. Which is to say that if you were a businessman in trouble and wished some advice from Sonnenberg, he might invite you to have breakfast with him at Number Nineteen Gramercy Park; the fee charged for any advice dispensed during the course of breakfast would be as much as twenty-five thousand dollars. It was a harmless way of supplementing an already substantial income, and the advice was given in so Delphic a fashion that after the businessman's troubles had been survived he would be hard-pressed to remember whether the advice had been good or bad, or even whether he had known how to follow it.

When Sonnenberg gave up his Park Avenue offices and retreated to the lofty Second Empire mansion on Gramercy Park, assuming the posture of an oligarch who dispenses wisdom because it is in his nature to do so, I found it possible to become his friend. The speed and ease with which I passed from deploring Sonnenberg's means of earning a living to becoming a beneficiary of those means because he had formally abandoned them raises some doubts as to the strength of my ethical standards. I suppose my sense of the distance between who Sonnenberg had been and who he was bent upon becoming helped me to establish a similar distance between his past and me. *My* Sonnenberg was a pleasing recent fiction; a roly-poly Edwardian gentleman, tucked into the corner of a large sofa in a library whose eighteenth-century pine paneling had been plucked from a long-demolished English country house. The twinkle in Sonnenberg's eye was that of a practiced rascal, but I endow the word, as he did, with an admiring connotation. "You rascal!" he would exclaim, complimenting a friend upon the happy outcome of some adventure. "You rascal!" was to say, in effect, "We know the ways of the world, do we not? And so we can afford to be merry as we make our way among its innumerable perils."

It was in that library that the self-invented Sonnenberg was at his best. I would put a question to him about the career of some former client of his, knowing that I would acquire much entertaining information along the way but that no substantial answer would ever be arrived at. He had an exceptionally quick mind, which he would slow down for the convenience of others by turning ordinary discourse into a game of cat and mouse, with himself playing both roles. "First of all," he would say, giving the phrase the authority of a papal bull, and as the years passed I came to see that the purpose behind the phrase was both to entrap a listener and keep him at bay. "First of all" served to introduce one or another of his scores of entertaining cautionary tales, which he would himself interrupt from time to time by asides that bristled with names, dates, and voluptuously veiled hints of the never-wholly-to-be-explained. These labyrinthine asides, prolonged silences, fixed stares under quizzically lifted brows, and a dozen procrastinative ritual gestures of pipe-cleaning, pipe-filling, pipe-lighting, and pipe-smoking, would themselves gradually acquire asides; in the mind of the hypno-tized listener, they gave the impression that they were accumulating strings of footnotelike dependencies, making the smoky blue air about Sonnenberg's head seem to sparkle with asterisks, daggers, brackets, virgules, and printers' fists. But a straight answer to a straight question? Certainly not.

How proud Sonnenberg was, and with reason, to be in Number Nineteen! And proud, too, that from its windows he could look out over

Gramercy Park, which, small as it is, can claim to be the largest private park in the city. That patch of green lawn was all the more precious to Sonnenberg because it had been designed in imitation of the squares of his cherished London, source of his wardrobe and of much of his collection of antique furniture. Like all property owners facing the park, Sonnenberg had in his possession a key to its locked gates, though he felt no desire to frequent it. (Sonnenberg was an intensely urban person; however pretty nature might be, it was not for him. Once, staying with Hellman at a house in the Connecticut countryside, Sonnenberg jumped restlessly to his feet and said, "Let's go out and kick a tree.") In his view, the gravel paths of the park were best suited to the trundling of baby carriages and the early-morning constitutionals of elderly widows. Among the adornments of the park are a small bronze statue of Edwin Booth and a large green-and-white gabled wooden birdhouse on a pole; in his prime, Sonnenberg would have snubbed both of them.

Nevertheless, Sonnenberg was eager to speak of the park, or of any other subject that was at a measurable distance from himself, if it promised to delay the dread moment when one or another of his listeners might say something of an admiring nature about him. Though he rejoiced to pay compliments, he was made miserable by having to receive them. His feelings in this regard used to puzzle me. The eccentric elegance of his dress and the extravagance of his hospitality had made him one of the most readily recognizable men in New York and on the Continent, but it appeared that he had chosen to be conspicuous in the hope of rendering himself invisible. Like many of the artists and writers whose works he felt drawn to, he preferred to be at once famous and unknown.

Thus, if on occasion Sonnenberg set off, seemingly without reason, upon some prolonged zigzag narrative path that led from a history of Gramercy Park to a history of Number Nineteen, one learned to detect a stout thread of meaning in these meanderings. Fearing to hear himself praised, he had developed a verbal sleight of hand that deflected any such potential praise from himself to the house, which, though a mirror of its master, could be treated as an object separate from him and therefore a permissible topic of conversation. And what a house it was! Certainly in the days of his and its glory, it was by far the biggest and most luxurious private house in New York City, and there was scarcely a square foot of it—a square *inch* of it—that was without interest, whether to connoisseurs or to mere party-going, rubbernecking chief executive officers.

The entrance to Number Nineteen faced upon Irving Place; affixed to the big black front door in the paneled vestibule of the house was a polished brass knocker in the shape of a lion's head, which glowered not in the least fiercely at approaching guests. (Sonnenberg used to say that when he took title to the house and discovered that the vestibule, having been built in part on what was public sidewalk, belonged in part to the city and not to him, he came close to bursting into tears. To have worked as hard as he had in order to possess a kingdom, and then not to possess *all* of it!) If, to Sonnenberg's delight, Gramercy Park looked back over its shoulder to England, so by his efforts did Number Nineteen. In the 1870s the house had belonged to Mrs. Stuyvesant Fish, who at some point during the following decade called in her neighbor from across the park, Stanford White, to smarten up the house. Like Sonnenberg, Mrs. Fish loved giving parties. (Unlike him, she once gave a dinner party solely for dogs; Sonnenberg felt an alert suspicion of all four-footed creatures and wouldn't have them around.)

Despite the awesome abundance of rooms in Number Nineteen—upwards of forty—the first impression that one gained on stepping past the lion-headed knocker into the broad, low-ceilinged, oyster white front hall was that of a cozy homeliness. It was as if one had been quite unexpectedly ushered into some delightful snug cave of a country house, ample and opulent and yet taking care to be more comfortable than opulent. Deliciously and mysteriously—a mystery that, as far as I was concerned, never diminished with familiarity—the air smelled of spices, and the old parquet gave up out of its waxed, dusky depths reflections of innumerable brass objects of every size and purpose. Buckets, caskets, candlesticks, and graduated pound weights are what I recollect over the gap of years, but no doubt I have omitted many other singular treasures; the polishing of all the brass in the house (so Horne, the butler, once informed me) kept a below-stairs houseman occupied from morning to night.

To the left of the front door was a small, oak-paneled room, whose deeply embrasured windows looked out at ground level onto the park, and in whose handsome fireplace (an improvement of the early 1890s?) one wondered, even in midsummer, whether a fire hadn't just gone out, for standing by it one caught the bittersweet scent of woodsmoke and ashes, mingled with that of the flowers which were everywhere in the house. Many friends of the Sonnenbergs used to call this little room, filled with books and drawings and with, here and there, something silvery glowing in the shadows, their favorite; it was every bit as satisfactory of its kind as the large red-and-white-confectionery ballroom on the fifth floor, which also looked out over the park but did so from a height and therefore with a difference. If there are ghosts of rooms as well as of people, then the ghost of a studio hovers near the windows of the ballroom, for in pre-Sonnenberg days the top floor of the house had been divided into apartments, one of which was occupied by the artist and writer Ludwig Bemelmans.

Number Nineteen was the prize that Sonnenberg had wrested from the world, but it would be but the crudest "first of all" of a cautionary tale unworthy of his high standard for anyone to turn this extraordinary achievement into a conventional American success story. If Sonnenberg had reason to be skeptical of plinths, he was still more skeptical of monuments that impose themselves upon us whether we will or no. Number Nineteen was a work of art that held and enfolded many works of art, and it held and enfolded Sonnenberg as well, but it was never intended to serve as a monument. Though Sonnenberg had strong feelings on the subject, he nearly always preferred to disguise them behind a scrim of bantering; he made a sophisticated collector's usual deprecating remarks about his "bits," as he called them, but given the quality of the "bits," they were falsely humble remarks. And given the ego that had driven him so unremittingly over so many decades, they were also falsely humble with respect to Sonnenberg himself.

Quickly (and there were those who teased me about how quickly) I became a member of that army of protégés with whom Sonnenberg had made a practice of surrounding himself. Hitherto, many of them had been of a pliability convenient for his purposes; now he was free to choose protégés who amused him and who were therefore eligible to join an inner circle of true friends. The members of this circle ranged in age from the journalist Alistair Cooke, then in his sixties, to Robert Pirie, a lawyer in his twenties. In my time, other members of the circle were my colleague Hellman; the British historian Jack Plumb (later, augustly, to become Sir John); Charles Ryskamp, the director of the

Pierpont Morgan Library; and John Calmann, a brilliant young British publisher, who was soon to be murdered under particularly gruesome circumstances in the south of France.

Sonnenberg and I shared an incurable anglophilia—no doubt an emotion as odd to encounter in me, with my Irish ancestry, as in Sonnenberg, born in a *stetl* near Brest-Litovsk. England at its most opulent gleamed and shimmered and winked from top to bottom of Number Nineteen, in objects of brass, silver, crystal, pewter, and gold; paintings by Sully, Sickert, Tissot, and Augustus John crowded the walls, along with marble busts by Nollekens and Roubiliac (a birdy-looking Pope, an equally birdy Sterne), while Sargent's enormous portrait of the fifteenth Duchess of Sutherland led the eye upward from landing to landing as one mounted the great white-balustered central stairway. Having a wide acquaintance in London, Sonnenberg was accustomed to receiving many invitations to parties there. Some of these invitations would prove irresistible to him. He would ring me up and say, "My dear boy, make your arrangements as fast as you can. We're off to London Friday morning!" (When I wasn't addressed as a rascal, I was apt to be addressed as a dear boy, though by then I was a middle-aged grandfather.) And off we would go to London, on the one flight by day that was then available and that Sonnenberg much preferred to the inconvenience of flying by night. Needless to say, we flew first class, on BOAC, amidst a scatteration of British newspapers, magazines, and books, to be met at Heathrow by a chauffeured Rolls ("Delighted to see you again, Mr. Sonnenberg, sir!"). In the hushed limousine, we would be sped through the late English twilight to Claridge's, where the Sonnenberg suite was in readiness and we would have time for a stroll about the neighborhood and a nightcap in some nearby bar.

At breakfast the next morning, in the drawing room of the suite, Sonnenberg would open his engagement book, pull up a telephone, and set about confirming the arrangements that he or his secretary had made days earlier in New York. Luncheon at the Littmans', in Chester Square. A visit to Colnaghi's, where a small charcoal drawing by Couture promised to be worth glancing at. A preview of some fine "bits" of silver soon to be auctioned off at Sotheby's. Peggy Willys stopping by for a drink at teatime. Dinner at the Michael Lindsays', in Holland Park. After an hour, the telephone is dropped in its cradle, the engagement book slammed shut. "You rascal!" he says. "They all send you their love and can't wait to see you." A barefaced, kindly lie: these are his friends, acquaintances of mine through him.

I am Sonnenberg's guest on these holidays, and it is the firmest of rules that he must pay every expense incurred on them. To preserve the self-respect of the beneficiary vis-à-vis his benefactor, one exception is permitted: I may treat him to lunch at a certain favorite restaurant of his off Jermyn Street—Wilton's, a tiny, skylit establishment with perhaps a dozen tables and a bill of fare that exists mostly in the mind of its elderly proprietor, along with the famously high prices that he charges and that alter in amount from one moment to the next, according to whim. A light luncheon for two, with a bottle of wine, will come to perhaps a hundred pounds—by my comparatively humble standards, enough to assuage a portion of the guilt that I feel over what my presence in London must be costing Sonnenberg.

Not that the cost of anything in actual money is ever visible on these impromptu London jaunts of ours. As we wander through Mayfair, stopping at twenty or so galleries and shops in the course of a day, Sonnenberg is invariably recognized and made much of, and if his eye is caught by some desirable object or other, he will say, "Charge it to my account at Claridge's and send it along to Number Nineteen." To which the answer is an immediate, "Very good, sir, happy to have been of service to you, sir!" It appears that every shop in London is familiar with Sonnenberg's charge account at Claridge's and with the street, city, state, and country in which Number Nineteen is located. Moreover, it is Sonnenberg's practice to pay an extra 25 percent of the purchase price for shipping and, at the New York City end, another 25 percent to have the "bit," whatever it may be, taken through customs, delivered to Number Nineteen, and unwrapped there. The object he has seen for the first time in a London shop or gallery he will see for the second time on his desk in the library at Gramercy Park.

Observing Sonnenberg on one or another of these shopping expeditions, I used to reflect on how simple life can be for the rich, if only they will consent to let it be so: a principle that Sonnenberg had evidently mastered the moment he learned that it was possible for people like him—a Lower East Side ragamuffin, son of a failed pushcart peddler—to become one of their company. In contrast, the kind of rich to whom I was exposed in youth were the puritanical rich of New

England, who start with the uneasy feeling that whatever they may have paid for some pretty *objet* picked up in the course of a trip abroad, it is almost certainly too much; their happiness in possessing the object is diminished by the fear, habitual among them, that they have been taken advantage of *because* they are rich: the very thing that their parents long ago warned them that they should never allow to happen. They proceed to carry the souvenir about with them in their luggage, fearful at every stopping place that they will leave it behind or that some unscrupulous hotel chambermaid will steal it. They carry it laboriously through customs along with the rest of their luggage, and expose it at last on the dining-toom table at home. There it is! But had they been flimflammed in the buying of it? Somewhere in Europe, were people laughing at them behind their backs?

Sonnenberg was a disciplined traveler. He displayed no impatience at delays that were beyond his control. True, in unfamiliar towns he grew restless when no English-language newspapers and magazines proved to be available—the *International Herald Tribune* was the least of the many lifelines that, in his view, were required to keep travelers in touch with civilization. Buying things was also an indispensable aspect of his life; acquisition was a form of good health. Once, we were visiting friends of his in Lugano. Though he looked at many choice things in the shops of that sybaritical city, he saw nothing that he felt inclined to send home to Number Nineteen. He grew pale as we neared the end of our stay. Hoarsely, in a voice charged with bewilderment, he exclaimed, "But, my dear boy, I've never left a country in my life without buying something!" Luckily, at the last moment we came upon a shop that dealt in Roman antiquities. Zestfully, Sonnenberg purchased an ancient marble table-leg, crowned with a lion's head, and a bronze grapple out of the second century B.C. Within an hour, the color had come back into his cheeks. He had found something in Switzerland to buy. He was himself again.

The occasional gaucheries I committed in the presence of my London betters greatly amused Sonnenberg. At such moments, he was able to enjoy the best of two worlds. Wearing the disguise of an Edwardian gentleman, he was at liberty to share the upper-class Englishman's contempt for the raw heartiness that even the so-called nice American visitor unwittingly conveyed. At the same time, who could be thought to be more nearly an epitome of the brash American-ness of Americans than Sonnenberg himself—a person who at the age of thirteen, speaking not a word of English, had journeyed by steerage from a European ghetto to the ghetto of the Lower East Side and who by the age of thirty had achieved the grandeur of residing in Number Nineteen?

One gaucherie of mine that especially delighted Sonnenberg was committed at a convivial dinner party at the Michael Lindsays', where late in the evening and after a considerable amount of wine-bibbing, I settled down on a sofa beside the Duke and Duchess of Devonshire and began to exhort them to give up old, worn-out, and impotent England in favor of the vitality and promising future of the United States. Unbeknownst to me, Sonnenberg across the room was listening as I pleaded the case for our great open spaces—it is even possible that I resorted to a few bars of ". . . where seldom is heard a discouraging word, / And the skies are not cloudy all day"—and the poor Duke and Duchess, thoroughly baffled by my jingoism but retaining their perfect good manners, kept assuring me that, marvelous as America must be, they were perfectly comfortable at Chatsworth, the family seat in Derbyshire. Sonnenberg never let me forget that evening. "You rascal!" he would say. "What do you hear from the Duke and Duchess? Are they emigrating soon?"

With age and ever-increasing wealth, Sonnenberg became a backer of several of the philanthropic causes in which I took an interest—causes having to do with city planning, architectural preserva-tion, and the like. He and a couple of neighbors purchased a nineteenth-century Quaker church on Gramercy Park in order to keep it from being demolished and replaced by a sky-high condominium. (Happily, it is now a synagogue.) His financial support included giving parties at Number Nineteen for various philanthropic purposes: New Yorkers are eager to prowl about in other people's houses, and in the Sonnenberg house everything was open to inspection, including bath-rooms, dressing rooms, and closets. Visitors would admire Sonnen-berg's shirts, fresh from the hand of the resident laundress and stacked in readiness on a marble counter, and his rank upon rank of ties, shoes, and tweed jackets. They would admire, too, in one of the guest bathrooms, a large, circular, many-nozzled, turn-of-the-century shower, said to have come from the house that Stanford White and his family lived in for many years on the north side of Gramercy Park.

Sonnenberg and I had it in common that we both despised illness and had no patience with it, whether in ourselves or in others. He had a robust physique and enjoyed a freezing New York City snowstorm as much as he did the hot sun of Cap Ferrat, or, for that matter, the hot sun of Provincetown, where he had purchased and made over a charming blue-and-white wooden beach house for his wife, Hilda—a house that, as the years passed, she came to feel more cozily at home in than she did in Gramercy Park. With a seeming suddenness, Sonnenberg fell ill, of a cancer that may have been usurping his body more or less stealthily over a long period. When he learned from his doctor that, even with such help as medical science could provide, he was almost certainly dying, he made his way back to Number Nineteen and asked the butler, Horne, for a key to Gramercy Park.

As far as Horne knew, it had been years since Sonnenberg had entered the park. He watched with alarm as Sonnenberg took the key, crossed Twentieth Street, and unlocked the gates. For a couple of hours he sat motionless on a bench in the park, then got up and returned to the house, speaking only a casual word or two to Horne as he returned the key. Much later, Horne surmised that Sonnenberg had isolated himself in the park in order to decide how to deal with the fearful news that he had just received. Whenever it may have been that he spoke to his family about his imminent extinction (and to him death was only that, without the least mitigating hope of a hereafter), he never spoke of it to me. Hilda said once, "Oh, Brendan! That little man of ours is very sick," after which, hugging each other, we found that there was nothing else to say. As for Horne, a high-spirited Britisher, the degree of his desolation could be measured almost daily. As Sonnenberg lay dying, Horne's head, hitherto crowned with clustering golden curls, yielded to a head of hair ever straighter and ever more gray.

Soon enough Sonnenberg was dead, and the family, unable to devise a funeral service not contrary to his wishes, permitted him simply to vanish, without the conventional punctuation of a ceremony. Moreover, the local newspapers were all on strike: the *Times*, in which Sonnenberg had found it so easy to spread favorable word of his clients, was unable to publish an obituary of him—an accidental demonstration, so one might have ruefully said, of Sonnenberg's lifelong aptitude for making quick and inconspicuous getaways.

The great house was emptied and put up for sale and its possessions scattered at auction, according to the terms of Sonnenberg's will. Not in that respect but in others the will was a disappointing document. Over the years, Sonnenberg had often hinted at generous benefactions to a number of museums and similar institutions, but the hints proved false. Including the sale of the house and the sale of the greater part of the contents of the house at Sotheby's, his estate must have amounted to many millions of dollars. It was left almost entirely to the family. Someone said of the will that it was what might have been expected of a small-town businessman, afraid of not having done enough for his wife and children; not what was expected of Sonnenberg. Immediately after his death, a fund to honor Sonnenberg's memory had been proposed by several friends, one of whom—John L. Loeb—started it off with a contribution of fifty thousand dollars; after the terms of the will were made known, the fund ceased to be mentioned. What long-harbored guilt, what irrational fear may have lain behind Sonnenberg's posthumous parsimony? I found it inexplicable in terms of the Sonnenberg I had known, but there had been many an earlier Sonnenberg, and it was surely one of them who, in the shadow of death, dictated the terms of the will.

Sonnenberg's wife survived his death by only a year or so. Hilda had little interest in the circus of celebrities of which her husband had been the most resourceful of ringmasters. Her devotion to her family—husband, daughter, son, and half a dozen grandchildren—was so fiercely protective that one spoke of her as a classic Jewish mother in order not to confront the question of what this protectiveness may have excluded. She was an intelligent woman, with a wit that turned out to be sharper than one had expected and that served to keep her at whatever distance from others she chose to set. She was affectionate with me, but it appeared that she wished me to see her as studiedly lazy—as someone who sat in her bedroom and read best-selling novels and looked at television and fretted over the well-being of her grandchildren. After Sonnenberg's death, when Number Nineteen was put up for sale, Hilda Sonnenberg was shown various attractive apartments into which she might move. I suggested an apartment in the Dakota, from which an especially pleasing view of Central Park could be had. "But, Brendan," Hilda said, "you know I never look out of the window." A droll remark, and yet concealed in it a truth—a harsh truth, perhaps a self-condemnatory truth—that retains its mystery for me to this day. She really *didn't* look out of the window, but why not? Why didn't she wish to take a more active part in the exceptionally varied life that her husband's success had made possible for her? No answer in her lifetime, no answer now.

In the course of preparing a catalogue for the auction of the Benjamin Sonnenberg collection—an auction that occupied three full days—Sotheby's small army of experts examined a certain handsome portrait sketch in charcoal of Augustus St. Gaudens, signed by Sargent and inscribed by him to Charles F. McKim. Sonnenberg had a passion for "association" portraits—pictures by a famous artist of a famous sitter (a portrait by Augustus John, say, of Lady Ottoline Morrell, or by Sargent of Ethel Barrymore)—and here was a triple-association portrait, for Sargent, St. Gaudens, and McKim had been close friends and fellow workers. It had pleased Sonnenberg to pick it up at a very reasonable price from a dealer in Dublin, who claimed to have received it on consignment from the estate of a member of an old and distinguished Irish family.

At my urging, Sonnenberg had taken the trouble to press the dealer for more facts about the provenance of the portrait. The dealer had written a charming letter to the effect that Sonnenberg as a collector and man of the world must know how protective old Dublin barristers were of the interests of their clients and therefore must be ready to sympathize with the totally impenetrable discretion of the particular old Dublin barrister who was in charge of the estate from which the Sargent portrait had come. For that reason and to his great regret, the dealer could offer no more information on the subject than that which he had already provided; at the same time, he congratulated Sonnenberg upon his good fortune in acquiring so great a rarity at so reasonable a price, and he remained, with sincere good wishes, Charles Merrill Mount.

The experts from Sotheby's pronounced the portrait a forgery, and it was omitted from the auction. Sonnenberg's daughter, Helen Tucker, asked me if I would like to accept the forgery as a memento, and I said that of course I would be delighted to do so. Handsomely framed— under the circumstances, the frame is worth far more than the portrait—

it is an excellent likeness of St. Gaudens, done in Sargent's best bravura style, and with a signature and inscription that look unchallengeably authentic to my amateur eye. Indeed, the only reason to doubt the authenticity of the portrait, which I glance at every day of my life with pleasure, is that the dealer, Mount, is alleged to have executed many similar forgeries, not only of works by Sargent but by Gilbert Stuart as well. In 1988, he was arrested, tried, found guilty, and sentenced to prison for stealing and attempting to sell to autograph dealers a number of precious historic documents from the Library of Congress. A gifted artist in his own right, Mount is a gifted author (his biography of Sargent is well worth reading), and a gifted scoundrel as well. If he was to be tricked at all, Sonnenberg's preference would be to be tricked by a master.

A glimpse of Sonnenberg in his late prime, at an especially notable moment of his life. It is the summer of 1971, when a selection of drawings of writers and artists from his by now celebrated collection is about to go on exhibition at the Pierpont Morgan Library. The opening party promises to be what Sonnenberg calls "a swagger affair." By this stage of his career, Sonnenberg is no longer eager to achieve publicity for himself; it is upon the collection that he wishes emphasis placed. Still, he is the person who has assembled the collection and who has been announced as the guest of honor at the opening. Charles Ryskamp, the director of the library, is a close friend of Sonnenberg's and has intended the occasion to serve as a sort of official stamp of cultural approval upon the Sonnenberg known to him and his fellow scholars—not the "what-makes-Sammy-run" Sonnenberg of whom Hellman had written long ago in *The New Yorker* in terms as mocking as they were admiring, but the Indian-summer Sonnenberg of proliferating good works, of a contented bookishness, of an endless procession of academics passing through Number Nineteen. At the Morgan Library that evening, in that vaulted marble lobby of the "old" building where champagne and other drinks and appropriate refreshments were being served, Ryskamp stood to greet his invited guests, and beside him was expected to stand, in the customary fashion, the honored guest of the occasion. At the hour that Ryskamp and he had agreed upon, Sonnenberg failed to appear. Minutes passed, and then an hour, and then two hours, and still no Sonnenberg. Concealing his bewilderment and wounded feelings, Ryskamp with his usual charm improvised excuses for the missing guest of honor.

The evening was a success—it has never been likely that any occasion at the Morgan could fail—but it was by no means the event that Ryskamp had been counting upon; from his point of view, it had been a fiasco. Why had Sonnenberg failed him? The reason was revealed to Ryskamp and me little by little in the days that followed, with more than the usual display of cat-and-mouse asides, silences, and pipe-lightings, and it was this: Sonnenberg had feared that people at the opening would be laughing at him behind his back. He had feared that they would misread the occasion: that they would suppose of him—him, of all people!—that he was capable of equating the value of his treasures with his own value, would suppose that he failed to comprehend the gulf that lies between the collector and his collection, would suppose that he could not measure to a millimeter the length and breadth and depth of that gulf, whether the collector was a Frick or a Getty or a Mellon. He had feared that they would suppose of him that he now took himself for one of them—for one of those toplofty, self-deceiving grandees.

And of course he did not. His ego was too big to contain an aspiration at once so conventional and so small. The possession of objects by any individual was so obviously temporary as to be almost laughable. Truly laughable to Sonnenberg was the hope entertained by some of his friends (one thinks of his crony Bobby Lehman) that if they gave a hundred million dollars' worth of art to the Metropolitan Museum they would secure at least some immortality for the family name. In Sonnenberg's view, this hope and all other such hopes were infantile. As well be remembered as the discoverer of the Islands of Langerhans, floating about somewhere in the human kidneys! That was why in his will Sonnenberg recommended a prompt scattering of the Sonnenberg collection. A lifetime of acquisition vanished in three days, leaving scarcely a trace. In his will, he also took care to order that all his personal papers be destroyed. And so he, too, effectually vanished from history, or sought to do so, and again it was a gesture based not upon humility but upon pride. Who could do justice to a man who felt so strongly that *nobody* could do him justice—who preferred leaving an empty space on the ground to leaving an imperfect monument, which was to say a plinth bearing the figure of a little top-hatted man with a potbelly and a droll mustache?

And yet even as I set down these words, I imagine his black eyes narrowing, the lid of one of them flickering in a fashion half-amusement, half-menace, and I hear his voice saying, "You rascal! Surely you don't believe that *you* have managed to see into me—see through me? Your Sonnenberg is all very well, but this I can promise you: he is not me."

Harry Mali

AMONG THE GREAT HOUSES of New York City—one that in its day easily rivaled the Fish-Sonnenberg house—was the mansion at the southwest corner of Fifth Avenue and Eighth Street occupied by John Taylor Johnston. It was said to have been the first marble house ever built on Fifth Avenue. At once plain and grand, with a high stoop and heavily framed windows, it survived until 1940, and I remember it well. Johnston (1820-1893) was a prominent businessman and patron of the arts; unlike most of the local connoisseurs of that day, he favored collecting the works of living artists, and in particular of living American artists, among whom he numbered many friends—Church, Homer, Whittredge, and the like. He turned the former stable of his house, facing upon Eighth Street (then known as Clinton Place), into a gallery for the display of his collection and opened it one day a week to the public; once a year, he held a reception for any and all artists resident in New York City, at which he served an "artists' punch" so potent that it became the subject of a celebrated poem. Johnston was one of the founders of the Metropolitan Museum of Art, to which he gave many notable paintings; as its first president, he also shared the financial risk when, on several occasions in its early days, the museum exceeded its budget in the course of acquiring certain exceptionally desirable items.

My friend Henry T. Mali—universally known as Harry—was a

39

grandson of Johnston's and grew up in the so-called Marble House, which his mother, Frances Johnston Mali, had inherited upon the death of her father. Of all the people I have known, Harry amounts to the greatest exception to a rule of life that, however hard we may struggle to outwit it, appears to govern our conduct: the rule that to survive in the world we must invent ourselves, and not once but many times, shaping again and again out of our past selves the succession of people we can bear to be. Not from pride—indeed, from a modesty that was authentic and therefore by no means a mere disguise for pride—Harry was content from the beginning with who he was. He accepted his nature and his place in life and the assortment of events that fate bestowed on him with an equanimity so unusual that it was often incomprehensible to others. At one point his gentle mother-in-law, with a mingling of affection and asperity, said to him, "Harry, you are a dreadfully moderate boy!"

Born in 1899, Harry was a couple of years older than Sonnenberg; the two men never met, and no wonder, because except for the near-equality of their ages, it would be hard to imagine two people who had less in common: Ben, the consummate outsider, Harry, the consummate insider. One a Russian-Jewish immigrant, born in poverty and with little formal education, who to his dying day spoke a vivid but imperfect English; the other, a wealthy and aristocratic American, who graduated from Groton and Yale and who spoke an old-fashioned, correct English that had no use for slang any later than—and any more vehement than—that of the Rover Boys. Ben dressed to be noticed at a distance of several blocks; Harry chose to remain sartorially inconspicuous in three-piece suits of a conventional Brooks Brothers cut. (As far as I know, the only exception Harry made to anonymity in dress was at a picnic that used to be held annually in Norfolk, Connecticut, the little town in the Berkshire Hills where both he and his family and I and my family spent the summer. At a certain moment during the picnic, Harry would appear in a long-skirted, blue-and-white-striped woolen bathing suit, a souvenir of his undergraduate days in New Haven. Harry's appearance in this apparitionlike form—which we other picnickers counted on from year to year and yet always found startling—brought loud cheers.) Ben was fiercely, restlessly eager to improve the circumstances in which he found himself; Harry preferred accommodating to them.

And in Harry's case, why not? His circumstances being so fortunate from the start, accommodation to them was the wisest course to follow. Meeting him for the first time, people sometimes mistakenly assumed that he was passive, but it was not so; what he felt and conveyed was happiness, an attribute so rare that it often goes unrecognized. Happiness is simple, and unhappy people are enviously apt to perceive a connection between what is simple and what is simpleminded. In Harry's case, nothing could have been further from the truth. Harry's intelligence was not in the least diminished by that inveterate happiness of his, which appears to have extended with no major interruption over the nearly ninety years that he lived. What was inexplicable in life he left to philosophers to brood upon; he accommodated to the unknowable as he accommodated to the inconvenient, with an acquiescent smile and, in an extreme gesture, a rueful shake of the head.

I assume that Harry's exceptional happiness began in childhood, where it begins for almost anyone who has a knack for it. In winter, the family lived in the big white marble house near Washington Square. To Harry it seemed that the mahogany banisters of the flights of stairs that led from one high-ceilinged hallway to the next had been designed solely for little boys to slide down upon. Long afterward, he remembered that in spite of the furnaceman tirelessly shoveling coal belowstairs, the house could never be kept comfortably warm in winter. So much for the rich, dwelling in mansions and wrapping themselves up in layers of heavy sweaters to avoid getting chilblains! (Lying in bed in the upper reaches of the house, Harry would be awakened at dawn by the sound, reverberating through the hot-air registers, of the grates of the furnace being shaken in the cellar; if he slipped back into a dream, the sound of the grates might transform itself into a distant sea-sound—the creak of a hull, say, as Captain Blood and his crew set out to gather booty on the Spanish Main.)

Big as the house was that the Malis occupied in winter, in summer they occupied an even bigger house, which Grandfather Johnston had built and frequently added onto, in Plainfield, New Jersey. As Harry noted in an autobiography that he wrote for his grandchildren and had privately printed, the house had nine master bedrooms and only two bathrooms; this meant, Harry wrote, "taking turns." Harry never saw anything wrong with taking turns: it was a part of that everlasting accommodativeness of his, which carried him through school and college and which I caught compelling glimpses of even in his middle years, when his children, then in their teens, would invite two or three of my children, accompanied by their father, to go camping in some remote corner of the Malis' summer place in Norfolk.

I am one who likes to dine at a broad table, sleep on a comfortable mattress, and have available at all times plenty of hot water with which to shave and shower. For that reason, spending the night in a damp woods (as like as not with sharp laurel roots making their way into my back as I toss and turn within a suffocating sleeping bag), eating ill-heated food by a smudgy fire, whose chief purpose appears to be that of attracting mosquitoes, and skinny-dipping at dawn in an icy stream, to the ear-piercing, merry shouts of innumerable children, is very far down on my list of favorite activities. Not so for Harry, and especially not so for Harry when it came to putting up with hardships, which to him amounted to welcome tests of character.

Camping out, like surviving the cold of a great house in winter, was to Harry the sort of experience that helped turn a boy into a man. Nor was one less a man for having acquired good manners along with fortitude. In his time, Harry was surely the best-behaved little boy in New York City. One day, he was walking up Fifth Avenue with his mother, who bending down to him whispered, "Harry, don't look now, but here comes Mark Twain." Well-brought-up Harry obediently didn't look and so lost an opportunity to see the great man. Moreover, he may well have aroused the great man's wrath, for Twain devoted much effort to making himself as conspicuous as possible, wearing a white suit winter and summer and washing his cockatoo's crest of hair daily with bluing to make it extra white. God damn and blast any little boy who failed to look at him!

On his mother's side, Harry's family had been rooted in America since the eighteenth century. On his father's side, he was a descendant of a well-known Belgian family, which has been manufacturing textiles in the town of Verviers for several centuries. Harry was proud of the fact that the Malis had long been the preeminent manufacturers of billiard cloth; in this country, the family firm continues into the fourth generation. In the trade, the name has been Americanized as "May-lye"; otherwise, among friends, it is "Mah-lee." One of Harry's great-uncles used to own a forty-acre country estate on a high, forested bluff in the Bronx. From his house (which still stands, in an altered condition), one gained in earlier days a view of the East River, the Hudson River, the mountains of New Jersey, and, far to the south, the many-steepled city of New York.

In the late 1890s, the Mali estate became the uptown campus of New York University, designed by Stanford White at the same time that his partner, Charles F. McKim, was designing the new campus for Columbia University, on upper Broadway. White was murdered by the cretinous Pittsburgh millionaire Harry K. Thaw in 1906; a year or so earlier, crossing the Atlantic by steamer on a holiday trip with his family, five-year-old Harry had had the good fortune to meet White, thanks to his having been assigned a deck chair next to the one assigned to White. No doubt White would have preferred to discover a pretty young woman in the chair beside him, but to his credit he proved an excellent companion to Harry, patiently playing tic-tac-toe with him throughout the voyage.

The velocity with which, in our day, the outsider becomes an insider makes it hard for us to realize how firmly established the boundaries were in the early years of our century. As a boy, Harry associated with members of old New York families, mostly cousins of his in one degree or another, whose very names—Minturn, Manice, Lockwood, DeForest—have been largely forgotten; he was allowed to play with his contemporary Henry Morgan (also nicknamed "Harry"), but not with a Rockefeller, the Rockefellers having arrived but recently from Cleveland and being known at the time only for their immense wealth and for the doubtful circumstances under which it had been accumulated. It was a predecessor of Sonnenberg, the great public-relations man Ivy Lee, who succeeded in conferring respectability upon the Rockefellers and hastened their entrance into New York society.

After graduating from Groton and Yale, Harry spent some time on the faculty of Yale-in-China. On his return, he joined the "May-lye" firm. Both his parents died when Harry was still in his twenties. In 1929, he married Katherine Lord Strauss, of a prominent banking family in New York. Kay was a great-granddaughter of the celebrated Quaker champion of women's rights, Lucretia Coffin Mott, and although her Strauss antecedents were Jewish and she was quick to identify herself with them, Kay was also quick to employ the Quaker "thee." She was an extremely good-looking woman, with big dark eyes, a prominent, high-bridged nose, and prematurely white hair. At our first meeting, which took place at a cocktail party in Norfolk, she made it clear that she was aware, as a newcomer to the town, of the strong strain of anti-Semitism that then permeated the community; the unspoken implication was that I wasn't for a moment to suppose that she would attempt to "pass" on the strength of her impeccable Protestant credentials.

As Harry recounted in his autobiography, he had proposed to Kay and been turned down; characteristically, he accommodated himself to this rebuff and when, a year or so later, Kay informed him that she had changed her mind, there stood the valiant Harry, ready to accept his prize. Kay and he brought up three sons, living in summer in an old remodeled farmhouse on a windswept Norfolk hilltop and in winter in a splendid townhouse on East Sixty-ninth Street, which had originally belonged to her parents. It had been designed for the Strausses in the Tudor style, with an iron-studded oak front door, leaded-glass casement windows, and a stairway whose broad, brilliantly polished treads gave off mirrorlike a reflection of one's feet mounting them. Over the formidable drawing-room mantelpiece hung a portrait of Grandfather Johnston; over the circular dining-room table hung an elaborately worked chandelier, whose fringed silk shade, also circular, provided a ring of gentle, pinkish light, reaching just to the outer rim of the table—a flawless light to dine by. I often congratulated the Malis on not having abandoned it when nearly every other possessor of such a chandelier (including my own family, in Hartford) had long since thrown it onto the dustheap. As usual, Harry was astonished that anyone would be tempted to cast aside something of value simply because it was out of fashion.

Kay Mali died in her sleep in the fifty-first year of their marriage, and Harry was able to accommodate himself even to that unlooked-for misfortune. He would have been ashamed to give way to self-pity; if it was his fate to be a widower, so be it: he wasn't the only widower in the world. In the concluding pages of his autobiography, three years before his death, he wrote, "I am eighty-four. At that age I do not have much longer to go . . ." Serenely he passed the days of his retirement, often lunching at his club and spending an hour or two in the library— "reading," he would emphasize, "and not napping." The humiliations of old age he confronted with his usual sunny resignation. Once, I encountered him in the lobby of the club, emerging from the men's room. "I'm down to about twenty minutes," he said, leaving it to me to deduce what it was that he had left unspoken. He was an old man approaching the end of his life, for whom everything had changed and yet nothing had changed. He was smiling, he was even perhaps happy as he stood there, at peace with what couldn't be helped. And so he slipped away, the uninvented man, as gently and good-humoredly and lovingly as he had lived.

Joseph Campbell

THANKS TO TELEVISION, people comparatively obscure during their lifetimes enjoy the possibility of becoming celebrated after they are dead. Indeed, they may do better than that—they may achieve what amounts to a substantial measure of immortality, which is to say that as long as tapes of them exist and as long as an audience can be found of a size sufficient to make it worthwhile to broadcast the tapes, they can go on occupying a prominent place in the world for many decades and perhaps even—who knows?—for centuries.

Of course I am thinking of a particular case: that of my friend Joseph Campbell, who taught at Sarah Lawrence College for almost forty years, his subject being the role of myth in human history. He wrote a number of books on this and related topics, the best known of them in his lifetime being *The Hero with a Thousand Faces*. He retired from Sarah Lawrence in 1972 and was at work on still another book when, in 1987, at the age of eighty-two, he died after what his obituary in the *New York Times* described simply as "a brief illness." That brevity was, so his friends thought, characteristic of him: why dawdle in the presence of the inevitable? At the same time, however, for Campbell to have consented to be sick at all seemed an impermissible aberration. Ordinarily, it isn't a reason for astonishment when an old man is called upon to die, but Campbell had seemed to us never to grow old. If by the calendar he had reached his eighties, in person he was a good twenty years younger than that, or so any stranger would have assumed on meeting him. He was slender and quick-moving, and because of his erect carriage gave the impression of being taller than he was. He had thick, dark, wavy hair, bright blue eyes, unwrinkled skin, and a pink complexion. He laughed readily, with a boyish glee, and his laughter remained especially attractive in age because, as far as one could tell, his teeth were his own, neither false nor capped. He was, in short, an invincibly youthful figure, so uncannily unaltered by time that I used to accuse him, to his delight, of practicing some hitherto unknown form of satanism.

We would encounter each other, Campbell and I, at monthly meetings of a club we belonged to in New York City. Handsome in black tie, he would be standing near one or another of the bars that were set up on such occasions in the art gallery off the landing of our grand marble stairway. Unlike many scholars, he was convivial and at ease meeting strangers; moreover, having enjoyed a cocktail or two before dinner, he participated with relish in the give-and-take of vigorous discussion, which is (or is reputed to be) one of the most welcome features of the club.

To the bewilderment of many members of the club, myself included, Campbell's lifelong study of conflicting points of view in a variety of world cultures had not resulted in his accepting a variety of conflicting points of view in his own culture. Scholar that he was, surely he could be counted on to observe with a scholar's detachment the aggressive upward mobility of minority peoples in the United States? Surely he would be the first among us to understand and forgive their crude and often dangerous patterns of behavior? Well, nothing of the kind! So far was Campbell from applying the wisdom of the ages to the social, racial, political, and sexual turbulence he found himself increasingly surrounded by that he might have been a member of the Republican party somewhere well to the right of William F. Buckley. He embodied a paradox that I was never able to resolve in his lifetime and that I have been striving to resolve ever since: the savant as reactionary.

It was also a paradox that, although Campbell had devoted most of his teaching career to Sarah Lawrence—and a brilliant teacher he was, the nonpareil of spellbinders—he never approved of the nature of the college, which was liberal if not radical with respect to politics and permissive with respect to personal conduct. He came from a middle-class Irish-Catholic background, which in his generation implied a certain Jansenist puritanism, and when he sought to describe the extent to which he believed himself to have escaped it—that is, to have successfully paganized himself—his words tended to grow at once lofty and mushy: he would suddenly be spouting language as coyly imprecise as that of any sentimental Victorian novelist. Of marriage, for example, Campbell would say that in undertaking it "we reconstruct"— Campbell's words—"the image of the incarnate God." Whatever that curious statement may mean, it certainly implies that marriage is an ambitious project and that we must therefore take care in choosing the correct marriage partner. How is this to be accomplished? According to Campbell, "Your heart tells you."

The bigotry that Campbell displayed toward blacks, Hispanics, and other minorities was so irrational that one hesitated to believe he was in dead earnest. (Having dinner one evening with Harold Taylor, the former president of Sarah Lawrence, Campbell spent much of his time arguing that it was of no use to admit blacks to the college because they were "unable to retain information.") His bigotry with respect to Jews was of an equal odiousness and seemingly ineradicable. By the time I came to know him, he had learned to conceal a few of its grosser manifestations, but there can be no doubt that it existed. For example, he was given to saying to Jews, with an enthusiasm to which they were evidently expected to respond in kind, "You're a Jew, aren't you? I can always spot a Jew." When the astronauts landed on the moon, Joe made a repellent jest to an immediate member of my family (a student of his at the time) that "the moon would be a good place to put the Jews." He avoided manifesting his anti-Semitism in my presence in order to avoid my attacking him, but a friend we had in common told me that Campbell, proud to be a member of the New York Athletic Club, often recounted the tricky means by which Jews were prevented from becoming members. This was ironic because, apparently unbeknownst to Campbell, the New York Athletic Club in earlier days had been every bit as violently opposed to Irish Catholics as to Jews. Campbell's father had been in a position to arrange for his son to become a member only because, in the Great Depression, the club had come so close to bankruptcy that its WASP members had grudgingly consented to elect the first of an army of what they called "the Irish swine."

Campbell's anti-Semitism tainted not only the man himself but the quality of his scholarship. For example, he despised Freud, and it would appear that he did so at least in part because of the fact that Freud was Jewish. He approved highly of Jung and not least because Jung *wasn't* Jewish. Freud had been, of course, anti-Nazi; Jung had been pro-Nazi, and Campbell had been heard to say, in a mock-humorous tone of voice, that not all of the Nazis' ideas had been so bad. In an episode unknown to me until after his death, Campbell as a young man had provoked an indignant letter from no less a person than Thomas Mann, one of his two literary heroes (the other was James Joyce).

In December 1940, with the Second World War already under way in Europe, Campbell gave a lecture at Sarah Lawrence on the topic "Permanent Human Values," urging the assembled undergraduates not to be caught up in war hysteria and not to be tricked into missing the education to which they were entitled simply because "a Mr. Hitler collides with a Mr. Churchill." Campbell argued that "creative writers, painters, sculptors, and musicians" ought to remain "devoted to the disciplines of pure art." In time of war, the fortitude of the literary man and artist consists of remaining aloof from the political cockpit, giving no thought to the "undoing of an enemy." At that very moment, Thomas Mann was devoting much of his energy to arousing the world to the menace of Hitler and his Nazis; for reasons difficult to imagine, Campbell sent a copy of his lecture to Mann, then living in Princeton, and received a civil but obviously angry letter in reply, which, translated from the German, reads in part:

> As an American, you must be able to judge better than I, in a country which just now, slowly, slowly, under difficult and mighty obstacles, I hope not too late, has come to the true recognition of the political situation and its necessities, whether it is appropriate at this particular moment to recommend political indifference to American youth . . .
>
> It is strange, you are a friend of my books, which therefore according to your opinion must have something to do with "Permanent Human Values." Now these books are forbidden in Germany and in all countries that Germany rules, and whoever reads them or

even should sell them, and whoever would so much as praise my name publicly would be put into a concentration camp and his teeth would be bashed in and his kidneys split in two. You teach that we must not get upset about that, we must rather take care of the maintenance of permanent human values. Once again, this is strange . . .

Campbell's speech did him no lasting harm; it was dismissed as the special pleading of a passionate young humanist, and with the eventual British-American victory over the Nazis (for Mr. Hitler did indeed collide with Mr. Churchill) even Mann may have found it in his heart to forgive him. Nevertheless, Mann's rebuke evidently galled Campbell. Many years later, he gave a talk in which he claimed that a monumental mistake had been made when Mann was invited to give the main address at the banquet held in Vienna in 1936 to celebrate Freud's eightieth birthday. According to Campbell, in the course of his eulogy Mann had criticized Freud—whom Campbell mistakenly believed to have been in the audience and whom he described as "that poor little old man"—for not being aware that most of his discoveries had already been made by earlier German writers. (In fact, Mann's admiration for Freud was unbounded and Freud was very much gratified by the eulogy.) Campbell wound up his speech by noting that Mann "had lost altitude" as an artist by descending into political activity and raising his voice against the Nazis.

During the course of Campbell's long career at Sarah Lawrence, his was a name well known in academic circles. In the narrower circle of admirers of James Joyce, he was revered as the coauthor, with Henry Morton Robinson, of a learned and amusing book called *The Skeleton Key to Finnegans Wake*. It was from this book that, according to Campbell, Thornton Wilder had pinched much of the material for his play *The Skin of Our Teeth*. (Campbell may have been justified in his accusation: Wilder was a notorious literary magpie.) It wasn't, however, until a series of television interviews that he undertook to record with Bill Moyers were first put on the air almost a year after his death that the quiet eminence he had enjoyed in life suddenly leapt skyward into posthumous fame.

These programs, six in number and lasting an hour apiece, were edited from some twenty-four hours of conversations between Campbell and Moyers which were taped during late 1985 and early 1986. The series was entitled "The Power of Myth," and a book was later published under the same title, drawing on both the broadcasts and on transcripts of the unedited conversations. The book became an instant best-seller, as did a new edition of *The Hero with a Thousand Faces*. By then, the series had attracted an audience far larger than anyone had expected. It was a hit, and probably in reruns and on cassette it will go on being a hit for a long time to come. Moreover, it was plain that the show's popularity wasn't simply a result of the awed praise of television critics or even of the almost universal respect in which Moyers has come to be held; among the kind of people who watch so-called talking heads on public television, Moyers has assumed a mantle not unlike that possessed on commercial television in a somewhat earlier period by Walter Cronkite, who was often described as "the most trusted man in America." No doubt Moyers himself would be the first to affirm that it was Campbell's personality, to say nothing of his message, that millions of people were reacting to and, it appeared, heartily agreeing with.

As he had done as a teacher at Sarah Lawrence, Campbell held a class spellbound—this time, one that consisted not of a handful of young women but of an audience beyond counting, of both genders and of nobody knew what range of ages, in a classroom that stretched from coast to coast. As interrogator, Moyers was playing with his usual sincerity the role of Brightest-Boy-in-the-Class. His questions were always simple but never to the point of being simple minded; reassuringly, they reflected a certain knowledge of the subject, which is to say that they took care to avoid that tiresome journalistic device, a pretense of ignorance as a means of securing information. Moyers had plenty of information, gained in part from a close reading of Campbell's books. Behind his rimless glasses, his eyes shone with an eagerness to be instructed in the means by which that information could be made to yield wisdom. In an article in the now defunct 7 *Days* magazine describing the program, Moyers' mouth was said to be "slack with rapture." Moyers was afterward to assert, in defending Campbell against the charge of anti-Semitism, that Campbell was the best Jew, the best Christian, and the best Buddhist he had ever known. Rapture could go no further.

A defect of Moyers' eagerness to sit at Campbell's feet and be instructed by him was the fact that the instruction would be a product of

Campbell's scholarship, which neither Moyers nor the television audience was in a position to pass judgment on. Many of Campbell's professional colleagues had found that scholarship faulty, and in the course of the programs Campbell himself would occasionally contradict, or turn upside down, some of the fundamental concepts that he had set out in print many years before. At one point, he tells Moyers that life and death are two aspects of the same thing (one of his characteristically undemonstrable formulations). He goes on:

> I know of no story in which death is rejected. The Mayan Indians had a kind of basketball game in which, at the end, the captain of the winning team was sacrificed on the field by the captain of the losing team. His head was cut off. Going to your sacrifice as the winning stroke of your life is the essence of the early sacrifice idea.

Moyers is suitably awed; his jaw falls and he says:

> The idea of sacrifice, especially of the winner being sacrificed, is so foreign to our world. Our ruling motif today is winner take all.

Campbell's statement, which comes as such a surprise to Moyers, exactly reverses what Campbell himself had written in *The Mythic Image*, where he describes the *losing* captain as being executed—in short, just what Moyers and the rest of us would expect.

Questions of accurate scholarship aside, what was Campbell's message to Moyers and the world? And why was it so astonishingly well received? Some of his listeners assumed that the message was a wholesomely liberal one. In their view, he was encouraging his listeners not to accept without examination and not to follow without challenge the precepts of any particular religious sect, or political party, or identifiable portion of our secular culture. By taking these precautions, his listeners would escape the conventional, unconscious blinders that all societies are likely to wear. That was the gospel Campbell had preached exactly forty years earlier, in the preface to *The Hero with a Thousand Faces*, where he wrote:

> There are of course differences between the numerous mythologies and religions of mankind, but this is a book about the similarities; and once these are understood the differences will be found to be much less great than is popularly (and politically) supposed. My

hope is that a comparative elucidation may contribute to the perhaps not-quite-desperate cause of those forces that are working in the present world for unification, not in the name of some ecclesiastical or political empire, but in the sense of human mutual understanding. As we are told in the *Vedas:* "Truth is one, the sages speak of it by many names."

Campbell's hero indeed had a thousand faces, which meant that he was equally authentic, equally to be admired, in whatever guise he might be seen to emerge. He was Christ, he was Buddha, he was Abraham Lincoln, he was John Lennon, he was whomever you chose as model for the nature of your own life, suffering, death, and (with luck) rebirth.

Superficially, this was indeed the message, or one of the messages, that "The Power of Myth" conveyed. In that case, why was it greeted so enthusiastically by millions of television watchers? By a million purchasers of the printed version of the program? For surely most Americans were not eager to hear that their fears and longings were identical to those of billions of other human beings, most of them illiterate, impoverished, and diseased, who lay scattered willy-nilly over the face of the globe; still less were they eager to hear that life itself ended in suffering and death, with (but also perhaps without) an eventual rebirth.

What I detect concealed within this superficial message and ready to strike like one of the serpents that are such conspicuous inhabitants of the Campbell mythology is another message, narrower and less speculative than the first. And it is this covert message that the vast majority of his listeners may have been responding to, in part because of its irresistible simplicity. For the message consists of but three innocent-sounding words, and few among us, not taking thought, would be inclined to disagree with them. The words are "Follow your bliss," and Campbell makes clear the consequences of doing so:

> If you follow your bliss, you put yourself on a kind of track that has been there all the while, waiting for you, and the life that you ought to be living is the one you are living. Wherever you are—if you are following your bliss, you are enjoying that refreshment, that life within you, all the time.

Now, it is hard to imagine advice more succinct and, at first glance, more welcome. Seek to do whatever it is that makes you happy,

Campbell tells us, and you will find fulfillment, you will have achieved union with the ineffable, you will be one with whatever form of godhead strikes your fancy. Eros will be there and so will agape; you will frolic in these and other delectable attributes as a dolphin frolics in the wine-dark sea, and if it happens that you are an ugly frog, sooner than you may expect you will be kissed by a virtuous maiden and become a handsome prince. In the world of mythic make-believe, out of which Campbell plucked his three-word precept, the miraculous is a gratifying commonplace.

At one point in their conversations, apparently seeking to pin down the relationship between miraculous myths and attainable bliss, Moyers asks, "What do myths tell me about happiness?" Campbell responds:

> The way to find out about happiness is to keep your mind on those moments when you feel most happy. . . . What is it that makes you happy? Stay with it, no matter what people tell you. This is what I call "following your bliss."

Moyers finds Campbell's circular, repetitive answer unsatisfactory and presses on: "But how does mythology tell you about what makes you happy?" Campbell replies:

> It won't tell you what makes you happy, but it will tell you what happens when you begin to follow your happiness, what the obstacles are that you're going to run into.

He then recounts three or four American Indian tales about maidens rejecting inappropriate suitors, and after the last of these tales Moyers gamely inquires:

> Would you tell this to your students as an illustration of how, if they follow their bliss . . . if they do what they want to, the adventure is its own reward?

Campbell says,

> The adventure is its own reward—but it's necessarily dangerous, having both positive and negative possibilities, all of them beyond control.

Plainly, to follow one's bliss is advice less simple than it sounds and also less idealistic. Indeed, under close scrutiny it may prove distasteful instead of welcome. For what *is* this condition of bliss, as Campbell has defined it? If it is only to do whatever makes one happy, then obviously it sanctions selfishness on a colossal scale—a scale that has become deplorably familiar to us in the Reagan and post-Reagan years. It is a selfishness that is the unspoken (the studiously unrecognized?) rationale of that contemporary army of Wall Street yuppies, of junk-bond dealers, of takeover lawyers who have come to be among the most conspicuous members of our society. Have they not all been following their bliss? But what of the fashion in which they have been doing so—is it not radically at odds with the Judeo-Christian traditions that have served as the centuries-old foundation of our society?

The precept to follow one's bliss is bound to interfere sooner or later with another precept that many Americans were brought up to believe and continue to believe, to wit: that we are our brother's keeper. And when that moment of interference arrives, what are we to do? If he were alive, what would my old friend Joe Campbell's advice to us be under such circumstances? No doubt he would begin by suggesting, with a gentle, rueful smile, that we had totally misconstrued the meaning he had assigned to bliss. But—we would protest—had he not said that bliss consisted of our doing whatever made us happy, and was it not possible for our happiness to spring from an unbroken series of self-aggrandizing acts? Upon which Campbell, smiling more ruefully than ever, might say that we had also totally misconstrued what he had meant by happiness. We would then protest that in fact we had done no such thing. For in other passages of his conversations with Moyers, Campbell had stated that what we perceive as good and evil are but two faces of a single entity, which is life itself, unchanging and unchangeable. ("The world," he assures Moyers, "is great just the way it is. And you are not going to fix it up. Nobody has ever made it any better.") From which it can be argued that selfishness and unselfishness, like good and evil, though contradictory in appearance are identical in nature, and may therefore serve equally well as a source of happiness.

Insouciantly permitting every concept to contain its opposite, Campbell expands on his recommendation that we follow our bliss by a further recommendation to the effect that we turn inward rather than outward in our pursuit of self-fulfillment. And again his words have, upon our first hearing them, the ring of a spiritual rather than a material enhancement, for surely nirvana is inward and the ignoble vexations of this world are outward. But again we had better take a long look at the possible consequences of choosing item A over item B: is it not perhaps only another way of elevating selfishness over unselfishness, of reiterating in a disguised form that we need have nothing to do with our brothers?

By now I have made plain why, in my view, the Campbell-Moyers conversations gained such an unexpectedly high television rating and why Campbell's books were found—and continue to be found—on any number of best-seller lists. It appears that Campbell's message is one that the great majority of Americans are eager to hear. Far from being spiritual, it is intensely materialistic; in a form prettied up with abstractions—bliss, happiness, godhead, ground of being, and the like— my old spellbinding friend is preaching a doctrine similar to that which Ayn Rand voiced in her novel *The Fountainhead*. Over four million copies of that trashy, imperishable work have been sold since it was published in 1943. Throughout its many pages, Rand tirelessly reiterates the gospel of individualism as a political and ethical ideal and denounces altruism in its practical applications—any species of philanthropy, whether private or public—as a demeaning weakness, unworthy of mankind.

The hero of *The Fountainhead*, Howard Roark, is widely assumed to be based on Frank Lloyd Wright, who, like Rand, was consummately elitist in spirit. As a friend of Wright's, I was well aware that he talked a great deal about democracy, as his *"lieber Meister,"* Louis Sullivan, had often done before him, but the word meant whatever those two cranky amateur philosophers wished it to mean, and in neither case did it imply respect for the masses. Wright wrote sneeringly of the common herd in his book on Sullivan, which he called *Genius and the Mobocracy*, and some of the words in that book might well have been lifted directly from the speeches that Rand put into the mouth of Howard Roark and that Campbell uttered in his conversations with Moyers. "The creator lives for his work," says Roark.

> He needs no other men. His primary goal is within himself
> . . . The man who attempts to live for others is . . . a parasite in
> motive and makes parasites of those he serves.

Two years before *The Fountainhead* was published, young Campbell was saying at Sarah Lawrence,

. . . the artist—insofar as he is an artist—looks at the world dispassionately: without thought of defending his ego or his friends, without thought of undoing an enemy; troubled neither with desire nor with loathing.

Had all of Campbell's experience over a long lifetime led to this, then—the continued championing of a right-wing antihumanitarianism that he and Ayn Rand and their like had first championed back in the forties? And if it is this doctrine that lies behind the exceptional success of the Campbell-Moyers conversations, then that success has for me the dead taste of the ashes of the Reagan years, in which so many of my notions of social justice, incorporated into law over the past half-century, have come under attack and in many cases have been reduced to impotence. I perceive now that in my years of poking fun at Campbell over what I called his antediluvian political views and his spongy, evangelical softness of reasoning, I had been far too easy on him and on myself. I had not striven hard enough to unravel the paradox that he embodied: the savant as reactionary. Listening to Campbell and Moyers, I was appalled to realize that what I had regarded as mere eccentricity in the private back-and-forth of conversation in a club was something altogether different when it took the form of a conversation on television—when by providing a national platform and the opportunity for fame (in Campbell's case, posthumous), television had succeeded in transforming my seemingly harmless companion into a dangerous mischief-maker. Which is to say, and with sadness, that my friend had become, if not my enemy, then at the least my adversary.

Louise Nevelson

LOUISE NEVELSON was celebrated in part for having achieved her deserved public success at a late age, which is to say in her sixties. She took care to diminish the significance of this fact by giving every sign, in the years and decades that followed, of intending to keep impertinent death at a distance for as long as she found it convenient to do so. If she had come late to fame, she would enjoy it long; her situation was as simple and amusing (and as serious) as that. Her friends were inclined to believe that she was indeed capable of outwitting nature in almost every respect: certainly in respect to old age if not to death. And this was because nature itself had granted her such an exceptional amount of energy—an energy that she radiated even in repose and that was as robustly and uninhibitedly of the body as it was of the mind. In her seventies and eighties, she gathered people in against her and hugged and kissed them with a relish that was both a sign of personal affection and the emanation of an impersonal—and seemingly unquenchable—physicality.

Some of this physicality Nevelson put to use in a form that, encountered in an actor or politician, we would call "presence." In a room crowded with people, one could almost always sense her arrival even before one saw her; the air in the room was mysteriously, unmistakably quickened, and one turned as if by instinct in the direction where she would be found. Again like an actor or politician, she was a master of the seemingly uncontrived dramatic entrance; as if she had no intention of creating a stir but had been helpless to prevent it, graciously she would yield to the sensation she had prompted.

The effect she wished to make upon her beholders was that of a gorgeous apparition not from outer space—outer space would have had for Nevelson a taint of the vulgar, of the conventionally anticipated— but from some inner space of which she was the sole proprietress and inhabitant. She dressed in a voluminous disarray, which tended to give her a shape architecturally pyramidal; she was at once a goddess occupying a shrine built in her honor and the shrine itself. Like an ancient Egyptian, she wore headpieces of one sort or another that covered her hair and left only the face exposed. By the artistry of her maquillage, that face became more nearly a likeness than an actual face—a mask that she had chosen to impose between the world and herself and out of which her black eyes, guarded by portcullislike false eyelashes, blazed with merriment or anger or mockery or love.

Louise and I had met when she was in her sixties as a consequence of a wedding—one of my daughters was marrying a nephew of hers, the son of her sister Lillian. As far as I could tell at the time, the bridegroom held no formal religious beliefs, but his family being Jewish, he had decided to make this occasion as Jewish as possible, perhaps in order to strike a vivid note among the comparatively colorless, largely non-denominational Gills. (As a collapsed Catholic, I was a sworn enemy of Christianity in all its forms; my wife was, if anything, an Episcopalian, and our children were an indiscriminate lot of believers and non-believers.) Non-Jews are inclined to practice the snobbery of congrat-ulating Jews upon the lofty ethics of Judaism, taking care to learn as little about the religion as possible. I have practiced this snobbery myself, with the especial delight of a Christian apostate, and I threw myself ignorantly but with ardor into preparations for the wedding.

The Gills were then living in a vast mock-Tudor-style house in Bronxville, New York, to which, back in the nineties, its then owner, the illustrator and portrait painter William T. Smedley, had added a sixty-foot-long, three-story-high studio. When we purchased the house from the Smedley heirs, we turned the studio into a gymnasium, with a basketball court, flying rings, a climbing rope, and other athletic facilities. In the past, in my role as an amateur carpenter, electrician, and stage designer, I had transformed the studio-gym on different occasions into a French cabaret, a Japanese geisha house, and an American circus tent; for the wedding ceremony, I erected in it an elaborate *chuppah,* under which the rabbi and the bridal couple could stand and the groom at the appropriate moment could smash a crystal goblet beneath his heel in a gesture that I was told symbolized abandonment of a life of frivolous self-indulgence upon entering into the responsibilities of the married state.

The wedding ceremony went off splendidly, marred only by an interruption on the part of my Yankee father-in-law, who was elderly and deaf and who at first supposed that the ceremony was being conducted by a Catholic priest speaking Latin (distressing enough from his point of view, he being a former deacon of the Brick Presbyterian Church and Catholics belonging in his view largely to the servant class). In a whispered conference with my brother, he learned that the speaker was a rabbi and the language being spoken Hebrew. "Do you mean to say," my father-in-law burst out loudly, "that my new grandson-in-law is a *Jew?*" The rabbi glanced over at the distinguished, noisy old man, his worst fears of Bronxville (once a well-known center of anti-Semitism) confirmed, and perhaps his worst fears about the Gills confirmed as well. "Shall we continue?" he asked, in an apprehensive voice. The goblet was duly smashed, though as time passed the consequences of this gesture left something to be desired.

After the ceremony, a dance was held in the gymnasium. Louise Nevelson stood on the sidelines, which simply by her standing there were no longer condemned to being considered sidelines. Grandly and as of right, she held court, while her pretty young granddaughter, among a number of other members of the wedding party, was whirling about the dance floor. At one point, a woman with whom I was dancing noticed, as I did, that the circular gold earrings that Louise's granddaughter was wearing pleasingly resembled in shape her breasts as we glimpsed them emerging from the low bodice of her dress. In the course of a moment's gossip with Louise, we mentioned this resemblance, and Louise responded at once, and characteristically, with a bawdy anecdote. She had given her granddaughter a pearl—natural, not cultivated—in the shape of a pear, hanging at the end of a gold necklace. One evening at a party the granddaughter was wearing the necklace, and the young man in whose arms she found herself kept glancing down as they danced. In all innocence, the granddaughter asked, "Oh, are you admiring the pear that my grandmother gave me?" Quick as a flash, the resourceful young man replied, "No, I am admiring the pair that your parents gave you."

Out of that wedding came, along with our friendship, the opportunity for Louise and me to pretend that we were "kissin' cousins"—I "Cousin Brendan" to her, she "Cousin Louise" to me. Because the relationship was a source of bewilderment to others it became, as one might expect, a source of conspiratorial satisfaction to us. We were like children keeping a secret that is of no value beyond the fact that it *is* a secret.

Louise had no patience with the Mrs. Grundys of this world. With respect to sex, money, and other important topics, she spoke her mind. In his biography of her, Arnold Glimcher recounts a characteristic anecdote:

> During an opening at the Martha Jackson Gallery, Nevelson was interrupted in conversation with friends by a man who suddenly hugged and kissed her. One of the men already talking to Nevelson turned to the interloper and said, "I didn't know that you knew Louise Nevelson." He replied, "I've known Louise for more years that I can remember. I know her very well." Nevelson raised her glasses suspended on a silver chain around her neck, looked directly into the intruder's eyes, and asked, "Have I ever slept with you?" Embarrassed, the quickly shrinking man nervously said, "Why, no, no, of course not." "Then you don't know me very well," Nevelson replied and, turning back to the man she was originally speaking with, continued the conversation.

Louise had in abundance that sense of personal worth without which an artist is unlikely to persist, as Louise was fated to do, decade after decade with little critical attention, until at last she found her way into that world of superbly spooky sculpture which earned her— suddenly and as if without effort—a worldwide fame. To the strangers engaged in discovering her, it was as if a locked door somewhere inside her had unaccountably swung open of its own accord, but Louise would have said that every step of the journey could be accounted for, in terms of trial and error; no one batters his or her way unscathed into the dark cave of the unconscious, and those matte black walls of hers (later sometimes to be white, sometimes to be gold) present themselves with the air of trophies brought back to us over the abysm of time and speaking with the authority of the primordial. The found objects out of which her sculptures are composed achieve an uncanny remoteness from us—put on a totemic sacredness that, like the animal hair, skin, and bone which serve to create the visage of the South Seas tribal god, seems wholly unrelated to their origins in the everyday world.

Louise was born in Kiev, Russia, in 1899, one of four children of Isaac and Minna Berliawsky. The family emigrated to the United States in 1905, settling in Rockland, Maine, where the father became a successful builder and where Louise attended the public schools. (She retained traces of Down East pronunciations throughout her lifetime.) As Orthodox Jews, the Berliawskys had been given little encouragement in the art of drawing human likenesses, yet no sooner did Louise and her family arrive in the New World than she revealed an exceptional gift for drawing—as, indeed, did other members of the family, implying that the gift had lain dormant among them over no telling how many generations.

Louise graduated from high school at eighteen and two years later married a wealthy young New Yorker named Charles Nevelson, younger brother of a business acquaintance of her father. The Nevelsons set up housekeeping in New York City, where in 1922 Louise had a son, Myron. Dissatisfied with marriage and motherhood (the Nevelsons were eventually to be divorced and Myron, nicknamed Mike, was to be her only child), Louise tested her talent in the fields of singing, dancing, and acting, as well as in painting and sculpture; she studied under Kenneth Hayes Miller at the Art Students League in New York City, under Hans Hofmann in Munich, and on her own in Paris. She had her first one-woman show in New York City in 1941, but it wasn't until the 1950s that she may be said to have "arrived," with purchases of her work by the Whitney Museum of American Art, the Brooklyn Museum, and the Museum of Modern Art. And it may be that arrived is too tame a metaphor for the sensation that her work caused and that Louise herself had long been ready for.

My last encounter with Cousin Louise took place in September 1987, when she and I shared a merry visit to Youngstown, Ohio. In that city, a new wing of the Butler Institute of American Art was being opened and the high point of the festivities was the presentation to Louise of the Butler Medal for Life Achievement in the Arts. We were flown to Youngstown in a private plane belonging to some local nabob. Louise talked a blue streak all the way and was in tearing high spirits throughout the ceremonies. She enjoyed being made much of in little Youngstown as fervently as she enjoyed being made much of in New York or London or Paris: a monarch as thoroughly at ease dispensing praise to others as accepting praise herself. She was eighty-seven and only a few months away from her death, but with what an air of being in the midst of life she presided over that occasion! Never was a medal presented to a worthier recipient and never was a recipient more confident of her worthiness. Her "dears" and "darlings" were scattered broadside; under the celebrated inch-long false eyelashes her black eyes gleamed with delight. Standing beside her, I could sense that her field of energy was expanding and that, whether the other guests were aware of it or not, the party would be a late one.

The next day we were flown back to New York, and nothing would do but that I climb with her up to the roof of her house on Spring Street and admire the roses still in bloom in the helter-skelter garden that she had fashioned there. All round us in the late afternoon sunlight shimmered the chimneys and wooden, spider-legged water towers of Manhattan. She was full of plans for the future. She might build an addition to the house (already a labyrinth, cobbled up out of two or three earlier, adjoining structures). If she hesitated over building, it was because she didn't want to shut off air and light from her neighbors. And speaking of neighbors, she said, it happened that one of them presided over a funeral home, the heat of whose crematorium furnaces helped to keep her house warm throughout the winter. How spoiled she was, and had always been, by happy accidents of this sort!

After an hour or so, we made our way down through the house, past room after room in which Nevelson stored not only fragments of works in progress but the inimitable debris—bedposts, legs of chairs, gunstocks—out of which the large finished works were wittily accumulated. We stood for a moment in the open doorway, facing the twilit side street, and then it was as it had always been—hug, kiss, and goodbye.

George Plimpton

FIRST, A LOVING FATHER fears that his son may fail. It then happens that the son, far from failing, enjoys a success that threatens to exceed the father's. At this point, the father begins to fear that in the world's eyes his own hitherto unquestioned success may come to seem, next to that of his son, markedly diminished. And so it turns out that the emotion of fear finds a new reason for existence, wholly at odds with the reason that had prompted it. But perhaps even this unexpected turn of events will turn out not to be the whole story. Perhaps that initial emotion of fear *doesn't* need to find a new reason for existence. For what if nothing has changed? What if the apparently unselfish desire for one's beloved son to succeed has been, in fact, a selfish desire for him to fail? The father is appalled; he denies to himself and to the world that any such reading of the situation is possible. As for the son, he is amused; he admits that his fame has sprung in large measure from a need to allay his father's concern for him. Strange, isn't it (the son speculates many years later), that his father couldn't have been more at ease with this question of motives? For the father, too, in his day, had been a son, which is to say that he, too, had had a father who expressed a fear of his son's failing . . .

I observed this classic Oedipal melodrama being enacted over a couple of decades by Francis T. P. Plimpton and his son George, and there was no more possibility of altering the course of it with advice, whether good or bad, than there would be of, say, preventing an automobile accident that was about to take place within one's sight but at a thousand yards' distance down a high-speed expressway. Not that the melodrama had the appearance of being a violent one; no voices were likely to be raised in my presence, much less limbs broken, for the Plimptons are a family whose ancient lineage has been accompanied, time out of mind, by exceptional good manners. They do not howl or beat their heads against walls or throw one another out of windows. Lady Violet Bonham Carter said once that "outer space is no place for a person of breeding." A possible corollary of this remarkable dictum is that for people of breeding, the disciplined inner space of the mind is where they breathe easiest, even when they are breathing hard. If Francis and George ever got past that sufficiently dangerous point—the point at which passion, jousting with civility, unseats it—the occasion was unknown to me.

Francis, who was born in 1900 and died in 1983, was for over half a century an ornament of the bar, on a national as well as a local level. In his youth, after graduation from Amherst and the Harvard Law School, he became a founding partner in the still flourishing firm of Debevoise and Plimpton. He served as president of the Bar of the City of New York and president of the American Bar Association, as well as the United States' ambassador to the United Nations between 1961 and 1965. He was married to Pauline Ames, a member of one of the few Massachusetts families in a position to look down upon Plimptons (not that an Ames would ever be so ill-bred as to do so, at any rate in public). Her brother, Amyas Ames, has long been a leading citizen of New York. Pauline and Francis had four children, of whom George was the firstborn.

George attended Exeter and Harvard (class of '48), where he distinguished himself both as a writer and as an athlete—a combination that is perhaps even rarer at Harvard than at most Ivy League colleges—and spent two years at Cambridge University. Conventional in his successes up to that point, he ought to have been conventional in his choice of a career, but no: off he went to Paris, where he became part of a group of writers that included Harold Humes (universally known as "Doc" in tribute to the breadth of his learning), William Styron, Terry Southern, and Tom Guinzberg. With them, he founded the *Paris*

Review, a literary quarterly of which he remains the editor to this day. It was during George's Paris period that Francis began to worry. From time to time, I would encounter him at the Century Club (of which he was for several years president), and sooner or later he would get around to the question that preoccupied him. "What are we going to do about George?" he would ask, usually with a sigh suitable to an inquiry into the health of a relative known to be dying.

In age, I was about halfway between Francis in his middle fifties and George in his twenties, and therefore ideally situated in Francis' mind to be a sort of go-between—a parent like him and therefore sympathetic to his alarm and yet a writer who was still comparatively young and therefore sympathetic to George and his literary aspirations. From Francis' point of view, I seemed to possess the further advantage of being able to earn a living as a writer, and this not very lofty capability of mine was something that Francis suspected his beloved harum-scarum George of lacking. To his experienced eye, the *Paris Review* did not promise to become a gold mine.

When Francis asked, "What are we going to do about George?" his use of the pronoun "we" in the reiterated question flattered me, as implying that I was fit to share an intimate family problem, but in fact I scarcely knew George at that time and could have had no influence over him. Moreover, if I *had* possessed such an influence, I wouldn't have exercised it in a fashion pleasing to Francis. From the beginning, I was on George's side and I constantly rebuked Francis for his fretful mother-hen possessiveness. "Leave George alone!" was my repeated answer to Francis' question. "He is doing exactly what he wants to do and needs to do." And to this unwelcome statement I would add, "The only thing a father should do in these circumstances is send his son money." Francis would wince; I had doubled the force of my rebuke by mentioning money.

What became of George is, of course, his biography: a story simultaneously personal and professional, with his two lives so intricately interwoven that not the thinnest of knife blades can be inserted between them. To have edited the *Paris Review* with such unflagging zest for over forty years might well be counted a sufficient career in itself. He has harvested a number of books from its pages, the latest of which is a compilation of witty and instructive literary obiter dicta entitled *A Writer's Chapbook.* He has also written eight or ten books on his own, including a brilliant work of fiction, *The Curious Case of Sidd Finch*, and (with Jean Stein) a biography of Edie Sedgwick. The exploits that have served as the raw material of his journalism (and sometimes of his appearances on television)—boxing with Archie Moore, playing football with the Detroit Lions, performing circus acrobatics at the top of the tent, playing an instrument or two (the triangle, the kettle drums) in the New York Philharmonic Orchestra under Leonard Bernstein—have long since made him a celebrity in his own right. Indeed, he has become far better known than most of the people he has written about; they have consented to bask in George's shadow, not he in theirs. One result of this fame is the number of sales pitches that he makes on television. Coming into a room, one hears his distinctive, faintly Bostonian upper-class voice seductively peddling some product or other, and there is no need to look at the screen; it can only be George.

Francis lived to see the transformation of George from an anonymous young man finding his way as a writer in Paris to a celebrity who maintained a salon in a remodeled tenement building on the East River (a salon that, though somewhat ramshackle, boasted a regulation-size pool table, convenient on occasion for the serving of buffet suppers); who enjoyed a close friendship with Jackie Onassis, encouraging her to enter that world of editors and writers where she is now so much at home; who masterminded an annual fireworks display on eastern Long Island; and who was himself a distinguished member of the very same clubs that Francis belonged to—the Century, the Brook, the Piping Rock, the River, the Coffee House. Francis marveled at this transformation and shook his head over these multiple sources of renown. He was a writer himself, who took pride in the elegance of his prose, whether spoken or written, and who composed verses that scanned and rhymed in the classical mode, and it was not at all clear to him that George was what the Plimpton and Ames families would ordinarily have called a *writer*, but there you were! The world certainly thought so.

It was then that I began to detect in Francis a wry vexation with the change that had taken place in his relationship with George. As someone who had acquired, over many years and with much honorable labor, a national reputation, it was both a source of pleasure and a source of displeasure to be introduced with increasing frequency as "George's father." With time, he adopted a pose of rueful resignation to his fate. Oh, dear, yes, wasn't George wonderful? And wasn't he—

Francis—lucky to share in some small portion of George's glory? A tincture of mischief-making often colors our conversation with old friends. I would put to Francis the question of whether he remembered the days when he used to ask me what we were going to do about George. "Vaguely," he would say. "Vaguely. I was worried about him, as any good father would be."

"And now what do you feel?" I would ask him, not without malice. "Envy? Perhaps even a twinge of disappointment in his success?"

Francis was shocked. "Certainly not! The nonsense you writers talk!"

"It's true," I said. "We spoil everything, we can never leave well enough alone."

Wisely, we would break off there, leaving unfinished a discussion that can never be brought to any satisfactory end. Francis has been dead for several years and the young George whom he and I once quarreled over has vanished almost without a trace. In his stead I see a white-haired man in his sixties, with deep lines in his face. And this George, what am I to say of him? Well, surely, to begin with, that he has a son . . .

John Betjeman

SOME YEARS before Sir John Betjeman was appointed poet laureate of England, he paid his first visit to this country, stopping over for a day or so in New York City on his way to what he plainly believed to be the Wild West—that is, Cincinnati. There, to his terror ("I don't much like the young. What ever shall I say to them? If only they were eighty-five!"), he had been persuaded to play the role of Poet-in-Residence for several weeks at the University of Cincinnati. Poets—at any rate, English poets—tend to be an endearing lot, attracting the protective instinct as a magnet does pins, and Sir John was no exception. He spent a lifetime taking advantage of his well-known ineptitude with respect to the mundane. In the belief that his sensibilities were far too delicate to survive the abrasions of ordinary life, in which plane tickets must be purchased and hotel accommodations secured, Betjeman used to be handed on from friend to friend like a morsel of fragile Dresden ware; this left him free to devote his energies and talents to what chiefly interested him.

A friend whom Betjeman and I happened to have in common and who arranged for the poet and me to have lunch together on the day of his arrival here took care to explain to me that the dear fellow had a tendency to turn green when things became too much for him, and while he had been lovingly bundled aboard a plane in London and had been no less lovingly unraveled from it at Kennedy, his first sight of the height and breadth of New York might well have had that effect on him. If so, if I found that his color was predominantly green, would I please keep my voice low and devote our conversation mostly to the weather? I assured him I would, but the request proved unnecessary. Betjeman and I met at the Brussels, which at the time was a fashionable restaurant on East Fifty-fourth Street. Since Betjeman and I shared an interest in Victorian and Edwardian architecture, I had chosen the Brussels as being likely to please him for architectural as well as for culinary reasons: it occupied what had once been the handsome town house of the banker Frank Vanderlip. The old Vanderlip kitchen served as the suave little bar of the Brussels, and the Vanderlip dining room had been expanded into what had been a considerable garden; windows in the east wall of the dining room looked out over a couple of adjoining gardens, striking an agreeable note of *rus in urbe.*

Far from having been caused to turn green by the jagged profile of our city, Betjeman was plainly in rude health and good spirits. An admirer once described Betjeman as looking like a highly intelligent muffin, and the resemblance was certainly there; a plump man in his fifties, with small, dark, shining eyes, negligible eyebrows, and an infectious, schoolboy laugh, he had no sooner seated himself at the Brussels than he ordered a bourbon on the rocks. "Because this is my first visit to the States, I want to do everything in the American style," he said. "I understand that bourbon is the authentic American drink. I mean to be intensely American during my stay at Cincy—I hope it isn't disrespectful of me to call Cincy Cincy so soon. The drive in from the airport this morning was an exaltation. The Woolworth building looks enchanting. All that Gothic work so high in the air, so close to eternity! I can't imagine what Cincy will be like. A city of hills, I believe, and then, of course, the river, and beyond the river, Kentucky. Everyone told me that I should be terrified out of my wits in America, and I'm not in the least frightened. I feel *very* brave."

Over a hearty, authentically American lunch, I learned that Betjeman, who chose to identify himself in *Who's Who* as a "poet and hack," had a Dutch great-great-grandfather; that his great-grandfather, a silversmith, founded the family fortune by inventing that extremely popular Victorian device, the tantalus, in which decanters of whisky, port, and the like can be locked up and thus prove no temptation to tippling servants; and that Betjeman himself was born in London, was an old boy of the posh Marlborough school and a graduate of Oxford, was married, had a son and daughter, lived in a tiny house in London, had a country place in Wantage, Berkshire, was a member of the Athenaeum and the Garrick, and had written more books than he could remember the names of. ("No matter," he said. "They're very *little* books.") His first job was as a schoolmaster. "Couldn't keep order and so got sacked," he said. "Then I tried insurance-broking and sacked myself. Then I served as secretary to Sir Horace Plunkett, who sacked me. Then I went back to schoolmastering. My great interest has always been architecture, so I left schoolmastering again and spent two years working on the *Architectural Review* and three years editing county guidebooks for Shell. In fact, I invented the guidebooks. There are those who would call me an 'architectural historian,' but I don't believe in such titles. To me, there are only the people who use their eyes when they look about and the people who don't. Once the term architectural historian is permitted, the door is open to other historians to start writing books about architectural historians. Ghastly! At the moment, I live by writing book reviews for the *Daily Telegraph* and a column—largely about architectural matters—for the *Spectator*, by appearances on the BBC, and by dipping into capital, as who does not?"

Betjeman finished a second cup of coffee, leaned back, patted his well-filled waistcoat, and asked me if I admired Henry James. I said I did. "Then you'll be interested to know that my body is exactly the same size and shape that his was," Betjeman said. "How do I know? Because I inherited his morning coat, waistcoats, and underclothes. After his death, his wardrobe came into the possession of one of the Oxford colleges and was up at auction, where I bought it. Lo and behold!— everything fitted me to a T. Exquisitely made, they are; over half a century since James died, and they show scarcely any wear. Of course, I get into them only on suitably august occasions, like weddings and funerals. Someday, if I think of it, I must present them to an institution over here. What more precious link between our two great countries than the linen drawers of the Master?"

After lunch, I took Betjeman on an architectural tour of midtown. Although in conversation we had already agreed that the first rule to be followed on such tours is "Look up! Look up! Always look up!", as we were making our way along Park Avenue, I urged Betjeman for once to look down instead of up. Calling his attention to the narrow slit of open space that separates the apparently solid masonry base of the skyscrapers along the avenue from the sidewalk on which we were strolling, I explained that the buildings rest not upon concrete foundations but upon slender steel pins springing up out of bedrock many feet below, in the maze of railway tracks that run beneath the avenue. Betjeman was aghast with admiration at this feat of engineering trompe l'oeil. Instantly he knelt down and then spread-eagled himself upon the sidewalk, pushing his muffin face close to the aperture I had indicated and thrusting his pudgy fingers into it. There prostrate on the sidewalk lay the future poet laureate of England; the crowd of pedestrians swept past him without a glance.

A couple of weeks later, finding myself on another pleasurable luncheon occasion seated next to Leon Edel, the biographer of Henry James, I eagerly recounted to him the story of Betjeman's having "inherited" the Jamesian wardrobe. After half a century of continuous marination in the Master, there is simply nothing about Henry James that Edel docsn't know, and the Betjeman inheritance was, as I ought to have expected, already familiar to him. "Such a pleasant story!" he said. "Too bad it isn't true." He was quick to add that Betjeman wasn't intentionally telling a lie. The facts were these: During the Second World War, an organization was formed in this country calling itself Bundles for Britain, whose purpose was to ship overseas to the beleaguered British anything in the way of unneeded clothing that we Americans felt moved to donate. One of Henry James' nephews—a son of Henry's brother William—bore the great writer's name. He lived in New York and in my youth I had encountered him from time to time on social occasions. He was a distinguished-looking old gentleman, of whom I once had the temerity to inquire, with a certain amount of preliminary throat-clearing, whether he thought his uncle was a homosexual. To which, after an equal amount of throat-clearing on his part, he replied, "Nothing like that, certainly not," and got up and left the room. In any event, this second—and secondary—Henry James having died at a ripe age, his widow had gathered up his clothes and handed them over to Bundles for Britain, which had duly forwarded them to England. They had reached Oxford, identified only as having belonged to Henry James, and of course it was that formidable name that had attracted Betjeman's attention.

To Edel, I protested, "But, Leon, the world must know the truth!"

"No, no, let Betjeman go on believing something so appropriate to his nature."

Which is how it happened that an eminent biographer made a gift of high value to an eminent poet, who was never to know that he had received it.

Eleanor Roosevelt

ONE EVENING in the autumn of 1932, as a freshman at Yale, I was walking along College Street on my way to a political rally in Woolsey Hall, the university's largest auditorium. As I approached its entrance, I noticed a tall woman in an emerald-colored evening gown standing alone in the dark at the top of a flight of steps leading to the stage door of the hall. I recognized her as Eleanor Roosevelt, the wife of Franklin Delano Roosevelt, governor of New York and Democratic party candidate for the presidency of the United States. The election was only a couple of weeks away. I had just turned eighteen and in accordance with the law as it then existed, I would not be eligible to vote until I was twenty-one; nevertheless, in principle I was ardently in favor of Roosevelt. The rally at Woolsey Hall was in his behalf, and I was attending it in order to make plain where I stood. The strongly Protestant and Republican Yale of those days was as indolent politically as a South Sea island; a straw vote recently taken on campus had indicated that the undergraduate body was overwhelmingly in favor of Hoover, the incumbent president.

My family was Irish Catholic, and in those days Irish Catholics were almost invariably Democrats; indeed, the only time my father ever voted for a Republican was in 1920, when, fearing that the party of Wilson would lead us into further foreign entanglements, he had voted

74

for Harding and Coolidge. He had never ceased to regret this momentary lapse. Helping to strengthen my Democratic ties was the fact that my brother-in-law, Thomas J. Spellacy, was the mayor of Hartford and the Democratic boss of Connecticut. By coincidence, Spellacy had been an assistant attorney general of the United States during part of the Wilson administration, at a time when Roosevelt was serving as an assistant secretary of the navy; they had attended the peace conference in Paris together. (I should add that in 1932 my brother-in-law, though as a Democrat he campaigned vigorously for Roosevelt, in private conversation, like so many of Roosevelt's colleagues at the time, dismissed him as a lightweight.)

I was startled to see Mrs. Roosevelt standing unattended outside the stage door of Woolsey. Running up the steps, I asked if I could be of any assistance to her. "I've knocked, but nobody appears to have heard me," she said. She seemed not in the least perturbed by the fact that the people in charge of the rally had counted on her to find her way to the hall without an escort. Seating herself on a stone parapet at the top of the stairs, she said, "I was told to come to the stage door. I assume this must be it?" Something in the tone of her voice—that curiously high voice, subject to change of pitch without notice—implied that if anyone had made a mistake, it was she; moreover, she would be ready to accept the blame. I assured her that she had done exactly right. I pounded on the door and no sooner had I done so than a couple of apologetic upperclassmen came tumbling out of the backstage area to welcome her.

Mrs. Roosevelt thanked me for volunteering my assistance and I said my goodbyes. She was one of several speakers at the rally, which, to judge by the smattering of applause it provoked, confirmed the straw vote: Yale saw Hoover as the man of the future. After the rally, when I reflected on my good fortune in having met Mrs. Roosevelt, I was surprised to realize that I found her good-looking. In the photographs of her that appeared constantly in newspapers and magazines, she was far from that; her buck teeth and receding chin were gross defects and had caused her to be described in print, with the usual harshness of journalists, as an "ugly duckling." It was to be said of her repeatedly throughout her lifetime that in person she had a "radiance" that made people forget her ugliness, but I perceived even then, on that long-ago evening in New Haven, that it wasn't a matter of having to forget: the ugliness simply wasn't there. Nor does radiance, unless we take particular care to define it, sufficiently explain the effect she had upon others. In most cases, what we think of as radiance implies the possession of a confidence in one's powers and in one's place in the world that causes people to follow wherever one leads. The radiance I sensed wasn't of that kind at all. Mysteriously, it appeared to consist of the opposite attributes—that is, of a desire and will to lead, coupled with a burden of self-doubt that kept her, though in constant motion, off balance: it was the radiance of vulnerability, of a feared imminent failure, of a Saint Joan without the voices.

Another surprising aspect of my minor encounter with Mrs. Roosevelt was that, while most boys of eighteen would have considered a woman of her age—she was then in her late forties—deplorably old, in her case I felt no such thing; she seemed extraordinarily young and vivid, with thick, glossy brown hair and fair skin. She had had six children and yet she was girlish, and I remember wondering then and in the years thereafter what this discrepancy signified. Was it a result of her continuing to believe in certain optimistic promises about life that the majority of people, as they grow older, relinquish? Plainly, Mrs. Roosevelt was still a believer; so, no doubt, was her husband, which was one of the reasons that I wished him to succeed the feckless Hoover.

In the years and decades that followed, I met Mrs. Roosevelt on a few other occasions, equal in unimportance to our meeting at Yale: a luncheon at the house of a New Yorker colleague (with a mynah bird strolling up and down the table, to Mrs. Roosevelt's evident alarm), a political gathering at her apartment overlooking Washington Square. She wrote a syndicated newspaper column about her daily activities, and when a play, The Day the Money Stopped, written by Maxwell Anderson and me, arrived on Broadway, she attended two performances of it and praised it highly. Among critics, whether amateur or professional, she was almost alone in doing so. This was kind of her, and it was also notably adroit—the play lasted only a few days.

On May 19, 1944, Mrs. Roosevelt wrote a letter to her close friend Joseph P. Lash (who was subsequently to compose an admirable biography of her). She was nearing sixty, and the Second World War had cast its shadow over much of the world. If she was still a believer in the intrinsic goodness of life, the prospect for her, like the prospect for the world, appeared to be darkening. She wrote, "I must really live in the Big House this year, but whenever I can I want to be at the cottage . . . I'll never like the Big House but suddenly F. is more dependent, the children and grandchildren look upon this as home and the cottage is just mine, so I must try to keep this lived in & really pleasant. Never from choice would I live here however & and never alone."

The Big House of that letter was Springwood, the Roosevelt place at Hyde Park, and the cottage was Val-Kill, which her husband had permitted her to build in a pleasant wooded corner of the property and where she could entertain with open affection a few close women friends. The other Big House in Mrs. Roosevelt's life—the White House—was also less appealing to her than the cottage, but it stood for duty, which she welcomed, and it held no continuously reverberating overtones of hatred and self-abasement, no sense of the fulfillment she felt that she had been denied as a woman, wife, mother, and grand-mother. Since she was never very good at slang (and had, moreover, so small a knack for strong language that her occasional use of the word "hell" was known to startle people), it may be that she was unaware of the fact that "big house" was in its day a common term for prison. However unconscious the link in her mind between the two half-rhyming Hudson River establishments, Springwood and Sing Sing, prison is what Hyde Park became to her at twenty, as the most innocent, tender-hearted, intelligent, and humorlessly ambitious of brides, and a prison it remained to her for forty years.

To make matters worse—and in Eleanor Roosevelt's private life, matters had a way of nearly always turning out worse instead of better—the tyrannizing old mother-in-law to whom Hyde Park belonged, and from whom even her world-famous son in his middle years had to beg domestic and financial favors, characteristically managed to remain in residence there after her death. The formidable ghost of Sara Delano Roosevelt stalked the tacky halls and tastelessly furnished rooms of Hyde Park, and her doting son saw no reason that it need ever be exorcised; it resides there today, as a part of his bequest to the nation. FDR was almost sixty when Sara died, but he put a mourning band on his sleeve and may be said never to have fully recovered from her death in the four years of life that were left to him. Like so many eminent Victorians, he enjoyed being tethered by his mother's apron strings; for all his reluc-tance to practice self-examination, he would perhaps have agreed with

Freud's dictum that no man who has been his mother's favorite knows what it is to fear failure.

FDR was the only child of a virginal matron of twenty-eight who adored her father and had come as close as possible to marrying him by marrying, against his wishes, one of his contemporaries, James Roosevelt. Franklin Roosevelt was so much hers, especially in the years of long widowhood that began for her at forty-six (she took a house in Boston in order to be near him while he was at Harvard), that she always thought of him as a Delano and not as a Roosevelt. She was made uneasy by the Oyster Bay, or Eleanor, side of the family because, though interesting, they were so pushy, so noisy, so *public*. If, in the nature of things, her darling had to take a wife, a Roosevelt was certainly better than nothing; the poor creature, orphaned and ill at ease, would be privileged to become Sara Delano's puppet, once she had proved capable of producing suitable descendants. Sara Delano was rather annoyed when the first of these descendants turned out to be a girl; luckily, the second was a boy, and could be given, according to her wishes, the first name of her late husband.

In Sara's eyes, Franklin's wife would always have a perfectly satisfactory goal in life, which was the perpetuation of the confident, self-delighting aristocracy that had flourished for generations on the banks of the Hudson, among the only kind of people that Sara thought counted: Delanos, Livingstons, Chanlers, and the like. She was proud of Franklin not because he had achieved the highest office in the land— after all, a member of the pushy side of the family had already done that. He had performed a feat that, creditable though it was, had the defect of obviously costing an effort to obtain. One had ever so vulgarly to want the presidency and to be seen to want it, by people who not only felt entitled to see but to *stare*. No, she gloried in Franklin for a much simpler and grander reason: he was her son, and for her, as for any aristocrat, that fact sufficed.

The contrast with the nonaristocratic Kennedys is instructive. It is hard to imagine Joseph and Rose Kennedy being proud of their children for any reason except accomplishment. In making accomplishment the criterion of a good life, Eleanor and Franklin Roosevelt were both going against their class, as her Uncle Theodore had done before them. As for Sara, it was always clear to her that to be was better than to do. In the late summer of 1939, it happened that several members of my family and I returned from Europe on the same ocean liner as Sara. Whenever my father encountered her on deck or in one of the public rooms, he would bow to her and say "Your Majesty." To my mind a risky jest, but my father knew her kind well: she had no difficulty accepting his greeting as a compliment and she bestowed upon him a pleased smile and a wagging of the royal wattles.

On one occasion—the hurly-burly of election night in 1940—Sara Delano allowed her aristocratic vanity to betray her. Reporters having asked her, in the usual fatuous journalistic fashion, how she felt, she replied, "Am I proud of being a historic mother? Indeed I am." Granted that she was repeating a reporter's question, still, what was going on in that imperious mind? She might have said a charming word or two about how lucky she was to possess a historic son, but how dared she accept the appellation of historic mother? One catches a glimpse of a bizarrely laicized Holy Family, with old Joseph safely put away and Christ and Mary in cozy rapture. Shaking one's head, one thinks, "Bone-breaking old harridan! Who could survive such serene effrontery?"

And then one thinks, "Well, but *did* anyone survive? *Has* anyone?" It was only when Joseph P. Lash published his book, *Eleanor and Franklin*, that I felt able to speculate with some confidence on these and other questions of a like nature. Lash was writing from Eleanor's point of view and not her husband's, and if there is another side of the story, FDR's biographers will be sure to recount it. Meanwhile, the Roosevelt marriage strikes me as having been simultaneously one of the most fruitful and most sterile on record—a marriage by which the world continuously profited but which left at least one of the parties to it feeling continuously cheated of her life. And formally outside the marriage but at the very heart of it stood Sara. What a tug-of-war she importunately presided over and helped exacerbate from year to year and then from decade to decade!

On the one hand, we have the handsome, tricky, and never deeply loving Franklin; on the other, the awkward, invincibly straightforward, loving, but unplayful Eleanor. No matter how much she gave, it either was not enough or, what was worse, it was the one thing not wanted. She could not bend to him, could not offer him the uncritical adulation that he craved from women and was nearly all that he craved from them.

There was no chance to make such a marriage turn out well; there was only the chance that it could be made to turn out as little badly as possible, but how was Eleanor Roosevelt, at twenty or even thirty, to concede such dire bounds to those imagined promises of life with which she had begun? For she always fiercely hoped against hope. It was a habit inculcated by the relentless, inescapable disasters of childhood— the beautiful young mother who mocked her and died, the handsome young father who cherished her and became an alcoholic and was sent away and died. Without the help of this habit of believing that what could never be was about to be, she might not have survived the series of deprivations that made up what the world assumed was an exceptionally rich and rewarding career. "It is a terrible thing to know me," she said once, in reference to the political insults addressed to friends on her account; in another sense, she could have said (and must often have thought), "It is a terrible thing to know myself."

In a great poem by Yeats one reads of "the folly that man does / or must suffer, if he woos / a proud woman not kindred of his soul." With the Roosevelts, it was the ironic case that he wooed a proud woman literally of his kindred and yet utterly alien to his soul—wooed her and won her, brought her home to an intolerable dragon of a mother-in-law, and was unfaithful to her with the pretty and lively girl who was her social secretary (it was like him to take the easy way and keep everything in the house—mother, wife, children, and mistress all mingled there together). Even after being desperately crippled by polio, he remained a flirtatious cavalier, seeking and finding—"for relaxation," Eleanor said with contempt—qualities and appetites that were the very opposite of his wife's. She was Duty, stern daughter of the voice of God, and he liked play as well as duty and was awfully good at play. So was Churchill, who invited Eleanor to Chequers during the war and appears to have found her a tiresome dinner companion; she wished to debate the question of Loyalist Spain with him, and he may have wanted to tell her some mildly risqué stories.

Growing older, Roosevelt became more dependent, as Eleanor wrote in her letter to Lash, but this was not to say that he was becoming more dependent on her. In age many married couples grow closer, in part faute de mieux and in part because their temperaments have tended to accommodate to each other over a long period of time. Contrariwise, the Roosevelts drew apart in age, for she remained as stiffly and indefatigably devoted to doing good as she had ever been, and he, as his labors mounted and his powers waned, required the consolation of untroubled social intercourse. It was a cruel fact that the less he saw of her the better he felt. He called in their daughter Anna to act as a shield between him and the hammer, hammer, hammer of Eleanor's arsenal of unresolved and perhaps unresolvable national and international problems. He liked dining with Anna, with his secretary, Missy LeHand, with his cousin Laura Delano, and with his former mistress, Lucy Mercer Rutherfurd, who would be smuggled into the White House without his wife's knowledge while she was off on one or another of her celebrated journeys. And it was Mrs. Rutherfurd who was to be in the room with him at Warm Springs when he died. On being told of Mrs. Rutherfurd's presence there on that occasion, Eleanor said not a word.

What a story it is—a melodrama that is of inexhaustible interest to those of us who observed (in my case, at a distance but with ever-increasing interest) the unfolding of its plot. Seventeen notably useful years of life remained to Eleanor after her husband died, and as if to signal the degree of her release from that unacknowledged bondage, she underwent a remarkable physical transformation. The Eleanor that the world had once cruelly called an ugly duckling and in whom I had found, to my youthful astonishment, lineaments of beauty, became in age a very handsome old lady. An automobile accident had knocked out her prominent front teeth and the plastic surgery that followed had improved her profile, but the change went far beyond any mere necessary cosmetic tinkerings. And it was a change that signaled a profound irony. For to resemble a dear old grandmother wasn't to reveal her true nature; rather, it was to conceal it. As ugly duckling had amounted to a disguise for the winsome embodiment of mingled hope and fear that I had encountered on the steps of Woolsey Hall, so grandmotherliness was a disguise for the skilled politician she had become. She was as hard as steel now, where people mistakenly saw an elderly softness. She was manipulative, she was arbitrary, she would have her way at almost any cost. The victim of a dragon had mastered a dragon's ways.

When FDR died, by his direction he was buried in the rose garden at Hyde Park and a large white marble monument was placed above his grave. On the monument were carved his name and the dates of his birth and death. Under his name were carved Eleanor's name and the date of her birth, with space left in which to carve the date of her death. At the time, many people considered it undignified for a widow to anticipate her own demise in so public a fashion—in a sense, didn't the uncarved death date impose a presence upon visitors by its very absence? There were those who said that Eleanor had chosen to share the monument with her husband as a gesture of loyalty. And there were those who said that she had chosen to share it as a gesture of revenge. After forty years of such a marriage, who could tell one gesture from the other?

Henry-Russell Hitchcock

THE PREEMINENT architectural historian in the United States in our time has been Henry-Russell Hitchcock. It has to be said at once that this distinction owes something to Hitchcock's having been one of the earliest surveyors of that corner of the broad field of history which devotes itself to architecture; mostly, however, it was a distinction earned by intelligence, effort, and an eye that served him as well in art as it did in architecture. For a number of years he was director of the art museum at Smith College, where with little money at his disposal he was able to purchase many exquisite paintings to hang upon its walls. Hitchcock's wit could be caustic when it came to private collectors of art; he said of Theodate Pope Riddle's house, Hill-Stead, in Farmington, Connecticut (open to the public as a museum), that its drawing room was the only one he knew of that had a Monet haystack at both ends of the room.

Hitchcock was eighty-three when he died in 1986. He had been ill with cancer for a long time; though his body steadily gave way, his marvelous mind remained intact, and he and his companion, Robert Schmitt, continued to entertain a constant procession of friends in their handsome old brownstone house on East Sixty-second Street in Manhattan. Hitchcock would be seated in his big chair by the fireplace in the ground-floor dining room, his back to the sunny garden; impenitently, he would be puffing away on his vile, beloved Gauloise cigarettes. He would let the ash at the tip of a cigarette accumulate unattended, centimeter by centimeter; one waited for gravity to gain its inevitable victory, whereupon down through his pepper-and-salt beard (pinkish red in youth), down over his vest, and down into his ample lap the nasty ashes would spill. In recent years, Schmitt had kept an ashtray in a water-filled vessel on a table by Russell's side, encouraging him to drown his cigarettes instead of risking inadvertent arson with them.

For over sixty years, Hitchcock gouged out one learned book after another—more than twenty in all, ranging over several centuries and half a dozen countries. In his youth, he and his close friend Philip Johnson introduced the American public to the International Style (the name was coined by Hitchcock) in the exhibition of contemporary architecture that they curated at the Museum of Modern Art in 1932. As a consequence of that exhibition, he and Johnson began a relationship with Frank Lloyd Wright that veered radically back and forth between friendship and hostility. Wright felt that the two young Harvard whippersnappers had neglected him in the Museum of Modern Art show and he was ever afterward to speak of them as "little Philip" and "little whiskery Russell." Since Hitchcock in his prime was as big and round and burly as a grizzly bear on his hind legs, the adjective "little" was singularly inept. Wright's wrath at Hitchcock led him to utter a boast that has entered history: "I warn Henry-Russell Hitchcock right here and now that, having a good start, not only do I fully intend to be the greatest architect who has yet lived, but the greatest who will ever live. Yes, I intend to be the greatest architect of all time."

By a pleasing irony, it was the much-abused Hitchcock who helped Wright to fulfill at least a portion of that prodigious boast. In 1942, Hitchcock brought out what was to become a classic work on Wright, the stout volume entitled *In the Nature of Materials*. In a comparatively brief text and with many photographs, it embraced most of Wright's work between 1887 and 1941 and saluted him in its final pages as a Titan, poised in the eighth decade of his life "for new triumphs at the opening of a great phase of his career." Wright, who had worked closely with Hitchcock on the book, found the praise just and proceeded with his usual formidable self-confidence to demonstrate its accuracy.

Hitchcock was one of the founding members of the Victorian Society in America and was for several years its chairman. Under his aegis, the society established headquarters in the Athenaeum building in Philadelphia. The handful of us who had founded the society had reason to hope that the ancient and august Athenaeum, a private library that was seeking to perform new and broader functions, would look kindly upon joining forces with our infant group. The day on which the two boards of directors sat down together at lunch and ceremonially pledged their troth to one another was of crucial importance to us, and it came close to proving a disaster. Hitchcock was our trump card; it was only he among us who was august enough to meet the Philadelphia Brahmins as an equal. Unfortunately, at that period in his life Hitchcock was a heavy drinker; he had long been extremely deaf (a deafness later corrected by surgery), and alcohol, which Hitchcock respected as a good in itself, was also a means of tempering the isolation that his deafness imposed on him, especially in large groups. Hitchcock had rejoiced that day to be served a few martinis before lunch, and when with some difficulty he rose from his chair after lunch to address the Athenaeum board, our bearded and handsome chairman began in his deep and (under the circumstances) all too arresting voice to utter perfect nonsense. Not a word of his gibberish emerged with clarity; he might have been speaking in tongues. Seated beside him at table in the office of vice-chairman, I sensed that our little society was teetering on the brink of involuntary suicide. At the first possible moment, when Hitchcock's grandiloquent farradiddle broke off long enough for him to draw a breath, I leapt to my feet, embraced Hitchcock as if congratulating him upon the admirable succinctness of his words of greeting, and with the pressure of my arm upon his back forced him firmly downward into his chair. He consented to this maneuver—he may well have believed that his eloquent words of greeting had indeed reached an appropriate end—and I called on another member of our group, a confirmed drinker of soda water, to offer a few concluding remarks.

Hitchcock's international reputation served to give the struggling little Victorian Society its credibility; moreover, the poverty of the organization's beginnings was ameliorated by a sizable gift in Hitchcock's honor from Philip Johnson. Still another friend of Hitchcock's, his British opposite number Nikolaus Pevsner (who was later to become Sir Nikolaus but remained Saint Nikolaus to most of his American friends), by his sympathetic patronage strengthened the public's interest in the Victorian period. Hitchcock was an authority on Victorian architecture, but then what period of architecture was he not an authority on? And the endless feats of scholarship that he performed were never known to diminish his sensual zest for life—he rejoiced to eat and drink (more nearly in moderation as the years passed, not because he enjoyed alcohol less, but because age and illness imposed a greater measure of abstinence upon him) among good companions, who, in the words of the poet Cory, would tire the sun with talking and send it down the sky.

Hitchcock was a giant, physically as well as intellectually, and with a giant's gentleness. He was happy among a galaxy of friends that, from Harvard days onward, included Virgil Thomson, Lincoln Kirstein, Buckminster Fuller, Isamu Noguchi, Ruth Emery, Joseph Brewer, and A. Everett Austin. Hitchcock was a homosexual, which in his generation was to say that he was a member of a large and flourishing secret society that readily assumed power in the conventional heterosexual world but reserved its emotional rewards for its initiates. Unless they were married, homosexuals were regarded socially by the heterosexual world as convenient "extra" men, suitable for completing the roster of a dinner party. Half a century ago, a hostess was expected to make sure that a seated dinner—and in those days of many servants there were few dinners that were not seated—consisted of an even number of men and women, seated alternately male and female, male and female, as if they were about to be marched up the gangplank into the ark. The statistical certainty of a prevalence of widows and otherwise unattached women caused single homosexual men to become, for hostesses, an indispensable resource. It was almost unheard-of in those days for homosexual lovers to be treated as a pair; one of them—the less distinguished one, of course—was left unacknowledged, or at least uninvited. In my youth, about the only homosexual couple that would be invited to parties as a couple was Glenway Wescott and Monroe Wheeler. Although Hitchcock lived well into the time when homosexuals "came out of the closet" (an ugly phrase, now sinking into disuse), he remained of the old school. Although he lived with the same man for over twenty years—indeed, slept in the same big double bed with him—on the social occasions when I encountered Hitchcock, his agreeable companion (a designer of jewelry) was never to be seen.

Like so many academics of his generation, Hitchcock was a snob, proud of his family background and of his social connections; he liked his friends to have the proper social connections as well, and it helped in the forming of our friendship that I had grown up in Hartford with the "right" people—Goodwins, Bulkeleys, Brainards, and the like. Snobbery is comparatively harmless, miserliness is not; moreover, it has the defect of being ineradicable. Reluctantly, one is bound to admit that Russell was a miser, to whom the spending of even the smallest sums of money came hard; for example, he would dragoon friends into typing letters for him, however badly, rather than pay a stenographer to type them well. (I have known many miserly males of his time and social position; without exception, they are either firstborn or only children and were toilet-trained at an early age by overfastidious nannies. The evidence is enough to convince me that psychoanalysts are correct in deploring the risks involved in being trained to be anally retentive in infancy.) But if Hitchcock, who had plenty of money, was unable to let even a few pennies go without anguish, he was generous in sharing his knowledge with colleagues and the endless procession of students who sat at his feet.

Hitchcock left his stamp upon every institution at which he taught: Vassar, Smith, Wesleyan, Yale, Harvard, and finally, in what would have been any ordinary professor's years of retirement, the Institute of Fine Arts of New York University. He was in scale with the noble building in which the Institute is housed (the old James B. Duke mansion, on Fifth Avenue at Seventy-eighth Street, designed by Horace Trumbauer), and his deep and resonant voice is missed there, as it is missed in the Athenaeum and in any place that he ever sat encircled by students and colleagues and, wreathed in the blue smoke of his Gauloises, opened their minds to wonders hitherto unknown or unremarked.

William
Adams Delano

To GLANCE for a moment at the subject of private clubs, commonly regarded today as having outlived their reasons to exist: the fact is that from the beginning these reasons were nearly always deplorable, pretending to be based upon fine discriminations with respect to interests and aptitudes but in fact being based upon prejudices either conscious or unconscious. Because the friendships that clubs foster are often of high value and because the taint of their origins is likely to be obscured by the passage of time, few club members trouble to examine the nature of clubs in general and of their club, or clubs, in particular. Moreover, it is fair to say that not *all* clubs are born in a state of original sin; some (like the little Coffee House Club, in New York) have been brought into being for purposes innocently merry and alcoholic, by artists, writers, and other reputed riffraff, and as far as I know without bias on the grounds of race, religion, or gender—only a bias against boringness, which, alas! being a filterable virus, is usually detected only after a candidate has been elected to membership.

Imitating their English betters, in the nineteenth century prosperous American males busied themselves with the founding of private clubs. They did so for several reasons, one of which was to provide an excuse for getting out of the house and away from their women, whom, again following the English pattern, they found tiresome; another reason was to establish publicly, by dint of flaunting the fact that the clubs were private, the superiority of men who were members of clubs over men who were not. Two simple, and simpleminded, reasons, and yet both of them were charged with a surprising degree of emotion, largely unexamined: a snobbery of gender in one case and a snobbery of class in the other.

In the eighteenth century, what we now call male bonding was, of course, already a cherished tradition in Great Britain and its American colonies. The form then preferred for this activity was the secret society—the Masons, for example, purporting to go back to the masonic guilds of the Middle Ages, and the Hellfire clubs, whose unspeakable practices were said to be traceable over several millennia to the devil himself. (The virtuous young men preparing for the ministry at Yale College in the 1830s founded a secret society called Skull and Bones, which to some extent parodied the Hellfire clubs, using Sterne's lubricious novel *Tristram Shandy* as its mock-Bible.) In New York and other large cities, clubs were founded in the early decades of the nineteenth century by artists and writers who, struggling to survive in a raw, business-oriented society, sought the comfort of their own kind. Money-grubbing entrepreneurs were quick to ape them, and by the end of the century there were at least thirty or forty private clubs flourishing in New York City. Certain prominent citizens, like J. Pierpont Morgan, thought nothing of belonging to ten or fifteen clubs in town (including, in Morgan's case, the Metropolitan, the New York Yacht Club, the Century, and the Union), and another ten or fifteen clubs out of town, whether in the countryside, at the seashore, or in London and Paris.

Where there were clubs there were clubhouses, which with the passing of years became increasingly grand and therefore, in terms of offering professional opportunities, were increasingly the plums sought after by fashionable architects. In New York City, the architects favored in the late nineteenth century for these commissions were the firm of McKim, Mead and White. From that firm's offices came—to count only extant buildings—the designs for the Century Club, the Metropolitan Club, the Lambs Club, the Harvard Club, the University Club, the Players Club, the original Colony Club (now the Academy of Dramatic Arts), the Harmonie Club, and the New York Racquet Club. In the twentieth century, the favored firm for the designing of private clubs was Delano and Aldrich, which won commissions for the Knickerbocker Club, the Union Club, the new Colony Club, and the Brook Club.

William Adams Delano (1874–1960) and Chester Holmes Aldrich (1871–1940) both attended the Ecole des Beaux Arts in Paris, and met as youthful employees of the famous architectural firm of Carrère and Hastings during the time that a major commission—the New York Public Library—was being planned in that office. Delano and Aldrich set off on their own in 1903. Along with clubhouses, their specialty was large city and country houses for very rich people, and to this day many specimens of their handiwork remain visible on the Upper East Side of Manhattan and along the so-called Gold Coast of Long Island: redbrick Georgian houses upon which they have succeeded in placing a highly individual stamp. Indeed, it would be an inept amateur of architecture who failed to recognize a Delano and Aldrich house wherever he happened to encounter it in the hidden green reaches of Locust Valley, Syosset, and Muttontown.

Delano was a smallish, delicate-faced man with a big nose and hair worn *en brosse*, and there was something so instantly appealing about him—some inveterate kindliness of spirit—that it seemed not in the least odd that even into old age he was addressed as "Billy." Though I marveled at the inappropriateness of the nickname, especially in proximity to the distinction implied by Adams and Delano, there was nothing else to call him. He was in his late sixties when we met and I was in my early thirties; the occasion was a talk that I gave one evening, at a monthly meeting of the Century Club. In those days, people who were deaf had to carry around with them quite sizable metal hearing aids, and to assist these aids in picking up sounds they would often hold them out in front of their chests, in what struck me as resembling an ancient priestly ritual of some kind.

At the start of my talk, a loud hum emerged from the front row of seats, and I realized that the old members' hearing aids were all going full blast. During my preliminary remarks, some of these members were sufficiently eager to hear what I had to say that they thrust their hearing aids in my direction—objects seeming to be sheathed in silver and gold and shining against the stiff white shirts of their evening dress. Little by little as I spoke, they began to tuck these objects back into their upper pockets; the gesture was by no means flattering, but I excused it on the grounds that to hold anything in one's hand for an extended period of time is bound to be exhausting. Then I noticed that the hum was falling off in volume; as discreetly as possible, one by one the members were reaching up and snapping off their hearing aids. Eventually, I could hear but a single, infinitesimal hum, and its source was a smiling old man in the middle of the front row. At the end of my speech he came up and introduced himself: Billy Delano.

Under such circumstances, who would not have been happy to meet him? Soon Billy and I had become friends, and knowing of my interest in architecture, he liked to reminisce with me about his professional beginnings. In the early years of our acquaintance, we would meet for drinks at one or another of Billy's clubs, but as he grew more infirm with age he was reduced to being pushed about in a wheelchair. This infirmity introduced a problem of whose irony he was keenly—and yet cheerfully rather than bitterly—aware, to wit: in designing clubhouses in New York City he had been so concerned with emulating the complex sets of stairways by which one gains access to the public rooms of British clubs that, imprisoned in a wheelchair, he could no longer readily make his way in and out of either the Knickerbocker Club or the Union Club. As for the Coffee House Club, of which he had been one of the founding members, it occupied quarters on the upper floors of a nineteenth-century building on West Forty-fifth Street and was accessible only by means of a narrow and precipitous flight of stairs, which meant that it, too, was lost to him. Only the Century Club was easy for a handicapped person to enter and wheel about in, and it was there that Billy spent much of his time.

A favorite story of Billy's was how Delano and Aldrich received its first commission. (My recollection of the story is accurate, but whether Billy was telling the story accurately I cannot guarantee.) He had roomed at Yale with a member of the Vanderbilt family and a few years later was invited to take a summer cruise on the family yacht. The yacht dropped anchor in Venice, at a mooring in the lagoon not far from the Doges' Palace. In the next berth was the yacht of the great Baltimore art collector Henry Walters, who invited the Vanderbilts and their guests over for dinner. At table, Walters drew the fledgling architect out about his hopes for the future. "I've been thinking of building a museum to house my collections," Walters told him. "I hear that Mr. Morgan had a good deal of trouble with McKim when he asked him to design his new library. If I were to hire you to design my museum, you wouldn't make a lot of trouble for me, would you?" At once, fervently, Billy replied, "Oh, no, sir, Mr. Walters! Certainly not!" And so, Billy would exclaim, leaning forward in his wheelchair, "I got the biggest commission of my life before I had designed so much as a doghouse!"

As a coda to this story, Billy related how, in the course of working on the plans for the Walters Art Gallery, he showed them from time to time to McKim, who was an old family friend. In the history of American architecture, nobody has ever surpassed McKim as a designer of beautiful and convenient staircases—one thinks at once of the stairs at the Harvard Club, which one floats up as if by an effortless act of levitation, or the entrance steps to the University Club, which I sometimes climb and descend, climb and descend, not in order to enter the club but in order to delight in the shapeliness of their design and in the physical pleasure of feeling them underfoot. The site of the Walters Art Gallery is a steep hillside. From the main entrance, opening off this hillside, one mounts a clifflike flight of stairs to the main floor of the building. "Looking over my plans," Billy said, "McKim seemed to lose his drift a little and instead of addressing himself to the actual museum building would start talking to me about the nature of stair design—the relationship of breadth and length of tread to riser, and all that. I thought impatiently that he must be growing senile. Much later, I realized that he had been trying to tell me, without hurting my feelings, that my stairs were far too steep—that they were *harsh* stairs, instead of being, like his stairs, gentle and friendly. So there they are, those brutal stairs of mine, because McKim was kind and I was obtuse."

Billy was far from obtuse when, a few years later, it came time to follow the instructions of the building committee of the Knickerbocker Club. The windows on the main floor of the old clubhouse, on Fifth Avenue and Thirty-second Street, had provided its members with an excellent view of the crowds of pedestrians flowing by. In those crowds, Billy was advised, were many pretty young women, who had begun at that time (the period of the First World War) to reveal daring, if fugitive, glimpses of ankle and lower shin. It was imperative that the windows in the new clubhouse, on Fifth Avenue and Sixty-second Street, should grant the same unacknowledged but indispensable satisfactions. Did the building committee make itself clear? Billy nodded: carefully he sketched sightlines on the blueprints to indicate to the building committee that a member seated in the library or lounge of the new building would have the same excellent view of passersby that he had been able to obtain in the old building.

The building committee remained skeptical; much was at stake. At last it was required of Billy that, before the walls of the new building had begun to rise out of its newly poured concrete foundations, he erect a scaffold at the same height above Fifth Avenue as the proposed library and lounge. Wooden planks were placed on the scaffold and with considerable effort big leather club chairs from the old building were hoisted into place on the platform. Then half a dozen portly, middle-aged members of the building committee were also hoisted into place and seated in the chairs. As the crowd of pedestrians flowed past, the committeemen sat eyeing them with their usual expertise. After an hour or so, they agreed that Billy's sightlines had been all that he had promised them they would be; let the building be completed as quickly as possible.

Seventy-five years later, there the building stands—in Billy's view and in the view of most architectural historians, his most distinguished work. It is safe to say that the sightlines from the windows of the library and lounge have not altered by so much as a hair's breadth during that long span of time, but the changes in women's fashions have been such that today it would take far more than the glimpse of a silken ankle on Fifth Avenue to prompt a sudden pounding of the heart behind the club's high windows.

Yale Kneeland

YALE KNEELAND paid me an unexpected compliment when I was young. He had an exceptionally varied collection of books, inherited in part from his father, a well-known bibliophile. One of the prizes in Yale's collection was a First Folio of Shakespeare. I had published a novel, *The Trouble of One House*, which enjoyed for a time as much fame as it deserved—looking back, I suspect it of having enjoyed perhaps *more* fame than it deserved. Be that as it may, one day I was having drinks at the Kneelands' apartment, and Yale led me over to the bookshelves. There stood his great leather-bound Folio and next to it stood my little *Trouble of One House*. "Shakespeare and Gill," Yale said. "How lucky I am! Both first editions."

Yale's kindly remark put me in mind of a story (which I took care not to share with him) about Henry James and the occasion on which some importunate woman hastened up to him at a tea party and gushed, "Master, I want you to know that I have all of your first editions." James stared at her with a certain coolness. "Ah, Madam," he said, "the second editions are much rarer."

Yale was the kind of person who, being distinguished in several fields of activity, was with tiresome regularity introduced at public gatherings as being a Renaissance man. As far as I am concerned, a Renaissance man is a man who lived during the Renaissance and no other; but since the word Renaissance as we use it was unknown during the period that we apply it to, in a sense there never was such a thing as a Renaissance man and never will be. In any event, Yale was a skilled physician and teacher, a scholar, a rider to hounds (for years he served as master of the Millbrook Hunt), and the beau ideal of a New York clubman.

In the 1970s, Yale was the much-admired president of the Century Club, whose charter stipulates that its members be artists, writers, or amateurs of arts and letters. Yale was the perfect amateur. Of so old-fashioned a courtliness was the language in which he conducted our monthly meetings that there were times when less courtly members were totally thrown off by his tropes. I remember that on one occasion he was introducing me as the speaker of the evening, and he described me as a "finished man." Some members of the audience thought that he had employed the adjective in the sense of my having failed in my career, as an aging boxer might be said to be finished on having been repeatedly knocked out. They came up to me afterward to express their regret at Yale's unfortunate slur. Of course I knew better; Yale had employed "finished" as meaning "accomplished," and I had been grateful for such praise.

Yale was amused by the ignorance of his fellow doctors: the more they specialized, the less they knew. One of his colleagues sought election to the Century on the grounds of his having invented a machine for milking mice—no doubt an invention of considerable importance in his particular field of research but one not easily accommodated under the rubric of amateur of arts and letters. Another colleague, also an aspirant to the club, had made a study of variations in body temperatures in patients suffering from a certain viral infection: temperatures would rise, then fall, then rise and fall a second time, which produced a curve that the doctor perceived as resembling the double hump of a camel's back; congratulating himself on his cleverness, he defined it as a dromedary curve. Unfortunately, the dromedary camel has but a single hump; Yale's colleague ought to have called it a bactrian curve, but all too quickly his mistake entered medical history and remains there to this day. It appears that we dare not quarrel with error once it prevails—an attitude that all too neatly and meekly parallels the attitude of the popes in Rome, who denounce freedom of the press on the grounds that error deserves no voice and need not be heard.

•

The Century yearbook contains the usual data of such pub-
lications—a brief history of the founding of the club in 1847; a list of
living members; a list of deceased members; and a sheaf of what are
called "memorials" of members who have died in the course of the
preceding year. These memorials are nearly always more entertaining,
because less guarded, than the conventional obituaries appearing in the
press; sometimes they climb up out of the ruck of a mere necessary form
of journalism onto the foothills of literature. Today the memorials are
signed by their authors; forty-odd years ago they used to be written
anonymously, by a remarkable man named George W. Martin. Yale
Kneeland and I were the self-elected officers of the George S. Martin
Fan Club, devoted (in spite of his continuously disowning us) to
outwitting his anonymity and spreading his fame.

We used to shake our heads in wonder, Yale and I, at the truths
George could find a way of relating without giving offense. For
example, of one newly dead member he wrote, "He had a bald head and
a big nose and nobody could stay angry with him for long." For long!
Which could only mean that one had occasion to be angry with him
often and was then—probably against one's better judgment—driven to
forgive him. On another member, an ancient gentleman whose departure plainly had left his fellow members with little to regret, George
managed to bestow what had the look of a hard-earned laurel wreath.
George wrote at the end of his memorial, "And so he got away ahead of
the rest of us." At first one was tempted to envy the old crock his celerity;
a moment later, one realized how little of the truly victorious his
seeming victory contained.

Enmities flourish in clubs as readily as friendships. Violence being
frowned upon (it is in the nature of house committees to fear the
smashing of china and glassware, to say nothing of furniture), the
weapons at one's disposal consist of whatever will serve to express rage
without causing outright physical damage. Yale and I were seated one
midsummer day in the East Room of the clubhouse (at a time before we
risked the high adventure of air-conditioning) when two elderly members carried out by the most trifling means possible a major skirmish in
what had evidently been a war of attrition waged by them over several
decades. Complaining aloud to nobody in particular of the uncomfort-
able heat, one of them got up, tottered over to a window, and after a

prolonged struggle succeeded in opening it an inch or two. Upon his return to his chair, his enemy got up, made his way slowly across the room to the window, and slammed it shut. Trembling with rage, the first elderly member then rose to his feet and, addressing his adversary in a voice loud enough to be heard by all the other occupants of the room, said, "Sir, this gives me the opportunity to assert that I have long found you, and continue to find you, the most disagreeable member of this club!" Having fired what was, for him, a tremendous salvo, he fell back in his chair, breathing hard. His adversary stood his ground, but could find nothing to say. Yale leaned over and whispered, "Do you see? They are keeping each other alive. At this rate, George Martin will never get a crack at them." And the words were prophetic: the embattled dotards hung on into their late nineties, while George slipped away in his seventies, long before anyone in the club was willing to let him go.

If, catching sight of Yale as he mounted the broad hall stairway of the Century, one asked, "Yale, would you like a drink?" he would reply at once, with vehemence, "Every fiber of my being is crying out for alcohol!" Given the eminence that Yale had attained in the world, I was impressed by the eloquence of his reply and I came to adopt it word for word as *my* reply to what is, after all, a by no means unwelcome inquiry. On one occasion, Yale and I having seated ourselves in the East Room, we signaled to a waiter and ordered drinks. Bearing our drinks on a tray, the waiter returned from the bar, but instead of coming directly to where Yale and I were seated at the south end of the room, overlooking the street, he undertook a long detour at the north end of the room, where two French doors led out onto an open porch. It was summertime, and the doors were ajar. The waiter stopped abruptly at the first of the French doors, facing us with his back to the porch, and a moment later we heard a report like a rifle shot—he had broken wind with extraordinary force, betraying his intention, which had been to break wind silently and at a considerable distance from us, thus sparing us the evidence of his little misadventure. Yale threw back his head in delight. "How privileged we are," he said, "to be in the presence of such good manners! *Quelle gentillesse!* This is the club for me."

Jay Rousuck

WHEN I FIRST MET E. J. Rousuck, he was second in command at Wildenstein & Co. in New York, which is to say that he had reached a very high rung on the ladder of prestige among art dealers in New York City. Rousuck was an exceptionally handsome man, tall and well built, with the head of a Roman emperor, or, rather, a head that I deemed fit for a Roman emperor, with a high forehead, large eyes, a strongly modeled nose, and a generous mouth. He carried himself superbly and took care to dress like a gentleman, which meant dressing better than most of the authentic gentlemen of his time. When he strolled the block or so of Madison Avenue that separated Wildenstein's from the Colony, a fashionable restaurant at which he liked to take lunch, men and women alike would glance at him with admiration. Observing his pearl gray homburg, his gray double-breasted Chesterfield with mole-colored velvet collar, and the black gloves carried loosely in the palm of his right hand, they would see him as maintaining an aristocratic standard of sartorial decorum all the more admirable for being by then a decade or so out of fashion.

To be regarded as the upholder of an aristocratic standard was pleasing to Rousuck, because his elegant dress and even (to his mind) his handsome countenance were but aspects of a lifelong masquerade; he was in constant fear of its being found out that he was not a gentleman—

that he had been a poor Jewish boy from Cleveland, who, thrown out upon his own following the early death of his father, had made his way up in the world with no protective cushion of money, family background, or education. Like his friend Ben Sonnenberg, he had invented himself almost literally out of whole cloth, but where the short and roly-poly Sonnenberg had chosen to present himself as the parody of an Edwardian gentleman, Rousuck had presented himself as the real thing. And the risk that this involved haunted him from one day to the next throughout his life. If people laughed at Sonnenberg's pretension to gentility, Sonnenberg could always reply that laughter was what he as a parodist had invited from them; to that extent, he had rendered himself (at whatever price) invulnerable. But if people were to laugh at the splendid figure that Rousuck cut in his prime, he would be done for.

Mary McCarthy was one of the people who laughed at Rousuck—at first privately, in her correspondence, and later publicly, in print—during that period of his life when he was still thrashing about as an impoverished outsider. Rousuck hired McCarthy as his secretary in the summer of 1933, between her junior and senior years at Vassar. The Great Depression rested heavily upon the land, and Rousuck was scratching the meanest of livings from the unlikeliest of enterprises: he spent his days feverishly seeking to persuade dog lovers to have their pets' portraits painted by a local woman artist of no particular merit. Sometimes it even fell to Rousuck or McCarthy to deliver the pets to the artist's studio; some of the pets were of an unamiable disposition, not only refusing to strike an affectionate pose but also snapping at their attendants. Rousuck was genuinely fond of dogs (during the course of his social ascent, he was selected to judge Boston bullterriers at the Madison Square Garden dog show); McCarthy disliked and feared them. In her biography of McCarthy, Carol Gelderman quotes a letter that McCarthy wrote to a Vassar classmate at about this time, describing Rousuck as "a nice, sweet, battered soul who spends his time skulking about, avoiding the sheriff."

A couple of years after graduating from Vassar, McCarthy went back to work for Rousuck on a part-time basis. By then he had moved up a notch or two professionally; contemporary dog portraits were out and eighteenth-century sporting pictures of horses and dogs were in, which eventually would provide him with an entrée into the world of the Mellons, Phippses, and Whitneys. McCarthy wrote about Rousuck in a short story, "Rogue's Gallery," which was published in her first book, *The Company She Keeps*. It is a funny and harsh view of the early Rousuck, who bears the fictional name of Mr. Sheer. One has no doubt of the authenticity of McCarthy's description of the quarters that Rousuck-Sheer then occupied:

> However unappetizing, however eccentric his gallery might appear to the sophisticated world, to Mr. Sheer these rooms with their dark velvet, their porcelain urns, their statuary, their dirty chasubles hung from the ceiling, their little rococo chairs, and their deep, velvet-covered sofa incarnated a double dream. From his Western boyhood, he said, he had loved dogs and culture. There was a rich man back in San Francisco whose dogs he had valeted and whose lawn he had watered; now and then he had been allowed to look at this man's fine library, which contained, he declared with reminiscent awe, "all these wonderful works on Shakespeare and vice versa." Today, as at that time, the dog was the natural highway to culture, and Mr. Sheer perceived no incongruity between the tarnished luxury of his setting and the homeliness of his liveliest line of goods . . . If Mr. Sheer loved culture, he loved Money too, and he could not always keep them apart in his mind (it was a *rich man* that had owned that library). Indeed it was sometimes difficult to tell whether he loved culture simply as an appurtenance of wealth or whether he loved it genuinely, for its own sake. He was fond of the fine arts, fond of long words, and fond of me, but was this simply because he felt that between us we could make a prosperous gentleman of him?

In the initial version of "Rogue's Gallery," McCarthy scarcely troubled to disguise her hapless hero: he was Rousuck to the life. (It was characteristic of McCarthy's fiction to be closely based upon fact. Over the years many a friend was shocked to find that he or she had been sitting for a pitiless McCarthy portrait unawares; some friends forgave her and others did not.) On learning of the existence of the story, Rousuck had contrived—was he not, after all, a rogue?—to purloin the manuscript; he read it and then furiously confronted McCarthy, threatening to sue her if she dared to publish it. She agreed to change a number of details in the story in order to make Rousuck less immediately recognizable (San Francisco instead of Cleveland, for instance). According to the version of these events that Rousuck related to me long afterward, McCarthy and he had been lovers at the time and it was as a lover and not simply as an employer that he felt betrayed by her. Be that as it may, when the book was published it was another of the stories that it contained—one entitled "The Man in the Brooks Brothers Shirt"— that created an immediate sensation, thanks to its sexual candor; Mr. Sheer was permitted to slink offstage unnoticed. With McCarthy's rise to fame and his own rise in affluence, Rousuck found it possible to forgive her. For almost forty years, until his death in 1970, they remained fast friends.

If it was true that McCarthy in her youth had been unkind enough to laugh at Rousuck, most of the clients that he acquired were too civil to do more than smile at him behind his back as the process of self-elevation continued. And continue it did, well beyond the usual goal of succeeding in a certain métier and gaining the friendship of one's peers within that métier. Rousuck wasn't content to be a peer of art dealers; he wished to be thought the equal of those people whose wealth provided him and his fellow art dealers with their livelihoods. Because fate permitted them to enjoy advantages that he had been born lacking, he had worked hard in order to make up the difference and he had become . . . well, what? A servant, and not a servant to one master but to many! It galled him to be an outsider, galled him to be a servant, galled him to be unable to resist the temptation of social climbing.

Rousuck knew well that he ought to have resisted this temptation. He had before him the example of Sonnenberg, who had made no effort to achieve a recognized social status. It was enough for Sonnenberg to be sui generis: a clever and amusing entrepreneur, who gave lavish parties that sooner or later proved to be at someone else's expense and who watched with cynical relish the skirmishing of the possessors of "new" money, exacting from them a substantial tribute in dollars and cents whether they eventually made good or failed. Rousuck was a romantic, not a cynic; like Gatsby, he hoped that a place could be found for him in that world which he wished so ardently to enter. It was true that he was only a salesman, as the people he sold to, though they were called collectors, were only buyers. It was true as well that although the commodity he sold was art—art of an extraordinarily high quality, thanks to Wildenstein's resources—the nature of the commodity was an irrelevance. He faced this odious truth reluctantly and mitigated its odiousness with the thought that it was far better for him to be selling art than to be selling stocks, bonds, or automobiles. That go-getting rascal of an earlier generation, Joe Duveen, had been a salesman in the same line of work, and look what had become of him! He had contrived to end up as Lord Duveen of Millbank, a much-admired benefactor of the British Empire. Rousuck would have liked to achieve for himself an American equivalent of that high place in the public esteem.

He had begun his professional career as E. J. Rousuck. The initials stood for Emmanuel Joseph, and the friends of his early days all called him Mannie. It was only as he moved up into the world of the Mellons, Phippses, and Whitneys that Mannie, with its faint, distasteful echo of the prophet Isaiah, was suppressed in favor of the insouciant and echoless Jay, which is the name by which I knew him. Not that, if challenged, he would have denied his Jewish origins or the straitened circumstances under which in Cleveland in the first decades of this century his widowed mother had valiantly confronted the task of raising seven children. He was the eldest, and his pride in her accomplishment and in the success of his siblings and of his siblings' children and grandchildren was an occasion for outbursts of affectionate boasting throughout his life. So, for that matter, was the city of Cleveland itself. Jay was convinced that no other American city had produced such a cat's cradle of relationships from coast to coast and even throughout the world. He bragged that there were Clevelanders and crypto-Clevelanders everywhere, and he rejoiced to spell out the refinements of their connections with the city, some of the more remote and intricate of which would turn out to be unknown to the very Clevelanders whom he might be engaged in addressing. The genealogies of the Hannas, Irelands, Humphreyses, Severances, Rockefellers, Harknesses, Zerbes, Halles, Frenches, Meads, and Johnsons were as familiar to him, so he made clear, as the back of his hand.

Rousuck himself was childless and whether this was an occasion for regret to him I never found it possible to ask. He was in his sixties when I met him, and much of his earlier private life remained unknown to me. From an old friend whom we had in common I learned that he had once been married, briefly and unsuccessfully. It was rumored of him that he had been jailed for falling behind in his alimony payments (shades of McCarthy's "sweet, battered soul"), and on a still more sordid level it was rumored that at one time he had enjoyed some illicit connection with the underworld. As to that, the only evidence I possessed was indirect; one day when we were having drinks in the lobby of a midtown hotel, Jay glanced across the room at a white-haired, benign-looking man, seated in a big armchair against the wall. He asked me who the man was, and I replied that he was the owner of the hotel—a millionaire who had come up out of the South and, as a stranger in New York, had purchased the hotel in an all-cash transaction. He had since made a name for himself as an exceptionally genial hotelkeeper, looking with especial favor upon actors and playwrights. "I've seen that man somewhere before," Jay said. "Maybe New Orleans. It was slot machines he made his money in." He shook his head, as if to free it of an unpleasant memory. "Slot machines! Big money, but dangerous."

From every side I heard of Rousuck's celebrity as a lover, and it appeared that this celebrity continued to justify itself as he advanced in years. Given his personal magnetism, his energy, and his good looks, he was bound to have attracted many women, but he was by no means a crude womanizer, interested solely in conquest. The running-up of a score as a proof of male puissance would have struck him as being, on the contrary, a proof of male weakness. He adored women and dealt gently with them. It was almost universally the case that the women with whom he had affairs remained, like McCarthy, friends and confidantes long after the affairs were over.

In the years that I knew him, Rousuck maintained a luxurious apartment on Park Avenue, furnished with handsome eighteenth-century English pieces (an octagonal rent table had been a gift from his friend Sonnenberg) and with splendid sporting paintings on the walls—horses by Marshall and Munnings, dogs by Stubbs. (No doubt the paintings were for sale; there were certainly more where they came from, in the great bins of paintings that filled the basement vaults of Wildenstein & Co.) Jay's bedroom was a dark cave of polished wood and shining brass, softly carpeted, fit for a pasha; on the bed lay a feather-light sable coverlet. A superlatively attentive butler presided over the apartment; he saw to it that a glass of well-chilled Reinart was always on hand to quench the thirst of unexpected guests. In the nature of things, they were often women, and if they were women in trouble, they might count on staying at the apartment for as long as they felt they needed to.

(At a couple of unhappy times in her life, McCarthy was among these guests.) And if they were in want of money, Jay would provide them with money as well.

It happened that I was a witness to the beginning of Jay's last affair. A late-evening reception was being held at Wildenstein's, for the benefit of some local charity. An immense crowd was milling about in the ground-floor and second-floor galleries and threading its way with the usual collisions and apologies up and down the grand lobby stairway. Resplendent in black tie, Jay was greeting guests, myself among them, near the open front door. A disturbance began in the street outside. With a show of anger—he had a famously quick temper and in his view any untoward interruption of the party would reflect badly upon him—Jay strode out to the sidewalk. A gleaming black stretch-limousine had pulled up in front of the building, evidently in order to discharge a passenger. The driver of the limousine appeared to be indignantly protesting something to a policeman, behind whom a few onlookers were starting to gather. From the doorway, I watched what amounted to a fast-moving dumb show, in the course of which Jay approached the driver, questioned him, ducked his head inside the limousine, straightened up, made a gesture of dismissal to the policeman, handed the driver some bills, stepped into the limousine, and was quickly driven away, abandoning the hundreds of guests whose official host he was.

Jay's abrupt departure from the reception astonished me because it seemed so thoroughly unlike him—ordinarily, he would treat the guests at such a function with a greater deference than they appeared to deserve, on the grounds that, being rich and social, their names would be found high on any list of his potential clients. But when, next morning, he telephoned me to explain the circumstances, I discovered that I had been wrong to be astonished: his conduct had been Jay at his most characteristic, for what he had done was to pitch himself headlong into an ideally romantic melodrama. Glancing inside the limousine, he had found curled in despair against the cushions, weeping hard, a pretty young woman in a ball dress. Between sobs, she had managed to let Jay know that she had been invited to attend the reception at Wildenstein's by a wealthy new acquaintance of hers; he had taken her to Twenty-One for dinner and on the way to the gallery had begun to assault her sexually, in a fashion repellent in itself and all the more repellent as a hint of what was almost certainly in store for her later in the evening.

She attempted to get out of the car; instead, it was the man who got out of the car, cursing her and leaving the driver to proceed to Wildenstein's. Having only a dollar or so in her evening purse, to her humiliation the young woman was unable to pay the fare; it was the driver's angry expostulations to the policeman that had attracted Jay's attention.

Given that the young woman was pretty and in trouble, Jay had known instantly how to proceed: he handed the driver fifty dollars and instructed him to drive the young woman and himself to the Plaza, where they spent the next couple of hours in the Oak Bar drinking champagne and seeking to expunge from her memory the unpleasantness that she had encountered earlier that evening. Jay took her by cab to her apartment building, where she refused to let him accompany her upstairs. She had given him only her first name, which was Marie, but she permitted him to scribble her telephone number on a corner of one of his calling cards. I congratulated him on the knight-errantry of his rescue of the young woman; was he planning to see her soon again? Ah, that was the difficulty! Or, rather, there were two difficulties. Thanks to the lateness of the hour and the amount of champagne he had drunk, he had no clear recollection of exactly which apartment house in the East Sixties he had brought her to. Moreover, he had jotted down her telephone number in such an illegible scrawl that he could make out only the first four digits. For the past hour, he told me, he had been dialing that fraction of the number, accompanied by random fill-ins, and again and again he had found himself talking to somebody at the Portuguese Airways.

Jay had telephoned me in order to seek my help: this pretty young woman was about to slip away from him forever. He added that I had no idea how lovely she was, how warm, how interesting! I must put aside whatever it was that I was working on and help him devise some means of tracing her. At that moment, there was an interruption on the line; Jay was accepting a second call, and . . . oh, Christ, yes! It was Marie. His voice assumed the lilting pitch of a lovesick twenty-year-old. Think of it! *She* was calling *him!* He would get back to me soon.

A year or so later, Jay died in his sleep, in the pasha's cave on Park Avenue, of just such a massive heart attack as the doctors had often warned him against. He was seventy-one. He had always eaten too much and drunk too much, and the five-minute walk between Wildenstein's and the Colony hadn't been what the doctors were recommending when they spoke to him about the need to exercise. Jay's family asked me to speak at his funeral service, which was held at Frank Campbell's, on upper Madison Avenue. Hundreds of friends of his had gathered in the chapel and among them I recognized a number of the women with whom, over the years, he had had affairs. Marie was there. I had met her half a dozen times with Jay; as Jay had told me, she was indeed pretty and intelligent and had a warm heart. She was in awe of Jay—his world was far grander than hers and the disparity in their ages served to heighten her awe. He had lived so long and had learned so much! Touchingly, she sensed intimations of the fragility of age behind his bluff vigor. She wished him to take better care of himself, but if she gave the slightest sign of mothering him in the presence of others—wiping a crumb from his chin, adjusting a scarf around his neck in cold weather—Jay would strike out at her with some remark so cutting, so unjust to her intentions, that tears would spring to her eyes.

At the funeral service, his sorrowing family sat in the front pew, only a few feet away from me as I spoke, and when I mentioned how reluctant Jay had been to grow old—how his death had at least this consolatory aspect, that it had kept him from experiencing any overt loss of the pagan zest and bodily prowess that had always meant so much to him—plainly it was not to the family that I was directing my remarks but to those women whom I saw scattered anonymously throughout the room. "Prowess" was a cold word for all that I intended it to imply in the way of affectionate friendship as well as sex, but it was the least false word at my disposal: the intense physicality that Jay had always emanated in life deserved in death to be recognized, if not celebrated—deserved, above all, not to be ignored.

Jay had taken much pride in being a Fellow of the Pierpont Morgan Library. The Fellowship consisted of a group of distinguished men and women drawn from the four corners of the earth, who shared an interest in arts and letters and who contributed financially to the varied purposes of the library—acquisitions, lectureships, and the like. A few weeks after Jay's death, a number of his friends suggested to Charles Ryskamp, then the director of the library, that a fund be set up for the purchase of books and drawings in Jay's memory. I was invited to take charge of the fund-raising. Among the people whom I felt at ease approaching for this good cause, having been friends of mine as well as of Jay's, were Paul Mellon and Mary McCarthy.

Paul Mellon replied to my letter of solicitation with a check in five figures, accompanied by a note that, with his accustomed humorous ruefulness, asked that the amount of the check be kept secret, since it was likely to be the largest that the library would receive in Jay's memory and he didn't wish it to prompt a lessened eagerness to give on the part of other donors. My major failure as a fund-raiser was with a certain Philadelphia dowager, the possessor of a fortune of perhaps a hundred million dollars. Jay had sold her many first-rate paintings, which, when I visited her at her big stone Tudor house a few miles outside Philadelphia, I saw hanging in profusion upon her walls. I arrived at the appointed hour to find that the old lady was suffering from what she called a severe migraine; perhaps we could discuss the Jay question on another occasion and meanwhile a delicious martini or two might make all the difference to her suffering head.

The next appointment that I succeeded in securing with her was at the Hotel du Cap, at Cap d'Antibes, where she spent a few days every year in a cottage on the grounds. I was at work on a story in the south of France and a stopover at Cap d'Antibes would not be inconvenient to me. I arrived at the cottage to discover her in bed, in a darkened room. Moreover, in a second bedroom across the hall lay a male friend of hers, also in darkness. It turned out that they had both had their eyes "done" a few days earlier and would be under bandages for a few days more. Perhaps I could meet her in Paris in a week's time? In the Ritz Bar, the one facing the rue Cambon? Meanwhile, a cocktail would surely brighten the dark to which she had been committed by her tiresome plastic surgeon?

It seemed a matter of ordinary good manners not to plead for money from a person with stitched-up eyes. In order to avoid a somewhat different form of discourtesy—that of asking for money from a person listening to one's words through a haze of gin and dry vermouth—I proposed that our appointment at the Ritz Bar be set for eleven in the morning. Surely at that hour I would be able in good faith to speak my piece on behalf of our deceased friend and the fund that would preserve his memory? But again the dowager was too clever for me. At the stroke of eleven, she slid unsteadily onto a banquette in the Ritz Bar, and I saw at once that if she had partaken of any breakfast at all, it had probably consisted of equal portions of vodka and orange juice. I spoke tenderly of Jay, of what he must have meant to her over the many years of their friendship, of the Fantin-Latours and other pictures that he had taken care to surround her with—charming pictures, to be sure, but as things had turned out such wonderful investments as well! Seemingly by way of reply, she undertook to describe in detail several frocks that she had seen at a couturier's opening the afternoon before and that she had it in mind to purchase. Blankly we stared at each other: the gap between my intentions on behalf of Jay and the Morgan and hers on behalf of herself was obviously unbridgeable, and so my pursuit drew to a sorry end.

McCarthy was another and far more agreeable story. In answer to my appeal for a contribution to the Rousuck Fund, she wrote at once, ". . . I enclose a small check. If more is needed, I can probably help again when I'm feeling slightly richer." The check was for five hundred dollars, which in proportion to McCarthy's means was indeed a generous sum. Like all Jay's friends, she was aware that his position as a Fellow of the Morgan Library had marked yet another milestone in his everlasting upward climb toward some lofty, seemingly unattainable, and perhaps nonexistent pinnacle of social acceptance. For how many years had she observed that climb, mocked that climb, forgiven him that climb! At the bottom of her letter she added a postscript. It contained fewer than a dozen words, and yet it struck me as being at once as long as a novel and as short as an epitaph. "I liked him as Jay," she wrote, "but I loved him as Mannie."

Edgar Kaufmann, Jr.

A DIFFICULT, prickly man: over the years, that was the impression I gained of Edgar Kaufmann, Jr. We were acquaintances, though not friends, and it may be that my recollection of certain occasions on which I was the butt of his dour humor has caused me to see him as a creature odder than he actually was. When he died in 1989, at the age of seventy-eight, the photograph that the *New York Times* published to accompany its obituary of him was itself an oddity: a close-up of Edgar wearing a debonair white Panama hat that appeared to date back to his father's generation and, under the broad brim of the hat, smiling the smile of an idling, mindless boulevardier. In short, not at all the intense and cranky Edgar Kaufmann, Jr., that I knew, or thought I knew.

He was a small man, and the delicacy of his bone structure hinted at something spidery; it was as if the meagre body supported only with a considerable effort the weight of the clothing that concealed it. For a long time, he suffered from Parkinson's disease, which accentuated the frailty of his appearance. He face radiated intelligence; again to suggest, not in the least disparagingly, a comparison with a nonhuman species, one observed in his bright, dark, darting eyes the high-strung intuitiveness of a lemur. If he were preparing to say something witty and malicious, the eyes would gain an extra brightness and his lips would begin to part over his big, prominent teeth—the telltale rictus of the predator approaching its kill.

The Kaufmanns were a wealthy mercantile family in Pittsburgh. The department store that bore (and continues to bear) their name guaranteed them a local fame; they entered history on a national level as a consequence of the fact that Edgar Kaufmann, Sr., became one of the leading patrons of the greatest of American architects, Frank Lloyd Wright. And it was Edgar, Jr., who brought them together—two men so like each other in their robust vitality and egotism and so unlike their soft-spoken little go-between. Edgar wrote a book that he entitled *Fallingwater* after the world-famous house that was the first of the commissions Wright received from the senior Kaufmann. In the book, published toward the end of his life, Edgar tells the story of the building of the house in his usual guarded fashion—although an architectural historian by profession, age had not encouraged him to tell all that he knew but only what he wanted to have known. His discretion leaves many questions unanswered, and one detects in it an element of the mischievous, like a child's singsong chanting of "I know a secret." Edgar did indeed possess a number of secrets and it was hoped that, as a historian, he would feel obliged to share them with us. Not he, not ever, and with his death they will remain tantalizingly undisclosed.

Kaufmann first encountered Wright in the early 1930s, upon becoming an apprentice at Taliesin, Wright's home and studio in Spring Green, Wisconsin. Kaufmann was then in his twenties, Wright in his sixties: symbolically, they assumed the traditional roles of the student-son looking up to the teacher-father. As the years and decades passed, Kaufmann gradually and perhaps unconsciously reversed their roles: he would speak of Wright as a kindly parent might speak of an errant child, not to rebuke him but to ensure that his beguiling exaggerations be kept in perspective.

Kaufmann, upon whom Wright bestowed the curious nickname of "Whippoorwill," spent less than a year as an apprentice at Taliesin. In *Fallingwater,* he asserts that "waking up in that marvellous place still seems one of my most profound experiences," but he doesn't say why, and his avowed reason for quitting Taliesin amounts to an illogical paradox: "So strong and convincing were Wright's principles that after a while—since I was not attuned to the Fellowship routine—it was time for me to leave." If Wright's principles had been so convincing, plainly young Edgar should have stayed on in spite of his failing to attune himself to the Fellowship routine; since Edgar was a homosexual and since there were many homosexuals among the apprentices, he may have been the victim of an unhappy love affair, in which case the convincingness of Wright's principles was an irrelevance.

Edgar in *Fallingwater* having characteristically hinted at something mysterious and having then revealed nothing, we can be sure only that there was time enough during his brief stay at Taliesin for his father and mother to pay a visit to him there and for them to form an instant and lasting friendship with Frank and Olgivanna Wright. The senior Kaufmann was then forty-nine. His wife was his first cousin—not an unusual occurrence in the days when Jewish families of prominence were accustomed, like royalty, to arranging marriages within a comparatively small circle. Still, it was against the law in Pennsylvania for first cousins to marry, and the young couple had to hold their wedding ceremony in New York. Edgar was their only child and he grew up to become in many ways the opposite of his sensual, extroverted, womanizing father. Of Edgar, Sr., the son says in his book that he was "a magnetic and unconventional person," adding that "Wright and my father were both outgoing, winning, venturesome men, and Father quickly felt the power of Wright's genius."

Within a short while, Kaufmann, Sr., was commissioning from Wright a planetarium for the city of Pittsburgh (a project never carried out), a new office for himself (now in the Victoria and Albert Museum), and a new weekend house at Bear Run, a woodland retreat that the Kaufmanns owned in the mountains some sixty miles south of Pittsburgh. The chief feature of the property was a waterfall, which the Kaufmanns had long enjoyed observing at different seasons of the year. They had hoped that Wright would contrive for them a house from which they could look out upon the waterfall, but it was not to be—with characteristic audacity, Wright saw to it that the house as he designed it was the one place from which it was impossible to gain a glimpse of the waterfall. He anchored the house to an outcropping of bare rock immediately above the falls, in order, so Wright said, that the family should be able to *live* with the waterfall and not merely *look* at it. In the course of designing the house, Wright gave it the name of Fallingwater, which nobody in the family noticed at the time was simply "waterfall" backwards. (The name also contains Wright's initials—FLLW—in the proper sequence. One wonders whether Wright, the consummate self-celebrator, was aware of this.) Recovering from their initial disappointment over the siting of the house, the Kaufmanns embraced the design heart and soul. All his life, Kaufmann, Sr., feared that the broad, cantilevered terraces of the house might someday tumble down into Bear Run, but of course they never did. Meanwhile he commissioned a number of projects from Wright not so much in order to have them built as to provide a reason for their keeping in close touch with each other.

In his history of the house, Edgar writes that "in 1952, beset by difficulties, my mother died at Fallingwater; this cast a long shadow over the place." Whatever his mother's difficulties may have been, the fact is that she killed herself at Fallingwater, with a rifle shot, a few yards downstream from the house. As for his father, Edgar notes that by that time he "needed constant attention, and two years later he remarried. These family matters influenced the fate of Fallingwater. Father and I talked earnestly about what would become of the house when he died, in view of his plan to remarry and my decision to remain in New York. We agreed that sooner or later Fallingwater and its grounds should become accessible to the public. We also agreed that a good portion of his estate should be used to establish a foundation on whose board I, assisted by my uncle, would represent the family . . . My father died in 1955 in California, a few hours after Wright had come for a friendly visit." (Wright himself died in 1959, shortly before his ninety-second birthday.)

Over the years, Edgar and I had enjoyed a few unnerving collisions as well as a few successful collaborations. I had helped him to arrange for the publication of an earlier book about Fallingwater by the architectural historian and critic Donald Hoffmann; for his part, Edgar had been helpful to a small group of us who, as champions of nineteenth-century architecture, were striving to bring to birth the Victorian Society in America. Like most authors, especially authors in the groves of academe, Edgar had a highly developed sense of territoriality. Plainly, his territory was Frank Lloyd Wright, and he was quick to cast doubt upon the reliability of anyone who happened to hold an opinion contrary to his own. I remember an occasion at the Guggenheim Museum—something having to do with the raising of funds for Wright's home and studio in Oak Park—when a symposium on Wright, to which the public was invited, was held in the basement auditorium of the museum. Among the members of the symposium were Vincent Scully, Philip Johnson, Edgar, the actress Anne Baxter (a granddaughter of Wright), and me. Each of us spoke for a few minutes, asked questions of each other for a few more minutes, and then answered questions from the floor. Again and again, it would happen that Johnson, Scully, or I would tell some favorite Wright anecdote to our satisfaction and (as far as we could judge) to the satisfaction of the audience as well, upon which Edgar would break in to say that, while it was an amusing story, of course it wasn't true. What *was* true, or, rather, Edgar's version of what was true, we were never to learn; that day, the keeper of secrets was undoubtedly king of the roost. As for the rest of us in the symposium, we were less chagrined than the audience may have supposed. Edgar's mockery of us was, as usual, a form of warning: since I, for example, was at work on a book about Frank Lloyd Wright, Edgar had reason to suspect that I might be encroaching upon his personal domain. From a harmless acquaintance of many years' standing I had become an adversary. Let me be warned! The mischief-making lemur was on the prowl.

Mary and
Ben Bodne

THOUGH THE AVENUES of New York are justly admired by visitors from all over the world, local citizens are inclined to prefer its side streets, as offering pleasures all the more agreeable for being minor. If every New Yorker has his favorite side street, mine is West Forty-fourth, where nearly every day for over half a century I have been a part of the ebb and flow of its tides of pedestrians, whether early in the morning (with, in summer, the sidewalks newly hosed down and glittering in the eastern light) or late at night, when pyramids of black plastic trashbags are piled on the curb in hillocks that reach higher than my head.

At the time that I first went to work for *The New Yorker*, in the middle 1930s, the magazine was already occupying space, in what proved to be a permanently makeshift, ramshackle fashion, in the building at 25 West Forty-third Street. (The lobby of the building is an arcade that runs through the block; hence, the official address of the magazine has always been 25 West Forty-third Street.) Like any newcomer, I sought to make friends as quickly as possible with neighbors on both streets and the neighbor that I wished most to become friends with was the Algonquin Hotel, where my elders and betters on *The New Yorker* were very much at home. Harold Ross, the founder and first editor of the magazine, ate lunch there regularly, as did E. B. White, Katharine White, and a dozen or so of our best-known writers and artists. At twenty-two, I was eager to be thought one of them, so around lunchtime I would hasten into the lobby with the look of fearing to be late to an important engagement, circle the clusters of people seated drinking there, and then slip away to a nearby cafeteria for a grilled cheese on rye. In that brief, deceitful circuit, what gods and goddesses I encountered! H. L. Mencken, George Jean Nathan, Julie Haydon, Ina Claire, Benchley, Thurber, Alajalov, Arno—my eyes rolled in my head like marbles.

The Algonquin first opened its doors in 1902, so it is unlikely that many people remember it in the days when the stamp of mere novelty was a part of its attraction. By the time I was beginning to secure a tentative foothold in the crowded lobby (the drink I would order was a sidecar, because it was reputed to be the favorite drink of F. Scott Fitzgerald), the Algonquin gave the impression of being venerable. Everything that one's hand touched, whether of mahogany, brass, marble, or fabric, felt welcomely, affectionately crowned with age. The same feeling persists today. Over the years, many costly, invisible improvements have been made with respect to heating, plumbing, air-conditioning, and the like, and many costly improvements have also been made in the bedrooms and suites on the upper floors, but the heart of the hotel, which is to say its lobby, its three dining rooms, and its Blue Bar remain little changed from my first memories of them. The great black grandfather clock stands in its accustomed place, sounding the hours in bass notes that a Chaliapin might envy, while men and women come and go in a flurry of salutations and blurred kisses, as if they were meeting or parting in the paneled hall of some immense old English country house.

The magic by which the Algonquin outwits time, weaving the past and the present into a seamless whole, is practiced also by a number of its neighbors in the West Forties. New York is thought to be a city that continuously, recklessly throws itself down and builds itself up again two or three times in the course of a century (says the rube in the old saw, "It'll be a great place if they ever finish it"), but in fact there are many sections of the city where nearly everything one looks upon has remained contentedly in place for generations. A guest at the Algonquin who sets out for a stroll through the nearby streets will find that, ignoring the occasional impertinent glass-and-steel high rise, he is moving back through the years to the turn of the century and then, uncannily, beyond the turn. On West Forty-fifth Street, diagonally behind the Algonquin, one climbs a steep flight of stairs to the premises of the Coffee House Club, which occupies a couple of floors of a building that, in the 1920s, was an artists' studio, and half a century before that was a brownstone-fronted family residence. How pleasant to sit there in winter, surrounded by books and pictures, and watch the snow falling beyond its two-story-high windows! Again, if a stroller in search of the past were to glance across the Avenue of the Americas from the corner of West Forty-third Street, he would catch sight of some large, boarded-up skylights emerging from the roofs of the dilapidated buildings that face out upon Forty-second Street. Those skylights once provided abundant north light for the artists who worked in studios there a century ago.

In the 1870s, on the site of the Algonquin, wealthy owners of fast trotting-horses would forgather before setting out for a spin in Central Park. The little brick building to the west of the hotel, whose ground floor provides space for two of the Algonquin's public dining rooms (and space for private dining facilities on the floor above), was once a stable; so were the three little buildings that occur at intervals along Forty-fourth Street to the east of the Algonquin and that are currently occupied by restaurants and shops. In the 1880s and 1890s, many of the houses and stables on both Forty-third and Forty-fourth Streets were demolished to make room for hotels, clubs, and private schools, since by then the neighborhood was coming to be regarded as among the most fashionable in town.

Sherry's restaurant, designed by Stanford White, was on the southwest corner of Forty-fourth Street and Fifth Avenue; long ago, the structure was transmogrified into the Morgan Guaranty Bank, but many of the other buildings of that period continue to exist, undiminished in their ability to impress the gawking outsider. One thinks of the tawny limestone and terra-cotta exterior of the Century Club, of the old Hotel Renaissance building that rises directly across the street from the Century, of the formidable Roman temple that houses the Bar Association of the City of New York, of the Mechanics Institute, of the Harvard Club, and of the New York Yacht Club, whose second-story windows romantically pretend to be the high-pooped sterns of seventeenth-century galleons. Daily as I pass these buildings, I try to measure in my imagination the amount of merry and sad life that they have contained. Now and again, I look up to see whether a ghost or two may not be peering out from the embrasure of a window. Not seeing any ghosts is the least of my concerns; for surely they are there.

The Algonquin, designed by the well-known architect Goldwyn Starrett, was much admired when it opened for its elegant redbrick and limestone front. Though few people ever notice them, six large white lions' heads, carved in stone, adorn the entablature of the cornice; the lions are of African ancestry, but the hotel's thirty-six painted-iron bay windows have, to my eye, a distinctly Parisian air. From 1927 until his death in 1946, the hotel belonged to Frank Case, under whom the celebrated Round Table came into existence (in part because the food he served was cheap and the credit he extended was long). The hotel was purchased from his heirs by Ben Bodne, who with his wife Mary moved into an apartment on one of the upper floors. A handsome man with a thatch of white hair, in his youth Ben was a semipro baseball player, who, in the course of a visit to Baltimore, met Mary, an undergraduate at Goucher College. As Mary tells the story, she felt instantly that Ben "was too good a catch to let him get away. Oh, my! So I dropped out of college and grabbed him!"

Because none of the Bodne children or grandchildren was interested in taking over the operation of the hotel, Bodne sold it a few years or so ago to a Japanese-Brazilian hotel corporation, for a sum reported to be twenty-six million dollars. The hotel corporation has been spending several million dollars more on renovations, which to old friends of the Algonquin have the look of being harmless, which is to say that up to now they have been almost indetectable. Mary and Ben, both in their late eighties, continue to keep their apartment in the hotel and to hold court in the lobby. During the last years of his ownership of the hotel, Ben feared that it would be designated an official city landmark. Unwilling to surrender the least iota of his right to do whatever he pleased with his much-prized possession and knowing that I had been among those who had urged the adoption of the city's preservation statutes, he was often on the phone to me, pleading with me to help him outwit the very laws that I had been at pains to champion. A strange state of affairs, which ended when Ben sold the hotel and a new strangeness took the place of the old: Ben at once became as eager to have the hotel designated a historic landmark as earlier he had been opposed to it.

Mary Bodne has been the ideal proprietress of a hotel that is a favorite of scores of the most prominent actors, actresses, and playwrights of our time, and for this reason: she claims never to have seen a play she didn't like. One of her grandsons, himself a playwright, has offered a rather churlish explanation of her claim; he says that the moment the curtain goes up on a play, his grandmother falls fast asleep. Be that as it may, in the years when I was serving as a theatre reviewer for *The New Yorker*, Mary and I often disagreed about the quality of a play, but we took care always to forgive each other. And Mary was prepared to help me carry out my duties, no matter how wrongheaded I might prove to be. Once, dressing for an opening, I discovered that I had mislaid my black evening tie. I told Mary of my plight and she at once dashed upstairs and brought down one of Ben's black ties for me to wear. "Now, behave yourself!" she commanded me. *"Like the play!"*

The Algonquin is not only a theatrical hotel. Throughout its long life, it has also played host to innumerable novelists and short-story writers, with their attendant editors, publishers, and agents. (D. H. Lawrence used to stay at the Algonquin, though I find it hard to imagine his poor little bearded ghost wandering its corridors.) Mary Bodne was every bit as hospitable to writers as to theatre reviewers. Very late one evening, she found herself riding up in the elevator with Thornton Wilder and William Faulkner. The men were silent, and she glanced back and forth between them. "Don't you two boys know each other?" she asked. They didn't, and the two "boys" made their acquaintance then and there. Norman Mailer, Eudora Welty, John Updike—by now it's unlikely that they would be in need of introductions under the Algonquin's uncannily capacious roof, but if so, Mary would be on hand to do the job.

Over the years, the Algonquin has sheltered many of our leading moviemakers, especially those from abroad. Truffaut, Godard, Rohmer, Costa-Gavras, Ophuls—one listens and thinks at first *ici on parle français*, but the Germans and the Italians and the Swedes are also volubly on hand. As for the so-called intellectuals who frequent the Algonquin—the college deans, the judges, the men of science—they are content to be unknown to fame. Not every face one sees ought to be recognized; there is much to be said for an establishment that makes one happy to be among strangers.

West Forty-fourth Street is a friendly street; we are used to one another's faces and one another's habits. Still, there are times when old friends can take one by surprise. Following an electricity blackout of the neighborhood a few summers ago, I went at an early hour to my office, only to be told that nobody would be admitted to the building until the power had gone back on. Disconsolately, I made my way to the Algonquin. To my astonishment, there were the Bodnes, comfortably seated at tables on the sidewalk in front of the hotel. In the darkness of the lobby, the battery-powered emergency electric lights were growing dim; a few candles guttered on tables. It was a fine day, and the Bodnes in high spirits had decided to carry some of the lobby furniture outside and make a sort of impromptu drawing room of Forty-fourth Street. They had already asked a couple of guests of the hotel to join them for breakfast and they insisted that I should join them as well. We sat there drinking coffee in the bright morning sunlight, for all the world as if we were breakfasting on some leafy terrace in St. Tropez. The Bodnes had put in a strenuous night making sure that the guests of the hotel were as little inconvenienced by the blackout as possible; now they were engaged in their customary practice of holding court. One of their breakfast companions was an English actor making his first visit to New York. He spoke with admiration of the shiny wonders of Fifth Avenue, a few hundred feet away. I held out my arms as if to embrace not only our group but the hotel rising behind us. "Some of us," I said, "have reason to prefer the side streets."

Padraic Colum

THIRTY-ODD YEARS AGO, a prominent figure in the literary life of New York City was the Irish poet Padraic Colum. He was a faithful attendant at the meetings of the Joyce Society, held at intervals at the Gotham Book Mart, on West Forty-seventh Street, under the benign—though by no means always benign—eye of the owner of the bookshop, the high priestess of the local Joyce cult, Frances Steloff. Then in his eighties, Padraic was a marvel of indefatigability; he issued books as regularly as a hen lays eggs and at the same time darted about the United States—to say nothing of the Old Country—giving lectures and readings from his poems and keeping an eye on succeeding generations of Joyceans. Padraic had been a close friend of Joyce and he was justified in asserting a proprietary interest in his reputation and especially in seeing to it that the sharp features of the man himself didn't vanish into an impenetrable fog of finicky, Ph.D.-seeking scholarship.

Padraic was small and well made, with a ravishing tenor brogue, gray hair that flew up and away in every direction (one had a sense that a high wind was blowing all round him even when the air was perfectly still). He wore a porkpie hat as if it were the crown of the high kings of Tara and sandals through which one glimpsed unexpectedly jazzy, many-colored socks. He had got off to such a quick start as a poet that he had already achieved a secure place in Irish literary history by the time he was in his early twenties. He and Synge were among the discoveries of the Abbey Theatre, and his play *The Land* was the third the Abbey ever put on and the first to be a success.

I remember Padraic's telling me that it had become the fashion in those early Abbey days to be writing stories and plays in the country speech. "Yeats, Lady Gregory, Synge, and all were doing it, but the truth of the matter is that I was the only one of the lot that knew what the real country speech sounded like. I wouldn't want to say a thing against Synge's language, which is exquisite, very fine, but has no more to do with how people actually spoke than Oscar Wilde's dialogue in his plays has to do with how people spoke in London drawing rooms in the 1890s. You might say that I had the advantage of the disadvantages that Yeats and the others didn't have—I was born in a workhouse and knew common speech from my birth. I always say I was born in a workhouse to make a romantic story. The fact is, my father was the master of a workhouse, which isn't *quite* so good, not being quite so bad."

At the time of that conversation, Padraic had just published the latest of the thirty or forty books that he had either written or edited—a paperback edition of the selected poems of Jonathan Swift. Padraic's complaint was that while everyone knew Swift's prose, only the damned academics paid much of any attention to his verse. "Swift deserves better of us than that," Padraic told me, leaning forward and lowering his voice, as if to prevent an invisible army of academics from overhearing him. "An extr-r-raordinary mind! So strong and delicate and coarse! You know what Yeats says about getting a manful energy into one's verse? That's precisely what Swift does." Padraic quoted a few lines by Swift, which prompted him to quote a few lines by Yeats, which brought him by a commodious vicus of recirculation back to the Dublin of his youth and to his first encounters with Joyce. "He was two or three months younger than I," Padraic said. "We became good friends not in our student days but after. He used to give fine parties in Paris, when he had the money—the best was good enough for James Joyce! Whenever Nora's back was turned, there'd be another bottle of his favorite white wine. Joyce was convinced that the proper sacramental wine was white, not red—I don't know why. But then he had a theory for everything and would willingly have set Rome straight on sacramental wine, had Rome but asked. We Dubliners are like the Florentines, who were so fiercely proud of their mention in the *Inferno*. To be a contemporary of Joyce and not to be mentioned in *Ulysses* is a disgrace. I come off easy in it—in the National Library scene somebody says of me, 'He has that queer thing called genius.' Joyce later made a sneering remark about me in a satire on poets, but it often slips my mind—I remember the praise and forget the sneer!"

It was at just about that time that the Dublin architect Michael Scott, owner of the martello tower in Sandycove that provides the setting for the first chapter of *Ulysses*, made a gift of the tower to the Joyce Tower Association. The presentation of the gift was to take place on Bloomsday (known to the barbarian world as June 16), with a party being held on the lawn of the tower. Liquid refreshments were supplied free of charge by the brewers and distillers of Dublin and sausages—Mr. Bloom was very fond of sausages—were supplied on the same generous terms by the well-known Dublin sausage house of Hafner. Padraic was looking forward to the event, at which he was prepared to read his elegiacal-autobiographical poem, "In Memory of James Joyce," which he recited to me and which goes, in part:

> *I looked back to the days of our young manhood,*
> *And saw you with the commons of the town,*
> *Crossing the bridge, and you*
> *In odds of wearables, wittily worn,*
> *A yachtsman's cap to veer you to the seagulls,*
> *Our commons also, but your traffic*
> *Sombre: to sell your books upon the quay.*

André Kertész

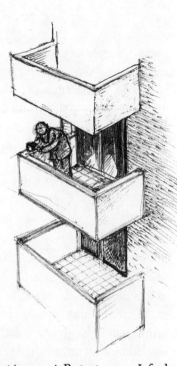

Oh, what an irritating man André Kertész was! But at once I feel inclined to lessen the harshness of that view of him, not out of compassion (André in heaven is presumably past having his feelings hurt) but out of a desire to be as precise as possible. For it may be that at least a portion of what I perceived to be André's irritatingness was his failure to measure up to a rule of conduct that I subscribe to but that André himself may never have heard of, or, having heard of it, may have rejected half a century or so before I met him. And this is not to alter the fact of how irritating he was, but to leave open the question of whether it was a deliberate practice or simply—and sadly—an unexamined attribute.

The rule I speak of holds that if one has been exceptionally fortunate in the course of one's life, one is forbidden to complain when some stroke of ill fortune interrupts the good. The privilege of whining—and it *is* a privilege, not a right—is reserved to those who have been plagued by true bad luck, and not from time to time but most of the time, or even, in rare cases, all of the time. In my judgment, and in the judgment that I believe history will take of him, André led a fortunate life, though he always vehemently argued otherwise. In his moaning and groaning, he broke my rule twice over, not only because he complained during the sombre passages in his life but also, and much

123

more disagreeably, because he complained nonstop, by the year, month, and day, seemingly without regard to the circumstances in which he found himself. The weather of his soul was charged with gloom and he was determined to share that gloom with all the rest of us. If his fifty years in New York City were spent incessantly griping, so, I suspect, were his early years in Paris, to say nothing of his youth in Budapest.

I have a friend who has been dealt many hard knocks by life. If one asks him, in the usual way, how things are, he invariably replies, "Never better!" I admire that sunny-sounding lie with all my heart. To the same question, André would have replied, "Never worse," punishing his questioner with what he believed to be the truth. But the truth in an exchange of conventional civilities is so unexpected and so unwelcome as to amount to a blow in the face; it places a strain upon small talk that small talk cannot support. Interestingly enough, André's difficulty in pronouncing English correctly, or, rather, in an understandable fashion, somewhat diminished the impact of his inveterate depressingness. For even in uttering small talk he could render the simplest of monosyllables incomprehensible and therefore harmless. Friends could tell by the sound of his voice that he was protesting some indignity unjustly inflicted upon him, but the nature of the indignity often, to our relief, eluded us.

If André were engaged, for example, in one of his habitual attacks upon those colleagues of his who, he feared, had gained a greater fame in the world than he, scarcely a single word would emerge from his lips unmangled. Listening closely—and one had to listen closely or not at all—from time to time one caught a verifiably coherent ejaculation, which I will set down phonetically as "Yunnerstan?" Early in our friendship, I learned to translate this as "You understand?" and I guessed that it must be an anglicization of the "*tu comprends?*" with which the French pepper their conversation and which André would have picked up in the course of his long stay in France. At first I assumed that, faulty as André's English pronunciation was, his French must be far more accommodating, but I was later to hear from French friends that this was not the case; a certain glottal thickness of utterance made him difficult to converse with in any language except Hungarian. We nodded when he said, "Yunnerstan?" but that was not because we actually understood him—it was only to keep our discourse with him from suffering a last, fatal stumble into chaos.

Luckily for André, the language in which he was incomparably fluent was that of images, not speech. Critics and historians of photography consider him to have been one of the handful of great photographers of this century. Having lived to be over ninety and having never stopped working, his professional oeuvre covers a span of seventy years. And what an awesome accumulation of exquisite photographs he produced in the course of that long career! Hundreds of them are works of art that find a place comfortably within the limits of a prescribed, conventional beauty; others (the result of experimental manipulations of camera lenses and darkroom techniques) are works of art that remain outside the canon of beauty to this day—I am thinking of his *Distortions*, in which women's naked bodies assume the slithery contours of ectoplasm—and that serve to provoke in us the unease that some of Picasso's more extreme anatomical perversions also provoke. In Paris in the 1920s, André earned two reputations: one as an innovative and commercially successful photojournalist and the other as an artist who had undertaken a double mission: like Atget, to record the city as it existed in his time and, like Man Ray, to extend the camera's aesthetic and intellectual range (in Ray's case, often to the point of prankishness). André shared with his near-contemporary Walker Evans, whom he evidently admired but never met, a knack for introducing wit into his handiwork without the dread taint of the merely jokey; and along with the wit one sometimes sensed (again as in Evans) the presence of ghosts, not all of them necessarily of a friendly disposition.

Yeats speaks of a man's having to choose perfection of the life or of the work. Few among us would risk choosing the work over the life, for once we had made that choice, we would have to possess the strength of will not to abandon it if the work failed to measure up to expectation—an expectation that, as Yeats defines it, amounts to nothing less than perfection. And yet in André's case the disparity between the life and the work appears so great—that grumpy man, those lyrical images!—that for once we feel that we may be in the presence of a deliberate choice and that the choice has been in favor of the work over the life. Nevertheless, I suspect that André would deny that he had ever been in a position to enjoy the luxury of making choices. In his bitter view, it has

been his fate as a giant to be ignored and rebuffed while pygmies—
Cartier-Bresson, Brassaï, and the like—stared enviously up at him,
sought to imitate his skills, and usurped his rightful place in history.

André and his wife, Elizabeth, came to the United States in the
middle 1930s, on a visit that they expected to last for only a year or so.
André had been invited to join a well-known news agency in New York
City for that period of time, but the job soon proved unsatisfactory. After
quitting it and after making a number of false starts, he began a career as
a photographer on hire to a series of magazines, including *Vogue* and
Town & Country. When the Second World War broke out in 1939,
Elizabeth and he were still carrying Hungarian passports and had to
register as enemy aliens. Elizabeth went on earning a good living in a
cosmetics company that she had helped to found, but André gave up
magazine work almost entirely, on the not very convincing grounds that
when he went about the streets with his camera, people looked upon
him as a spy. A more likely explanation of the period of professional
despair through which he passed was that many other photographers, of
a generation later than André's and in some cases disciples of his, had
been driven out of Europe by the war and were being hailed by editors
and critics in New York City as the last word in geniuses, while André's
name was rarely mentioned and his services rarely sought. He was right
to feel neglected, but his touchy temperament—his quickness to take
offense—unquestionably made matters worse, as seeming to account
for and justify the neglect.

After the war, it was too late to think of returning to Paris; André
and Elizabeth had become naturalized American citizens and it was
plain that their future lay in the States. André joined the staff of *House
and Garden* magazine and remained there for almost twenty years,
providing the magazine with the astounding total of over three thousand
photographs. He was often to tell me that the time he had spent there
was hell—"a beeg vayste of my life, yunnerstan?"—but the evidence of
the immaculate work itself strongly asserts otherwise. (At least one of his
outbursts against *House and Garden* was prompted by my asking, in
connection with a book I was writing about Cole Porter, whether I could
make use of certain color photographs that he had taken of Porter at his
house in Williamstown. "There *are* no such peectures!" André shouted.
"They're gone, all gone, faded to nuttin'! What do you expect with color
after twenty years?") He worked hard and well at the magazine and his

habitual querulous pursuit of perfection was accepted by the staff as a price well worth paying.

I had come to know a number of photographers—Evans, Steichen (whose work André disliked), Man Ray, Avedon, Wolf—but it was not through these anointed dignitaries that I happened to make André's acquaintance; rather, it was through a group of younger photographers living in Greenwich Village, to whom André had come to seem a sort of tutelary god, conveniently resident among them. From their point of vantage (in some cases, basement apartments), he possessed at least one of the customary attributes of a divinity: the boon of dwelling in a high place, whence he could look down upon the world and pass judgment upon it. For thirty years, André and Elizabeth occupied an apartment on the twelfth floor of Number Two Fifth Avenue, overlooking Washington Square. From the balcony of their apartment, one gazed out over much of Manhattan island, lying in the embrace of its two rivers and with the harbor gleaming far to the south. (The apartment was a cozy one, filled with a helter-skelter assortment of European furnishings. Given André's complaints over his lifetime of unbroken hardship, one was startled at first to find the Kertészes occupying expensive quarters on Fifth Avenue; then one recalled that Elizabeth was a successful businesswoman, earning an income that was probably at all times more substantial than André's.)

André had taken many hundreds of photographs from the balcony of the apartment, and in the middle 1970s I was invited by a friend of André's, the publisher Nicolas Ducrot, to write an introduction to a small book of his photographs of Washington Square. It was an agreeable task, which gave me an opportunity to "place" André for a public that was still largely unaware of his existence. Needless to say, from André's point of view this placement was long overdue. I wrote of their little cantilevered balcony that it hung in space like the crow's nest of some impossible high-masted barkentine:

> All the year round, winds blow fiercely across it, in summer the sun bedazzles it, in winter the snow silently doubles and redoubles the thickness of its railings. One is close to the elements up there and feels the force and hazard of them; at the same time one becomes part of an immense cityscape of shining towers, tarred roofs, and zigzag, bonneted chimney pots . . . As an old mariner might arm himself with a sextant to shoot the stars, so Kertész on his balcony

arms himself with a camera and bulky zoom lens to shoot the many lives of the square, of the narrow streets that bound it, and of the nearby roof gardens and terraces . . . Now and again he descends to encounter his fellow creatures—men, women, dogs, cats, and birds—on terra firma, eye to eye. Washington Square is hard-used. It is not the gentle, flowering Luxembourg that Kertész once frequented; rather, it is a palimpsest well worth an artist's careful reading, well worth recording a thousand likenesses of by day and night and in all weathers. Kertész likes to recall those distinguished predecessors of his, the artists and writers who have strolled through the square since its beginnings in the eighteenth century as a swampy potter's field: Walt Whitman, Winslow Homer, Edith Wharton, William Dean Howells, Willa Cather, John Dos Passos. Today bronze Garibaldi drawing his sword and the bust of stolid Holley, maker of Bessemer steel, stare from their plinths upon a turbulent playground, whose air is alive with song, aglitter with bicycle wheels, ashiver with frisbees. Young and old cram the little park to bursting, and dustily, raucously, amorously, dangerously, the little park survives.

Kertész, observing it all, preserves it all, for he is one of those upon whom, in a phrase of Henry James (born just off the square), "nothing is lost." His subject matter is ever before him, his eye and hand are at the ready. He scans his chosen domain with relish. The light of afternoon falls benignly athwart the square; a squirrel leaps from bench top to bench top, a girl and boy pass through the Washington Arch, an old man lies crumpled in sleep against a tree—likenesses modest and precious, about to put on immortality.

In the course of working on the book with André, of course I heard a great deal about the perpetually rising sea of troubles that daily—or hourly, or even from one moment to the next—threatened to engulf him. At least one of these innumerable troubles was authentic: several hundred of his glass-plate negatives that had long been in storage had developed a species of fungus that was threatening to destroy them, and André claimed that he lacked money enough to have them restored. I suggested that he should apply for a Guggenheim Fellowship, which at the time had a value of twelve or fifteen thousand dollars. What better use could a Guggenheim be put to than to rescue a portion of the lifework of one of the greatest of living photographers? André shook his head. The very mention of a Guggenheim appeared to depress him. It was of no use to ask anyone for money. When he was young, nobody had ever given him any help. Now that he was old, the Guggenheim people would only laugh at him. "Do something nice for a man in his eighties? Forget it! That's how life is," he said, adding the inescapable interrogatory, "Yunnerstan?"

Over André's prolonged objections, Nicolas Ducrot and I secured an application blank from the John Simon Guggenheim Foundation and filled out the necessary particulars with respect to the proposed project. All that André had to do was sign the application. Reluctantly he did so. Months passed, and André squeezed the last drop of sour pleasure out of the silence that ensued. What had he told me? Hadn't I known that money doesn't grow on trees? A few months later, a missive arrived at Number Two Fifth Avenue. It was from the Guggenheim Foundation, and André was indeed the recipient of a grant; his glass plates would indeed be saved. Desperately, André cast about for some reason to disbelieve the good news and could find none; grumblingly, he consented to acknowledge that something fortunate had at last befallen him. "The first time, yunnerstan?"

Years passed, and at last a true misfortune befell him: Elizabeth died. The funeral service was to take place at the Frank E. Campbell Funeral Home, on upper Madison Avenue, and on the evening before the service I paid the customary brief call during what are peculiarly called "visiting hours" at the funeral home. A room on the second floor had been assigned to the Kertész family; André was standing in the doorway, a few friends were visible in the shadows behind him, and at the end of the room rested Elizabeth's coffin, with the usual embankment of flowers. I embraced André and spoke a word or two of sympathy. In previous generations, Elizabeth's family, like André's, had been Orthodox Jews, but neither of them had practiced any formal religion, and there was certainly nothing in the way of religious consolation for me, long a collapsed Catholic, to offer him. As I turned to go, André mumbled something; I shrugged to indicate that, as usual, I hadn't been able to make out his meaning. He repeated the words and it became clear that he was inviting me to step over to the coffin and see Elizabeth. I realized then that the coffin was open. My heart quailed; long ago in childhood, I had had enough of open coffins—my mother's, my grandmother's. "André," I stammered, "dear André, thank you, but you know—well, I don't think so!" Though I had been caught off guard,

I was determined not to let some conventional and, to my mind, ghastly funerary practice entrap me. I patted André's shoulder. As I crossed the threshold into the hall, I saw André approach the coffin. He began to speak to Elizabeth, and it was obvious that he was voicing a complaint. I was sure he was telling Elizabeth that I hadn't wanted to see her. Sorrowfully he wagged his head. Wasn't that the way things always turned out—that even old friends weren't to be counted on?

The last time I saw André was at a party held in his honor on a sunny terrace high above Fifth Avenue, in a grand apartment house a couple of miles north of André's own snug eyrie at Number Two. He was ninety years old and, unbeknownst to him and to all the rest of us, he had only a few months to live, but there was no way of predicting that from his stalwart posture and the animation with which he spoke. He had never been handsome; his face had grown chunky with age and now the hair on the top of his head was scant and blowing in wisps, uncontrollably, in the breeze off Central Park. A wen on his left cheek that he had never troubled to have removed seemed to me more prominent than ever, or perhaps it had become more nearly indispensable to my sense of him—no longer a disfigurement, that is, but an earned emblem of the naturalism that André had always practiced in his art. Let be whatever is: ugly or beautiful, surely it is all one to the camera's eye.

The crowd of young people who had gathered round him on the terrace were there to celebrate the publication of a book of his photographs, the latest manifestation of his now all but universal fame. The temptation to tease him at that climactic moment was irresistible. "Now, then, André," I said, "surely today there isn't a single thing in the whole world for you to complain about.'"

André threw back his head and stared at me in disbelief. How could I dare to make fun of him at such a time? Indignantly and for once with clarity, he exclaimed, "The book is out but not out, yunnerstan? No copies in the bookshops, a disaster, a catastrophe! Am I a saint, is that what you think, a holy man, I should not complain?" Happy in his misery, plainly he had much to say.

Brendan Behan

BRENDAN BEHAN came to New York City in the late 1950s, when his plays *The Quare Fellow* and *The Hostage*, both of which had been hits in London, were put on here and received favorable reviews. An auto-biographical work entitled *Borstal Boy*, dealing with the years he had spent in reform school in England, had already been published in England. (As a sixteen-year-old member of the Irish Republican Army, he had been convicted of attempting to blow up a British battleship. Subsequently, he had been imprisoned for other terrorist activities.) If Behan had earned a just measure of recognition in theatrical and literary circles, he was not yet famous, and oh, how eagerly he coveted fame! In his early thirties, he was a short, plump, aggressively unathletic-looking young man, with a thick shock of black hair, vivid blue eyes, and skin of an uncanny pale whiteness—a color, or absence of color, that could be attributed in part to the fact that he had been born and bred in rainy Dublin and in part to the fact that it was his habit to collide as little as possible with broad daylight: he bloomed at night, in bars where the stink of sweat, smoke, and spilled beer was perfume to him.

Long before arriving here, Brendan had been an impassioned devotee of New York City. He had read about it in books and magazines and—since he always preferred the spoken word to the written one—had seized upon every scrap of gossip about it in the course of conversation. Living in Dublin after the Second World War were many former GIs; at least nominally, they were taking advantage of the opportunity to acquire an education at the expense of their government, whether at Trinity College, which young Irish Protestants of good family traditionally attended, or at University College, which the Catholic Irish attended. Brendan educated himself by hanging out in the pubs that students favored, mingling his drunken good humor and his occasional drunken truculence with theirs. (Glimpses of him are to be found in J. P. Donleavy's classic novel of the period, *The Ginger Man*.) Whatever the rowdy Yanks told Brendan about New York City he believed: it was the Land of his Heart's Desire.

One of the first stories that Brendan told me after his arrival in New York City was of how he had come to marry. The setting of the story was, of course, a pub. Brendan had been lounging at one end of the bar, nursing a pint, while at the other end of the bar, but still well within earshot, a distinguished-looking middle-aged man was holding three or four Trinity scholars enthralled with his rhetoric. Brendan was playing his usual role of penniless laggard; he had a lively sense of the gulf that lay between the likes of him, the son of a house painter, and the Trinity lads and their eloquent companion. With delight he heard the gentleman wind up a particularly lofty passage with the words, "Man stands sentinel to the nullity of the void." "Ah, by Jesus!" Brendan thought, "that's the grandest remark I ever heard in me life!"

The Trinity scholars at last took their leave, and Brendan, perceiving that the gentleman intended to remain and continue his drinking, summoned the courage to sidle along the bar to the gentleman's elbow. "Excuse me, sir," he began. (When I quote Brendan, the burden of imagining his strong, lower-class Dublin accent is upon the reader; to reproduce it phonetically would make it seem more overbearing and untranslatable than it actually was. Let me just mention, as an example, that his "sir" was pronounced "sor" and that the final "g" of any verb form never sullied his lips.) "Excuse me, sir," he repeated, when the gentleman acknowledged his presence, "but what would be the meaning of that fine thing you were saying just now?"

The gentleman looked blank.

"The fine thing," Brendan pressed on, "about how man stands sentinel to the nullity of the void. What would *that* be meaning, sir?"

The gentleman, genuinely astonished: "Did I say that? Be damned if *I* know what it means. But I've a daughter at home in want of a husband—come along with me, lad!"

And so Brendan met Beatrice Salkeld and they entered into a marriage that proved equally unsuitable to both of them.

On his first visit to New York City, Brendan and Beatrice stayed at the Algonquin. He had been bound to choose that celebrated hotel to stay in; he had been accumulating lore about it for many years and would have known, for example, that D. H. Lawrence, Douglas Fairbanks, John Barrymore, and Tallulah Bankhead were among the great dead who had stayed there before him, and that Alec Guinness, James Thurber, William Faulkner, and Thornton Wilder were among the living whom he might hope to encounter in the hotel's little bar or in its single, slow-moving passenger elevator. At the start of our acquaintance, we two Brendans had thought that it might be a good idea for me to write a Profile of him for *The New Yorker*. William Shawn, the editor of the magazine and a man temperamentally as unlike the hooligan Behan as it was possible for a human being to be, had urged me to try my hand at it. Like many another of my attempted Profiles, it came to nothing—or, rather, what it came to was a few years of troubled friendship with Brendan and never a word set down in print until now.

Brendan enjoyed my taking him to the Coffee House, a small private club occupying rooms on the upper floors of a shabby pre–Civil War brownstone building on West Forty-fifth Street. The club set an excellent table, and Brendan was especially drawn to their steaks, which he washed down with glass after glass of beer and whisky. Young as he was, he had lost most of his teeth and he would continuously put off getting false ones because, he claimed, dentists in Dublin were so incompetent and dentists in New York were so expensive. He had but one tooth left in the front of his mouth and he would use it as a sort of combination hook and auger, snagging a large slice of steak with it, sinking the tooth well down into the steak, and then worrying it with his bare gums into small, edible portions. It was not an agreeable sight, but one shared his pleasure in a feat that appeared at first glance impossible to accomplish.

One evening, Brendan huffed and puffed his way up the stairs of the Coffee House Club carrying a newly arrived copy of a Finnish edition of *Borstal Boy*. He was boyishly proud of having been translated into a language so exotic and he regretted that he had no way of testing the accuracy of the translation. Lo and behold! Our faithful waitress Marie was a Finn and we all sat ourselves down by an open fire and over brandy and walnuts listened to her admirable reading of Brendan's failed attempt to assassinate a large number of innocent British subjects. On other evenings, especially when he was on his way from amusingly tipsy to disagreeably drunk, Brendan would insist on going backstage at the theatre where *The Hostage* was playing and would take advantage of the opportunity to pick up a bagpipe and march out onto the stage, interrupting the action of the play and thereby bringing down the house. For it quickly became known that Brendan was given to this calculatedly mischievous prank and the producers of the play and its sorely tried cast forgave him for it because it sold tickets and because . . . because Brendan was Brendan and there was no way to reason with him, ever.

The Algonquin being directly across the street from the West Forty-fourth Street entrance to the building that housed (until 1990) the *New Yorker* offices, it was easy enough for Brendan and me to meet. Like me, he was an early riser, and we often breakfasted together. In those days, there was a Schrafft's restaurant in Times Square. The Schrafft's chain belonged to the Shattuck family, which was Catholic and which made a practice of hiring as waitresses young Catholic girls fresh from farms in the stony countryside of the west of Ireland— hopeful immigrants of the sort that used to be called "greenhorns." Brendan would always pronounce the word "Schrafft's" as "Scrap's." "Let's go get a bite at Scrap's," he would say, and on our way to the restaurant he would stop and pick up the morning papers and a magazine or two at a newspaper kiosk in Times Square. If he failed to find his name mentioned in one or another of the gossip columns in the *News* or the *Mirror*, he would toss the papers into the nearest trash basket. As for magazines, he liked sampling them, especially the newly invented ones. He doted on *Playboy* and the other so-called girlie magazines, which were hard to obtain in Ireland at that time. One day he picked up a novelty: a magazine devoted to homosexuals, featuring nude "studies" of handsome young male models. Brendan pretended to be astonished and shocked by this publication. To the kiosk attendant he said, with a show of indignation: "Who would be buying a rag like this?" The attendant gave Brendan a sour look and replied, "People like you." Brendan was delighted with the quickness and accuracy of the reply.

"B'God, you have me there!" he said. "Where can I take out a lifetime subscription?"

At "Scrap's," the waitresses made much of Brendan and, despite their Irish primness with respect to sex, would allow him to take considerable liberties with them. Under their uniforms they wore medals that bore a likeness of the miraculous Virgin Mary. In the course of ordering breakfast, Brendan would impudently reach out and attempt to grab one or another of the waitresses around the waist or even make a pass at their breasts, saying, "Gimme a feel of your miraculous middle." And the waitresses would giggle and blush and thrust his hands away from their persons but at the same time convey their delight with him as well; wicked as he was—oh, a matter for confession!—he could do no wrong in their eyes.

Brendan was taking certain astonishing liberties at the Algonquin as well. Accompanying Beatrice and him to New York, in the guise of a secretary and all-purpose social buffer, was a pretty young Irishwoman of conventional upper-middle-class Dublin background, whom I will call Lydia because that was not her name. Like most girls brought up in Dublin at that time, she hadn't troubled to continue her education beyond the high-school level and had taken care to avoid acquiring any skills that might have helped her find a place in the world of business. At seventeen, she and an American girlfriend had drifted into Ernest Hemingway's entourage in Spain. Years later, when Hemingway was breaking down mentally and physically, he came to believe that he had sexually abused Lydia, although in fact he had done no such thing. Lydia had an innocent passiveness about her, which translated itself into seductiveness; men wanted to sleep with her because it was so plainly impermissible.

Lydia and I became friends in the course of my becoming friends with Brendan and Beatrice. She had a room near theirs at the Algonquin, and she got into the habit of telephoning me in the morning, asking me in a sleepy voice for news of the day. Often, she would run across the street from the Algonquin and drop off for me at the receptionist's desk on the twentieth floor an Old Nick candy bar, which came to serve as an outward and visible sign of the bond of friendship we had forged and which also served to baffle the receptionist: was it really possible that the way to Mr. Gill's heart was paved with Old Nicks?

In the midst of a telephone conversation one morning, Lydia began to chuckle—a muffled, throaty chuckle that I was hearing for the first time—and I said at once, "Lydia, you wretch! There's someone in bed with you. How dare you phone me at such a moment?" She swore that she was alone and we went on gossiping in our usual vein. Later in the morning, I went over to the hotel to pick up Brendan for a luncheon engagement in the Village, and he suddenly burst out, "Well, what do you know! Fat and ugly as I am, I succeeded this morning in ravishing a pretty young Irish virgin." For once, I was angry with him, and I burst out, "You *are* fat and ugly, and your success disgusts me." "Well, now," he said, with a sullen look, "I didn't expect you to agree with me so fast."

Neither Brendan nor Lydia had the least knack for discretion; soon enough the slovenly openness with which they conducted their affair (an openness emphasized by the narrow boundaries of the settings in which it took place: the Algonquin, Jim Downey's bar, and the like) caused it to become common knowledge, and Beatrice, understandably indignant, had no choice but to retreat to Dublin. Unbeknownst to me at the time, she had had far more than Lydia to put up with in the course of the years of her marriage to Brendan; he was a bisexual who, in his recurrent, constantly accelerating bouts of drunkenness, chose companions in the lowest and most dangerous of gutters—that is, in actual gutters, where he would be beaten up, robbed of his money, and left unconscious.

Sometimes Brendan would invite unsavory companions back to the Algonquin, hoping to take them up to his room to sleep off drugs and drink, and would scandalize other guests in the hotel by making a noisy scene in the lobby when he wasn't permitted to do so. Proud as the management of the Algonquin was of its reputation for giving shelter to writers and other unpredictable characters, it found Brendan too much to put up with. He was told that his presence there was no longer desired, and his astonishment and dismay at this news—his feeling of actual heartbreak at being, so he felt, unjustly abandoned—was touching to observe.

Despairingly, Brendan moved to the Chelsea Hotel, itself a citadel of despair. Meanwhile Lydia, careless as ever, loving as ever, had a baby by Brendan, whom he officially acknowledged and who was given his name. (Beatrice and Brendan had never been able to have children. Years later, when the Behans were living in Dublin, Beatrice bore a daughter. The world assumed that the daughter was Brendan's, but Brendan, perhaps out of malice or perhaps out of loyalty to Lydia, when speaking with American friends would always hint otherwise.) Brendan would carry his namesake to a bar near the Chelsea, prop him up against the draft-beer handles, and encourage him to take a swig from his father's seidel. On one occasion, Lydia and Brendan brought their winsome infant out to the Gills' house in Bronxville, where a snapshot was taken of four Brendans in a row: two Brendan Behans, me, and my eldest grandchild, Brendan Larson. A superb actor, Brendan entertained us throughout the afternoon with imitations; my favorite was his imitation of a pious adolescent boy advancing to the communion rail, accepting on his tongue the unleavened wafer—by then, nothing less than the transubstantiated body of God—and returning down the aisle with hands reverently clasped and with his tongue feverishly working away to get God down off the roof of his mouth and duly swallowed.

Meanwhile, Brendan's professional life was deteriorating. He had written *The Quare Fellow* and *The Hostage* in collaboration with Joan Littlewood, who took public credit only as the director but who had her just, if secret, share of the author's royalties. This collaboration was a source of embarrassment to Brendan, who wished to be seen as a genius in his own right. Bad enough to live with the often-voiced accusation that he had lifted the plot and emotional ambience of *The Hostage* from Frank O'Connor's short story "Guest of the Nation"; worse to be thought a sort of literary grab bag, to be plucked from when he was more or less sober and ignored when he was drunk.

For years, Brendan worked with Littlewood on a play, *Richard's Cork Leg*. When their collaboration was dissolved by Brendan's envy and by his increasing inability to concentrate (one sorry factor feeding the other), Brendan turned with mounting desperation to selling the tatters of his talent here and there, to purchasers unworthy of them. The English editor who had patched together and rendered publishable *Borstal Boy* was brought over to the Chelsea to help wrest from Brendan, paragraph by paragraph and even sentence by sentence, a sufficient number of observations about his beloved New York City to make up a book. Brendan was aware that I had known Dylan Thomas and that I feared, as Brendan approached the age at which Thomas had died, that he might suffer a similar grotesque fate. Thomas at thirty-nine had, in effect, inadvertently committed suicide, by drinking so many neat Scotches one after another that they amounted to what the doctors at St. Vincent's Hospital, struggling in vain to save his life, described as "a massive insult to the brain." Brendan was engaged in massively insulting his brain, in a way that even his exceptionally strong constitution could not long withstand. I would plead with him to seek medical attention for his alcoholism and he would say jeeringly, "Ah, you think I'll be pulling a Thomas on you, but I won't! Remember, I have a Swiss bank account and nobody with a Swiss bank account has ever died young."

Whether Brendan had a Swiss bank account I was never to learn. He had assured me that there would be no difficulty about his supporting Lydia and his namesake, but the erratic hurly-burly of his life both in New York and in Dublin made it hard for him to keep his word: the money, if it came at all, came by fits and starts. Lydia and little Brendan were living in a dismal basement apartment on the West Side of Manhattan; while Lydia was at work in midtown, Brendan was cared for by the Puerto Rican superintendent of the building and his family and so came to speak excellent Spanish before he spoke a word of English. Lydia deputized me to telephone Brendan in Dublin whenever she was financially in dire straits—a deputy was needed because of the likelihood that it would be Beatrice and not Brendan who would answer the telephone—and as time passed I became to him not so much a trusted American friend as an irritating voice, reminding him of an obligation that he had failed to live up to. Guilt was transformed into anger and anger must find an object; far better that the object of his anger should be me rather than Lydia or the child.

Brendan died in Dublin in 1964, his wasted lungs drowning in pneumonia. He was forty-one, which is to say that he had managed to outlast Thomas by two years. He had been many days a-dying, his death was much written about in the press, and his funeral was counted upon to be a notable event. Beatrice, Beatrice's daughter, Brendan's mother, his innumerable aunts, uncles, and cousins would all be in attendance. In New York, Lydia felt strongly tempted to attend the funeral, however inappropriate her presence there was apt to strike the Behans and her own family as being—her mother, a highly respectable Dublin matron, had often expressed contempt for Lydia's adulterous carryings-on with a married man (a drunken, lowborn lout of a married man, at that), to say nothing of her unsanctioned motherhood. What would her mother say if Lydia turned up at the graveside and was to be caught by the lenses of a dozen television cameras? There was also for Lydia the problem of the cost of flying over to Dublin and back. At the last moment, Jim Downey, the owner of the Eighth Avenue bar in which Brendan had often held court, decided that he wished to attend the funeral and he invited Lydia to come along at his expense.

The funeral was indeed the grand affair that everyone had been predicting it would be, thoroughly covered by the press and television. By bad luck, the plane carrying Downey and Lydia arrived late at the Dublin airport and Brendan's coffin had been lowered into the grave and the funeral obsequies concluded by the time they arrived at the cemetery. To Lydia, the funeral was a botch, as so many of the events in Brendan's life that she had tried to share had been a botch. This time, at least, the fault was neither Brendan's nor hers. Nevertheless, it turned out that fault would indeed be found with her, that she would indeed be blamed for something. And the blame reached her from a totally unexpected quarter. For when she stopped off at her mother's house to say a hurried hello and goodbye before returning to New York, she discovered to her astonishment that her mother was furious with her for not having been present when the television cameras were scanning the mourners at the grave. Her mother had assured all her friends that Lydia was bound to be at the ceremony. The friends had been advised to keep their eyes peeled for Lydia on their "tellies." And she had failed them. Sitting in her mother's parlor, Lydia thought of how delighted Brendan would have been to hear the old harpy's complaint: that the absence of a sinful daughter from an event that she had no right to attend had succeeded in causing her virtuous mother embarrassment. That was the sort of two-faced, upside-down, Humpty-Dumpty hypocrisy that Brendan had relished and mocked throughout his lifetime; for him to have helped expose it even in his coffin would have struck him as adding a certain welcome savor to the inescapable necessity of dying.

Simon Verity

IN DESCRIBING Simon Verity, the British sculptor who for the past year or so has been carving great chunks of limestone into major and minor prophets on the main portal of St. John the Divine, one may as well begin with his hair; it appears to be made of some spiky, indestructible material, in which grayish stone dust readily accumulates, sometimes to the point where it has been mistaken for frost. Verity himself thinks that people passing him in the street, especially in warm weather, suspect him of being an apparition. Beneath the nimbus of hair is a handsome, fine-boned face and a body whose trimness is accounted for by the fact that hitting a chisel with a mallet is excellent exercise; moreover, the harder the stone that one seeks to wrest an imagined figure from, the more muscular one becomes.

Verity is forty-six and could pass for a boyish thirty; this deceptiveness with respect to his age is but a trifle compared to the deceptiveness of his dress. In hand-me-down tweeds, moth-eaten sweaters, and scuffed sneakers, he has the look of a hard-pressed ragamuffin, but since he numbers among his patrons the Prince of Wales, the Countess of Rosse, the Honorable Jacob Rothschild, and a notable assortment of wealthy lesser mortals on both sides of the Atlantic, one assumes that he is occasionally rewarded for his handiwork and that his waiflike appearance serves some obscure personal need. As to that need, the reticent

Verity is willing to grant this much—that almost from the cradle he has rebelled against the conventions of class that he was expected to uphold. And almost from the cradle he has possessed an enviable talisman of the rebellious spirit: a silver-headed walking stick—complete with concealed sword—that was once the prized companion of that fiery literary rebel, G. K. Chesterton. (The midwife who delivered Simon was a friend of Chesterton's; at his death, the sword-stick was bequeathed to her and by her handed on to Verity as soon as he was of an age to brandish it.)

Verity's father, grandfather, and great-grandfather were all trained as architects—his great-grandfather designed the celebrated Criterion Theatre in London—and it was supposed that Verity would follow in the same path. But far from it; upon graduating from Marlborough, a fashionable public school, he chose not to trundle along to Oxford or Cambridge. Unhappy at home, he went to spend a weekend with his great-uncle, the architect Oliver Hill, and spent the next seven years under his roof. (When his great-uncle was pleased with Simon, he would refer to him as "our boy." When he was displeased with him, he would complain to Simon's parents about "your boy.") The first vocation that ever seriously attracted Verity's interest was printing. From the craft of printing, he proceeded to the art of hand-lettering and from lettering in ink he proceeded to carving letters in stone. It happened that his great-uncle employed the services of the sculptor and master letterer Eric Gill on several big commissions, and Verity may have been inspired in part by that connection; be that as it may, he learned how to letter and cut stone by himself, mostly from books.

One of the first jobs that young Verity tackled was the task of carving a memorial tablet to Thomas à Becket, set in the stone floor of Canterbury cathedral. Since the cathedral was visited by upward of ten thousand visitors a day, Verity had to do much of his carving by night, with a single spotlight high in the nave illuminating the tablet. Memorial tablets led quite naturally to tombstones. Among the tombstones that he has designed and lettered is a particularly merry one, filled with dancing Victorian curlicues, for Sir John Betjeman, the late poet laureate, a champion of Victorian exuberance. For Nancy Mitford, who was said to have been mad about moles, he designed a tombstone bearing a couchant mole. When he met Nancy Mitford's sister, the Duchess of Devonshire, the Duchess inquired tactfully of him, "Do please tell us, Mr. Verity, because we have all been so unsure—is it a mole or an armadillo?" Verity was able to assure the Duchess that it was indeed a mole.

When Sir Roy Strong stepped down as head of the Victoria and Albert Museum, his colleagues wished to offer him as a farewell gift an ornament for his garden. Verity carved a medallion in which at first glance one sees only Queen Victoria and the Prince Consort, carved in profile; at a second glance, one sees that the bespectacled profile of Sir Roy has been cunningly inserted between the royal couple. In recent years, there has been a revival of interest in what had been a leading eighteenth-century passion throughout the British Isles—the building of grottoes, especially grottoes every inch of whose mossy, dripping walls and vaulted roofs would be covered with exotic shells. Verity has restored some elegant old grottoes—"Our British climate," he says, "lends itself to architecture intended to be damp"—and has been engaged in building several new ones as well, in places as remote from one another (and as dry) as Corfu and Fort Worth, Texas. He has also been carving bigger-than-lifesize baroque statues representing the twelve months of the year, to be placed on the parapets of a sumptuous Palladian villa that is now under construction in the Cheshire countryside.

Verity was interrupted in this task by a summons from the Cathedral of St. John the Divine; a jury at the cathedral had chosen him to be in charge of the carving of statues to be placed in the empty niches of the central portal. (The cathedral has long supported a program in which the stonecutter's craft is taught to young New Yorkers, many of whom come from the immediate neighborhood. Out of the stonecutters' big steel sheds on the cathedral grounds emerge those ornamental crockets and finials that bestow on the sombre mass of the building its unexpected delicacy.) A visitor to the cathedral will see perched on scaffolds and hammering away under Verity's guidance six or eight apprentices; they are encouraged to make individual contributions to the storytelling symbols that decorate the columnar bases upon which the statues of Ezekiel, Jeremiah, and other Old and New Testament figures, now mostly blank cubes of limestone, will eventually emerge. On the base of the statue of gloomy old Jeremiah, for example, is carved a likeness of New York City, bristling with skyscrapers, and above the city rises the mushroom cloud of an atomic explosion.

Back home in England, Verity has made use of many varieties of stone—Purbeck, Portland, Harnton, Ham, and the like. Much as he admires them, he has become infatuated with the far greater variety of stone available to him here in the States. "Why on earth do you Americans bother to import stone from anywhere else in the world when you have so many marvelous kinds of stone right here?" he asks, striking a note of well-bred, infinitesimal exasperation. "And stone available in such large sizes! Everywhere I look, I see another stone I want to set to work on, including in some cases the very pavement under my feet. Those enormous slates in front of St. Thomas's on Fifth Avenue, for example, and those even bigger pink granite sidewalks that one sees down in Soho and in Tribeca, ten feet across and a foot thick—what wouldn't I give to get my hands on them!"

Verity is keen not only about the stones out of which New York is built (including our lowly brownstone) but also about the city itself; in token of which he has bought a house in Harlem, at the foot of Morningside Park, from which he can gaze up at the great apse of the cathedral. Four stonecarvers share the house with him, and he has it in mind to use the house and its adjacent garden as the scene of certain experiments with stone, both as elements of structure and as freestanding objects, such as outdoor furniture. (Some of his furniture is already on sale in the gift shop of the cathedral.) Verity is hopeful that recent advances in the technology of stonecarving, much of it based upon the use of computers, may lead to a revival of the use of stone as an integral part of the design of buildings—"New designs for a new century," he says, "and in buildings of every kind, public and private. Today we can do in stone what has never been done before. I would like to see a dozen young Frank Lloyd Wrights bringing to us stonecarvers a sheaf of new designs and saying, 'There! Let's see what you can do with *that!*'" Not that Verity is waiting impassively for the dozen young Wrights to appear on his doorstep. "In all modesty," he says, looking his most ragamuffinlike and therefore the embodiment of modesty, "I should like very much to do a few of those designs myself."

Dorothy Parker

THERE ARE WRITERS who die to the world long before they are dead, and if this is sometimes by choice, more often it is a fate imposed on them by others and not easily dealt with. A writer enjoys a vogue and, the vogue having passed, either consents to endure the obscurity into which he has been thrust or struggles against it in vain, with a bitterness that tends to increase as his powers diminish. No matter how well or badly he behaves, the result is the same. If the work is of a certain quality, it survives the passing of the vogue, but the maker of the work no longer effectually exists. Even though he goes on writing, he dwells in the limbo of the half-forgotten, and his obituary notices are read with a flippant, unthinking incredulity: who would have guessed that the tattered old teller of tales had had it in him to hang on so fiercely?

A protracted life-in-death is all the more striking in the case of writers who make a reputation in youth and then live on into age. It is most striking of all in the case of young writers whose theme is the pleasingness of death and for whom it amounts in the world's eyes to a betrayal of their theme when they are observed to cling so tenaciously to life. Dorothy Parker's career was of this nature. She enjoyed an early vogue, which passed, leaving her work to be judged on its merits, and because the subject of so large a portion of her verses was the seductive-ness of a neat, brisk doing-away with herself, many people were astonished to read of her death from natural causes in 1967, at the age of seventy-three. Under the circumstances, it seemed to them a tardy end, and by an irony that had been one of Mrs. Parker's chief stocks-in-trade, she would have been the first to agree with them. She had indeed taken an unconscionably long time to leave a world of which she had always claimed to hold a low opinion. Her husbands, her lovers, and most of her friends had preceded her; for a person who had boasted of wooing death, she had proved the worst of teases—an elderly flirt of the sort that at thirty she would have savaged in a paragraph.

There had been, of course, more at stake for Parker than a reluctance to keep old promises made in poems. The gap between her life and her work had grown very wide. The fact was that, though in her thirties she had attempted suicide (her friends considered the attempt nominal), as she put on years she seemed unable to make a favorite of either life or death. She refused to take sides; it was as if she had hung on not fiercely or grimly but because she lacked the tiny tremor of will required to give up. She had had fame, and for long periods in Hollywood had enjoyed a very large income. The world would have said that she had had every opportunity to fulfill her talent, and now she lived alone, with a raspy little concierge of a dog, in a hotel room in Manhattan, and waited for nothing and hoped for nothing and got through the day, often enough with a bottle. She had been tiresome when she drank in youth, and with age she could scarcely be expected to improve; the occasions for drink were not cheerful ones. There were, besides, no suitable companions left to raise hell with—no incomparably comic Benchleys to babble nonsense to, no Hemingways to hero-worship. She was a friend of Jerry Zerbe's, who had photographed her with one of her lovers, John McClain (of whom she said later, when the affair was over, that his body had gone to his head), and with her second husband, Alan Campbell, but Zerbe's invincible high spirits were unable to overcome the intimations of misery (and, more surprisingly, of fear) that her round, pleasing face revealed. And even if old friends had found her better company, she would no doubt have sought out ways to alienate them. Early in life she had developed a strong bent for cutting ties with friends; to the born wisecracker, uttering the one funny word too many is the last appetite that fails.

Parker had been a writer whose robust and acid lucidities had been much dreaded and admired, and it was too bad that she should be making such an awkward finish; she was never so muddled as not to see this and to make her apologies for it. By the standards of her prime, what she was engaged in committing—what, plainly, she was helpless not to commit—was an inexcusable social and aesthetic blunder: she was becoming the guest who is aware that she has outstayed her welcome and who yet makes no attempt to pack her bags and go.

It was in her sad old age that I first encountered Parker. The occasion was a cocktail party given by the artist Charlie Addams and his first wife, Barbara—the slender, black-haired witch of those early Addams drawings in *The New Yorker*. I remember that at least two other *New Yorker* artists were present that afternoon: Alan Dunn and his wife, Mary Petty. Dunn possessed—and, indeed, may be said to have cherished—every phobia known to man, pyrophobia prominent among them. He informed me that earlier in the week, before accepting the Addamses' invitation, he had taken the trouble to send a messenger down to the hall of records in order to obtain a copy of the floor plan of their apartment. Being unfamiliar with it, he had to make sure that the fire escapes in the building were sufficient to permit Mary and him to save their lives in case a fire were to break out in the course of the party— a disaster that struck him as being very likely to take place.

Alan introduced me to Parker. Among friends of long standing, like the Dunns, she was Dottie; to me, a latecomer in her life, she was— and could only be—Mrs. Parker. In speaking her name, she took care to give both portions of it a derisive ring, and I was soon enough to learn why. The respectability implied by being a Mrs. and the still greater respectability implied by being a Parker—her first husband had been the scion of an old Hartford family—was in both cases emphasized in order to be mocked: she had never been a proper upper-middle-class matron and she had never been a WASP. On the contrary, she was a Jew named Rothschild. Or, rather, she was not a Jew, having had a Christian mother and a Jewish father, but she was also not *not* a Jew. Was that perfectly clear? As clear, she hoped, as mud?

In those late years, there was no praising her—her life had failed, and so her work had failed, and it was equally the case that the work of all her early colleagues (Benchley, Robert Sherwood, Marc Connelly, Donald Ogden Stewart) must also be seen to have failed. The posture she assumed that afternoon at the Addamses' was an especially painful one for a new acquaintance to be forced to observe, and of course she had assumed it for that reason among others: perhaps I was being punished for not yet having failed, or perhaps for supposing that, because I had written a few short stories for *The New Yorker*, I was a success. She knew better—she who had helped, after all, to invent *The New Yorker*, she who had been the most formidable wit at the Algonquin Round Table. There were, it appeared, certain truths for me to bear in mind.

If it was true, for example, that she had been hailed as one of the leading lights in the literary world of New York in those far-off days, people like me should remember that it hadn't been a world at all—it had been only a province, or maybe no more than a parish, made up largely of second- and third-raters. To be a leading light under such conditions it would have sufficed to be a glowworm. None of the major American writers of the period had been members of a set; they had lived and worked far from the coterie of self-promoters who gathered at the Algonquin Hotel. Hemingway, Faulkner, Lardner, Fitzgerald, Dos Passos, Cather, Crane, and O'Neill were not to be found cracking jokes and singing each other's praises or taunting each other into tantrums on West Forty-fourth Street.

So far, true enough, but what Parker appeared to have banished from her mind and was urging me to banish from mine was the quality of the work she had accomplished; there it stood, and stands, and will stand, refusing to be dismissed. Astonishingly, if one considers her harum-scarum ways, it is a body of work ample as well as of high quality: verse, short stories, theatre and book reviews. The titles of her books amount to a capsule autobiography: *Enough Rope, Sunset Gun, Laments for the Living, Death and Taxes, After Such Pleasures, Not So Deep as a Well, Here Lies*—with a single exception, they all speak directly or indirectly of death, and the exception is concerned with man's loss of something profoundly good: the contentment after making love that is more than satiety. In a poem that Parker cherished, John Donne had asked, "Why cannot we / As cocks and lions jocund be / After such pleasures?" Why cannot we turn away even at the moment of highest joy from the distress of our continuously prefigured death? Under whatever disguise, this was Parker's theme, and she never feared to sound its heartbreaking note throughout fifty years of writing.

Parker was one of the wittiest people in the world and one of the saddest; if even now we go on laughing at something she happened to say very late at night in some long-since-vanished bar, we do so at our peril. Man is the animal that knows he dies, and the death's-head grinning in the mirror back of all those lighted bottles is our own. There is nothing good in life, Parker held, that will not be taken away. One of the things she admired most in Hemingway was how he had struggled to face this problem both in his life and in his writing. He had been so sure in youth that he would not choose his father's way out of life, by suicide, and Parker had been so sure in youth that she could find no other means of dealing with the pain of being; and so Hemingway had killed himself and she had lived on, and toward the end there were only ghosts in the corners of the hotel room, silently reproaching her for having had the cowardice to live. It was no use asking them when she had ever claimed to be brave. If, as she said, she had always been the greatest little hoper in the world, she had known that hope was a form of folly and had nothing to do with either courage or wisdom. "People ought to be one of two things, young or old," she had written. "No; what's the use of fooling? People ought to be one of two things, young or dead."

But she had been young, and it had not been satisfactory. Her mother had died when she was five, she had intensely disliked her stepmother, she had grown apart from her father and her jolly, noisy, gregarious Rothschild relatives—not the world-famous rich Rothschilds but only simple American Rothschilds—and she had detested the Catholic education she received at the hands of nuns. Delicate and bold and virginal in her teens, she must have been determined even then to be found worthy of heartrending misadventures. There are hints of them in the early poems—hints that, given a choice between happiness and unhappiness, she would be prompted by some imperious devil in her to choose unhappiness. She had the imagination of disaster, as so many people do who have lost a mother in childhood, and she cultivated this form of imagination and made it flourish. Her knack for making things end badly amounted, in her friends' eyes, to genius, and one cannot help thinking with sympathy of the wretched nights and days through which she drove a succession of distracted lovers. Edna St. Vincent Millay's confident "We were very tired, we were very merry, / We had gone back and forth all night on the ferry" would not have served the purposes of Dottie Rothschild Parker, standing tiptoe on the brink of doom: "Lips that taste of tears, they say, / Are the best for kissing." The lines are from the first poem in her first book, and we are not surprised to see that the poem is entitled "Threnody." She began her career as a poet with a song of lamentation and she ended it with what she called a war song. In the last poem she ever wrote, she urged her soldier-husband to be unfaithful to her. Since he was a bisexual, the poem contained more ironies than her readers would have been likely to perceive.

The savage witticisms, the exquisite threnodies, accumulated over a lifetime—to think of discarding them as valueless in the fretful loneliness of age! Listening to her that day of our first meeting at the Addamses', I but half-listened, for by then the work itself had come to stand between me and the little dumpling of a woman who, dressed all in black, with a broad-brimmed black hat hiding her fallen face, sipped her drink and sought in the gentlest of voices to expunge herself and her sorry past. The attempt failed, as once the attempt at suicide had failed. She shrugged her shoulders and made some conventional, unpleasant joke about another guest at the party. Plainly, so her shrug implied, it was her doom to succeed only at failing.

Even in death that doom may be said to have prevailed; the messiness that characterized her life was manifested in the circumstances of her cremation. In her will, she had asked that there be no funeral ceremonies, but her bossy friend and benefactor Lillian Hellman insisted that a service be held at the Frank E. Campbell Funeral Home, where Hellman delivered what was less a conventional eulogy than a public address. Afterward, it was unclear what disposition should be made of Parker's ashes. No instructions having been received from Miss Hellman, they were mailed to the law firm of O'Dwyer and Bernstein, which had drawn her will and which represented her sole heir, Martin Luther King, Jr., as trustee for the National Association for the Advancement of Colored People. Parker's estate amounted to approximately twenty thousand dollars, which the NAACP was surprised and delighted to receive.

For twenty years the Parker ashes remained in a filing cabinet in the offices of O'Dwyer and Bernstein. In 1988, Paul O'Dwyer sought to secure an appropriate last resting-place for the ashes, but even this kindly intention met with rebuffs. Because of the long and notable association between the Algonquin and Parker, O'Dwyer offered the ashes to the hotel, which declined to accept them. So did *The New Yorker*, which pleaded that it had trouble enough providing space for living writers without finding room for the remains of dead ones. In the fall of 1988, the NAACP headquarters in Atlanta agreed to accept the ashes and secure for them an honored place in an agreeable setting. One of Parker's early witticisms had been that she wished the epitaph on her tombstone to read "Excuse my dust." As usual, the note of mingled apology and mockery had proved accurate.

Wallace K. Harrison

WALLACE K. HARRISON was one of the best-known American architects of this century, as well as one of the most misunderstood. In his
lifetime, it was difficult for critics to maintain a sympathetic balance
between the architect that the world saw him as being and the architect
that he and a handful of close friends believed him to be. Which is to say
that there was always a gap between the public figure whose skill in the
management of headstrong peers brought many a complex architectural
project to a satisfactory conclusion and the private figure whose talent,
eager to express itself in surprisingly radical terms, was all too often at the
mercy of circumstances that held it in check.

Throughout history, it has often been the case that the more
successful a man is as a member of the architectural profession, the
more likely it is for him to fear that he has failed as an individual artist.
This is thanks in part to the fact that the profession is at best impure,
subject by its nature to factors often obdurately at odds with art. Unlike a
painting or a musical composition, the purpose of a work of architecture
isn't simply to give delight; it must also carry out efficiently the various
down-to-earth functions for which it has been designed. Moreover, the
architect often finds himself at the mercy of unlooked-for obstacles—an
importunate client, say, or a parsimonious budget. For that reason, the
lives of even the most celebrated architects are apt to possess an

151

undertone of sadness, and Harrison's is no exception. His arduous career ought to have earned him a long and not unfruitful twilight; instead, though he lived to be eighty-six, the dark came comparatively early, and with his accustomed stoic Yankee valor he was obliged to suffer the most unwelcome of fates—not to be used up but simply to be cast aside.

To make Harrison's story all the more poignant, what an attractive young man he had been and how hard he had worked to fulfill his promise! Born in Worcester, Massachusetts, in 1895, to a family without means and frequented by troubles, as an architect he was virtually self-taught. Earning his keep in the offices of McKim, Mead and White, while attending the atelier of Harvey Wiley Corbett, he was able to save enough money to enter the then indispensable Ecole des Beaux Arts in Paris. Back in New York, he worked as a draftsman under two superb architects, Bertram Grosvenor Goodhue and Raymond Hood, and won a traveling fellowship abroad. Then, once again with his purse empty, he returned to New York and found employment with Corbett and Hood.

A tall, broad-shouldered, handsome young man with old-fashioned good manners, he soon found himself at home in the "best" New York City circles; in 1926, he married Ellen Milton, who happened to be a sister-in-law of Abby Rockefeller. In later years, it was often stated that much of Harrison's success was owed to his Rockefeller connections, but this is too simple (and malicious) an explanation; on the contrary, it appears to have been the case that he was already making a name for himself as one of the cluster of architects engaged in designing Rockefeller Center before John D. Rockefeller, Jr., the family patriarch who closely supervised the building of the center, became aware that Harrison had any marital link to him. It was during the building of the center, which took place with exceptional speed during the early years of the depression, that Harrison demonstrated his capacity for fashioning a consensus among warring factions—young as he was, he embodied a firmness of will and a probity of character that brought even the most impetuous of his elders to the conference table.

By 1939, Harrison and a newly acquired partner, the brilliant young Max Abramovitz, had been commissioned to design the main theme buildings for the New York World's Fair: the trylon and perisphere, which for the past fifty years have continued to serve as romantic symbols of a longed-for, unattainable "world of tomorrow." When, after the Second World War, it was decided that the United Nations' headquarters buildings should be located in New York City, Harrison, assisted by Abramovitz, was placed in charge of the overall design. An international advisory committee was invited to participate in the undertaking, and it was in the course of presiding over this band of prima donnas that, to Harrison's dismay, his reputation as an achiever of useful compromises began to outstrip his reputation as an architect. A man who could keep such an overbearing and meddlesome member of the advisory committee as Le Corbusier from usurping the project was plainly, when called upon to be so, hard as nails. Out of years of struggle emerged the General Assembly building, the Secretariat building—one of the first of our glass-walled, high-rise office buildings—and other subsidiary UN structures, all bearing to a greater or lesser degree the stamp of Harrison and Abramovitz.

In the early 1960s, Harrison and Abramovitz were given what ought to have been their greatest plum—the project called Lincoln Center for the Performing Arts. Harrison again served as the Grand Panjandrum, coordinating the work of Philip Johnson, Eero Saarinen, and several other architects. Abramovitz was to design the Philharmonic Hall; Harrison himself took on the design of the Metropolitan Opera House. As the project proceeded, committee piled atop committee, and many members of these committees turned out to be ardent amateur architects disguised as bankers and insurance executives. The brave hopes with which Harrison had begun designing the opera house were continually dashed, not only by unsuitable suggestions but by escalating costs. As built, the opera house was so far from being what Harrison had intended that for him to appear at the gala on opening night, smiling, in white tie and tails, was an act both courageous and mortifying.

It was during the course of Harrison's work on the opera house that I first became a friend of his. Looking back, I realize that he must have had to forgive me silently for the auspices under which we met: one of those damnable committees that was constantly tripping him up. The chairman of the building committee for Lincoln Center was a charming middle-aged lawyer named Charles Spofford, whom I had encountered through some remote Yale connection and who had learned of my interest in architecture. Spofford confessed that he knew little or nothing about the subject and he invited me to serve as a sort of unofficial adviser to him when, from time to time, he would stop by the offices of Harrison and Abramovitz to check up on the designs for the opera house.

Leading us into the room where various models in clay and plaster of alternative designs for the opera house had been constructed, Wallie (as one came to call him within a few minutes of meeting him) would show off the models one after another, pointing out the nature of the differences between the designs and accounting for each difference according to whether the reason behind it was aesthetic, financial, impractical in terms of physical comfort, or, in some cases, open to objection on all three grounds. For example, in order to bring in x amount of dollars in revenue, the auditorium would have to have y number of seats, which would be several hundred seats more than the z number of seats that the acoustical engineers had stipulated as ideal; one was expected to weigh the oranges of high-quality sound against the apples of prudent bookkeeping.

To make matters worse, some members of the building committee were opposed to having boxes in the auditorium, on the grounds that boxes were undemocratic; other committee members were adamantly in favor of retaining as many boxes as possible, in imitation of the golden horseshoe of the old opera house. On the one hand, boxes guaranteed their possessors a certain social prestige; on the other hand, they cut down on the total number of seats available. As for correct sightlines, they, too were a vexation; having been consulted, the singers on the Metropolitan roster had unanimously agreed that they wished their audiences to be packed into a tight semicircle just outside the proscenium arch, almost within touching distance. No matter that this might produce a number of seats from which the stage would be partly invisible: for the singers, the important thing was to be heard if not seen.

I recall that in one model of the opera house the flyloft rose in a great swoop skyward, like the grotesquely elevated rear-fender fins of the Cadillac automobile of that day; in another model, the flyloft was surmounted by a square office tower of considerable height, which would generate a regular income even when the opera house itself was dark. What alarmed me was not that Harrison and his colleagues had produced so great a number of alternative designs as that he seemed to be about equally pleased to champion each of them in turn. As an amateur of architecture, I had always enjoyed the luxury of assuming that one solution to a problem was better than another—was inescapably bound to be better than another—and was therefore worth defending at all costs. However hard Wallie may have fought with others for a preferred solution to the problem of the opera house, in conducting Spofford and his committee about the model room he was always that equable, accommodating presence upon whom his professional detractors were used to pouring their scorn.

Sorriest of all Harrison's failed successes was the most ambitious project of his career—the immense government mall that Nelson A. Rockefeller as governor of New York insisted upon creating south of the capitol building in Albany. An entire neighborhood of run-down but habitable housing was wiped out to build, at a cost of billions of dollars, a futuristic cityscape of marble and concrete. It is the only true embodiment in this country of the principles of urban design that Le Corbusier enunciated in the twenties and thirties: endlessly multipliable vistas, airy and yet airless, half park and half necropolis. Like the embodiments of these principles on an even vaster scale in Brasília, the capital city of Brazil, and at Chandigarh, the capital city of the Indian Punjab, the Albany experiment proved that Corbu, the grand enunciator—always so sure of himself, always so ill-disposed to rivals—was a success in book form, as a theorist of architecture, but a failure in practice.

Harrison had been Corbu's chief sponsor in this country and had arranged for him to be given more credit than he was entitled to in the preparation of the designs for the United Nations. In carrying out a Corbusian program at Albany, Harrison granted himself but a single personal eccentricity—what he called his egg, an ovoid structure perched rakishly aslant on a pedestal along the eastern parapet of the mall. Ingeniously stacked within the arbitrary shape of the egg are a couple of theatres and the usual complement of lobbies, greenrooms, and dressing rooms; the theatres are said to serve their purpose well enough, though less agreeably than if they had been placed within a conventional structure, accessible at ground level to audiences and performers alike.

In the course of attempting to humanize the icy colossus at Albany, Harrison found that the close friendship between him and Rockefeller (once Harrison's protégé and later for many years his chief patron) was steadily deteriorating. Before the project was completed, Harrison was tacitly dismissed. Soon thereafter, without a word to anyone, he cleaned out his office at Harrison and Abramovitz and set up in practice on his own: an old man eager for work, but alas! the work was hard to find. For by then architectural critics and the public at large had also dismissed Harrison; his lifelong championship of the experimental over the conventional was forgotten and his own novel and sometimes reckless essays—the cylindrical pavilions of glass and steel that he designed for himself and his family on Long Island, the fish-shaped church in Stamford, the Nelson Rockefeller hideaway cottage at Pocantico Hills, whose concrete-shell roof seemed to float as weightlessly over one's head as the wings of a giant moth—were taken to be mere aberrations, handiwork of a sort uncharacteristic of the compliant servant of the rich that he was thought to be.

In so many ways, then, a sad story, but in other ways a heroic and not unhappy one: the forging of a worthy life against what had seemed in youth the highest possible odds, with a constant display of generosity to others and with personal reverses staunchly borne. One day when Harrison was in his early eighties, he and I had lunch together at the Knickerbocker Club—that masterpiece of William Adams Delano, an architect of an earlier generation, whom Harrison and I had known and revered—and we began to talk about the zestful, frantic period in which he and half a dozen distinguished colleagues (Hood, Fouilhoux, Corbett, and Stone among them) were engaged in designing Rockefeller Center. John D. Rockefeller, Jr., had purchased the leasehold to the property for a philanthropic purpose that, thanks in part to the stock-market crash of October 1929, was no longer capable of being fulfilled. He was understandably eager to turn the property to commercial advantage as quickly as possible; to that end, the architects worked more or less around the clock for many weeks, pooling their ideas and their energies with an abandon that left no room for personal vanity.

According to Harrison, "young" John D.—young because his father, the first John D., was still clinging greedily to life in his late nineties as the center went up—was an ideal client, keeping close watch on every aspect of the project (even to checking with a pocket measure the mountains of blueprints that would be daily unfurled before him) and rejecting almost every opportunity to impose his personal notions of good design upon the architects. Harrison remembered as the only exception to this remarkable feat of self-discipline that Rockefeller had initially had his hopes set upon a Gothic treatment of the exterior detailing of the buildings, as being appropriate to St. Patrick's Cathedral, directly across Fifth Avenue from the center, and to his own taste. (His major benefaction to the Metropolitan Museum had been the Cloisters.) The consortium of architects had agreed to employ a severely stripped-down limestone exterior not unlike that which Raymond Hood had employed on the *Daily News* building, but to placate Mr. Rockefeller, they threw him the sop of some bronze railings in a vaguely Gothic style on the observation deck at the top of the RCA building—railings that, so they thought, no pedestrians would be able to detect from the street and channel gardens far below. To their dismay, when the building was erected, the Rockefeller Gothic railings were readily visible, and they remain so to this day.

At lunch that day, and on other occasions as well, in the course of our reminiscing about the building of the center, I would ask Harrison who among the architects in the consortium had designed such-and-such a detail in the center—the handsome brass stair railings in the lobby of the RCA building, say, with their brass-ball banisters and newel posts—and again and again, as the last survivor of the group, he could easily have claimed them as his own, but he would smile and shake his head and say, "Honestly, I can't remember. We were all working so fast, you know. . . . Wait! I think it must have been Ed Stone who did those railings. Ed, the big bear! The lobby of the Music Hall, that was Ed for you—on his scale. What a talent he had!"

As for Harrison's own talent, which with his usual old-fashioned good manners he was reluctant to speak of, luckily for him a year or so before his death it was made manifest in an exhibition of his life's work organized and curated by the young Dutch writer and architect Rem Koolhaas. It was held at the Institute for Architecture and Urban Studies (now defunct) in New York City, and Harrison himself was able to be present, claiming to feel—as the subject of any exhibition is bound to feel—at once intensely present and no less intensely posthumous. Thanks to his great height and erect posture, at the well-attended opening his bald head could be seen moving about among the portable screens to which were affixed a host of his sketches, elevations, and renderings. When I congratulated him on the show, joyously he burst out, "Everything's here but the doghouse!"

Of all the people at that gathering, I was surely the only one able to appreciate that obscure reference. Harrison and his wife had often visited the country house of Henry and Kay Mali, in the hills above Winsted, Connecticut. The Gill family had—and has—a country place in Norfolk, a town a few miles northwest of Winsted, and the Malis were among the oldest and dearest of our friends in that neighborhood. Arriving at their house for dinner one summer evening many years ago, we had no sooner shaken hands with our host and hostess and with Harrison, their weekend guest, than we were all marched round to the back of the house. There, in a place of honor adjacent to the kitchen door, was a brand-new miniature building of considerable elegance: a gable-roofed doghouse neatly assembled out of ancient planks and a few dozen secondhand shingles.

The designer-builder was no less a person than that distinguished Fellow of the American Institute of Architects, Wallace K. Harrison. Drinks were served and toasts were proposed not only to the architect but to the occupant of the doghouse as well—a basset hound with the dolorous countenance characteristic of its breed. The Malis assured us that, in spite of appearances, the basset hound was smiling. And so was Harrison, and with reason, far from New York and from the responsibilities that were continually thrust upon him and that he never shirked. It is that tall figure standing there in the late summer twilight, boyishly elated by his prowess as a carpenter and half a lifetime away from the disappointments of old age, whom I recollect now.

The Irish:
Barry, O'Neill, Fitzgerald, O'Hara

EVEN IN A PALACE life can be lived well. Marcus Aurelius' stoic witticism offers a clue to the fortunate life of the American playwright Philip Barry, who with his wife, Ellen, were among the earliest of the friends I met through my colleague on *The New Yorker*, the cartoonist Charles Addams. Barry and I turned out to have many things in common, and not least that we were partial to palaces and to the people who lived in them, especially if the palaces were small and sunny and the people smiling. We were still more partial to people who might have lived in palaces and who chose instead to live in pavilions and pleasances, accepting with light hearts the responsibilities that their good luck imposed on them.

Barry liked to be around lucky people and he set lofty standards for them. He wished them to be every bit as disciplined in their happiness as unlucky people are obliged to be in their misery. For both sorts of people the goal must be the same—grace of the body, grace of the spirit. Grace is whatever is fitting, whatever flourishes within bounds. Barry was a lucky man and very hard on himself; sooner than most, he achieved the grace he sought and, the price proving higher than he found it possible to pay, sooner than most, he died.

Barry's sense of the appropriate manifested itself in his work as it did in his life: nothing bigger than need be. No matter how ambitious the

159

intentions of his plays, he kept them modest in scale. He wrote often in the now little-favored genre of high comedy, but his comedies strove to be deeper than they were high, and he could write a tragedy low enough, bleak enough, coarse enough, to take place in a saloon. Among other plays, he wrote *Holiday, The Animal Kingdom,* and *The Philadelphia Story,* but he also wrote *White Wings, Hotel Universe,* and *Here Come the Clowns.* He had many hits and many flops, and little as he enjoyed the drudgery of putting on plays, he mightily enjoyed the drudgery of writing them. As far as he could tell, it was the task he had been born into the world to perform, and it was agreeable to be well rewarded for what he was almost helpless not to do.

The characters that Barry invented for his so-called drawing-room comedies have tastes that run to simple, costly things. His heroes and heroines state and resolve their problems as best they can over drinks in deluxe farmhouses, villas, and seaside cottages. Barry shared the tastes of his characters, as he shared their appetites and pursuits. One has only to glance down a list of the places where Barry and his family chose to live over the years—Mount Kisco, Cannes, Hobe Sound, East Hampton, and the like—to see where his preference lay. He was born in 1896, in a plain wooden house on a humdrum side street in Rochester, New York, and he died in 1949, in a big apartment high above Park Avenue, in the most fashionable section of New York City. (On his desk at the time was the typescript of his latest play, *Second Threshold.* Typically, its setting is the library of an elegant old town house on West Tenth Street.) On any map that one can buy, the distance traveled between the points of Barry's birth and death is not very great; on maps of the sort that one cannot buy, it is very great indeed. Given the light that it throws on the unexpectedly ample body of his work—twenty-one plays on Broadway in less than thirty years—it is a distance well worth taking the measure of.

More than most American writers of his day, Barry was drawn to the rich and wellborn. To their astonishment, he found them interesting and therefore to be cultivated. They were seductive in their good looks and good manners, and so he was careful to remain unseduced by them. They might take him up, those charming insiders, but they couldn't take him in. He had been born an outsider, and that gave him a certain dark advantage. He stood his ground among them, sometimes at moments when they were unaware that he felt any need to do so. He would eat with them and drink with them and at parties and on other social occasions he would give what they spoke of as excellent value—civilities of attentiveness, of badinage, of flattery—but he watched them warily. Some of them he loved, a few of them he admired without love; as for the rest, he might have been content to echo Mark Twain, who on being asked his opinion of the Jews replied with asperity, "They are members of the human race; worse than that I cannot say of them."

Twain was like Barry in being fascinated by the rich and in being uneasy over the degree of that fascination. Twain liked the excellent whisky and cigars of Carnegie, Rogers, and the other new, brigandly millionaires, and he stepped with relish into their carriages and onto their steam-yachts, but he kept himself on sentry-alert. Eager to amuse them and avid for their admiration, he was yet ineradicably of Hannibal; he never made the mistake of supposing that he was one of the moguls. His white suits and his mop of preposterously unruly white hair served as the credentials that established his separateness from them. He called attention to himself in a way that "nice" people shrank from and could find acceptable only in a mountebank. Though Barry and Twain shared the same temptations with respect to money, fame, and social position, Barry was of a temperament radically at odds with Twain's; his credentials of separateness were inward and therefore not to be detected by eye or ear, and "nice" people approved of him whether he sought their approval or not.

Barry's wife, Ellen, an able artist, once painted a portrait of him as a birthday present. Thanking her for it, Barry said, "I see you have caught my fox's eye." And so she had. Nearsighted from birth, Barry wore thick-lensed, steel-rimmed round spectacles, behind which his eyes shone with an exceptional intensity. Their blue irises seemed to gather up brightness like a burning glass. His scrutiny was so sharp that, standing before him for the first time, you suspected that he was not only seeing you but was also seeing into you and perhaps seeing through you. That was a chance you were prepared to take, in the hope that you deserved to be his friend. (My own first experience of that fox's eye occurred at a cocktail party given by Charlie Addams. Barry's gaze slipped sideways from me to fall upon a young woman just then entering the room. Her name was Kay Draper and she was a new member of *The New Yorker* staff. "Now, *there's* a pretty girl!" Barry said, as indeed she was. That day my worthiness to be his friend went unexamined.) What that fox's eye observed, the writer's mind never failed to take note of; in mental equivalents of the little brown-paper-covered schoolboy pads in which he jotted down ideas for possible plays, Barry tucked away names, slang phrases, and physical resemblances, to be pondered on and found room for sooner or later, transformed and illuminated.

In his comedies, Barry was an accurate chronicler of a tiny but important fraction of the American population. One of the curious attributes of that fraction is that it has no desire either to be chronicled by others or to chronicle itself. The rich and wellborn produce few historians and even fewer novelists, dramatists, and poets, and perhaps this is less curious than it appears at first glance. The fact is that they have little reason to go to the trouble of telling us who they are, or where they came from, or where they may be going. In the most serious sense, they have got past having to know *any*thing about themselves. It is the middle-class stranger on sufferance among them who has something to gain by a close examination of their ways. For him they are instructive; the more he learns about their class, the better able he will be to pass over into it, if that is what he intends to do, or to behave correctly in their presence, if for some reason he should wish to remain outside the pale. When the stranger is also, like Barry, a writer of drawing-room comedies, then his surroundings become doubly precious to him; he will immerse himself in them in part because he finds them agreeable and in part because they contain material out of which he will be able to fashion his works. He remains ignorant of even the smallest social details at his peril. Care must be taken to distinguish one club tie from another, one symbolic rosette from another, and upon inventing as a character an old lady on the Main Line he will see to it that she says "go to bank" and not "go to the bank," and that she "posts" a letter instead of mailing it. To a certain kind of writer, and especially to a certain kind of playwright, milieu and métier are one.

Among the things that Barry and I had in common was that we were both of Irish-Catholic descent. It would be hard to exaggerate the degree to which, in the period during which he—and, some twenty years later, I—were growing up (that is, during the first quarter of the twentieth century), our ancestry served to mark us as outsiders. On his father's side, Barry was a first-generation American; on his mother's side, he was of the third or fourth generation, but her family—Quinns, long resident in Philadelphia—had remained devout Catholics and so had failed to assimilate themselves into the dominant Philadelphia culture. Not that their chosen isolation would have struck them as a sign of failure; on the contrary, it was proof of their success in having preserved a precious religious heritage. For it was religion rather than race that, upon their arrival in this country, encapsulated the Catholics who had come from the south of Ireland. The Irish in the north were Protestants, being, in fact, mostly Scots, who had been planted in Ireland in the seventeenth century by Cromwell in a vain attempt to subdue that unsubduable country. Emigrating to the States, these Scotch-Irish were quickly swallowed up in the indiscriminate mass of Presbyterians, Congregationalists, Baptists, and Episcopalians. Almost at once they fell in with American vernacular traditions, while the devout Catholics living beside them remained generation after generation Irish and therefore foreign, a minority conspicuously and perhaps dangerously at odds with the majority.

The injustice of the situation was especially painful to the descendants of the tens of thousands of Irish who had settled in this country in the eighteenth century and who fought as patriots in the Revolution. In my case, the story goes that my grandmother Bowen's family established itself here as a result of bringing thoroughbred horses over from Ireland to sell in the colonies some time during the 1750s and 1760s. Another branch of the family boasts of a Captain Jack McManus, who certainly fought in the Revolution, but whom I suspect of having promoted himself to a captaincy long after the war was over. In a similar fashion, a later ancestor, a veteran of the Civil War, is always referred to within the family as a general, though the official records indicate that he was nothing of the kind.

By an irony of history, these early Irish-Catholic settlers felt obliged to identify themselves with the millions of immigrants who swarmed here from Ireland in the years immediately following the Great Famine of the 1840s and who established a stereotype of rude manners, boisterous humor, alcoholic belligerence, and political chicanery to which all people of Irish descent were assumed to conform. (A few generations later, a similar irony of history played a similarly unfair trick upon the long-established American Jews of Portuguese and German descent; the waves of Jewish immigrants arriving from Poland and Russia around the turn of the century soon came to stand for all Jews. In both cases, it was a matter of pride for the early comers not to deny fraternity with the latecomers, though in fact little or no fraternity existed.)

Of the postfamine Irish, many of the women went into domestic service, while many of the men dug ditches, built railroads and subways, and worked their way up to being policemen, firemen, and, with an extra pinch of ambition, saloonkeepers. For a long time, the bulk of the Irish were thought to belong by nature to the servant and laboring classes; the white Protestant middle class that was later to be succinctly categorized as WASP looked with amusement on the efforts of these gross underlings to better themselves socially. As late as 1920, in help-wanted advertisements in newspapers, it was a commonplace to encounter the phrase "No Irish need apply." If they were not to be welcomed as employees, how likely was it that they would ever be welcomed in WASP homes, clubs, and other self-perpetuating, self-aggrandizing organizations? There was but one way to achieve such a reversal of fate, and it was the oldest way in the world—a way that no WASP ever jibbed at, which is simply to gain more money than other people. For money always talks and sometimes money shouts, and even when it whispers, the deafest of the deaf can hear it and make obeisance to it.

The first rule for achieving what sociologists call "upward mobility" is to acquire as much money as possible. The second rule is to acquire it as quickly as possible, and the third rule is to pretend that one has always had it. In Barry's case, both sides of the family made good remarkably soon after their arrival in this country. His father founded a successful marble and tile business in Rochester, New York, but died at forty-five, when Philip was only a year old. Brought up largely by his mother and sister, possessing faulty eyesight, and undergoing an unusually profuse number of childhood diseases, Philip was never an athlete, never a "joiner," and became known instead for a quick wit and a sharp tongue. He made jokes and, as he grew into adolescence, developed a "line" that girls found delightful and that boys envied. He also became an excellent dancer; it was in him to wish to shine before women more than before men, though, like most Irish-Americans, he always preferred flirtation to commitment.

From early childhood, Philip was preoccupied with books. They were the chief reward offered in the Barry household for good conduct and were the looked-for gifts at Christmas and on birthdays. In the aspiring middle class of those days, books stood for culture and culture for prestige; as soon as possible, one put together what could be spoken of with pride as one's "library." Philip memorized scores of poems, which he and his sister would recite antiphonally, stanza after stanza. By then, like almost all writers, he had provided the obligatory evidence for his literary bent; indeed, at the age of nine he had published a short story called "Tab the Cat" in the children's supplement of a Rochester newspaper, and trifling as the story was, it had the effect that all such precocious debuts have on all born writers: he burned to be published again.

The most important event of Philip's life in Rochester may well have been his enrollment in a public high school. The accident of there being no Catholic high school for him to enter after his graduation from a Catholic grammar school caused him to move at a single stride away from a religiosity that was threatening to suffocate him into the seemingly ample air of those well-bred, well-to-do Protestants among whom, as it turned out, he was to spend the rest of his life. Unlike the other Barrys, Philip had never been a devout Catholic; it was characteristic of him that he objected strongly to his sister's decision to become a nun and that he resented serving as an altar boy at Mass—one day, taking advantage of the sticky misery he felt on an exceptionally hot Sunday morning, he cast aside his churchly vestments and swore that he would never wear them again. "Where," said his pious mother, "did I get that boy?"

East High was a welcome revelation to Philip. The boys and girls that he met there—especially the girls—were so good-looking, so easy of manner, so clever at his kind of repartee, and so easy a match for him in scholarship that he was at once enchanted by them. He was enchanted by their surroundings as well. He had chafed at the effortful, lace-curtain gentility of his Irish-Catholic neighborhood; he felt himself coming into his own on East Street, the grand residential boulevard of Rochester. There the big houses sat ranged in self-congratulatory propinquity on their level green lawns, like so many stout matrons seated elbow to elbow, implacably chaperoning a ball. Soon he was being invited to tea dances and birthday parties in those houses. He was carefully dressed, he had excellent manners, he was eager to please— oh, dear, yes, in spite of the fact that he was Irish and Catholic and without money and without connections, he was worthy of a conditional acceptance. He would be given a chance to see whether, on further testing, he might not, after all, do!

The milieu into which Barry slipped with such grace and alacrity—the upper middle class of a prosperous small provincial city—was one that was proving of interest to a number of other Irish-American young men who would one day be writers. Prominent among them were Eugene O'Neill, in New London, Connecticut, and F. Scott Fitzgerald, in St. Paul, Minnesota; a little later, there would be John O'Hara, in Pottsville, Pennsylvania. Like Barry, they were all outsiders and they were all intent upon acquiring the perquisites, both outward and inward, of their Protestant betters, with their country clubs and their cars and chauffeurs and, above all, their assurance—the conviction that whatever they might do was all right because of who they were. In the degree to which this made life easier for them, it was an attribute that deserved emulating. One might affect to despise them, as O'Neill did, but no sooner did he begin to have their kind of money than he began to build their kind of houses—in Sea Island, in Danville, in Marblehead—and to put on their kind of airs; he took care to drive a Cadillac like their Cadillacs and he rented in the French countryside a château on a scale of splendor that would have struck most of them as being, in their accustomed phrase, "too rich for our blood."

O'Neill had felt snubbed by the not very lofty aristocracy of New London—old families with old money, who were almost certainly unaware of any slight that they had administered to the extremely good-looking if often drunken young man who was to be seen mooning about the streets and beaches of the seaside town. They liked his father, the celebrated actor James O'Neill, who was glad to encounter them at the bar of the Mohegan House and who never supposed that because of a drink or two together and a few pleasantries exchanged he would become a friend of theirs and frequent their houses. As an Irishman-born and an actor, Jim O'Neill knew his place and was comfortable in it; little Monte Cristo Cottage was good enough for him. Besides, he admired the rich and was determined to become rich himself. He was given to speculating in land, and it was true that he once had a run-in with the immensely rich Harkness family over a parcel of land that he had bought adjoining the Harkness estate in Waterford, but for the most part he held in awe the millionaire yachtsmen who dropped anchor in the harbor at New London (then a rival of Newport); they showed what American go-getters with sand in their gizzards could do.

It was Jim O'Neill's son Eugene who was the parlor radical and railed against the injustice of capitalism. Still, he was not averse to going to Princeton and would have liked still better to go to Yale—institutions not known in his time as champions of social justice. Moreover, when he proclaimed his fraternity with sailors, roustabouts, and the boozy, homeless losers of the world, he was careful to forget (and wished later for his biographers to forget) that he first shipped out not as a sailor before the mast but as a passenger—doting Pa had paid a considerable sum to see to it that his boy had a cozy cabin to himself. Young Gene studied the rough comradeship of the fo'c'sle from a fastidious distance, soiling his hands only with ink. Even as a drunken down-and-outer, he was a self-conscious imitator of the real thing; whenever he and his ne'er-do-well cronies ran out of funds for liquor, Pa could be reached backstage for a quick touch. James O'Neill was by no means the compulsive miser that he is depicted as being under the name of James Tyrone in *A Long Day's Journey into Night*. An indulgent, much put-upon man, he was a hundred times more generous as a parent than his son as a parent would eventually prove to be.

Resenting the WASP elect, O'Neill pretended to embrace its opposite. The pretense was unconvincing in the actuality of his daily life but it led to valuable consequences in his work. One never doubts the sincerity of O'Neill's sympathy for the penniless failures who people his plays. As for the rich in his plays, they are merely caricatures. One guesses that he may have lifted their lineaments and their utterance—especially their utterance—out of cheap novels (he was an addict of trashy detective stories and murder mysteries); he certainly never troubled to study them at first hand, as, living among them, he might so easily have done. (The highly cultivated Edward Harkness turns up in *A Moon for the Misbegotten* as the ranting character named J. Stedman Harder.)

In this respect, the outsider O'Neill was wholly unlike the outsiders Barry, Fitzgerald, and O'Hara. Fitzgerald in particular sought out the rich and stared hard at them. They were a delectable puzzle to him, well worth the effort of solving. When, according to Hemingway, Fitzgerald once commented to him that "the rich are different from you and me," and Hemingway replied, "Yes, they have more money," the wisecrack would have struck Fitzgerald as simplemindedly missing the point. In fact, the anecdote is Hemingway's and is one of his usual light-fingered borrowings from a colleague; it lifts words that Fitzgerald had written in all seriousness on another occasion and trashes them. To Fitzgerald, money, and especially old money, alters the nature of the possessor of it; he is set apart from birth, precisely as the possessor of noble blood is set apart. Moreover, in wealth as in so many things, a difference of degree, if great enough, becomes a difference in kind. The very rich are far more different from the ordinary rich than the ordinary rich are from the rest of us; they are a mysterious species and therefore to be pursued, described, and accounted for. It was this truth about them that Fitzgerald would no doubt have conveyed to Hemingway if Hemingway had not been so eager to make a joke at his old friend's expense. No American writer of importance has yet made the super-rich the subject of a novel. Fitzgerald would have liked to try his hand at it, but he had so little knowledge of how wealth works that even the disposition of the financial resources of his friends the Gerald Murphys, who were merely well-to-do, appears to have baffled him.

Growing up on Summit Avenue in St. Paul, Fitzgerald began higher on the social ladder than O'Neill, Barry, or O'Hara. For a couple of generations, there had been a certain amount of money in the family, and there was even a distinguished, if only a collateral, ancestor: the Francis Scott Key after whom Fitzgerald was named was not so close a relative as Fitzgerald liked to pretend, but the relationship was an authentic one and could be trafficked in. Fitzgerald had a sufficient entrée to the right houses and country clubs and, coming home on vacation, he would be asked to the right winter dances and summer picnics. If he believed himself to be an outsider and drew much of the energy for his writing from this belief, it was less because he was Irish and Catholic than because, having gained acceptance inside the WASP pale, he wished to rise there. He reached out and he reached up, not always wisely. He was brave and reckless, and no doubt it was to increase his bravery that he fell back upon alcohol, though what it chiefly increased was his bad manners. (Janet Flanner, looking back in old age upon life in Paris in the twenties, observed: "Scott could be very tiresome when he drank.")

As Fitzgerald eventually came to see, it was his fate to be always overextended, emotionally as well as financially. He would have liked to possess the unassertive security of place and family manifested by Nick Carraway, the narrator of *The Great Gatsby*—Nick, who was able to repeat without irony his father's genteel aphorism, "Just remember that all the people in this world haven't had the advantages that you've had." The fact was that Fitzgerald more nearly resembled Gatsby, with his "extraordinary gift for hope" and his "romantic readiness," than he did Carraway. Gatsby was the quintessential outsider, who made the mistake of supposing that money would instantly win him his heart's desire; it is money plus a long period of time patiently endured that usually achieves this goal. Fitzgerald may have known this, even if he saw to it that Gatsby didn't, but there were other things that Fitzgerald himself didn't know. His ignorance was profound, and his curiosity, though keen, was short-lived. He was like Henry James in having a first-class mind and therefore first-class intuitions and in having at the same time very little practical information upon which to base them. James, for example, adored motoring and hadn't the slightest idea of what made an automobile run. Fitzgerald was fascinated by Hollywood as an industry, but he never did the donkeywork of discovering how the industry operated. For that matter, how did Gatsby operate? Fitzgerald didn't trouble to find out, simple as it would have been to do so, but oh, how ingeniously that huge hollow place at the heart of the novel is patted over and concealed!

Fitzgerald saw himself as an outsider in terms of geography as well as in terms of wealth and social position. St. Paul was middle-western, and Fitzgerald's idea of an earthly paradise was the East Coast: Princeton, New York City, the golden scimitar of Long Island. The Alleghenies were not only a mountain range, a thousand-mile-long continental divide—they were the grim heights that divided people as readily as they did earth and water and divided them, moreover, into categories not necessarily sympathetic to their desires. Fitzgerald would have liked to come from that ancestral Maryland which had been the birthplace of Francis Scott Key; he would have liked to boast a name—Hadley, Saltonstall, Baker—immediately recognizable in the remotest cranny of the Ivy League. He was confident of his intelligence, his talent, his good looks; still, there were barriers that appeared insuperable, and the older he grew (not that he was ever to grow truly old: he was dead at forty-four), the more bitterly he resented them. He worked so hard, against such high odds, to make a lot of money, and then the money trickled away—*rushed* away—leaving him penniless, with his energy diminished and his talent in jeopardy. He could even make heartbreaking jokes about his plight: "It grows harder to write, because there is much less weather than when I was a boy and practically no men and women at all." Though his income was at times torrential, he never acquired any capital—that prize which others possessed without effort by a gorgeous accident of birth. More and more he found it necessary to blame his vain attempt to escape financial pressure—for once, to manage his talent well instead of badly—upon the elegant enemy beyond the barriers. "That was always my experience," he wrote, in his last years. "A poor boy in a rich town; a poor boy in a rich boy's school; a poor boy in a rich man's club at Princeton . . . I have never been able to forgive the rich for being rich, and it has colored my entire life and works." A statement all the more touching because the rich in question wouldn't have been aware that they were in need of being forgiven for anything, by anyone—certainly not for the fact of being rich and certainly not by a drunken failed writer the most celebrated of whose peers—the cruel cock-of-the-walk Hemingway—had long since publicly dismissed him as "poor Scott."

John O'Hara, the last of my quartet of Irish-Catholic writer-outsiders, cultivated the rich throughout a much longer lifetime than Fitzgerald's—O'Hara died in 1970, at the age of sixty-five—making them the objects of an intense, ice-cold scrutiny. Unlike Fitzgerald, he had a curiosity that never flagged and was never satisfied. He took care to know where everybody's money came from and where it went. He prided himself on measuring with precision every infinitesimal gradation of wealth and social status that he came in contact with, from Pottsville in childhood to Princeton in maturity. (Being an outsider, of course he ended up living in Princeton, as, for much briefer periods, O'Neill and Fitzgerald had done. Princeton in the twentieth century has been the nirvana of the fortunate arriviste.) The range of O'Hara's knowledge of how Americans live was incomparably greater than that of any other fiction writer of his time—a statement that O'Hara himself often made in life and that he repeated even in death, in words that he ordered cut on his tombstone. One would have to go back to Norris,

Crane, or Dreiser to find a hunger for knowledge on the scale that O'Hara hungered for it, and with his degree of particularity.

The world both high and low fascinated O'Hara and revolted him; no doubt correctly, he assumed that there had never been a time when it wouldn't have fascinated and revolted him. He was a Jansenist in spite of himself, loathing his body for committing sins that he no longer believed in but that yet succeeded in costing him remorse. (Like many people who loathe their bodies, in age he let himself grow coarse with fat; his face came to resemble an uncooked side of beef.) Though not a practicing Catholic, he continued to believe, straight out of the penny catechism, that man was a fallen creature, subject to the most fearsome carnal temptations. To resist these temptations was to love the God that had invented them; not to resist them was somehow to hurt God's feelings and delight the Devil.

Few of O'Hara's female characters are able to remain chaste for long; indeed, he wrote about women and their unbridled sexual feelings so often and with such relish that many reviewers accused him of seeing all women as nymphomaniacs. (Reviewers used to be as quick to assert the prevalence of nymphomania in our society as O'Hara was to provide them with suitable opportunities for making the assertion. It appears that as the number of priggish reviewers has declined, so has the number of supposed nymphomaniacs.) The truth was that O'Hara's dark view of women's chastity was but the manifestation of a profound and typically Irish-Catholic disappointment. Almost without exception in O'Hara's day, the puritan Irish, brought up by nuns and priests, wished that every woman, even every mother, could remain a virgin, as the blessed mother of God had managed to do. The fact that women made love, or had once made love, was intolerable. (That we had to be born, in St. Augustine's words, *"inter faeces et urinas"*—that is, "between shit and piss"—was surely unpleasant enough; couldn't nature, so extravagant in other respects, have spared us the humiliation of that extreme economy of means?) O'Hara's male characters are less to blame for their sins than his female ones, for the reason that man in his simplicity is never a match for woman and her wiles. It is Adam and Eve all over again; the bitch is a betrayer, who cannot leave well enough alone. How much better if she had remained a rib!

O'Hara trusted his eye and ear only to the extent that he could keep them free of admiration and pity. In this he was like O'Neill and radically unlike Fitzgerald and Barry, who found much to admire and pity in their fellows. Barry in particular was pained by the evident malignity of the world and sought with increasing despair to find some reasonable explanation for it. The more troubled he became, the less he was able to write and the less confidence he had in what he wrote. To his friend O'Hara, no explanation of the malignity of the world was necessary; mankind was vile by nature and without surprises. His grim view, far from paralyzing him, seemed to give him extra energy. Following an operation for a bleeding ulcer and a warning from his physicians that if he didn't give up alcohol he would die, he stopped drinking and turned himself into a machine for writing. He was obsessed with composing what he believed to be an accurate record of the social structure of his time—hard news, not soft, in a prose pared of every superfluous adjective and adverb. He faced the ugliness of this record with equanimity, in story after story, novel after novel. The items in the indictment of mankind that he was prepared to draw up were many, and he was confident that they would last him as long as he lived, and they did.

As for the rich, in O'Hara's view they were no better and no worse than the poor—he would never have been so sentimental as to speak, as Fitzgerald did, of not being able to forgive them. For O'Hara, the question of forgiveness didn't arise; there they were, such as they were, and he would tell us honestly everything he had found out about them. He would be honest, too, in admitting that he wanted to be one of them. By the time of his death, he had long been a millionaire. It pleased him that by a tireless, forty-year-long flogging of his remarkable talent he had become one of the richest writers who ever lived. Still, he would have preferred to have been born rich, and he was given to pretending that his father, a physician in Pottsville, had been far richer than he actually was. It was true that Dr. O'Hara had lived well and, if he had not died comparatively young, might have achieved moderate wealth, as Barry's father had been on the way to doing when *he* died; but neither the senior O'Hara nor the senior Barry would ever have become rich in their sons' ambitious interpretation of that word. To the sons, the really rich were the Whitneys, the Morgans, the Goelets, and the Johnny-come-lately Mellons and Rockefellers.

Much has been made of O'Hara's yearning to attend Yale. He blamed his failure to do so on his father's death and the family's subsequent impoverishment, and it may be so, but there is evidence that O'Hara, an indifferent student, might not have succeeded in entering the university even under the best of circumstances. All his life, he was so boyishly eager to fulfill that early fantasy that his close friend Wolcott Gibbs spoke of raising a purse to send him off to New Haven. Other friends pleaded seriously with the university to bestow an honorary degree on O'Hara, always in vain. As a former friend of O'Hara (he had come to perceive me as his enemy, as a consequence of events the details of which I related some years ago, in my book about *The New Yorker*), I was among those who sought to gain this distinction for him. In my undergraduate days at Yale, I had been able to help gain an honorary degree for Sinclair Lewis, but O'Hara's case was more difficult, in part because Lewis was a Yale alumnus and O'Hara wasn't. The main difficulty was that the stuffed-shirt members of the faculty who had it in their power to recommend candidates for honorary degrees to the Yale Corporation thought of O'Hara as a dirty writer, preoccupied with sex; they felt far safer in recommending that honorary degrees be awarded to E. B. White and Walt Disney, since neither *Stuart Little* nor *Snow White and the Seven Dwarfs* was likely to bring a blush to the cheek of even the primmest member of the Yale academic establishment.

O'Hara was haunted by the mystery of Skull and Bones, the oldest and most distinguished of the secret societies at Yale. He accepted it as an indisputable fact of life that the fifteen men elected every year to Bones became a part of the tiny, never openly acknowledged power structure that ran the country. He believed, too, that being a Bones man guaranteed you certain privileges throughout your life—for example, that you would never be allowed to experience total financial failure. According to legend, the Russell Trust Association, the legal entity controlling the Bones endowment and real-estate properties (including an island in the St. Lawrence River, to which devout Bones men make annual retreats), would always arrange to set you up in some reassuring fashion. There was plenty of evidence to disprove this hypothesis—at least one famous Bones man, in the course of his descent to Skid Row, had been obliged to pawn his Tiffany-manufactured gold Skull and Bones pin—but O'Hara, in most such matters so scrupulous a reporter, in the matter of Skull and Bones chose romantic make-believe over reality.

Statistically, it was the case that there were only a few hundred

Bones men alive at any given moment; nevertheless, O'Hara saw them as forming an intricate network of elite operators throughout both hemispheres. How many Bones men were openly exercising power in Washington, New York, and throughout the country! (In his view, it was only to be expected that a Bones man, Prescott Bush, was for many years a senator from Connecticut; if he had lived into the 1980s, O'Hara would not have been surprised when Senator Bush's son George, also a Bones man, was elected president of the United States.) O'Hara would recite with reverence the names of the great men who had been tapped for Bones—the innumerable Tafts, Bundys, Stimsons, and Binghams—and he would take pride in mentioning the names of several personal friends of his in Bones—Bob Lovett, Gerald Murphy, Archie MacLeish, and the rest. They were names that resounded on Wall Street and in Locust Valley and on Fishers Island and at Kennebunkport: bell-like names, which gave off a formidable hum for a long time after they were dropped.

Throughout its long history, Skull and Bones has kept what it considers to be the barbarian world from acquiring any substantial knowledge of the rituals practiced inside its immense, windowless, brownstone tomb on High Street, in the heart of New Haven. (The tomb itself, vaguely Egyptian in style, is held to be so sacred that, according to undergraduate lore, a plumber or electrician entering it in order to make some necessary repairs must first become a member of the society.) Over the years, O'Hara contrived to accumulate a startling amount of Bones information, which he would reveal only to Bones men; sharing with them his little scraps and samples of their secrets made him, in a way and for the time being, one of them. It was the most cherished of all O'Hara's daydreams that if he had gone to Yale he would have been tapped for Bones. The touching truth of the matter is otherwise. Of the four Irish-Catholic outsider-writers I have been glancing at—Barry, O'Neill, Fitzgerald, and O'Hara—O'Hara was the crudest and most contentious. He lacked the good manners and cheery flights of fancy of Fitzgerald and Barry; he was less amiable and therefore less "nice" than even the mordant O'Neill. He was a grudge-bearer—a master of the fancied slight, as Harold Ross, the founder and first editor of *The New Yorker*, was later to say of him. Acrimoniously at odds with the world, though the world could not be sure why, he was the last person likely to be tapped for Bones. He would have stood waiting in vain on Tap Day, and afterward he would have found reason to believe that unknown enemies had ruthlessly conspired to deprive him of the honor he so richly deserved. But there would have been no enemy, no conspiracy; there would only have been his truculent chip-on-the-shoulder self.

Barry shared O'Hara's preoccupation with Yale and, although the family had begun to suffer financial reverses, he could afford to go there. Never was a young man from the provinces more eager to enter the great world and be transformed by it, and the Yale of that day was an ideal place in which to effect the transformation. Barry studied diligently and earned high enough grades to permit him to engage in the extracurricular activities that would make him, he hoped, a big man on campus. He wrote for the Yale *Daily News* and for the Yale *Lit*, and a trifle tardily—shyness? outsiderness?—was elected to the Elizabethan Club, which came as close as any single institution to being the intellectual center of Yale. The club occupied (as it does today) a pleasant old white clapboard house on College Street, and in the late afternoons book-loving undergraduates and members of the faculty would gather there for tea and cakes and conversation. As its name implied, the "Lizzie" contained an extraordinary collection of ancient volumes; one sniffed Marlowe and Shakespeare in the very air and was perhaps able to be infected by them. The infection was strengthened when living writers—in Barry's day, John Masefield, Vachel Lindsay, Rabindranath Tagore—stopped by for a quiet chat. The literary life was bathed in a romantic glow, to which Barry responded; the outsider in him was quick to note how attractively it paved the way into the heart of the Yale establishment.

The supreme sign of one's having made good at Yale was, of course, how one fared on Tap Day. There were several secret societies, and one could hope that if one weren't to be among the fifteen men tapped for Bones, one might be tapped for Scroll and Key, Wolf's Head, Elihu, or Book and Snake. To Barry's profound disappointment, he failed to be tapped for any of them. His disappointment was all the keener because some of the men he admired then and continued to admire throughout his life—Donald Ogden Stewart, Archibald MacLeish, John Farrar, Robert Lovett, Gerald Murphy, Artemus L. Gates, and F. Trubee Davison—were Bones men. Long after college, he remained aware that they had something in common with one another that they were never to have in common with him. (During the period when O'Hara and I were friends, he was constantly dropping asides to let me know that he was aware of my membership in Bones; it was beneath Barry's dignity—his prized sense of his own high worth—to do so.)

Barry's failure on Tap Day was especially galling to him because it was so public; it was also, in his eyes, mysterious. Unlike O'Hara, Barry was not paranoid and could draw no comfort from a hypothetical conspiracy. He was a practical idealist, who had worked his way up to the top of the class, or close to the top, and he had been flagrantly passed over. The injustice of his fate puzzled him. An apprehension of having been unfairly dealt with by life was to afflict him often in later years, when those of his plays that he most believed in would prove, on opening night, to be the ones that the critics least respected. A classmate of Barry's, S. Wilmarth Lewis, later to become a celebrated Walpole scholar, once said of Barry that he wasn't "terrifically one of the boys" and that "nobody would have been surprised if he had been tapped, but then nobody was surprised that he hadn't been." Lewis' testimony contains a minor mystery of its own. An elegantly turned-out, handsome young undergraduate, Lewis himself was very far indeed from being "terrifically one of the boys"; nevertheless, he was tapped for Scroll and Key. Plainly there was more to Tap Day than met the eye. Lewis was a well-connected WASP, who had come East to Yale from the fashionable Thacher School in California, and Barry was an unknown Irish Catholic from a public high school in upstate New York. No wonder that Barry came to be partial to palaces and to the lucky people who lived in them! Even more clearly than in Rochester, he saw how much harder than for rich aristocrats it was necessary for ordinary folk to run, simply to catch up with them. Passing them was out of the question.

Having graduated from Yale and enrolled in the famous forcing-house for dramatists presided over by Professor Alfred Pierce Baker at Harvard, Barry was hard at work on his first professionally produced play when he met and fell in love with a girl named Ellen Semple—the most fortunate event in Barry's exceptionally fortunate life. It is rare to be able to speak with confidence of the place a man's marriage occupies in the scheme of his life; still more rarely can one speak with confidence of the degree to which a marriage is fortunate, but in Barry's case the evidence is overwhelming: he married the woman best suited to him in every way.

Ellen Semple was tall and slender, brown-eyed and brown-haired, with a delightful smile. Her voice was low and thrilling, with an unusually warm timbre. How different she was from him, in how many enviable ways! Her nature was joyous and unguarded; she was at ease with strangers and it seemed to cost her no effort to give back more to the world than she took from it. Parties were meat and drink to her. (Over sixty years later, vigorous in her early nineties, Ellen Barry still takes delight in giving and attending parties.) She was a natural athlete, who swam and rode and played excellent golf and tennis. She was gently born and carefully reared, and she was also—and startlingly—a Catholic. Whether the young Barry would have married a non-Catholic we have no way of knowing; Ellen rendered the question academic. We do know of Barry's astonishment and pleasure at encountering a fellow Catholic in the very heart of the WASP establishment. He was a lucky man, and Ellen's background, like Ellen's affectionate nature, was a part of his luck.

Ellen and Philip were married in 1922. Her father, Lorenzo Semple, was a partner in the celebrated international firm of Coudert Brothers. Among the wedding presents from her parents was a pretty cottage on her parents' country estate in Mount Kisco, New York, and a wedding trip abroad. Within a few months of their return, Philip had his first play, called *You and I*, on Broadway. The reviews were uniformly favorable and the play became a hit. Money rolled in upon the young playwright, who proved then and thereafter to be an adept businessman. So began a career that was to last for almost thirty years. By the conventional standards of wealth and fame, over that long period Barry became one of the most successful playwrights in America. He was proud to find himself achieving a permanent place in the history of our theatre and he was grateful for the monetary awards that that place assured him. It was important to him to feel on a comfortable financial footing with those worldly and well-read insiders—the elect of the elect, like Jock Whitney and Bob Lovett—who enjoyed the company of playwrights, novelists, and poets. One had to have money enough to share the give-and-take of pleasant social occasions without strain—something the Scott Fitzgeralds were doomed never to achieve. The

Barrys and their close friends the Gerald Murphys learned to use their money wisely; the outward grace with which they lived was the sign of an inner grace that they never stopped seeking to possess in greater abundance.

Among other early, characteristically generous benefactions of Ellen's father was a villa at Cannes, which the Barrys gratefully named the Villa Lorenzo in his honor and which they kept until Philip's death. The Barrys at the Villa Lorenzo in Cannes, and the Murphys at the Villa America, a few miles along the coast at Cap d'Antibes, were known for their exquisite manners and exquisite taste; important as these attributes were, they concealed as much as they made plain. The paradox faced by Murphy the painter and Barry the writer was that good fortune already bestowed could yet require to be earned, and not once but many times. The means of earning it was the fulfillment of their talent in daily hard work. Murphy mysteriously broke off painting at what amounted to the beginning of his career; Barry never stopped writing, though with every passing year the task grew more difficult, the self-doubt more grave.

And with reason, for an oddity was invisibly present inside his success, and the oddity was failure. Of the twenty-one plays that Barry had on Broadway, the majority enjoyed short, unprofitable runs. His fame and his wealth came from the drawing-room comedy hits, like *Paris Bound, Holiday, The Animal Kingdom*, and, above all, *The Philadelphia Story*, but no less important to Barry, and often more interesting to his admirers, were the plays in which doggedly, year after year, working outside the conventional drawing-room setting, he struggled to express his ever-darkening view of life. What these plays sought to state was often hard, if not impossible, to dramatize; moreover, they were the very plays in which Barry was at his most experimental. The new forms that he essayed were often as intractable as the ideas they were intended to embody. Barry found himself committed to a contest that he was both too brave to withdraw from and too weak to win. To the degree that he chose to go on experimenting, one might say that, whether consciously or no, he was choosing to fail. The defeats he suffered were galling to him and yet he never gave up.

Given the ease and agreeableness of Barry's life in the late 1920s, it is at least superficially ironic that he spent the last summer of that decade in Cannes writing the sombre *Hotel Universe*. It is a play beautiful as well as sombre; many students of Barry consider it his best work. The setting, borrowed from the Murphys' Villa America, is a terrace overlooking the Mediterranean. On the terrace are gathered half a dozen attractive men and women of varied backgrounds; at first glance, they would seem to be among the most fortunate people alive, but one soon perceives that something dreadful has happened: a malignancy no more palpable than air has put them in jeopardy. Death hovers all around them, not so much a threat as a temptation. Only recently, death seduced a delightful young acquaintance of theirs, who smilingly dove into the sea and committed suicide.

Barry has given the play the appearance of a drawing-room comedy, and it is no such thing. On the contrary, it is a fantasy, whose theme is existential despair and whose subject matter concerns the grim fact that people's lives often come to an end before they die. All those nice people on the terrace in *Hotel Universe*—like all those nice people on the Murphys' terrace at Cap d'Antibes? the Scott Fitzgeralds, the Robert Benchleys, the Ring Lardners, Dorothy Parker?—are engaged in a desperate struggle to find themselves by finding meaning in their lives, or, failing that, by finding meaning in the universe. This was a struggle that Barry remained a party to until his death. Despite the skepticism that he felt in regard to the church and its conduct in the world, he was never not a Catholic; he was bound to the church by emotional ties that no reasoning could loose. Once, when long after Barry's death I was talking about him with his old friend Katharine Hepburn, she told me of an occasion on which he had confessed to her that he would find it impossible to get up out of the chair in which he was then sitting if he weren't able to believe in some sort of God—some divine principle, however little aware of man—at work somewhere beyond us. *Hotel Universe* was one of the several attempts he made to give philosophical speculations a dramatic form; that he was able to provide the play with a happy ending is a tribute not only to his ingenuity as a playwright but to his courage: he would live with his doubts as other men live with an incurable malady.

Hotel Universe was treated respectfully by the reviewers, though many claimed to find it baffling. It failed to catch on with the public and closed after eighty-one performances. Within a year, Barry was back on Broadway with another serious play, *Tomorrow and Tomorrow*, which did well and was followed by *The Animal Kingdom*, which was the last success that Barry was to enjoy until *The Philadelphia Story* seven years later. It starred Katharine Hepburn, for whom Barry had written it. The play ran for over four hundred performances and grossed the then staggering sum of two million dollars. Hepburn had taken the precaution to purchase the movie rights to the play before it opened and was able to sell them to Metro-Goldwyn-Mayer for $150,000—she was always as good at business as Barry was. "Phil and I were both box-office poison at the time," she told me once. "Moreover, our producer, the Theatre Guild, was on the verge of bankruptcy. It was very pleasant indeed for the three of us to make our comebacks together."

Barry was to experience nothing as gratifying as the triumph of *The Philadelphia Story* throughout the rest of his career. During the forties he had a couple of extreme failures and a couple of mild successes, one of which, *Without Love,* starred Hepburn and the other of which, *Foolish Notion,* starred Tallulah Bankhead. Both shows did well on the road, and it was unquestionably their stars that carried them. This was satisfactory to Barry in the case of Hepburn and unsatisfactory to him in the case of Bankhead; in or out of the theatre, it would be hard to imagine two people with less in common than the mannerly, soft-spoken Barry and the joyfully foulmouthed Bankhead.

Barry worked intermittently for many years on the play that was to become *Second Threshold.* From his notebooks, it appears that at some point it was to have been about his friend Benchley, who died in 1945 (it was a matter of astonishment to the fastidious Barry that Benchley had numbered among his many mistresses the unruly Bankhead; indeed, Benchley had broken off the affair only because, as a married man, he couldn't endure Bankhead's indiscreet public praise of his sexual prowess.) Little by little, the play altered and darkened in tone as Barry grew older. By 1949, its central character was a wealthy man in middle age who, after a distinguished career in government, finds so little of interest left to him in life that he contemplates doing away with himself in the guise of a hunting accident. Barry's friend and neighbor at Hobe Sound, James V. Forrestal, committed suicide that spring, and Barry feared that his play might be thought to be based on that event. More revisions would be needed, to keep real life from blundering in its usual clumsy fashion into the precincts of art. After Barry's death, *Second Threshold* was completed from his notes and revisions by his friend and colleague Robert E. Sherwood. It opened in New York in January 1951, in the very theatre in which, thirty years earlier, Barry's first play had been performed. It was directed by Barry's old friend Alfred de Liagre, Jr., and had a handsome setting by still another old friend, Donald Oenslager. The play received the now all but obligatory mixed reviews, in which Barry was praised for his witty dialogue and damned for his bleak thoughts. Seemingly, it was the case that even posthumously, Barry was expected to embrace the sunny views of the young man who had written *You and I* and *Paris Bound*. Grace of the body, grace of the spirit—they had been goals far harder to achieve than that eager and diligent young man had supposed. With luck, over the long years of one's life the cost of achieving them would be only just bearable, and no man could bear the cost of them alone. That was the theme of *Second Threshold*—a fitting one for a playwright in his middle years to dramatize. And the title of the play was charged with promise. Barry had weighed both words with care.

Barry died of a massive heart attack on Saturday, December 3, 1949, in the family apartment on Park Avenue. A requiem Mass was celebrated next day in the Church of Saint Vincent Ferrer. Among the honorary pallbearers were Robert Lovett, Artemus L. Gates, John O'Hara, and Charles Addams. Barry was buried in the Catholic cemetery in East Hampton. Later, Ellen Barry arranged to have placed above his grave a small white marble monument in the shape of an open book. On the left-hand leaf are carved his name and the dates of his birth and death. On the right-hand leaf, in a flowing script, are two lines from *Hotel Universe:* "All things are turned to a roundness. Wherever there is an end, from it the beginning springs."

Ellen Stewart

IN THE ALMOST thirty years that Ellen Stewart has been presiding over the Café La MaMa, down on East Fourth Street in New York, some fifteen hundred plays, musicals, and theatre pieces of no conventionally identifiable sort have been put on there. The first Café La MaMa was a basement space containing fifteen seats; today it consists of two big buildings furnished with four stages and a total seating capacity of several hundred. A handsome black woman in her late sixties, Ellen was enjoying a career as a dress designer when she undertook to finance the first Café La MaMa out of her own pocket; she did so in order to help her brother, an aspiring playwright, get his early works staged. That was in 1961. Now, as always, Ellen sees her role as a producer in terms that Broadway producers would doubtless turn up their noses at: her purpose is not to pass judgment on the aesthetic quality of a particular work but to offer an opportunity for voices to be heard that might otherwise be forced to remain silent. She is, in short, just the kind of fostering mother that her chosen nickname, "La MaMa," implies: a source of unquestioning affectionate support and encouragement.

A fierce champion of anyone under her roof, Ellen is impatient with adjectives like "provocative" and "experimental," which theatre reviewers tend to fall back upon to conceal their professional unease in the presence of the new and which, whether interpreted as being favorable or unfavorable, define and therefore set limits on the nature of Ellen's intentions. Ellen will have no truck with limits. Moreover, while a large number of first-rate works have emerged from her seemingly helter-skelter approach to theatre (one thinks of playwrights that, in alphabetical order, range from Sam Beckett to Sam Shepherd, among literally a thousand others), Ellen hesitates to boast of them, lest she be thought to share the entrepreneurial world's high regard for success and low regard for failure.

In my theatre-reviewing days for *The New Yorker*, I was often in and out of Café La MaMa, though it was my colleague Edith Oliver who, being assigned to cover Off Broadway and Off-Off Broadway (as I was assigned to cover Broadway), had far closer ties to Ellen and her projects than I did. Edith never employed the shorthand of weaseling adjectives that I mentioned above; she was every bit as forthright as Ellen and they got on splendidly by dint of a shared truth-telling. At that time, I attended productions at La MaMa as a busman on holiday; having given up writing about theatre in *The New Yorker* in order to write about architecture in its pages, today I am able to attend performances at La MaMa as an ordinary member of the audience. And yet not quite an ordinary member, for whenever Ellen in her usual fashion introduces a performance by getting up in front of the audience and ringing an old-fashioned brass schoolbell to secure its attention and then happens to catch sight of me out front, a big smile crosses her face and I smile back. What we are both likely to be recollecting with pleasure at that moment is that once upon a time in Salzburg, at my urging, she brought off something that we thought would be only a trifling theatrical prank but that turned out instead to be a moving and much-admired work of art. And it was Ellen, carrying out the task of director as well as producer, who accomplished this memorable feat.

First, as to why Ellen and I happened to be in Salzburg. From the shore of a small lake some twenty minutes' walk from the center of the city rises Schloss Leopoldskron, a romantic baroque castle built in 1736 by Leopold Firmian, the archbishop of Salzburg, for a favorite mistress. (The story goes that his heart lies buried under the marble floor of the chapel of the castle.) In the 1920s, Leopoldskron was purchased and lavishly restored by the Austrian theatrical impresario Max Reinhardt. The Reinhardts being Jewish, the Nazis were quick to take it away from them at the beginning of the Second World War; after the war,

Leopoldskron became the setting for a gathering that assumed the impromptu name of the Salzburg Seminar: it consisted of a group of scholars brought together by a young Harvard instructor and a couple of Harvard undergraduates with the idea of helping to reweave some of the cultural ties between the Old World and the New that had been severed by the war.

So successful was the first session of the seminar, held in 1947, that it was decided to set up a permanent body under that name—what is today officially described as "a private, independent, nonprofit educational organization, committed to the study . . . of contemporary issues of worldwide scope and of significant aspects of American society. . . . Eminent thinkers and practitioners meet with midcareer professionals for a period of from one to three weeks to address a subject chosen from the realms of politics, international relations, education, economics, business, the environment, or the arts and humanities." Over the years, some thirteen thousand men and women have attended sessions of the seminar. I have served for many years on the board of directors of the Salzburg Seminar and on two occasions have been invited to conduct seminars dealing with the state of contemporary theatre.

It was at the second of these seminars, in 1981, that Ellen served as one of my "faculty," along with the Irish dramatist Hugh Leonard, the Turkish director Oya Bazak, and the American actor and director Austin Pendleton. I have been told that Austrian nomenclature with respect to academic rank is so highfalutin that, as the nominal dean of this little faculty, I was entitled to be addressed as "Your Magnificence." Had I attempted to exact this salutation from my students—an exceptionally merry and energetic group of Fellows, recruited from all over Europe and mostly in their thirties and forties—they might well have booted me out of the schloss and into the lake. Ellen became an immediate favorite, and not least because to an assortment of Europeans drawn from a dozen or so cultures she was the ideal of an American black woman—noble in demeanor, queenly in bearing, earthy in speech. They admired her gray hair set in cornrows, her gypsy costumes, and her unflagging determination to get the best out of them, either by cajolery ("Hey, honey, let's try it this way") or by a drill sergeant's bullying ("I don't give a damn if we stay here all night, we gonna get it right, y'hear?").

Boldly, Ellen had decided to put on a workshop production of Romeo and Juliet. She had seven days in which to stage it, and to her the obvious inadequacy of the time span was one of the most exhilarating aspects of the project. Certain traditions long practiced at La MaMa would be embodied in the workshop: for example, use would be made of whatever talents happened to be available and of whatever props lay to hand. The chief props turned out to be the castle itself and the extensive garden surrounding it, once Max Reinhardt's particular pride but abandoned for so long that it had become a nearly impenetrable jungle. As the roles in the play were being assigned, it became apparent that English, at best the second or third language of most of the actors, would be too hard for the cast to memorize and give dramatic utterance to—Shakespeare's golden words would have to yield to approximations in a variety of tongues. To the general astonishment, the total number of languages employed in Ellen's Romeo and Juliet came to seventeen. Juliet spoke Hebrew, Romeo spoke Maltese, Capulet spoke German, and Montague spoke French. In the crowd scenes, one heard minglings of Gaelic, Turkish, Polish, Russian, Hungarian, and Norwegian—indeed, the only language one didn't hear was Shakespeare's own.

Because the play is so familiar, on the evening of its single performance the audience had no difficulty in following the twists and turns of the plot; more difficult to follow were the twists and turns of the settings, for Ellen staged the play both in- and out-of-doors, with the audience trooping after the actors as, scene by scene, they moved from the majestic dining hall of the schloss to the stone-paved lakeside terrace and then along paths newly hewn out of the underbrush of the garden. Flaring kerosene torches held by members of the company illuminated the settings, always with the great moony-white ghost of Leopoldskron leaping skyward above us. The music that Ellen had devised to accompany the scenes was produced by an orchestra of pots, pans, and jelly jars from the castle kitchen, and by sheets of tin hung from the branches of trees in the garden; on being struck with rakes and brooms, the sheets yielded sounds eerie enough to make one's hair stand on end.

I have said that the production was intended as a prank, perhaps to be moderately instructive of La MaMa's methods but not to bear much weight of emotion. Nevertheless, the triple enchantment of Ellen, the play, and the place where the play was being enacted gave it an unlooked-for power. As its last lines were being spoken, many in the audience—many in the cast as well—were weeping. In the dark garden, in the flickering yellowy light of the torches, Ellen had caused us to confront not only the outrageous sequence of events that led to the deaths of Romeo and Juliet but the sequence of events (perhaps no less outrageous) that in our own lives we consent daily to be shaped by and that, though we take care to keep them secret, put us from one moment to the next in jeopardy.

Jerome Zerbe

JEROME ZERBE, who died in the summer of 1988, would have been delighted by his obituary in the *New York Times*. When one is old and has been long retired, the odds against being publicly remembered in print become high, but Zerbe achieved the accolade of several substantial paragraphs in the *Times*. Moreover, by chance he enjoyed the good fortune of having his obituary bracketed top and bottom by those of people every bit as worthy of notice as he was, though light-years away from him in their natures and careers—the designer Ray Eames, dead at seventy-two, and James Hubbell, former headmaster of the Buckley School, dead, like Zerbe, at eighty-five.

The *Times* obit read, in part:

> He was one of those who in the 1930s pioneered the type of photography adopted decades later by the paparazzi: candid shots of socialites and entertainers out-on-the-town and eager to be seen. His pictures appeared in many national magazines and books. [He] helped turn El Morocco into one of the world's best-known night-clubs. His photography became one of the elements on which cafe society thrived.

In 1973, Zerbe and I published a book together called *Happy Times*, and the title was an unusually apt one. Even the portion of the book dealing with the Second World War managed to reflect some of the sunnier aspects of that tragic event; as a nephew of Lieutenant General Robert Eichelberger, Zerbe, officially a chief photographer's mate, was in a position to mingle with and photograph the great ones of the earth—Churchill, General MacArthur, Admiral Nimitz. And if it happened that such old friends of his as Moss Hart and Gertrude Lawrence happened to journey to the South Pacific to entertain the troops, Zerbe was on hand to photograph them swimming in remarkably elegant-looking lagoons and pretending to climb unclimbable palm trees.

In war or peace, Zerbe was a dedicated hedonist, with convictions as strong as any follower of Calvin. To him it was evident that to be joyous, even selfishly joyous, enriches life, while to be despairing, even unselfishly despairing, cheapens it. As Sarah Bernhardt had her gallant *"Quand même!"* and Tallulah Bankhead her "Press on!" so Zerbe had his smiling, invariable "Why not?"—a response so characteristic of him that his friend Mrs. William Waldorf Astor embroidered it on a pillow, which one would catch sight of at once upon entering the drawing room of his apartment on Sutton Place. In Yeats' words, "Hearts are not had as a gift but hearts are earned," and Zerbe held that a likely place to start earning them is in the merrymaking thick of things, among the dancers and singers and talkers and topers and players of games. It is they, the seemingly profane ones, who turn life into a sacrament by consuming it. They eat, drink, and seize the day, knowing how soon it will end.

For Zerbe, the merrymaking lasted longer than for most of his companions. He came of exceptionally hardy stock—his father lived to be eighty-eight, his mother eighty-seven, and his sister, Margot Larsen, is at the moment of writing a spry ninety-two. The punishment to which Zerbe subjected his body might well have dispatched any ordinary mortal in his middle fifties. He drank far too much and exercised far too little, and as an amateur chef he was not above providing himself and his guests with such hazardous delicacies as butter-pecan ice cream with cold mincemeat sauce. Born and raised in Cleveland, he was shipped East to prep school in Connecticut. At Yale he was voted the second-greatest social celebrity in the class of '28 (in first place was Charles Tiffany Bingham, son of the then governor of Connecticut, Hiram

Bingham), as well as the fifth most gentlemanly member of the class, to say nothing of the sixth most original and eighth most entertaining.

By his senior year at Yale, Zerbe was maintaining a distinguished salon on the so-called Gold Coast in Harkness Quadrangle. He had a living room with a wood-burning fireplace, two bedrooms, and a bath, and his furniture, books, linen, and silver were much admired. On his walls hung drawings by De Wint, Kneller, and other artists of conse-quence. (One of his professors having told him that the Kneller was far too valuable a work of art for any mere undergraduate to possess, Zerbe obediently presented it to the Elizabethan Club, of which he was not a member.) Football players were prominent frequenters of his salon, in part because they liked him and in part because, themselves hard-driving puritans headed for Wall Street, marriage, and all their atten-dant responsibilities, they were puzzled by his carefree pagan attitude toward life. They also enjoyed the liquor that, despite Prohibition, Zerbe was able to keep flowing in abundance. "New Haven was a very active port in those days," Zerbe once told me. "I had a lover, a Greek sailor, who was a member of the crew of a rum-running boat, and whenever it docked in New Haven he would walk through the streets of New Haven to my rooms at Harkness with a case of gin on his shoulder. Such a darling boy!"

In his prime, Zerbe was often described in the local press as the second-handsomest man in New York. (The handsomest was said to be one Larry Doyle, a broker and playboy.) The number and variety of his sexual conquests was for years the admiration of the homosexual world. He was a reckless, inexhaustible flirt, and in his heyday at El Morocco he set a standard of achievement that even the hard-boiled heterosexual world felt obliged to pay sullen tribute to. In the New York *Mirror*, the vituperative macho gossip columnist Walter Winchell called attention to an affair that Zerbe was having with Lucius Beebe, a columnist on the *Herald Tribune*, by commenting that Beebe's column, filled as it was with constant references to Zerbe, should be headed not "This New York" but rather "Jerome Never Looked Lovelier." The affair was perhaps less satisfactory than Winchell supposed—Beebe was more aggressive physically than the gentle Zerbe wished him to be.

In Hollywood, Zerbe and Cary Grant were so often to be seen in each other's company that Grant's studio felt compelled to cook up a synthetic newspaper romance between him and Betty Furness. Among Zerbe's lovers in Hollywood were Randolph Scott and Errol Flynn; of the latter, Zerbe used to say that Flynn would sleep with anything that moved and with one or two things that wouldn't or couldn't move. When I asked Zerbe once what women had meant to him, he said, "Friendship." And when I asked him what men had meant to him, he replied, "Excitement." Like many homosexuals, he chose as close friends women of his mother's generation—Hedda Hopper, Elsie De Wolfe, and the like—and so as time passed he was confronted with the loss of a number of his most trusted companions.

Zerbe in age remained flirtatious, but it had become a role that he played out of habit, requiring little energy. I remember that once, when Zerbe was in his seventies, we were having lunch at a bar-and-grill on East Fifty-seventh Street. A handsome, white-haired priest, perhaps in his fifties, was seated directly across the room from us. After a few minutes, I noticed that Zerbe was striking a pose—he had straightened his shoulders and cocked his head at an odd, roosterish angle. In a low voice, he said, "The holy father is making eyes at me. Another conquest! Oh, dear, at my age I can't help feeling flattered."

Zerbe spoke with candor of the loneliness that he would face as what he mockingly called himself—"an old queen." He said to me, "I think I can stand the loneliness. I *hope* I can stand the loneliness. In any event, I don't intend to be the very last to leave the party. Mrs. Harvey Cushing remarked to me when she was dying that dying was a very boring business, and I would hate to be one of those who linger over it."

And yet it happened that Zerbe was indeed among the last to leave the party. Moreover, as the end approached he contrived to make an unlooked-for mess of the disposition of his estate—a mess that his Larsen nieces and nephews, presumably his heirs, make an effort to treat lightly by calling it "Jerry's last prank." He had written a will, naming his nephew Jonathan as his executor, but the day before he died he chose to write a new will, naming as his executor the male nurse who had been attending him. At the present moment, two sets of lawyers are seeking to work out a compromise satisfactory both to the nurse and to the Larsen family.

If it was sad that Zerbe lived far longer than he wished to, he would have no patience with our dwelling upon that accident of his indefatigable genes; the Jerry he would have us remember and salute is the zestful, blue-eyed, loving, and generous Jerry, the sound of whose voice asking "Why not?" made everyone who heard it happy.

Our *Happy Times* book came about as a consequence of a chance remark by Zerbe, to the effect that among the photographers at work in New York City in his time he was scorned as a mere amateur, in part because he had never troubled to learn even so much about the technical side of photography as to be able to develop a roll of film. I asked him how many pictures he estimated that he had taken in the course of his career. When he replied that he had about fifty thousand negatives on file, I assured him that I would have no difficulty in selecting from this large number at least five hundred publishable pictures—more than enough to make a book and enough to secure for him the professional standing that he longed for and deserved.

My confidence in Zerbe's pictures was based upon my knowing that from early manhood he had chosen to frequent and record with one or another of a succession of cameras a world not familiar to most of us—the world of the young and the rich and the beautiful. Zerbe himself had been born into that world: his father was a prominent Cleveland businessman, in possession of an ample amount of old money, and his mother was a vigorous and amusing grande dame, who kept in touch with an army of similarly vigorous and amusing grandes dames from coast to coast. Almost from the cradle, Jerry had been aware that he and his lucky companions had reason to wish full records kept of their pleasures and revels, even of their follies. How else were they to outwit the enemy they had in common: implacable time? Documents in the form of words and pictures, but especially pictures, would be their means of stating, each in his own way, "Mark me. Envy me. I was this person in this time and place. And I was happy."

Memories of good days fail, or are altered by needs unknown in youth, but what the camera registers and preserves unchanged becomes an earnest of immortality. For it is a fact that the camera's eye is able, among many other remarkable things, to stop time; long after the young and the rich and the beautiful are dust and up to the far-off moment when the last printed image of them is also dust, photographs will bestow upon them a posthumous existence, shining with promise. Not the past but the fixed present blazes all round them in its early-morning freshness, thanks to the handiwork of someone who, in the course of taking their likenesses, can be said in a sense by no means ironic to have saved their lives. That was precisely the sort of lifesaver that I knew Jerry Zerbe to be. I had only to cull from his files the evidence—young "Babe" Paley in tennis shorts on her wedding morning, truculent young Marlon Brando after the Broadway opening of *Streetcar*—that would assure him a just place in the history of his time.

Zerbe spent upwards of half a century depicting attractive people on delightful occasions—christenings, birthday parties, debuts, weddings, hunt breakfasts, costume balls, cocktail parties, dinner parties, supper parties, yacht races, picnics, clambakes, croquet and tennis matches, theatre openings, and excursions to fashionable resorts and watering places. Christenings and weddings aside, these occasions might strike the historian's eye as trivial; Zerbe—and I—would argue it was not so, or not necessarily. For the sharers of such occasions are to be seen under their most favorable aspect, and this is a fact well worth calling attention to; in practice, we rarely attain the high standard of deportment that we tend to think of as our habitual one.

Days of feasting are days of forgiving. Our moments of celebration are almost always kindly as well as courteous. The sorry truth that much of history is an account of mankind at its worst is reason enough to offer as footnotes at the bottom of the page a few glimpses of mankind at its best, or at any rate at its merriest. And there are other reasons, not least among them that even this late in the twilight of the twentieth century, most of us are brought up with a nineteenth-century puritan distrust of good times, and particularly of other people's good times. Some of us consider party-giving and party-going the ideal means of eradicating this dour and miserly emotion. Eagerly we make our way out onto the polished ballroom floor, under all those winking prisms and pink balloons. We say with Jane Austen, "Everything happens at parties!" For something *is* always just about to happen on such occasions—an adventure that has the disadvantage for the more cautious among us that we must be willing to assent to it before we have learned its nature. Best to be brave and say "Why not?" then quickly hold out our hands to hands waiting to be taken and drawn close.

Zerbe became the country's first society photographer by chance, and it may be that, by the same chance, he will be seen to have been its last. The reason for his singularity is not that what we think of as "society" is dying, though its death is announced in newspapers and magazines with tiresome assurance from year to year. (The fact is that in numbers and in amount of wealth, society is continuously on the increase. So-called old members of society can be heard fretting over the unfitness of new members within a few years' time of their having become themselves new members; it is they who encourage the rumors that society is nearly extinct.) What made Zerbe singular was his combination of exceptional energy and exceptional entrée. Despite the *Times'* obituary, Zerbe was no frantic precursor of the paparazzi hovering outside the gates. His invitation with its gilt coat of arms tucked in his dinner-jacket pocket, he would ride through the gates and up the long drive to the brightly lighted portico in somebody's ink black and almost certainly not rented limousine. His camera was always at the ready, but no more significance attached to it than to the flower in his buttonhole. Dear Jerry clicking away was first and last dear Jerry.

It was the case, moreover, that Zerbe had never been known to publish an unfavorable picture; the unlovely negative of a haggard eye, a wrinkled neck, a hand like a claw was at once destroyed. A professional disguised as a kindly amateur, for decades he crisscrossed the United States and Europe, moving from great house to great house, from party to party, inexhaustibly. With every evidence that he was enjoying himself to the fullest, he was forever turning up as a valued guest at Palm Beach, Madrid, Northeast Harbor, Kansas City, Key West, Nassau, New Orleans, Florence, Nantucket, Chicago, Cuernavaca, Glouces-ter, Deauville, East Hampton, San Francisco, Paris, Oslo, Macon, Akron, St. Tropez, London, Dublin, Versailles, and a hundred towns too small to find their way into atlases but not too small to possess, for Zerbe's pleasure as a connoisseur of architecture, a well-staffed Palla-dian villa, a honey-colored château, a pillared plantation house behind its stout levee.

Some fifteen years before his death, Zerbe officially retired as a photographer; soon thereafter, he claimed to have unofficially retired as a celebrity as well. Back in the thirties and forties, a party that Zerbe had failed to attend and take pictures of could scarcely pretend to have been a party at all; without Zerbe, the participants were but miserable nonen-tities, glumly living it up in limbo. Toward the end of his life, Zerbe affected to believe that he was totally forgotten in New York. If this passing of his fame caused him any measure of regret, it was mitigated by the fact that, looking back, he saw everything in his life as having happened for the best. Scattered about him in his dangerously overfurnished apartment ("I have far too many things: mind you don't trip") lay the fruits of a long and happy career—in something over a hundred stout scrapbooks of photographs, an accumulation of thousands of intimate, unpremeditated moments. Taken as a whole, these moments become a social history unlike any other in the world—a pictorial *roman-fleuve* in which scores of characters are introduced and carried from youth to age, with who they were and what they have become stamped unmistakably upon their faces and bodies.

Some of the characters are unknown except to their families and close friends; we watch them grow up and grow old in the comparative privacy of houses, country clubs, hotels, and nightclubs. The names of pretty girls change once, then again, and often for a third or fourth time. Strangers become friends, become lovers, become husbands and wives, become ex-husbands and ex-wives, become strangers. The men dancing with these elegant women, or lying beside them on the deck of some sloop in the Caribbean—who is to say whether they have been found to be better companions than their predecessors? Practice does not always make perfect, especially in marriage; so Zerbe, having escaped marriage, insouciantly believed.

Others in the large cast of characters in Zerbe's scrapbooks are plainly used to being thought of as members of a cast. They are the innumerable actors and actresses that Zerbe knew and photographed in unrehearsed encounters over the years: the Lunts, Noël Coward, Ina Claire, Gloria Swanson, Tyrone Power, Mary Pickford, Errol Flynn, Ethel Barrymore, Charlie Chaplin, Carole Lombard, John Garfield, Paulette Goddard, W. C. Fields, Katharine Hepburn, Greta Garbo, Clark Gable (who in his youth in Ohio worked in one of the coal mines owned by Zerbe's father). In the scrapbooks, which Zerbe bequeathed in his will to the New York Public Library, we see Shirley Temple grow from a tiny child to a woman in early middle age; Gary Cooper passes from being a fantastically handsome young man at a cocktail party in Hollywood to being a fantastically handsome older man in a sunlit garden in France. The fate we all have in common deals with us in different ways; some of us manage to hold age at bay indefinitely, while others alter so quickly that it is hard to recall what they were like in youth. Cary Grant becomes with every birthday better looking and more confident, while Judy Garland plunges headlong into woeful, puffy-faced decay.

The Hollywood that Zerbe photographed in the thirties and forties was also the Hollywood of Nathanael West, of Scott Fitzgerald and Aldous Huxley and Evelyn Waugh. These writers saw rightly that movies were a new and incalculable force in our culture; their mockery of Hollywood was not without awe, and Fitzgerald in particular studied the leading members of the movie colony as closely and warily as Stendhal had studied his careerist Parisians. Nothing in Hollywood existed on an ordinary scale or in an ordinary hue. The great stars of the day might have been so many gods and goddesses. They accepted their worshipers with equanimity, for it was simply the case that they were far above ordinary mortals in the perfection of their hair and teeth and skin and features. Their supple bodies deserved to be adored, as the nearest mirror could not fail to tell them and as Zerbe's informal snapshots of them revealed more accurately than any stilted, airbrushed studio photograph could be counted on to do.

These stars led lives of conspicuous splendor, which they shared with millions of people drudging in circumstances irredeemably commonplace. The means of sharing were in large part gossip columns and articles in newspapers and movie-fan magazines, and it was a becoming irony that many stars reached Hollywood as a result of reading gushy fictions about their predecessors in the very magazines that were later to publish gushy fictions about them. Hollywood was indeed a dream factory, and the workers were tempted to believe that the dreams they manufactured were the real thing. A few of the stars that Zerbe knew were wise managers of their small talents; still fewer—among them his friend Garbo—were wise managers of great talents. Zerbe used to say that in the golden age of the Hollywood that he had known, it was hard for anyone to keep his head, especially if that head was silly as well as pretty. In Hollywood as in New York, one was obliged to live not according to principles but according to a single rough-and-ready rule of thumb: good luck gave one fame and bad luck took it away. It was only to be expected that most stars rose and blazed and then burned out, but there were other stars who rose and blazed and, though dimmed, remained in the firmament.

If Zerbe's scrapbooks are a novel written by a camera, that is because behind the camera was a man with a novelist's eye and sensibility. Not so much a novelist, however, as to seek to impose upon his enormous work a formal ending; he was satisfied to let it follow life and peter out untidily, wherever it willed. "No doubt I am growing untidy myself," he said to me once, on the eve of an unwelcome birthday. "Not that it upsets me. I read somewhere that the dying brain is calm, and why should it not be? What has it got left to be excited about?" He beamed and lifted a glass. His blue eyes were merry and his voice was strong. The wind off the East River, freshening, rattled the sashes of the drawing-room windows. The sky was filled with scudding clouds. "To give my doctor some satisfaction, I take care to drink as little as possible until dark," Zerbe said. "One of the nice things about winter in New York is how early it gets dark."

Maxwell Anderson

TODAY THE PLAYWRIGHT Maxwell Anderson is all but forgotten. A few decades ago, he was a highly esteemed figure on Broadway, taken seriously by critics and audiences alike. Not that the critics themselves, especially those who wrote for the daily New York City newspapers, deserved to be taken with any great degree of seriousness; many of them reflected the tradition of a somewhat earlier day, in which hard-drinking reporters who failed even at the lowly task of covering the police beat were assigned to reviewing plays and movies. In Prohibition days, the much-admired critic of the *Herald Tribune*, Percy Hammond, used to write his reviews with a coffee can full of gin beside his typewriter; by the time the review was finished, the gin was finished.

The drama critics employed by weekly magazines tended to display a lighthearted—equated with a gentlemanly—irresponsibility with respect to their duties. Most of my predecessors in the "Theatre" department of *The New Yorker* were alcoholics; among them was the universally beloved Robert Benchley, who, having enjoyed a few martinis before an opening-night curtain time, would often take advantage of the opportunity to slump down in his seat and enjoy a much-needed nap. On one occasion, the sound of a telephone ringing on stage startled him into wakefulness, and to the dismay of the cast he called out, in a loud voice, "I'll get it!"

As for the high esteem in which Anderson's audiences held him, I remember thinking in those days, no doubt with the uncharitable arrogance of youth, that the source of the popularity of his plays lay in their being so accessible; the plots nearly always concerned historic personages familiar from one's schooldays—Joan of Arc, Queen Elizabeth I, and the like. Moreover, the texts were often composed in blank verse, which the public was overly impressed by, imagining it to be a difficult literary feat. In truth, as most writers discover early in their careers, it is far easier to write blank verse than good prose; the iambic pentameter beat takes over like some sort of automatic pilot and mere rhythmic logorrheic gush emerges in an all but unstoppable flow. As a child, I wrote a bombastic melodrama about the long-drawn-out struggle that took place in Florence in the late Middle Ages between the Guelfs and Ghibellines. Today I recollect very little about that struggle and I suspect that I had very little knowledge of it at the time that I chose it as a subject, but oh, how the iambs flew! If not a word of my text made sense, every line of it scanned, and now and then, as an extra flourish of virtuosity, I would cause the verse to rhyme, in order to indicate to my imaginary groundlings, as Shakespeare did to his real ones, that a scene was coming to an end.

Maxwell Anderson—always Max for short—was a genial, modest man, and I am glad to think that, at the very least, some measure of fame will always accrue to him as the author of the lyrics of "The September Song." That romantic ballad was part of the score of the highly successful musical comedy *Knickerbocker Holiday*, which Anderson wrote with the composer Kurt Weill. It was Walter Huston (father of John, grandfather of Anjelica) who played the role of Peter Stuyvesant in the original production and sang "September Song" in a reedy, old man's voice, to touching effect: "The days dwindle down to a precious few . . . September, November . . . and these few precious days I'd spend with you."

Anderson and I were brought together in the 1950s by the coincidence of our sharing literary agents—Brandt and Brandt, the most prominent firm of agents operating in New York City in those comparatively innocent days, when writers hoped to be well paid but didn't expect to become millionaires. (We saw nothing strange about our agents becoming millionaires; after all, they were in business to make money and we were not.) Deals with magazines were handled by Carl Brandt, deals with book publishers by Bernice Baumgarten—wife of the novelist James Gould Cozzens—and deals with theatre and movie people by Harold Freedman, who was celebrated not only for his astuteness but also for the fact that when he got angry, he lowered his voice. The angrier he grew, the more inaudible he became; when he whispered in your presence, you knew that you were in serious trouble.

I had published a novel, *The Day the Money Stopped*, which received exceptionally favorable reviews. In *The New Yorker*, the playwright S. N. Behrman topped off his praise with the suggestion that the novel could be turned into a hit on Broadway with scarcely a word changed. As a result of the reviews, several Hollywood studios sought to purchase the novel for (by my standards) very large sums. Richard Morrow, the hero of the novel, is quoted in its epigraph as saying, "I've always been so ready to be rich," and this was a cry from the author's own heart; now for the first time in my writing career I saw myself standing tiptoe on the threshold of considerable wealth. Impatiently I waited for Freedman to bring off a big deal, but unbeknownst to me, and remaining unbeknownst to me for some time thereafter, he had prepared an agenda in which I was to serve as the means to an end and not be an end in myself.

First of all, Freedman said, it would be wiser—which is to say more profitable—if the novel were to be turned into a successful play before selling it to Hollywood. I said that that would be fine with me; I'd be glad to try my hand at its dramatization. No, no, Freedman went on, he was very much opposed to writers turning their novels into plays; it was a different line of work altogether. I should let an already well-seasoned playwright adapt my novel. Moreover, he might just possibly be able to persuade one of the most famous of his clients, Maxwell Anderson, to undertake the task. Maxwell Anderson! How lucky I was! Of course I consented to hand the novel over to Anderson and the rest of the all-star team that Freedman assembled: Stanley Gilkey as producer (soon to be joined by Robert Whitehead, as coproducer); the eminent Jo Mielziner as the designer of the set and lighting; the no-less-eminent Harold Clurman as director; and a cast consisting of Richard Basehart, Kevin McCarthy, Mildred Natwick, and Collin Wilcox. Even the press agent for the play, Richard Maney, deserved to be called eminent; at the time, he was the leading figure in the peculiar calling of press agentry, eventually being granted the honor of a Profile in *The New Yorker*, written by Wolcott Gibbs.

Historically, it is the case that novelists tend to protest any changes that may have to be made in the course of transforming their handiwork into an actable play or movie; for that reason, which I respect, I was not encouraged to observe at first hand the preparation of the stage version of *The Day the Money Stopped*. It wasn't until after the play had opened out of town, in Wilmington, Delaware, to unfavorable reviews, that I was invited—begged—to come down and take a look at it. I was shocked by what I saw. First of all, Jo Mielziner, an old friend of mine, had provided what was surely the ugliest and most boring stage set of his entire career. It was supposed to represent the office of a senior partner in a long-established law firm in some such proud old New England town as Hartford or Worcester; it consisted of little more than a desk, a couple of chairs, and a secretary-bookcase that contained a few leather- and buckram-bound law books, lending a sketchy verisimilitude to the whole. On the top shelf of the bookcase was a gilded plaster bust, which at the cost of a few dollars Mielziner had picked up many years earlier in a junk shop; he had made use of it in several earlier productions, including *The Barretts of Wimpole Steet*, one of Katharine Cornell's greatest successes. The bust had become a sort of good-luck charm to Mielziner, and no doubt he felt greatly in need of it on the occasion of designing *The Day the Money Stopped*.

The play itself was no better than the set. Anderson's adaptation of the novel had failed to sustain—indeed, had managed to obliterate—the tone of self-mocking, self-destructive gallantry with which I had attempted to endow its protagonist. And Richard Basehart, a conscientious actor, lacked the charm and debonair physical presence that would have made Richard Morrow's self-mockery appealing; what the role required was an actor like Cary Grant, which poor Basehart was far from being. Moreover, it was obvious from the very first performance I sat through that Harold Clurman was as ideally unsuitable as the director of this supposed comedy as Anderson was as its author and Basehart as its star. A leftist intellectual (and in any event always a better critic than he was a director), Clurman must have been contemptuous of the content of the play, which superficially was concerned with the financial bickerings of a wealthy WASP family; it may have been chiefly his close friendship with Robert Whitehead that kept Clurman from throwing up his hands and departing. As it was, he kept throwing up his hands and not departing. Clurman was a master of the sudden, explosive temper tantrum, which left his victims cowering and him radiant, instantly ready to forgive and forget.

I was invited to join the hapless little company and, with Anderson's permission, do what I could to improve the play. After our stay in Wilmington, we were scheduled to put in a week in Philadelphia and a week in Boston before our opening night in New York City. It became obvious to me that Anderson was a man far older than his years (he was then in his late sixties) and in consequence had suffered a severe loss of energy. It also became obvious that Freedman had offered him my novel as a means of keeping him active in the theatre when he was no longer independently capable of it—a kindly service to Anderson, though not to me. Anderson was too proud to admit it, but he had given up on the play; if it was to be rescued at all, Whitehead and I would have to accomplish the task.

First in Wilmington and then in Philadelphia, Robert and I set about feverishly rewriting the play. The cast accepted our rewrites with heroic good humor, memorizing the new lines day after day even as they were speaking the old ones. Robert and I spent much of every night bent over my portable typewriter, and the new material would be professionally typed and copied the following morning. Robert has recalled that just before curtain time at one matinee, as he and I were hurrying down the aisle of the Walnut Street Theatre to deliver to the actors waiting backstage a freshly copied new version of the play, I turned to him and whispered, "This isn't likely to induce much confidence on the part of the audience." Nor did it induce much confidence in us: trying to improve matters in such circumstances nearly always leads to their disimprovement.

In his distress, Max Anderson hit upon another reason that the play wasn't all that it should have been. The room that he and his wife occupied at the Barclay Hotel, on Rittenhouse Square, happened to adjoin on one side the room occupied by Basehart and, on the other side, the room occupied by Collin Wilcox. Collin was a pretty young woman with a pleasingly pert bosom, and Max, lying sleepless in bed, became convinced that he could hear Basehart stealing along the hall to Collin's room late at night and then stealing back into his own room early next morning. "He's using up all his energy at night," Max would complain. "He's being drained. He has nothing left for the play."

Robert and I knew that the flaws lay within the play and not with the noctambulations, real or imaginary, of our star. For that reason, we were dismayed but only moderately astonished when, following the play's opening night in Philadelphia, a reviewer for one of the morning newspapers began his notice with the sentence, "The Walnut Street Theatre is the oldest legitimate theatre in America and never in its 128 years has a play as bad as *The Day the Money Stopped* appeared on its stage."

Before we left Philadelphia, Max called me aside. He was sipping a cup of cold coffee in the Barclay lobby. I had learned by then that he *liked* cold coffee and always waited for hot coffee to cool, saying that cold was how people who worked in the theatre must expect their coffee to be. (Because I liked Max, I came to like cold coffee as well. I drink coffee cold to this day.) Max had called me aside in order to tell me that, since I had labored so hard on the play, he wished me to share billing with him as its coauthor. It was a generous gesture and one that there was no way for me to brush aside, although it had already begun to look as if the farther the author of the novel kept from the play, the better it would be for his literary reputation. With a false show of gratitude, I accepted Max's offer, and we proceeded to our next station of the cross, which was Boston.

In Boston, we stayed at the Ritz, tinkered in vain with the play, and kept our courage up with walks on the Common and shopping for sale-priced clothes in Filene's Basement. If the reviews proved to be better than they had been in Philadelphia, that was because it was scarcely possible for them to have been worse. We opened in New York at the Belasco Theatre. It was snowing hard that evening and Robert and I, pacing up and down at the back of the theatre, heard the snowplows grinding along West Forty-fourth Street and got ready to blame the weather and the snowplows for whatever bad news the next day's papers would contain. A muted theatre party was held in the grand offices that Robert shared with his partner, Roger Stevens, and some time after midnight one of Dick Maney's assistants began to telephone the papers and call out to us dejected party-goers snippets of the reviews. Negative, negative, negative, though Brooks Atkinson in the *Times* did his best to distribute a few alms of praise. Three days later, the play closed. A small army of children—classmates of one or another of half a dozen Gill children attending school in Bronxville—were invited to the last performance. One little girl sought, with some effort, to pay me an appropriate compliment. She said, "Oh, Mr. Gill, I think it's a fine play"—to which I was about to assent and say "Thank you," when she added, "for children."

Collin Wilcox was the only person to attain a measure of glory out of *The Day the Money Stopped*—she won the Clarence Derwent Award as the most promising new actress of the year. Nevertheless, it is a mercy of the world of the theatre that one is thought to have gained a permanent foothold there simply by having entered it. Given that failure is far more common in the theatre than success, a cynic might scoff at the nature of the foothold as being born of necessity rather than kindness. Be that as it may, I have enjoyed the sense of participating in theatrical matters not only as the Broadway theatre critic of *The New Yorker* for some eighteen or twenty years but also, on at least three occasions, as a writer for the theatre and therefore a member of a much-extended and nearly always affectionate family.

All three of the occasions I have in mind were failures, painful enough at the time; no matter, for the long-range consequences proved in each case so agreeable. Writing books is a lonely, molelike occupation; lonely, too, may be the publication of what one has written—for reasons totally beyond one's control, a story or poem or novel may drop out of sight as swiftly and silently as a stone in snow. Writing for the theatre is a communal enterprise, and what one remembers afterward is not the earned misery of a project that has seemed to come to nothing, but the forging of bonds that in the course of time transform one's initial despair into a sort of rueful merriment.

I cherish as a symbol of such a transformation the gilded plaster bust that Jo Mielziner had employed in so many productions before finding a place for it on the top shelf of the secretary in *The Day the Money Stopped*. When the play closed and the set was being dismantled, Jo asked me if I would like the bust as a souvenir of the misadventure we had shared. I replied that I felt in need of a consolation prize and that the bust would serve that purpose admirably. Jo sent it over to me from the theatre and a bracket was built for it high on the wall of my office at *The New Yorker*. I had asked Jo if he had any idea whom the bust might be a likeness of; no, he had told me, as far as he was concerned its provenance began and ended with the junk shop.

Over the years, I would glance up from my desk and wonder idly about the identity of the handsome stranger who had become my ever-watchful, never-aging officemate. In 1975, I published a photograph of the bust in my book about *The New Yorker* and soon thereafter I was in receipt of a letter from a curator in the National Portrait Gallery in Washington, D.C., informing me that the bust was a likeness of the nineteenth-century American artist J. Alden Weir, executed by a sculptor friend of his. The gallery possessed a copy of the bust in bronze; scholars had been aware that the bust had first been modeled in plaster and had hoped that this plaster version would some day turn up. Moreover, if I were to make a pencil rubbing of the back of the bust at approximately the neckline, I would almost certainly find the sculptor's name incised there.

Down came the bust from the bracket and with equipment no more professional than a piece of Kleenex and a Venus pencil, I set to work. Sure enough, in the course of a vigorous rubbing the name Olin Levi Warner, hitherto illegible, came up in a ghostly fashion white on black out of the plaster and onto the sheet of Kleenex. Lightheaded with the excitement of discovery, I assured the staff of the National Portrait Gallery that some day before I died (though as close to that date as I could manage) I would see to it that the bust found a permanent home at the gallery; and so it will.

Offenbach and Ives

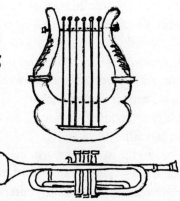

MY SECOND ADVENTURE in the theatre was prompted by a death. One summer in the late 1950s, in Cambridge, Massachusetts, the director Albert Marre, his wife, the actress Joan Diener, and the elderly Yiddish actor Menasha Skulnick put on a spoofed-up tent-theatre version of Offenbach's *La Belle Hélène*. Offenbach's comic opera is itself a spoof, melodiously toying with the plot of the *Iliad*—young Paris falls in love with the beauteous Helen, wife of Menelaus, the aging King of Sparta, and carries her off to Troy; Menelaus asks his brother Agamemnon, leader of the Greek kings, to join him in rescuing Helen, and so the bloody Trojan Wars begin. One might not have expected Offenbach's spoof to survive a secondary round of spoofing; nevertheless, the knockabout Cambridge version proved a success, with the usual optimistic, imprudent result: a producer was persuaded that it ought to be brought to Broadway.

The producer was a man named Gerard Oestreicher, of a well-known New York City real-estate family. Gerry was stagestruck and had recently enjoyed the rare good fortune of achieving a hit with his first Broadway show, a musical comedy called *Milk and Honey*. The show had starred Molly Picon and was in the genre vulgarly known as a "Hadassah musical," meaning that it attracted an audience of middle-aged, middle-class Jewish women. (*Fiddler on the Roof* was also a

Hadassah musical. When Hal Prince brought Anthony Quinn to Broadway in *Zorba*, some reviewers mocked the show as a Greek Hadassah musical, which indeed it was.) Oestreicher drew up a schedule that allowed him several months in which to secure the requisite number of backers, rent a satisfactory theatre (the Plymouth, on West Forty-fifth Street), select a set designer, a costume designer, and a lighting designer, and round out a cast that came to consist of Diener, Skulnick, George Segal, Howard da Silva, and a television horror-show actor known only as Zachary. The musical would rehearse in New York City, open out of town in Philadelphia, and have its Broadway premiere in the fall.

As the months passed, everything was falling nicely into place with *La Belle*—Hélène had been dropped from the title, perhaps for copyright reasons—when the young writer engaged in providing the book of the musical dropped dead of a heart attack. As the director of the show, Albert Marre was aware that to cancel or postpone the already contracted-for rentals of the theatres in New York and Philadelphia might put an end to the project. Plainly, a person was needed who was capable of writing at high speed; if he was able to accomplish the task with some wit or elegance as well, so much the better. Because I was known to write rapidly and to relish the pressure of deadlines, Oestreicher and Marre offered me the job.

I was flattered to be asked, even under such comparatively morbid circumstances and with the knowledge that velocity and not wit or elegance was considered my most valuable attribute. Moreover, having tasted defeat in the theatre with *The Day the Money Stopped*, I might hope to taste victory with *La Belle*. I was certain that *The New Yorker* would scarcely notice my taking on extra work—moonlighting was a way of life on the magazine for those of us who had long ago observed that the moon was coin-shaped and of golden hue. The one substantial reason for rejecting the opportunity was that the Gill family had been counting on a summer holiday abroad. A sister of mine who had recently died had left me a bequest of ten thousand dollars. With a tender sternness, she had stipulated in her will that I was to spend the entire amount on something that amused me and not on the usual drearily inescapable daily and weekly expenditures, like groceries and mortgage payments. (Plainly, my sister had taken to heart the degree to which *The Day the Money Stopped* was autobiographical.) Being eager to follow her instructions, I had rented from a friend a commodious villa in the south of France, in the flowering hills above Grasse; the villa would have plenty of room for the Gill family and for the usual number of summertime visitors.

If it was suspected that I was using *La Belle* as a means of avoiding several uninterrupted weeks in the bosom of the family, no formal protest ever reached my ears—on the contrary, I was simultaneously congratulated upon having been chosen for so interesting a task and commiserated with for the loss of a vacation that everyone generously pretended I had been long in need of. My admired father-in-law was pressed into service in my place. He had always loved France, it had been many years since he had been in a position to visit it, and he was delighted to be offered an opportunity to brush up on his French accent, which, though he appeared never to have noticed it, bore the unmistakable Down East Yankee stamp of his birthplace: Calais, Maine. (A town whose name—speaking of French accents—the natives have always pronounced to rhyme with malice.)

Rehearsals began on the bare stage of the Plymouth Theatre. Most of the new lyrics for the Offenbach melodies were in usable if not excellent order; I was to fashion a book that would provide a plausible reason for getting from one song number to the next, and to that end I was supplied with a desk, chair, and typewriter directly under the stage. So urgent was the process that day after day I would be typing out a new version of a scene in my cramped, airless quarters below-stage and handing it up, page by page, through an open trapdoor in the stage floor to the actors running through the scene a few feet above my head. If a certain line failed to please, the piece of paper on which it was typed would be crumpled into a ball and hurled down through the trapdoor to land at my feet: instant rejection followed by instant rewrite.

If the method of composition practiced by Robert Whitehead and me, laboring all night on the script of *The Day the Money Stopped*, had not been calculated to induce confidence on the part of an audience, how would my subterranean method of composition at the Plymouth have struck them? Luckily, only the cast, engaged in frantic bouts of memorization, was aware of the thin ice upon which they were skating, or perhaps (to put it more accurately) skidding, sliding, and falling. To our distress, Howard da Silva, a veteran of many stage disasters, never troubled to learn any of the lines, whether new or old, assigned to him in his role as a meddlesome high priest; mumbling a kind of gobbledegook of approximately the right duration, he left it to the other actors to pick up their cues as best they could. Their difficulty was heightened by the fact that da Silva spoke this gobbledegook from behind the shield of whatever newspaper happened at the moment to attract his attention.

Da Silva put on the airs of a star, though he had never been one. Menasha Skulnick had indeed been a star, in the Yiddish theatre if not on Broadway, and he was rightly irritated to find himself immersed in what struck him as a highly unprofessional state of chaos. To placate him, we left his role as Menelaus nearly intact, though with every change we introduced into the book poor Skulnick became more and more bizarrely isolated from Joan Diener as Helen and George Segal as Paris. Diener was a good-looking young woman, with blond hair, blue eyes, a voluptuous figure, and an admirable singing voice. Segal may have lacked the male equivalent of a voluptuous figure (the long hose he wore when in costume were padded to fatten up his skinny shanks), but his countenance was pleasing, and compared to the curious croaking sounds that Skulnick uttered when called upon to sing, Segal's croonings struck us as those of a veritable Caruso.

While the *La Belle* company was rehearsing at the Plymouth, my family set off by ship for France. On previous family trips abroad, we had always favored a small ship of the French Line called *Le Flandre*, which took eight days to make the voyage and gave one a sense of how vast the Atlantic is and how bold our ancestors had been to undertake the western crossing of it in earlier centuries in ships that took weeks and sometimes months to complete the voyage. Once more it was *Le Flandre* that the Gills had booked passage on, and after seeing them safely aboard (champagne and flowers in the cabins, an orchestra playing on the deck, the ship's foghorn gallantly tooting—all those merry accompaniments of setting sail that are now ancient history), I waved farewell from dockside as *Le Flandre* slipped slowly downstream into the Narrows.

After another week or so of labor on West Forty-fifth Street, the *La Belle* company moved en masse to Philadelphia. There for the first time we were able to rehearse inside the clever, mock-classic stage set that Ed Wittstein had designed; meanwhile, members of the cast began to familiarize themselves with their costumes, at once gorgeous and comical, and with singing not to the tinkle of a single upright piano backstage but to the sound of a full pit orchestra. We had fractured Offenbach's original and had put the pieces back together in a contemporary form that was at least moderately entertaining; it now appeared that the major difficulty confronting the production was the cast. As the director, Albie Marre struggled in vain to fashion an ensemble. Making matters worse than they would otherwise have been was the fact that he was married to Diener and understandably wished to emphasize her role and so bring her stardom on Broadway. Again and again she would blow up in the course of rehearsing a scene and as if in an unconscious response to this momentary failure she would begin frantically to peel off her clothes. The first few times that this happened, I was as delighted as if I had been one of those lascivious old Parisian rakehells whom Zola described in his novel *Nana*, their faces suffused with blood as the music-hall dancer who is the heroine of the novel raises her naked arms aloft. Soon enough, however, it became the case that whenever Diener gave the first hint of imminent disrobement my heart would sink instead of leaping. I saw that my efforts, and the efforts of all my colleagues, were at the mercy of Diener's failure to portray a convincing Helen of Troy. Beautiful as Diener was, alluring as she strove to be, she was never the queen who had launched a thousand ships and caused the topless towers of Ilium to burn, and her own occasional toplessness was an insufficient compensation for this failure.

After a couple of costly postponements (with Gerry Oestreicher, rich as he was, quite rightly wringing his hands), we opened to what are known as "mixed" reviews—a theatrical euphemism for "mostly bad." Given the cost of the production, what we needed and what we knew in our hearts we didn't deserve were rave reviews. Two or three days of heated discussion ensued, the topic being whether to kill the show outright in Philadelphia or to continue getting ready for the scheduled Broadway opening in September. A couple of well-known play-doctors were flown in from New York and Hollywood to pass judgment on the show as it stood and on the likelihood of its improvement. Marre and Diener were for pressing on; I was for giving up inconspicuously in Philadelphia in order not to risk the probability of a much greater financial loss than Gerry and the other backers had already suffered, coupled with the near certainty of a public humiliation. No doubt I was being selfish in respect to that second argument—I had had enough of theatrical humiliation with *The Day the Money Stopped*.

The play-doctors took a pessimistic view of our prospects, the backers were reluctant to advance more funds, and Gerry concluded that the show must be abandoned: along with money, so much time and talent and energy expended, leaving not a trace behind! Over a gloomy farewell round of drinks, we commiserated with one another. Had they been able to read the future, Marre and Diener would have been less gloomy than the rest of us, for their next production was the Broadway hit *The Man of La Mancha*, which Marre directed and in which Diener starred with Richard Kiley. I told Gerry that I had but a single consolation: at least I would be able to join my family in France just as their summer stay there was drawing to an end, and so demonstrate that I had not altogether forsaken them in the course of my failed pursuit of glory. With characteristic generosity, Gerry informed me that since he had a certain amount of credit with El Al, the Israeli airline, he would be happy to arrange for me to be put on a free-of-charge, first-class flight to Paris.

By long-distance telephone to the villa at Grasse, I learned that the Gill party would be setting out for Paris in a few days' time, in the Volkswagen microbus that they had rented for the summer. Consulting road maps, we decided that I might count upon meeting them at about noontime a week later, at the entrance to the château in Blois, a couple of hundred kilometers southwest of Paris. At the appointed hour, I was seated, a glass of vermouth in hand, on the terrace of a bistro close to the great, shouldering bulk of the château when round a distant bend and up the street came the little microbus, gaily bedecked with American flags. I raised my glass to the bus, which returned my salute with vehement horn-tootings, and so the family reunion was accomplished.

My third and—up to now—final misadventure in the theatre was indeed an ambitious project: the writing of a libretto for an opera the musical portion of which consisted of some seventeen songs by Charles Ives. The libretto was intended to tell the story of Ives' life from birth to death by means of a series of brief recitatives linking the songs, accompanied from time to time by appropriate folk and ballet dances. The well-known conductor Richard DuFallo had assembled the songs. The forging of the biographical links was to be my task, and for this purpose I introduced as the leading characters Charles Ives; his father, George (every bit as remarkable a composer as Charles himself);

Charles' wife, Harmony Twitchell; and a few supernumerary characters. The project was sponsored by the Lenox Art Center, under the guidance of the redoubtable Lyn Austin. The center then occupied a grand turn-of-the-century neo-Renaissance mansion in Lenox, Massachusetts, not far from the grounds of the Tanglewood Music Festival, and it was there, in the great hall of the mansion, that we rehearsed and gave our premiere performance of the opera, which we called *Meeting Mr. Ives*.

An odd and agreeable thing happened during the course of my writing the libretto. Charles Ives and my father had been members of the same class at Yale—the class of '96, remarkable for the variety of distinguished alumni that it produced (including George Case, a founding partner of the law firm of White and Case and, as an undergraduate, inventor of the squeeze play in baseball). Although I was fairly certain that Ives and my father had never met, the more I familiarized myself with Ives' life, the closer he came to resembling my father. The two had much in common. They were poor boys, born in small towns in rural Connecticut; they had to work their way through college; they were excellent athletes; they were emotionally inhibited (with this difference, that Ives had a violent temper and manifested it in repeated, howling tantrums, while my father took care never to lose his temper at all); and, finally, they became rich not because it was their primary goal to do so but because wealth was a natural by-product of an exceptional devotion to their chosen careers—my father as a physician and surgeon, Ives as the founder of a life-insurance agency.

My father had long been dead at the time I began work on the opera, and Charles Ives was newly dead. He had lived on East Seventy-fourth Street, in New York, and I could easily enough have met him through friends of his or relatives of his wife. (Harmony Ives—and what were the odds against a composer marrying a young woman named Harmony?—was the daughter of the Reverend Joseph Twitchell, who in the late nineteenth century had been pastor of a church in Hartford and Mark Twain's close friend during Twain's Hartford years.) I had heard many stories about Ives in age: for example, of his standing in the window of his brownstone, across the street from the Mannes School of Music, and, as students were making their way into the school, of his shaking his white-bearded old head and mouthing a silent, vehement "No! No! No!" For as a student at Yale he had despised his professor of music, the academically correct Horatio Parker, and he felt that beginning musicians and composers were hindered rather than helped by any formal musical instruction whatsoever.

At Yale, Ives had written some "rags" for undergraduate shows, which Professor Parker had forbidden him to play in class. Ives had a friend who played piano for some blackface comedians at Poli's Theatre, in New Haven. The friend liked reading the newspaper while he played an accompaniment to the comedians, so Ives wrote him some music for the right hand, leaving his left hand free to turn the pages of the newspaper. My father used to tell me about attending performances at Poli's, where the air was, so the saying went, "chained to the floor." Naturally, I wanted my father and Ives to have met on some convivial occasion. In writing the libretto and, with an author's customary temerity, putting thoughts into Ives' head and words in his mouth, I found his image beginning to blur with that of my cherished father. In my imagination, the two men became friends, became twins, became at last one man, whom I proceeded to believe in and dote upon. I see now—but was far from seeing then—that my fondness for the creature I had invented was detrimental to *Meeting Mr. Ives*, whose hero was expected, after all, to bear as close a resemblance as possible to the actual, historical Charles Ives.

The premiere, given in Lenox before an audience of friends, was considered a success—sufficiently a success, at any rate, to persuade the San Francisco Opera Company that it ought to be put on as one of its summer novelties. In the summer of 1976, the *Meeting Mr. Ives* company put in a few happy days in San Francisco, and enjoyed an after-opening party that Gordon and Ann Getty gave in their splendid big square house on Broadway, looking out over the bay and thence to the rim of the world. The opera was reviewed in the two morning papers; one review was favorable and the other unfavorable, and I had to admit to my colleagues that I found the unfavorable review more accurate than the favorable one. For the opera was really a sort of television documentary of Ives' life, carried out with a certain zest and charm but wholly dependent for any inner life that it might possess upon Ives' crotchety tunes and parodies of tunes.

Still, as with *The Day the Money Stopped* and *La Belle*, the degree to which I saw *Meeting Mr. Ives* as failing bore almost no relation to the amount of pleasure it gave me, both at the time and in memory.

Speaking with my old *New Yorker* friend William Maxwell about the difference between writing for publication in a magazine or book and writing for the stage, I contrasted the loneliness of the one with the incessant huggings and kissings and reiterated exchanges of praise ("Darling, you were *mar*-velous!") of the other. And Maxwell, smiling at my naïveté, said of the theatre as a whole, "Remember, dear Brendan, it is all marzipan." To which I could think of no reply except the truth. I said at once, urgently, "But I like marzipan!" And so I do.

Arnold Whitridge

ONE SUMMER EVENING in the 1980s, I was leaving a dinner party on Park Avenue. It was almost midnight—an awkward hour at which to hail a cab. As I reached the curb, I saw that someone with the same goal in mind had preceded me: running up the avenue in the light of a full moon was a tall, slender figure in black tie and white evening scarf—black and white against the black surface of the avenue, like a photograph all the more authentic for its lack of color. The figure was moving lightly and jauntily—rather as if, I remember thinking, he were a young tennis player rushing the net. A cab responded to the vigorous, repeated waving of his right arm and screeched to a stop. As the tall figure bent down to enter the cab, I caught a glimpse of his face; it was that of an old friend of mine, Arnold Whitridge. He was then perhaps ninety.

While I stood there, a thought came into my mind—one of those thoughts that we keep at a distance, to toy with but not subject to a rigorous scrutiny. And the thought was this, that I had reason to be grateful to Arnold for putting off the threatened imminence of *my* old age by dint of having so successfully put off his own. For if as my senior by twenty-odd years Arnold was still usefully, happily among us—was still, after all, hailing cabs at midnight on Park Avenue—then it was not altogether bizarre of me to feel that I might also have a good many years of usefulness and happiness before me.

Arnold Whitridge was named for his maternal grandfather, the English poet and essayist Matthew Arnold, who was born in 1822. It pleased me to think of Matthew Arnold's grandson strolling the streets of New York so late in the twentieth century. What would the doleful author of "Dover Beach" have made of the city in which his daughter had found a husband and of which his grandson had become so august an ornament? No doubt he would have been appalled by New York, as Arnold himself was often, and candidly, appalled. In cultural matters, to say nothing of matters of politics, Arnold chose the conservative side, which in our local affairs was rarely the popular side. And yet sometimes he surprised us. For example, he was a member of the Art Commission of New York City when a colossal bronze sculpture by Henry Moore was offered as a gift to Lincoln Center. The commission had to approve all such gifts, and Arnold was vocal in his dislike of the Moore; nevertheless, when it turned out that the vote in the commission was a tie between for and against, Arnold in sultry summer weather hastened in from the country, climbed the many flights of stairs to the attic of City Hall, where the commission sat, and cast the deciding vote in favor of the Moore. "In my opinion, it is not sculpture," he said, "but if the board of Lincoln Center thinks otherwise, I will not stand in its way." The sculpture now occupies a conspicuous place in the center of a reflecting pool between the Vivian Beaumont Theatre and Avery Fisher Hall, where (to take Arnold's side for a moment) it does in fact resemble nothing so much as a wad of decaying greenish dough.

Arnold and I met when I was an undergraduate at Yale. He was the Master of Calhoun College—one of the half-dozen colleges that the ardent Yale philanthropist Edward S. Harkness had arranged to have built (in a quaint Tudor Gothic style that was supposed to borrow the appearance and atmosphere of the various colleges at Oxford and Cambridge) in order to provide the unwieldy mass of Yale undergraduates with a sense of identity on a small scale inside the cumbersomely vast scale of the university as a whole. Calhoun College was located next to Berkeley College, of which I was a member, and was just across College Street from the white clapboard house that sheltered the Elizabethan Club, in whose rooms at teatime Arnold and I would often encounter each other. (Yale at the time was saturatedly British in tone: Shakespeare and Gilbert and Sullivan were held in about equally high repute; Tennyson and Browning were the poets that mattered.)

Arnold was a handsome man, with a big straight nose, prominent teeth, and close-cropped hair. He was an authority on French history, told stories well, had a rich, charming wife, Janetta, and dressed in English country-gentleman style, wearing, on occasion, tweed golf-knickers with thick woolen hose instead of the obligatory collegiate gray flannel trousers. His shoes had spongy, light-colored, crepe-rubber soles, upon which he visibly bounced as he walked. How I envied him those soles! It was a sorrow to me that they had gone out of fashion before I was able to take advantage of their incomparable elasticity. I had to content myself with red rubber soles affixed to brown-and-white saddle shoes identical in appearance to the shoes that every other undergraduate at Yale was then wearing. Sartorially, my only notable Anglicism was a tweed deerstalker cap, which made me resemble some ancient species of bird of prey and which I left behind in New Haven when, not a moment too soon, I left New Haven itself behind.

After Arnold's retirement from Yale, he and Janetta divided their time between an apartment in New York and a big old eighteenth-century farmhouse in Salisbury, Connecticut, overlooking lawns and gardens and the nearby Taconic mountain range. Some years ago, when I was working on a book about Cole Porter, I paid Arnold a visit that I warned him was to be of a professional nature. He and Porter had been members of the class of '13 at Yale, had been members of the same secret society (Scroll and Key), of the Glee Club, and of a small band of undergraduate humorists known as the Pundits. At what were then called "smokers," Arnold sang many of the first songs that Cole Porter ever wrote. Moreover, it was Porter who in Paris, toward the end of the First World War, had introduced Janetta and Arnold to each other. For the purposes of my book, I was eager to hear whatever Arnold might be able to tell me about those far-off days.

To my dismay, Arnold proved to be very much on his guard. It dawned on me after a while what the difficulty was. Arnold was what would have been called, in the slang of a few years ago, a "straight arrow" or perhaps even a "jock," and he was fearful of being thought to have been one of that group of homosexuals in which Porter, himself a homosexual, had been a conspicuous figure throughout his lifetime. Even as an undergraduate, Porter's close friends had included Leonard Hanna, Monty Woolley, T. Lawrason Riggs, and other homosexuals, and Arnold wished to make it clear to me, without letting down his guard sufficiently to utter the actual words, that he was not of their kind. The closest he came to making a definitive statement was to say, "The fact is, Brendan, I was never very close to Cole during the years when he was mixed up with that theatrical riffraff."

I pretended to take offense. "Theatrical riffraff!" I said. "But, Arnold, that's what *I've* been mixed up with for twenty years—writing plays and musicals, working as a movie and drama critic!"

Arnold remained the soul of equanimity: with no injury to good manners, he saw to it that what he wished to exclude from conversation did not exist. "My dear fellow," he said, "I'm not talking about people like you and me."

"But think of Cole's friends in the theatre—Noël Coward, Moss Hart, Clifton Webb! To call them riffraff!"

Coolly ignoring my protest, Arnold the perfect English country gentleman: "I may say that it was different toward the end, when Cole was old and sick and in constant pain. Janetta and I would have dinner with him at his apartment in the Waldorf Towers, and after dinner I'd sit by him and sing from memory, stanza after stanza, some song of his from an undergraduate smoker of forty years ago. And Cole would smile and say, in the saddest voice, 'Did I write that? Is that really mine?'"

Janetta Whitridge suffered a stroke in her early seventies, from which she made an excellent recovery. During the period of her illness, lying in bed in an upper room of the farmhouse in Salisbury, she was astonished to realize that, although she was unable to recall the name of her daughter when she came to pay a visit, she could remember with ease something that she had learned years ago in school, the Latin name for the maple tree outside her window. During her convalescence, she wrote a poem about this phenomenon and sent it on to me at *The New Yorker*. The poem was a long one—far longer than it needed to be. The portion of it that dealt with the daughter and the maple tree was charming; the rest of it, seeking to draw a moral, was both conventional and gratuitous. I told Janetta that if she were prepared to let the magazine reduce the poem to what it considered an appropriate length, we would be willing to publish it. Janetta was delighted with this news. The poem had reached the stage of galley-proofs before she telephoned me and, with some embarrassment, confessed that Arnold felt that she had spoiled the poem by permitting the magazine to edit it and that her permission to do so amounted to a betrayal of her gifts as a poet and should therefore be rescinded.

Mildly, I objected that no such betrayal was involved: many first-rate poets whom the magazine published were glad to receive editorial advice with respect to their handiwork. Janetta remained adamant; she said that Arnold had consulted with other writers, who had agreed that Janetta must not yield to the magazine's blandishments. And so the poem—such a touching and original poem!—was killed in galleys. Ever after, I suspected that Arnold's insistence upon Janetta's retrieving it from the magazine contained at least a measure of self-interest, not to say envy. For it was he who was the writer in the family, and it cannot have pleased him to perceive a rival so near at hand.

A year or so after this decorously conducted literary skirmish, I found myself in the not altogether comfortable position of asking Arnold a favor. I had inherited from an uncle a share of stock in the New York Society Library, which, founded in 1764, is the oldest private library in the city and a source of reading pleasure and scholarly assistance to thousands of subscribers. Only a few shares of the stock are outstanding; handed down in families from one generation to the next, they are rarely bought and sold. I was proud to have been given this connection with an institution that I admired and that satisfied my desire, as an amateur antiquary with no roots in New York City, to possess something of high sentimental (if not financial) value dating back to a time when New York was a British colony—the library's charter had been signed by George II.

When Arnold, as chairman of the board of trustees of the library, learned of the transfer of the share of stock from my uncle's estate to me, he congratulated me on my good fortune, and I replied (boldly, for me) that while I had long served on the boards of directors of a variety of not-for-profit institutions throughout the city, I had done so as a civic duty; the board of the library was the only board I could imagine serving on not as a duty but as a pleasure. Arnold received this broad hint silently and we changed the subject. About a year later, he caught up with me on the street. "My dear Brendan," he said. "I have just come from a meeting of the board of the library, and I am instructed to inform you that you have been elected a member of the board." Magisterially, he raised his hand to forestall any thanks that I might be preparing to offer. "I may as well tell you," he said, "that I have grave doubts as to the wisdom of the board in acting in this fashion. The fact is that you are a much older man than we like to recruit these days." At the time, I was in my early sixties; Arnold was eighty-seven.

Arnold continued to preside over the board of the library for several years after my election to it, and I observed with delight the covertly arbitrary fashion in which he conducted our meetings and brought them to a close at whatever juncture suited his convenience. At a certain moment, he would clear his throat and say, "Ladies and gentlemen! I would be happy to entertain a motion to adjourn, as there is somewhere else that I would much prefer to be." Instantly, the motion would be made and carried, and off Arnold would stride to his next engagement, perhaps at the house of a lady friend, somewhat younger than he, with whom he was reputed to be enjoying a romance.

Arnold died at ninety-seven, regretting as the end approached only that he had failed in his ambition to reach a hundred. My last glimpse of him was at ninety-five, on a day when he came to the Century Club for lunch. We greeted each other at the foot of the long flight of stairs leading up to the dining room. After the usual exchange of small talk and just as he was turning away, on an impulse I said, "Arnold, this may be an impertinent question, but I can't help wondering—at your age, do your legs ache when you climb stairs?" "Certainly not!" he replied. "*Nothing* aches yet, nor do I see any reason that it should." And with a wave of his hand, impatiently he started up the stairs.

Alec Waugh

ALEC WAUGH was a trim little man with nut-brown skin and the alert, bright-eyed look of a chipmunk. Everyone who knew him was quick to say how unlike his brother Evelyn he was, and this was intended to be perceived as a compliment, which indeed it was. For Alec was charming and kindly and without, as the British say, "side," while Evelyn was a viperish and pretentious snob. Alec was content to be an upper-middle-class Protestant; Evelyn would have liked to be a member of the ancient Catholic gentry. Lacking that (to him) enviable ancestry, he produced an imitation that deceived no one and that cost him much of his humanity.

Alec was the older brother and gained his first recognition as a prodigy—his first novel, *The Loom of Youth,* was published in 1917, when he was nineteen and serving in the British army in France. As was only to be expected, the novel was a thinly disguised autobiography; it enjoyed a considerable succès de scandale because it revealed more than was then thought permissible, much less in good taste, about the homosexual aspects of British public-school life. (To be just in looking back at the period, reticence in dealing with the subject of homosexuality wasn't merely a function of the hypocrisy of innumerable Mrs. Grundys; homosexual practices were deemed to be criminal in England as late as 1957.)

Alec wrote agreeable, conventional novels that earned him a living and a reputation as an entertainer. Evelyn having written *Decline and Fall* and *Vile Bodies*—two of the funniest novels in the English language—he was judged to have far surpassed his brother in talent. However galling to his ego Alec may have found this judgment, he behaved well about it, which is to say, among other things, that he didn't make the mistake of publicly challenging it. In the years that I knew him, I don't remember his ever saying a word in derogation of Evelyn as a writer, though from time to time he let his friends see that, if pressed, he could point out one or two things to object to in Evelyn as a man. For example, he mocked the devout Catholic that Evelyn had become, pointing out that he wasn't so devout as not to have perjured himself with regard to his first marriage in order to obtain the blessing of the Holy Mother Church upon his second. The church frowns upon a man's having two living spouses; because a divorce has no standing in the eyes of the church, a marriage must be annulled, and the usual grounds for securing an annulment are, or used to be in the Waughs' time, notably embarrassing—impotence, madness, malformation of the sexual organs, and so on. "At Evelyn's urging, I, too, p-p-perjured myself at the annulment hearings," Alec told me once. (Alec had an upper-class English stammer, which helped to focus his listeners' attention upon what he said. Consonants were hurdles that he cleared only after a few preliminary balks.) "Evelyn had me lay it on good and thick," Alec said. "A whopper or two to help my saintly brother cost my conscience nothing."

As far as one could tell, the bonds of marriage, to say nothing of the usual sexual proprieties, cost Alec's conscience little more than did his lying on behalf of Evelyn. All his life, he was mad about women; he married several times and had scores of mistresses over a period of fifty years. In his seventies, one of his novels, *Island in the Sun*, became a best-seller. At last and (given his age) in the nick of time, he had what he called "pots of money," and he squeezed every drop of pleasure out of his tardy fame and good fortune. Like W. Somerset Maugham, Graham Greene, and a host of other British writers (his brother included), he had spent much of his life traveling to exotic places throughout the world and writing well about them. Now he was able to settle down, dividing his time happily between Tangier and New York City. He had always liked coming to America as much as his brother Evelyn had disliked coming here—or claimed to dislike it, even when he was handsomely paid for doing so. (It is worth mentioning that Evelyn always took more than money away with him when he left: much of his little novel *The Loved One*, set in Hollywood, is brazenly lifted from Nathanael West's *Miss Lonelyhearts* and Aldous Huxley's *After Many a Summer Dies the Swan*.)

Alec maintained a fixed schedule in New York City. He was a much-sought-after guest at luncheon and dinner parties, and I doubt if he ever dined out fewer than four or five evenings a week. He was a skillful storyteller (as a great many writers are not: an author eloquent on paper often proves tongue-tied in person), and he had accumulated a seemingly bottomless supply of entertaining anecdotes about grand and celebrated personages. These anecdotes he dispensed ad lib at social gatherings, with a verve and professional polish that Mark Twain himself might have envied. Alec's New York base was the Algonquin, a hotel much favored by visiting Britishers, not least because the bedrooms were small, the bathrooms archaic, and the one elevator slow and noisy; the absence of up-to-the-minute luxuries gave the Brits a reassuring sense of being close to home.

In terms of its location, the Algonquin was especially well suited to Alec's needs. Of the clubs that he enjoyed lunching at when he wasn't committed to a party on Beekman Place or some other fashionable quarter of town, the Coffee House and the Century were but a five minutes' walk away. Still, I came to suspect that perhaps the happiest portion of Alec's day had already been experienced by the time he turned up at one or another of his clubs and began to hold his companions spellbound. This happiness was linked to another establishment on West Forty-fourth Street, only a few hundred feet from the Algonquin: the turn-of-the-century Hudson Theatre, which at the time I am speaking of had fallen upon hard times and was no longer being used as a legitimate theatre. It had been reduced to showing movies, and not ordinary movies but hard-core pornography, of a sort so flagrant that it often led to public protests by priests, ministers, and rabbis, to indignant newspaper editorials, and even to police action.

In old age, his once hectic sex life reduced to a jumble of delectable if no longer accurate memories, Alec took comfort in attending these pornographic movies. The first show at the Hudson began promptly at 11 A.M., and Alec arranged his schedule accordingly. He woke just before ten, bathed, shaved, and ate a leisurely breakfast. After breakfast, he would step outside the hotel, form an opinion on the weather with the help of the doorman, and retreat to his room to dress in an appropriate fashion. Many years earlier, a splendid overcoat, sable-lined and with a caracul collar, had been given to Alec by the widow of his friend and contemporary, the novelist Michael Arlen. The coat had been a favorite of Arlen's, and his widow had rightly supposed that Alec would be grateful to possess it as a keepsake. From the point of view of a professional critic of male fashions, the only drawback to the overcoat was that, Arlen having been a taller man than Alec, the coat was too long for Alec, reaching almost to his ankles. This wasn't a drawback from Alec's point of view; the exceptional length of the coat helped to keep his old bones warm in the cold of a New York winter, when the wind blew in off the New Jersey meadows and rushed through the narrow, high-walled trough of Forty-fourth Street.

Nevertheless, there *was* a drawback to the coat, and that was its mass. As Alec grew older, he grew smaller and lighter, while the coat remained of exactly the same size and weight. On a chilly, blustery day, one would see Alec leaving the Algonquin, heading west toward the Hudson Theatre, and at first one got the impression that an exceptionally well-cut dark winter overcoat was making its way unaided, under its own mysterious power, along West Forty-fourth Street. It wasn't until a moment or so later that one noticed, at the bottom of the coat, Alec's small feet valiantly thrusting themselves forward against the wind, and, at the top of the coat, Alec's small bald head tucked well down into the caracul collar. One was tempted to hail him, old friend that he was, but no—he had an important appointment and nothing must cause him the least delay in keeping it. Eagerly, the overcoat moved on.

Emma
Jane
Bowen

WHEN MY GREAT-AUNT Emma Jane Bowen sat down to compose an autobiography, she began it with a sentence fairly sure to capture a reader's attention: "It was just over a hundred years ago that, holding me in his arms, my father quarreled with his parish priest." Aunt Emma wasn't a professional writer; though she wrote many short stories and a couple of novels, they found no market. Neither did her autobiography, which I possess in manuscript. As far as I can tell, she wrote it in that comparatively idle period of her life between her hundredth birthday and her death at the age of a hundred and four. Having worked hard all her life, she had not taken readily even to the degree of idleness that had been imposed on her by the flagging of her exceptional energy. Her mind never failed, and the niece with whom she lived became aware that Aunt Emma had decided to die—characteristically, it was a decision and not a mere consenting to the inevitable—when she told the niece that she needn't bother to bring her a copy of *The New Yorker* on the day that it ordinarily arrived in Hartford, where they lived. Aunt Emma had always been impatient to hold the latest issue of the magazine in her hand; not to wish to see it at all was so obviously a portent that the niece, herself a woman of considerable age, felt her heart flutter at Aunt Emma's words: with dread, she perceived that something awful was about to happen, and such was Aunt Emma's iron will that it would be of no use to plead with her to change her mind.

Aunt Emma had read *The New Yorker* regularly over many years, in part because I was a member of the staff but also in part because it maintained a literary standard that she found worthy of her respect, which was to say a standard of good English of the kind that she had been brought up to employ during the middle years of the nineteenth century. The magazine was old-fashioned in an affirmative sense of the word. Unlike other magazines, in her view it had resisted spreading those dire contemporary infections: slovenly grammar and odious slang. Often enough, she would sit down and dash off a letter to me appraising the contents of a given issue; only I, being family, was exempt among its contributors from the rigor with which she expressed her views. And even I was not truly exempt: when she failed to pay me a compliment, I learned to assume that I was being reproached. It was up to me to discover what it was that I was being reproached for—perhaps for what she regarded as a lapse of taste on my part, perhaps only for a split infinitive.

Aunt Emma wrote her autobiography in blue ink in a bold, unwavering hand, line after line marching across the page with inexhaustible zest. She had a strong sense of what the accident of her great age had made valuable with respect to her store of memories of the past. Born on a farm in Southington, Connecticut, during the Civil War, she was the last of the children that her father, Patrick Bowen, had sired by his second wife. Patrick himself had been born in the last decade of the eighteenth century and he would often tell little Emma Jane stories about his father, Andrew Bowen, born in 1732, who as a young man had been put in charge of bringing over from Ireland blooded horses for sale in the American colonies. Andrew was a vivid figure to Aunt Emma; she spoke of him not only to my father and me but to my children and (at the very end of her life) to my grandchildren, which is to say that a single voice became the family voice, sweeping us along through six generations and four centuries—the eighteenth, nineteenth, and twentieth as a certainty, and (almost as certainly in the case of my grandchildren) the twenty-first as well.

I speak of her voice both as a metaphor and as an actuality. She pronounced words as they had been pronounced correctly in a small town in Connecticut in the first half of the nineteenth century; for example, the word "Indian" was then still being pronounced "Injun"—

philologically, the "i" followed the "d" in order to procure that sound—
and the final "g" in most words ending in "ing" was never sounded.
Thus, to Aunt Emma, "Indian pudding" was "Injun puddin." The
proper name "Goodyear" was pronounced "Gudger," and "Renwick"
was "Rennick." Many of the pronunciations of the old-time Connecticut Yankee persisted into my youth; it is only as a result of having lived
for so long outside Connecticut that I unconsciously gave up calling
milk "melk" and a roof a "ruff."

If Aunt Emma was a kind of library for genealogical and philologi-
cal research (which, as she sometimes protested, was all that the world
appeared to think her fit to be), she was also a source of knowledge about
customs common in her childhood and long since abandoned. One
especially bizarre custom of which she wrote in her autobiography was
intended to protect children from the then prevalent scourge of tuberculosis (in those days called consumption). Laboriously, a large pit,
some four or five feet on a side and of about equal depth, would be dug
in the backyard of a house and little children would be made to scramble
down into the pit and lie there on the bare earth for a couple of hours, in
the superstitious belief that some healthy emanation of Mother Earth
would strengthen their lungs against a disease whose cause had yet to be
discovered. Forcing a child to lie on the damp soil of what was, in effect,
an open grave might well have been thought to provide an occasion for
catching the disease and not for preventing it; Aunt Emma set down
without prejudice the fact that her parents thought otherwise.

Aunt Emma was a lifelong spinster; in a phrase that would only
have been used behind her back, she was an old maid. What her
chances for marriage may have been I never heard. In the years of our
friendship, she was tall and slender, with shining black eyes and white
hair, and I assume that she must have been a very good-looking young
woman. She had an animated manner and a notable grace of carriage—
even in her nineties, she was remarkably nimble—and she had talents
that were then much prized in young women: she painted in watercolors, she sang, she wrote stories, and, like Curlylocks in the nursery
rhyme, she could sew a fine seam. She ought to have been a catch, and
perhaps she was, but a stroke of ill fortune befell her. A younger sister,
remembered now only for her nickname, which was "black-eyed
Susan"—black eyes ran in the Bowen family—had married, produced

two daughters, and had then suddenly died. Aunt Emma assumed the task of bringing up the motherless children.

There being little money in the family, Aunt Emma turned the most practical of her gifts—her skill as a needlewoman—into a career. She earned a moderate living and gained a moderate fame by making exceptionally pretty dresses for wealthy society women in the community. Sometimes the women brought Aunt Emma photographs or drawings that they had snipped out of magazines and asked Aunt Emma to copy them, which she did so well that it was often said of her handiwork that it surpassed the originals; at other times (but not as often as she would have liked), she was allowed to design her own originals, which were also much praised. About once a month, she would travel by train to New York, to buy the gorgeous materials—silks, taffetas, and the like, to say nothing of fancy enameled or cloth-covered buttons and trimmings of lace and velvet—out of which her dresses (yard upon yard of convoluted, richly colored fabric) were cunningly fashioned.

The trips to New York were a joy to Aunt Emma. Tiring as it was to tramp up and down Sixth Avenue in search of appropriate materials at an appropriate price—for one's clients' sake, one couldn't afford not to purchase the best of everything, but one also couldn't afford to be cheated in the course of doing so—the evenings provided her with an incomparable reward for the days' labors: dressed to the nines, she would make her way unaccompanied to the Metropolitan Opera House on Seventh Avenue, buy a standing-room ticket in the back of the house, and listen bewitched to her pantheon of heroes and heroines—Jean de Rezske, Gigli, Melba, Mary Garden, Caruso. They sang as if especially for her, and she carried the memory of their voices back to Southington, to be listened to again and again during all those hours of handstitching in the glow of a kerosene lamp.

Over the years, the nieces that Aunt Emma brought up proved a credit to her in their schooling, in their business careers, and in their marriages. Well into old age, having retired from dressmaking, she took care of a house and a big, rambling garden (a cutting of bittersweet, which Aunt Emma gave me some fifty years ago, now threatens by its profuse growth to topple a stone wall at whose base I planted it), and it was only with reluctance that in her late eighties she consented to move into the house of one of the nieces. Even so, she claimed that the single argument worth paying attention to was that she would be far more of a worry—and therefore far more of a nuisance—at a distance from the family than within immediate sight of them. "Better to be dead than to be a nuisance," she said, "and I'm not yet ready to die."

Nor was she—on into her nineties Aunt Emma sailed, undiminished in energy and intellect. As her one-hundredth birthday approached, the family gathered to discuss the question of a suitable birthday present. What on earth ought one to give a centenarian? Foolishly, too hastily, we chose an easy way out. At the time, large-screen color television sets had just come on the market and we decided that Aunt Emma could not fail to be impressed by their novelty, if by nothing else about them. How wrong we were! The gift was a disaster. Aunt Emma turned out to have stronger feelings about television than we had supposed—all negative. If she had despised television in its small-screen, black-and-white period, she despised it far more in grandiose, large-screen color. "Do you think that just because I am a hundred I am going to be content to sit staring at that ridiculous object?" she asked. "Do you think I am so far gone in senility as to satisfy my mind with gruel of that infantile nature? With nursery porridge? With milk toast? Take the thing away at once! Out of my sight it goes! Out! Out! Out!"

Being Irish, Aunt Emma had been raised as a devout Catholic and, to the best of my knowledge, she remained one. (We never discussed religion, partly because Aunt Emma was aware that, as believers would say, I had "lost my faith"—a condition that I called being a "collapsed" Catholic.) Whatever she may or may not have accepted of the church's teachings, evidently the notion that on Judgment Day we are all to enjoy the privilege of a bodily resurrection did not cause her to hesitate in making plans for a radical (if perhaps only temporary) scattering of her remains. To have survived the century mark in undisputed full command of one's mind and body was a highly unusual feat, and it was a characteristic of Aunt Emma not simply to take pride in the feat but to perceive that it imposed a certain responsibility upon her as well. Not for her to go down into the earth—the dark earth that she had been repeatedly lowered into as a frightened child—as an embalmed and intact corpse when something of value might be gained in behalf of science by being chopped up and scrutinized. To the scandal of the more pious members of her family, having made the decision to die, she made the further decision that her cadaver was to be sent down to the Yale Medical School, in New Haven, for the doctors there to do with it whatever they chose.

Reluctantly, Aunt Emma's orders were obeyed; gratefully, the Yale Medical School accepted her donation of herself. Two or three times during the course of the ensuing year I made attempts to find out what an examination of Aunt Emma's body had revealed, always without success—certain regulations were said to prevent the giving-out of such information, especially to laymen, and I sensed, moreover, that inquiries of that nature on the part of a relative of the deceased were considered morbid, if not downright pathological: I was threatened with the possibility that the authorities at Yale had begun to take me for some sort of weirdo. If that were the case, they might well charge me with some legal transgression hitherto unfamiliar to me, or (to look on what amounted to the bright side) might request that I, too, leave my body to the school, and the sooner the better. I stopped making inquiries, and now the consequences, if any, of Aunt Emma's donation will never be known, except, it may be, anonymously, in the fine print of some statistical footnote.

"It was just over a hundred years ago that, holding me in his arms, my father quarreled with his parish priest." That opening sentence of Aunt Emma's autobiography embodies a greater melodrama than most of us, living in the last years of the twentieth century, may suppose. For in an Irish-Catholic parish in a small town in Connecticut almost 150 years ago, the local pastor was a tyrant. However benign a tyrant he might be, he was never to be disobeyed. For in such a town the Irish were an isolated minority; they felt threatened by the Yankees who surrounded and dominated them, who owned the mortgages on their farms, who employed them as hired hands and house servants. In any crisis, whether temporal or religious, the Irish invariably closed ranks behind the pastor: he was to them literally the surrogate of God, and to quarrel with him, even in a matter of private concern, was almost unthinkable.

And that was what Patrick Bowen did. When his last child was born (and perhaps assuming that she was to be his last child), he wished at the baptism ceremony to have her named Jenny after Jenny Lind, the Swedish diva whom he had heard singing at Castle Garden in the 1850s. (The structure had been built as a fort at the southern tip of Manhattan island, to guard the city against naval attacks in the years before the War of 1812; later, it was converted into a place of entertainment, then into a depot for immigrants, and finally into an aquarium. In recent years, what remains of the original fort has been turned into what preservationists call a "stabilized ruin.") Hearing Jenny Lind sing had been one of the superb adventures of my great-grandfather's life, and he was determined to celebrate it in a permanent form; by the magical power inherent in naming, perhaps he would bend his infant daughter toward the world of music that had meant so much to him. (One thinks of Aunt Emma standing entranced at the back of the Metropolitan. The magic had worked.) On the morning of the baptism, the infant was carried to church and held above the marble font, to be sprinkled with holy water and touched on the lips with salt. The pastor: "And what is the child's name to be?"

Patrick Bowen: "Jenny, Father."

The pastor, with a show of irritation: "You can't name a child Jenny, man."

"Why not, Father?"

"Because it isn't a saint's name, that's why. Only a saint's name will suffice in the eyes of God."

"But, Father, I heard Jenny—"

Furious now, his authority challenged, the pastor growls: "Let's get on with it, man. What about Emma Jane? There's a fine saint's name for you, and as close as two pins to Jenny."

"Pleasing Your Reverence—"

"Silence, you puppy!" (My great-grandfather was then in his late sixties.) The pastor makes a sign of the cross above the swaddled infant. "In the name of the Father, Son, and Holy Ghost, I baptize thee Emma Jane."

Georges Simenon

AS I WRITE these words, news comes of the death of the French novelist Georges Simenon, in his eighty-seventh year. A lifelong hypochondriac, in youth he expected to die young and in middle age, during the time that he was a resident in this country and he and I became friends, he counted on dying within a year or two at the most. I would not be surprised to learn that, toward the end, he had been predicting his death on a day-to-day basis. The morbid relish that he had always taken in the prospect of his extinction was unlikely to have grown any less as he approached the certainty of its being fulfilled. I can imagine him saying, as hypochondriacs invariably do when their tough old bodies begin to break down, "There! You see? Didn't I tell you that I was a sick man?" Voltaire spoke thus in his eighties, after complaining for seventy years of ill health, and Simenon would have said that what was good enough for Voltaire was good enough for him—all the more so, indeed, because, like Voltaire, he had chosen Switzerland as the refuge of his old age: Voltaire in Ferney, Simenon in Lausanne.

Because I am recalling Simenon as the *malade imaginaire* that I found him to be when he was living in the States, I risk sounding callous in mentioning at this moment his continuous preoccupation with death. It was a favorite topic, and the enthusiasm with which Simenon seized it and shook it and cuffed it about was such that to omit it would

231

be to render any likeness of him incomplete and inaccurate. More than once, Simenon claimed in my presence to regret not having died at the age of forty-four, as his father had done. A shy, decent man, Simenon's father worked as a clerk in an insurance office in Liège, where Simenon was born in February 1903. As for his mother, Simenon used to say that he and she strongly disliked each other and that he considered it characteristically unattractive of her to have lived well into her nineties. "She was a miser, a money-grubber," he told me. "She could never understand my becoming a writer. Her grand hope for me was that I become a pastry cook. Oh, how she wanted to see me at an oven and herself behind the counter! Once, I put her in a novel, called *Pedigree*. I admit that the likeness I drew of her was not only harsh but unmistakable, and at first she was very much offended. Then people started coming from miles around to look her over, and she turned out to enjoy it. She'd take visitors through the house and show them the table at which I wrote my first novel. But it wasn't really the same table. That table she sold."

Simenon's first novel, entitled *Au Pont des Arches*, was published when he was seventeen. It is an accomplished work, very much in that vein of unadorned candor and contempt for lower-middle-class life which he would be exploring throughout his career. One of the dozens of early novels by him that have yet to pass from French into English, it begins:

> On that particular Sunday morning, Joseph Planquet, who ran the drugstore at the sign of The Bridge of Arches, wasn't allowed to lounge about in bed. Promptly at eight, he was aroused by his wife on her return from Mass. Her nose was red and moist, her voice slightly hoarse. "Hurry up, now!" she said. "You know what a job we have to do today!"

As we read those sentences, we assume that the pharmacist, lazily lying abed on a Sunday morning, may well have been entertaining certain mildly lustful thoughts, but when his wife returns from Mass her nose is red and moist; instantly, we take in how the poor man's sexual desire would wither in the presence of that dreadful nasal moistness. This is Simenon at his best, incomparably terse and devastating. Only fifteen hundred copies of *Au Pont des Arches* were printed and there was no second edition; a sound copy might bring a couple of hundred dollars today. Simenon mislaid the manuscript of the novel following a party held to celebrate its publication. When he returned to Belgium many years later, to accept election to the Royal Academy of Belgium, he was astonished to discover the manuscript on exhibition in the Liège town hall. He had no idea how it survived the intervening years.

Simenon had dashed off *Au Pont des Arches* in ten days. Eight to twelve days soon became the usual span of time that he devoted to the composition of his novels, which total several hundred. In Europe, he has long been regarded as the most prolific novelist of the century, the fastest-writing novelist of the century, and the most popular novelist of the century. Nobody—least of all Simenon himself—has ever been sure how many millions of copies of his books have been sold throughout the world over the past sixty-odd years, nor does anyone know for sure how many languages they have been published in. Something like two hundred of his novels have been brought out in English, and although in extreme old age Simenon wrote no fiction, novels hitherto unpublished in English continue to appear in this country at the rate of two or three a year. Plainly, he has earned his possession of that supreme accolade for a novelist, the reduction of one's name from upper case to lower case: throughout Europe, his short, violent, and often terrifying novels are known simply as "simenons."

By the time he was twenty-one, Simenon had married—the bride was an artist, a few years older than he—and had moved to Paris, where he took an apartment in the Marais, on the place des Vosges, and announced (if only to himself) that he was preparing himself for a career as a serious writer. He was fairly sure that he would be unable to write a work of lasting value before he was thirty; therefore, he would spend the next nine years learning his craft. He would write anything and everything, he would write and write. Colette was then editor of *Le Matin*, and Simenon was soon contributing a weekly short story to that newspaper. Like most young writers of the day, he had fallen under the influence of Maeterlinck and the other symbolists. Colette told him sternly, "Be simple. Never try for a literary effect. Leave out every word and syllable you can." It was the only advice Simenon ever needed and the only advice he ever took. His writing is spare and fast-moving. Flaubert said that he would rather die like a dog than force out an immature phrase; Simenon would rather die like a dog than let slip a superfluous adjective.

While the novels of most prolific authors can be cut like butter, Simenon's novels can scarcely be cut at all. Once, chatting with him over a couple of mugs of beer in a New York City bar, I mentioned that some of our local critics had complained of him that he told too little, that among his novels were those that went from the breathless to the merely out of breath. Simenon shrugged with his usual vehemence—in his prime, his shrugs were as energetic as an African war dance. That particular shrug was the silent equivalent of *"Que voulez-vous?"* Surely I could see that a simenon that dawdled wouldn't be a simenon? Besides, fresh characters and plots were accustomed to break from the barrier of his typewriter as quickly as he was able to strike the keys. One relative clause too many, and they might outdistance him.

Living during the years of our acquaintance in a village in northwestern Connecticut and paying an occasional visit to New York City, Simenon was nourished by memories of his extravagantly success-ful youth in far-off Paris. How hard he had worked and how hard he had played! He remembered that one day when he and the century were in their middle twenties, he was summoned to a publisher's office and offered a contract for twelve novels. He signed the contract and took a taxi back to his apartment; he was never to ride in a bus or subway again. Soon he acquired a Chrysler Imperial limousine and a chauffeur, whom he would send into the publisher's office to deliver manuscripts. He dressed the chauffeur in a sailor's uniform, and for years the Paris police allowed the chauffeur all sorts of vehicular liberties on the assumption that he was driving for a high official of the Ministry of Marine. It became obvious that a month or two of Simenon's full-time writing was equal to a lifetime of writing by the usual torpid author. His output was too much for a single publisher to handle, and soon he had six. He wrote eighty pages a day, every day. He not only erupted prose, he erupted it in every form, turning out sketches and short stories by the thousands, novellas by the hundreds, and novels by the score. Nor was he in the least disturbed that nearly all of them were trash. He was serving his apprenticeship and was being handsomely paid to do so.

It was also the case that the Simenons were having a marvelous time. They installed a large bar in their apartment and gave a succession of nightlong parties, to which the only drawback was the singular early-morning habits of the host. At 6:30, party or no party, Simenon started work. Often it happened that guests were sprawled on the floor about his desk and at every piercing click of the typewriter keys—for Simenon hit the keys vigorously as well as fast—they would rouse themselves with a groan and beg him to have pity.

Once, Simenon had six stories in a single issue of a magazine, each story signed with a different name. At the peak of what he has termed his preliterary period, he was juggling a total of sixteen pseudonyms, among them Georges Sims, Jean du Perry, Christian Brulls, Georges Martin-Georges, Poum et Zette, and Gom Gut. (These pseudonyms have long played hob with collectors of Simenon first editions. Some collectors, convinced that Georges Simenon is merely another pen name for Georges Sims, would rather invest in old Sims than new simenons.) Many of his novels were Westerns, for which the French had, and have, an insatiable appetite. They bore such titles as *The Black Panther* and *The Eye of Utah*, Simenon having chosen Utah for reasons of euphony rather than geography. Others were adventure stories laid in faraway places—*The King of the Pacific, The San Francisco Chinaman, The White Monster of Terra del Fuego*—that Simenon knew little about but was eager to visit someday. The rest were what are known in France as *"romans galants."* Recollecting for me the delight he had taken in writing them, he took pains to hit upon an exact translation of the phrase as it applied to his work. "'Spicy stories' would do," he said, "but 'juicy' is better. Truly, they were more juicy than spicy." Notable among his juicy stories were *Fever, Forbidden to Love, Lily's Luck*, and—in French as in English—*Miss Baby*. "It was the hot twenties and I made those novels as hot as I could," Simenon said, with a craftsman's pride. "Some of them were illustrated, and oh, what a waste of the artist's time! I had given the reader more than enough to picture in his imagination."

By that time, Simenon had acquired an eighteen-foot boat, which he kept moored in the Seine. The royalties from his juicy stories made possible the commissioning of a stout thirty-six-foot sloop, the *Ostrogoth*, named for an early and savage tribe of European marauders from whom Simenon liked to think that he was descended. He cruised in the *Ostrogoth* through most of the canals of France, Belgium, and Holland, as well as in the Mediterranean and the Atlantic, and for two years never spent a night ashore. It was during this period that he received one of his few official honors—a post as private literary consultant to His Highness the Prince of Monaco, grandfather of Prince Rainier. The duties attached to the honor proved welcomely indetectable. Simenon found writing even easier aboard the *Ostrogoth* than it had been in the place des Vosges. For one thing, he had fewer guests to step over on his way to work. For another, every day's travel brought him fresh material. One *Ostrogoth* novel, *The Dancer of the Gai-Moulin*, was composed in exactly twenty-five hours. Simenon's fans are certain that this is the world's record for speed in the novel; certainly Simenon regarded it as his record, recalling that the typewriter went lame in the last paragraph and had to be destroyed. It was said in Paris that Simenon would compose his next novel in public, in a glass cage hung outside the office of one of his numerous publishers. Simenon would have been glad to oblige, but somehow he was unable to stop writing long enough to get to Paris and make a clean start. Occasionally, he would tie up at the stone pier of some seaside village, hoist his typewriter onto the stones, and type away like mad, to the distress of nearby fishermen. They protested that artists and their dirty paints were bad enough but that Simenon was worse, because his machine-gun-like typing caused the pier to vibrate, roiled the harbor bottom, and made the fish seasick.

At twenty-seven, perceiving that he had pretty well exhausted the technical fascination of trash, Simenon plunged into what he has called his semiliterary period. In it, the *roman galant* gave way to the *roman policier*. The switch was signaled by the arrival of Inspector Maigret, a fat, pipe-smoking, middle-aged Parisian, more interested in learning what has led to a crime than in apprehending the person who has committed it. Like his creator, Maigret is contemptuous of banality above all and sees loneliness as the greatest of human hardships. As a literary character, Maigret promises to go on living as long as people go on reading crime fiction, and there are those who say he will live longer, being superior to his genre and therefore outside it. He is, in any event, far enough outside it to be a familiar figure to readers who abominate ordinary mysteries.

Inspector Maigret was born aboard the *Ostrogoth*, somewhere between Le Havre and Hamburg, and the first two Maigret novels were published together, in February 1931. To mark the occasion, Simenon decided to give a *bal anthropométrique*, naming it for a department of la Sûreté, the police headquarters in Paris. He persuaded his publisher to let him draw on funds that had been set aside to advertise his two novels, and hired a nightclub, La Boule Blanche, in Montparnasse. He sent invitations to four hundred well-known actors, writers, artists, and other celebrities, including high officials of la Sûreté. He also arranged for the Paris office of MGM to film the ball, though why the movie company should have troubled to do so was never clear to either Simenon or MGM. The ball was a raving, staving success. His four hundred invited guests were joined by seven hundred outsiders, who gamely fought their way into the club and raised no objection to the overcrowding.

At Simenon's insistence, the proprietor of La Boule Blanche kept sending out for more cases of caviar and champagne, and by nine the next morning, when the party reluctantly broke up, Simenon had spent every sou of the publisher's advertising budget, as well as what he estimated would be his royalties on both novels for several years to come. Nevertheless, he was delighted, for the ball was the talk of France and Inspector Maigret was famous before he had a single reader. In a matter of months, the novels had been translated into eight languages and the inspector's name was a byword in Europe. Rare as it is for an author to achieve the glory of lower case, still rarer is it for an author's character to achieve an equal glory; be that as it may, it is a fact that one can speak today with equal readiness of both "simenons" and "maigrets." Facile as Simenon was, he was always hard-pressed to keep up with the public's demand for maigrets. The best he could do was twenty in the first two years. The total number of maigrets now stands at around eighty, while serials featuring the inspector have long been a staple on radio and television in half a dozen countries. Maigret has also been the hero of a dozen or so French movies.

Simenon's semiliterary period, far from letting the young man in a hurry be in less of a hurry, proved twice as strenuous as its sexy predecessor. In the course of it, he wrote more, earned more, spent more, and traveled more than ever. Though he was rarely at home, he accumulated five houses here and there in France and kept a hundred-foot schooner in the Mediterranean, with a crew of seven who spent most of their time patiently standing by. Between 1931 and 1939 he made extended visits to Russia, the Near East, the United States, Scandinavia, South America, the South Pacific, and Africa. His novels became a sort of log of his voyages. Whereas, if one forgets such preposterous thrillers as *The White Monster of Terra del Fuego*, the settings of his novels had been the cities and villages of France, Belgium, and Holland, they were now the cities, villages, islands, and continents of the entire world. Bordeaux, Brussels, Amsterdam, Fécamp, and Porquerolles were supplanted by Istanbul, Brazzaville, Berlin, Trondheim, the Galápagos, Panama, Chile, and New Zealand. Never before, say his admirers, has a novelist attempted to assimilate and depict so many and such varied cultures. (Simenon even wrote a song—in English, at a time when he knew no English—about the blacks who helped build the Panama Canal. In his library was a recording of it, as sung by the distinguished black American baritone Roland Hayes.)

Wherever Simenon went, he would stop off long enough to rent a house, explore the surrounding countryside, and try to lose his identity in that of one or another of the hundreds of acquaintances he made. The photograph albums that he preserved from this period afford glimpses of a man in khaki shorts and topee, in swimming trunks, in white ducks, in a leather windbreaker, in a stout winter overcoat and bowler. Behind him is the jungle, the sea, the desert, a walled garden, a waste of snow. The man is always Simenon, but he is never the same Simenon. The actor is nimble, the roles are many. Also in the albums, neatly named and dated, are snapshots of pretty black girls in the Congo, pretty brown girls in Tahiti, pretty yellow girls in the Orient, and pretty white girls in Cannes. As much as he contrived to change from one civilization to the next, Simenon's eye for womanly beauty never faltered. In respect to scientific matters, his eye may be said to have faltered fairly often, perhaps for reasons having little to do with reason. I remember Simenon showing me photographs he had taken of a Watusi tribe—seven-foot-tall warriors, standing storklike on one foot. Simenon assured me that these splendid specimens of manhood were incapable of having an erection: their great height had deprived them of the privilege. Incredulously, I asked how the Watusi succeeded in reproducing themselves in the face of that unlucky circumstance. Simenon merely shrugged: the world was full of wonders, was it not?

Little by little, to keep the mass of his readers from guessing what he was up to, Simenon moved into his third period. At twenty-one, he had hoped to write a work of lasting value by thirty. Thirty came and went, and he conceded that he might require another decade of preparation; at forty, he raised his sights to fifty, though by then the world had long since assured him that he had successfully met that early, self-imposed goal of his. From being a writer of crime fiction, he became a writer of what he called "*le roman crise.*" The acts of violence in his novels were no longer merely literary devices that set in motion a tantalizing series of bafflements and explanations. They were, to him, tragic consequences of the fact that for many men and women life is sometimes, if not nearly always, unendurable. In the moment of crisis, they are driven to affirm themselves, and, human society being what it is, they can affirm themselves only through murder, rape, arson, suicide, and the rest of the long and sorry catalogue of crimes familiar to us in our culture. It was one thing for a writer to believe this; it was another to set it down without diminution or cheapness within the framework of a popular novel.

From the first, Simenon possessed the "imagination of disaster" that Henry James thought indispensable to a writer. With the development of a style that was more and more savage and staccato, more and more a kind of shorthand of anguish, Simenon released that imagination. In novels where the barometric pressure seems always to be falling and the knife coming closer to one's own or another's throat, he wrote, as he said, "of the fact that every man feels that he is lonelier than every other man and of the implacability of day following day." Simenon's first duty to his readers had hitherto been to knock them for a loop. Now he tried to knock them for a higher and more significant loop. "I knew where I was going," he told me once, speaking of those first years of the third period, "and I was determined to take my readers with me. I was writing better than they wanted me to write. Often, I would put in a few pages or even a whole chapter of a novel for my pleasure, not theirs. Those pages would be completely different from the rest of the novel. It must have confused my readers very much. *Tant pis.*"

Meanwhile, Simenon was taking other chances in his writing. As he risked using foreign settings, where a single false note might turn melodrama into farce, so he risked dealing with a variety of professions and occupations—a greater variety, it has been claimed by scholars, than either Balzac or Dickens ever dealt with. And if it is nervy to write about faraway countries, it is ten times nervier to write about near-at-hand occupations. Comparatively few readers are able to tell whether an author made an idiot of himself in describing the flora of Christmas Island (the scene of Simenon's novel *Evil Star*). Thousands of readers will howl if he blunders with regard to the most trivial particulars of their job. *De minimis non curat lex*, but lawyers are slow to apply this principle to novels that concern the law. Or let a novelist who has made his hero a distinguished surgeon mislocate the carotid artery, and his doctor readers will turn on him as if he had been caught practicing medicine without a license. Among the characters Simenon has managed to portray to the satisfaction of their counterparts in real life are not only lawyers and doctors but grocers, movie directors, mayors, stagehands, judges, night watchmen, sailors, planters, factory managers, diplomats, actors, wine merchants, professors, policemen, prostitutes, housewives, working anarchists, and—by far the greatest sticklers for accuracy—thieves.

In 1939, when his son Marc was born, Simenon resolved to move to the United States. He was eager to have Marc grow up as an American and he was scarcely less eager to match himself against the American public. Unlike his contemporary Hemingway, who tended to see writing as a form of combat between himself and other writers, Simenon always saw it as a form of combat between himself and uncountable hosts of unknown readers. He felt that he was as widely read and as famous as he could ever be in Europe (Simenon would tell me, "A writer in Europe is like a movie star here. He is given or may take whatever he pleases"); it was time for him to challenge new adversaries. Before he could complete plans to come to the States and enter the ring against the average light-heavyweight reader, the Second World War broke out and in 1940, being a Belgian national, he retired with his wife and son to a farm outside the village of St. Mesmin-le-Vieux, in the Vendée.

In the quiet of that remote village, during the first years of the war, Simenon worked on two autobiographical books. They were wholly unlike anything that he had written before, perhaps because he wrote them in anticipation of death—this time, a reasonable anticipation of death and not his habitual hypochondriacal one. Chopping wood at the farm, he injured his chest with the axe helve. When the pain persisted, he walked ten miles to visit the nearest X-ray specialist. The specialist examined Simenon's heart, pronounced it the organ of a seventy-five-year-old man (Simenon was then in his late thirties), and forbade him to smoke, drink, have sex, or engage in any physical exertion whatever. Simenon tiptoed the ten miles home in the conviction that every step would be his last. "I was the man who had done everything and now I was ordered to be the man who did nothing!" he said many years later, his face crinkling at the recollection as if he were about to cry. "My own doctors were far away in Paris. I thought I had better sit down at my desk and say what I had to say, for I was seventy-five and couldn't afford to waste a moment."

Simenon's first autobiographical book, entitled *I Remember*, was addressed to Marc and begins, "My dear boy." Simenon sent several chapters to his admirer André Gide—Gide had called Simenon "perhaps the greatest novelist in contemporary French letters"—and Gide suggested that he tell the same story in the guise of fiction. Simenon put aside *I Remember* and began the long autobiographical novel called *Pedigree*, which some critics consider his finest work. In it, he recalled his early life in Liège with such fidelity that when the book was published in 1948, it led to a brisk flurry of suits for libel by litigious Liègeois; a couple of these suits took most of a decade to settle. In 1944, the nondrinking, nonsmoking, nonexerting Simenon managed to get to Paris, all but holding his worn-out heart in his hands. He was given a thorough examination by three leading heart specialists and was told that he was in perfect physical condition. The provincial specialist had apparently misread his fluoroscope. Simenon was astounded. He could smoke again? But of course. And drink? Certainly. And even exert himself a bit? It would do him good. When his next novel was ready for the press, Simenon dedicated it to the three specialists, *"en souvenir de février, '44."*

The Simenons landed in New York in the fall of 1945. Though he spoke no English, he got the feel of the country with his accustomed speed. If one ignores the trashy Westerns written in his youth, his first novel with an American setting was *Three Rooms in Manhattan*, which was brought out in France in 1946. Simenon and his entourage set out to explore the United States and Canada, with the usual Simenon intention of finding a place in which to establish a permanent home. The entourage consisted of his wife and son; Boule, the housekeeper who had been employed by them for many years and with whom Simenon had long had a sexual relationship, consented to but by no means approved of by his wife; and a young Canadian woman, Denyse Ouimet, whom Simenon had recently hired as his secretary. Traveling by car through a number of states, they sampled for months at a time Florida, Arizona, California, and the province of Quebec. Soon enough this itinerary yielded the usual harvest of convincing local backgrounds: a novel published in 1947, *Les Frères Rico*, is set in Brooklyn, Florida, and California. The brothers are gangsters, and an American reader of the novel cannot help being startled when he first comes across Eddie Rico on the telephone to Boston Phil:

—*Eddie?*
—*Oui.*
—*Ici, Phil.*

By the time the Simenons had completed a couple of years of zigzag-voyaging back and forth across America, Simenon had begun an affair with Denyse and had arranged to divorce his wife—an action made all the more necessary because Denyse had become pregnant. As Simenon had learned to his dismay, it was legally possible that as a resident alien he might be subject to deportation on the grounds of moral turpitude for practicing with Denyse what the immigration authorities called concubinage, to say nothing of violating the Mann Act by transporting her (and, for that matter, Boule as well) across state lines for carnal purposes. In recounting this period of his life to me, Simenon confessed to looking back on it as an intolerable mingling of tragedy and farce. He had always boasted quite openly of what he believed to be his exceptional sexual prowess, claiming to have made love to many thousands of women over his lifetime. Making love to two or three women concurrently was not an unprecedented feat for him; it was the confined circumstances in which the feat had to be performed that taxed his ingenuity. "Imagine what it was like in that automobile!" he exclaimed. "*Quelle horreur!* I might have been driving a Frigidaire."

Divorced, remarried, and for the second time the father of a son, Simenon purchased a house in the small town of Lakeville, Connecticut. (He also purchased a house nearby for the first Mrs. Simenon and the eleven-year-old Marc, in order that, according to the terms of the divorce settlement, she could conveniently share Marc's custody with him.) The house into which Simenon, Denyse, baby Johnny, and Boule moved had formerly belonged to Ralph Ingersoll, a journalist who had worked for *The New Yorker* and *Time*, had founded a liberal daily newspaper in New York City called *P.M.*, and after its failure had retired to Connecticut and set himself up as the publisher of a chain of small-town newspapers. Ingersoll had added ten or twelve rooms and four bathrooms to the two or three rooms and no bathrooms of the ancient original house and had installed an intricate heating system, which Simenon, having often experienced the cold and damp of country houses in Europe, greatly admired but claimed to be unable to comprehend.

Simenon had been eager to buy the Ingersoll place within a few minutes of seeing it. Close to the heart of the village but remarkably secluded, it consisted of forty-eight acres of fields, woods, cliffs, and swamp. Near the house, which was built on different levels over a number of rocky ledges, was a small swimming pool and beyond the pool were a brook and the remains of a stone dam and millrace. Simenon used a barn on the property as a garage for his two cars—a Jeep station wagon and a Chrysler sedan, in which Simenon pretended to find a family resemblance to the Chrysler limousine in which his chauffeur used to make weekly deliveries of the juicy masterpieces of Poum et Zette and Gom Gut. Scattered throughout the house were many evidences of Simenon's inveterate bent for acculturation. African masks, Spanish plates, an ancient French wall clock, an Italian refectory table, and sets of august authors in august bindings agreeably jostled plastic-covered maple rockers, television sets, and his son Marc's model airplanes. Bookshelf after bookshelf contained hundreds of paperback copies of simenons, many of them in languages of which Simenon could not read a word.

It was a year or so after the Simenons had settled in Lakeville that I met him. We had a friend in common, J. Campbell Beckett, a lawyer practicing in Lakeville; it was he who had arranged the purchase of the Simenons' house. The Gills' summer place in Norfolk was only a few miles east of Lakeville. One evening, the Becketts gave a dinner party for the purpose of bringing the Simenons and us together. It was a jolly assembly, towards the end of which Simenon performed one of his favorite "turns"—an imitation of Charlie Chaplin, carried out with the aid of a derby and cane borrowed from Beckett. We became friends and when, some months later, I had occasion to cast about for a likely *New Yorker* Profile subject, I thought at once of Simenon.

The prospect was a challenging one for me, and Simenon was amused to share the challenge. Our establishment in Norfolk consisted of a long, low-roofed, shingled bungalow set in a great sweep of lawn and meadow on a hillside on the edge of town. It had been built in the early years of the century and remodeled by me as an amateur architect at the height of my imitation–Frank Lloyd Wright period. Surrounded by many acres of pine and hemlock woods, it lacked but a single amenity: that of access to water suitable for swimming and sailing. One evening, I got a telephone call from a Norfolk friend, Jim Lawrence, whose first question was, "Are you the kind of man who likes to take chances?" The answer to that question is, of course, "Yes"—indeed, it *must* be "Yes," since the least equivocation in answering it would brand one forever as the most arrant of cowards.

Having proved myself sufficiently brave by an affirmative reply, I was told that a certain camp on Tobey Pond was for sale. Now, Tobey Pond is one of the few sizable bodies of water in or near Norfolk—a spring-fed glacial lake formed during the retreat of the last Ice Age, some ten thousand years ago. (It is called a pond instead of a lake because in the nineteenth century the water level was raised a number of feet by means of an earthen dam; literally, the lake was impounded.) With the exception of a small, pie-shaped parcel, all the land surrounding Tobey Pond belonged to half a dozen owners. It was this small parcel, known as the old Post camp, that had unexpectedly come on the market, and Jim Lawrence, a member of one of the families owning land directly across from the camp, was eager to make sure that no stranger gained possession of it. He had already approached another member of the Norfolk community with the "Are you the sort of man—?" question and that poor wretch, being a prudent Yankee, had failed to give the proper answer. Fortunately, I had been the second person on Jim's list. His next question to me was, "Have you ever seen the Post camp?" I had only the vaguest recollection of having done so, though I remembered hearing that my parents-in-law and even my grandparents-in-law had been accustomed to swimming there. "Buy it," commanded Lawrence, and "I will," said I.

Getting in touch with the owner, a Norfolk neighbor who had recently moved to North Carolina, I learned that he was asking a price of thirty-five hundred dollars for the camp—a low price even in the early 1950s. Still, it was a fact that I didn't have the thirty-five hundred dollars at that moment; as a writer, I had long practiced a system of deficit financing of which the federal government's version was but a timid reflection. What subsequently came to be known among businessmen as "a cash-flow problem" had long been characteristic of my fiscal arrangements; I had never been poor, but I had often been overextended. I told my former neighbor that I would like to buy the camp and added, holding my breath, that I would be glad to send him a check as a binder. I was aware that the check would have to be a "hot" one, drawn against insufficient funds, but I was determined not to let the camp slip through my fingers for so trivial a reason. To my relief, the neighbor said, "My dear fellow, don't bother! We know each other—just send me a check for the full amount whenever you like."

A welcome answer. The next day, I instructed a Norfolk lawyer to set about acquiring the property for me but to take a certain amount of time in searching the title. It happened that the payment I would receive for a Profile in *The New Yorker* at that time was the same as the price of the camp, and I wanted a few weeks in which to choose a subject, conduct interviews, and compose the piece. Most writers were expected to take several months over a Profile, but I was a notoriously speedy writer—according to William Shawn, editor of the magazine, only Edmund Wilson and Rebecca West exceeded me in that respect. I figured that I could accomplish the task in a couple of weeks at most. This was the challenging occasion that Simenon had consented to share with me, and I was later to realize that for him there was also something of value to be gained. In his very long, harshly written, and often unpleasant autobiographical work, *Intimate Memoirs*, published in English in 1984, he wrote that the Profile in *The New Yorker* (by a friend whom he described as being also an excellent novelist—praise from the master!) constituted "some kind of official recognition" in America, as did a picture story about him and his family that appeared in *Life* at a somewhat later date.

In order to interview Simenon as expeditiously as possible, I accepted his invitation to join his ménage in Lakeville for a few days. When I knocked on the front door of the house and Boule opened it for me, I guessed at once not only from her air of self-possession but from her air of possessing the premises as well that she was more than a mere housekeeper. Something in her posture—in what we would now call her "body language"—informed me of the power that she wielded under that roof. She led me to a guest room, where I deposited my gear, and then on into Simenon's presence. Ever the superb actor, that morning he was playing the role of Great-Writer-at-Home. A short man with a face as round and bright-eyed as a chipmunk's, dressed in excellent well-worn English tweeds and smoking one or another of his scores of pipes, he created an impression perfect of its kind: domestic bliss, or as close to domestic bliss as a literary man of genius could hope to attain.

Denyse Simenon joined us at lunch. She was then at the height of her triple career as wife, mother, and executive. Having begun as Simenon's secretary, she had advanced to being his business manager, with a secretary and office of her own. She was a dark-eyed, dark-haired, and pretty young woman and, I suspected, like her husband a superb actor; her role during my stay was that of a demurely civil *jeune fille bien rangée*. She looked up adoringly at the Great Man and even deferred (or so I seemed to detect) infinitesimally to Boule. Simenon had just finished one of his ten-day novels—not as exhausting an ordeal as a twelve-dayer but hard on him because one of the chief characters was an alcoholic and, in the days just before sitting down to compose the novel, Simenon had been drinking more than usual in order, so he said, "to keep the poor chap company." The Simenon family doctor had been asked to stop by several times during the course of the writing of the novel and had found that Simenon's blood pressure had been constantly falling. "Some day soon I will wink out like a candle," Simenon said, and Denyse Simenon uttered a little-girl moan of protest, while Boule, standing behind Simenon and with her face never changing expression, gently shook her head.

For several days, Simenon and I talked, whether in his study, at meals, or while running errands in the village, picking up Marc at school, or tramping over the grounds of the estate. Simenon had established only one proviso in respect to the Profile: that the proximity of the first Mrs. Simenon to Lakeville not be mentioned—the divorce settlement had rendered her nearby presence necessary, but dear little Denyse found it troubling. Simenon indicated to me, in the confidential tone of one man to another, that the possibility of his having sex with his ex-wife was far more upsetting to Denyse than the fact, openly acknowledged, of his having sex with Boule. "If one has a place in the country and if one has servants," Simenon said, "what can one expect? One must take care of their needs."

In a similar vein of preening reminiscence, over drinks at the local tavern, Simenon would deliver lectures by turns droll and disconcerting on the physiology of women and the remarkable range of sexual response that he had managed to induce in them. "Ah, that one!" he would say, singling out one or another of the hundreds of women that he apparently kept on file in his memory. "When she came, it was like a burst of summer rain—believe me, it flew out of her in torrents! That's how a man should make a woman respond." He would slap his hand down hard on the surface of the bar, startling our fellow drinkers. "Like a rifle shot," he would say. *"Un coup de fusil."*

Less disagreeable than Simenon's old-fashioned man-to-man sexual revelations were his writer-to-writer discussions of the art of the novel. With a bit of burnt match, he would draw diagrams on a bar napkin or beer coaster to show how the action in certain of his novels would hopscotch from climax to climax, while in others it would jog along *tchi, tchi, tchi.* Over the years, he had accumulated a few bold literary maxims. "The writer does not exist," he would say. "Only the novel and the reader exist. The more the novel seems to have been written by the reader, the better it is. The novel must be short and must be read at one sitting. It must not be a chronicle. It must not be picturesque. It must strike the reader a single terrible blow, like a blow in the face." Then he would add that none of these maxims was likely to be true of any novels except his own.

If I was aware that Simenon was playing a theatrical role as the central figure in a felicitous family circle, I was convinced at the same time that the role bore some relationship to the truth. Surely he *was* a happy man then, standing at the peak of his powers as a writer and at the beginning of a popular acceptance throughout America. He had a young and pretty wife, two sons, and the prospect of more children in the future. (A daughter and a third son were, in fact, soon to follow.) He was already rich and could only grow richer as, with his books selling at the rate of three million copies a year, royalties poured in upon him from all over the world. However morbidly obsessed by death he might be, he was an exceptionally vigorous fifty-year-old. Moreover, unlike most authors, he never feared going dry, never feared running out of material.

Having written hundreds of novels, Simenon felt himself to be hundreds of novels away from being written out. He had grown accustomed to a schedule as regular and relentless as the seasons, calling for six novels a year. Two of the novels were maigrets, which Simenon regarded as finger exercises; two were what he called "half-hard" novels; and two were "hard." (Pressed by me to describe the difference between half-hard and hard, he said that the former could be read on one or two levels of meaning, while the latter could be read on numerous levels.) He would begin each of his novels with no clear idea of where the course of its action would lead him; plots spun themselves out of the proclivities of the characters, over whom Simenon exerted, or claimed to exert, no control beyond that of choosing their names out of one of the twenty or so telephone books that he kept in his study and choosing their addresses out of another. After eight, ten, or twelve days of strenuous typing, mostly between six-thirty and nine-thirty in the morning, the manuscript would be finished. He invited me to look over a number of these manuscripts, which he kept neatly in binders in his study; they were marvels of immaculate typing, with here and there a blacked-out adjective or adverb, but with few additions; it was almost the case with Simenon, as Ben Jonson quoted contemporary Elizabethan players as saying of Shakespeare, that he never blotted a line.

A contented man, then, at an unusually fortunate moment in his life? That was how I saw Simenon and how I wrote about him in the *New Yorker* Profile, which, after a few days of interviews, I sat down and dashed off, Simenon-fashion, in something less than a week. The Profile having been accepted and paid for, I called my lawyer in Norfolk and told him that I was ready to complete the Tobey Pond transaction. To my dismay, the lawyer had taken me at my word with respect to making a particularly careful search of the title and had discovered a minor cloud on it dating back through several owners to the middle of the nineteenth century. It would be some months before this cloud could be effactually removed, most of the parties involved being long since dead. Irritating as the result of his obeying my orders proved to be, the Gills were in possession of the camp on Tobey Pond by early summer. We invited the Simenons *en famille*—that is, with the children and Boule, though without the ever-invisible first Mrs. Simenon—to have a picnic with us at the camp. I toasted Simenon for having made it possible for my family to experience, I hoped for many generations, the joys of that unlooked-for acquisition.

Two or three years passed. Depending on the season, Simenon and I would have drinks together in the country or in New York City, or we would encounter each other at cocktail and dinner parties. From time to time, I would hear stories about him from friends we had in common. One of his publishers told me, for example, of how Simenon had approached him on a delicate matter: that of giving Marc the Christmas present he had set his heart upon. How quickly the young grow up! For it turned out that Marc was now in his teens and that, in the immemorial tradition of like father, like son, what Marc wished for Christmas was a first visit to a prostitute. Simenon asked the publisher to recommend a house of ill repute in New York City, which the publisher was at first unable to do. Canvassing his colleagues, he learned that the Hotel Great Northern, on West Fifty-seventh Street (long since demolished to make way for the Parker Meridien Hotel), was said to be a comparatively attractive—or, rather, a comparatively unhazardous—place in which to pick up a prostitute. Shortly before Christmas, Simenon visited the hotel, chose a companion, found her satisfactory, and arranged with her a paid-in-advance assignation for his beloved Marc.

Simenon had said of the Lakeville house that it was the twenty-sixth he had lived in and that he counted on its being his last. "I have put down roots," he said to me once, stamping his foot on the ground and then pretending to be unable to lift it. But soon enough and for no reason that he was able to confess to at the time, he abandoned those roots and moved his household back to Europe. By then, a daughter, Marie-Georges (always known by the affectionate diminutive Marie-Jo), had been born; their last child, a son whom they christened Pierre, would be born in Switzerland in 1959. Thirty years later, in his *Intimate Memoirs*, Simenon wrote that he was still unable to explain the decision, except as a manifestation of the restlessness that was as integral to his nature as the equally strong desire to stop being restless. The Simenons moved first to a series of rented houses in the south of France, then to a rented château in Switzerland, and afterwards to a house designed largely by Simenon himself, set in a high meadow overlooking Lac Leman. It was the first house he had ever built and he took great pride in it. Not for the first time and not for the last, he was sure that he had found a place where he would be content to spend the rest of his life.

Of course, it was not to be so. Moreover, the family idyll that he had depicted so convincingly for me in Lakeville had been riddled with falsehoods—with those necessary falsehoods, Simenon would perhaps say, by means of which he had hoped to preserve a marriage that was even at that stage showing signs of disintegration. For according to the anguished *Intimate Memoirs*, which he wrote in his late seventies, Denyse Simenon in Lakeville was far from being the demure young matron who sat across from me at table and worshipfully regarded her lord and master. On the contrary, she was even then beginning that downward path which led her to grow ever more irrational, ever more impetuously tyrannical in the management of the household and of Simenon's business affairs. According to Simenon, she had slept with many men before marrying him, and soon after their marriage she indicated to him that she expected to share with him, if it amused her to do so, whatever sexual adventures he might happen to embark upon with other women. She would make love to him less and less. When he requested it, she consented to perform her "duties" grudgingly; on at least one occasion, she insisted upon performing them on a couch in her office, in the presence of an astonished and abashed secretary.

In the wreckage of a marriage, there is always much to quarrel over, and the temptation grows to conduct these quarrels in public. More and more readily as the years passed, the Simenons came to accuse each other of being mad. Meanwhile, Simenon's favorite child, Marie-Jo, gave increasing signs in adolescence and young womanhood of being emotionally disturbed on a level far more serious than that of her quarreling parents. Pretty, intelligent, and affectionate, from her earliest years she had doted extravagantly upon Simenon and he upon her. At the age of eight, she had pleaded with him to buy her a gold wedding ring, which she wore ever after. In *Intimate Memoirs*, Simenon confesses that he and she were both aware of the weight of meaning that the ring symbolized. It appears that never for a moment throughout her life did she wish to be anything other than his wife, his mistress, his consort. When in her late teens and early twenties she took lovers, they were always older men, surrogates for Simenon, and they were always bound to prove disappointing. She saw many psychiatrists, spent much time in clinics, sought a life of her own in Paris, in an apartment that Simenon provided for her. Meanwhile, he was living in a small house that he had acquired in Lausanne. With him was the latest and probably the last of his mistresses, whose presence, though Marie-Jo begrudged it, she saw as being indispensable to Simenon in old age.

Several times, Marie-Jo sought to commit suicide, perhaps always with the intention of failing—with the hope, common among so many would-be suicides, of being lifted up onto the threshold of a new and happy life through that failure. At last, in 1978, alone in her Paris apartment and after having written Simenon a long farewell letter, she succeeded in killing herself with a bullet in the heart. Simenon begins his *Intimate Memoirs* with a characteristically blunt account of the death:

> My tiny little girl,
>
> I know that you are dead, and yet this is not the first time I am writing you. You would have liked to go out quietly, without disturbing a soul. But your death touched off legal and other mechanisms, so that even now lawyers and counselors are trying to work out the problems created by your mother's obstinacy, which may sooner or later have to be settled in court.
>
> Our friend Dr. Jean Martinon, of Cannes, whom you were supposed to speak to by phone, was the one who gave the alarm. Martinon called over and over again, and finally found that the line had been disconnected. He called Marc, the one of your brothers who lives closest to Paris. Marc and Mylène rushed to the Champs-Elyées and found the door to your apartment locked from the inside. The concierge did not have a duplicate key, so they had to call the police, who came right away and got a locksmith.
>
> Your apartment was impeccably orderly and clean, as if, before leaving, you had given it a thorough going-over, including laundering and ironing your clothes and linens. Everything was in its place. And you lay on the bed, with a small red hole in your chest.

For what are asserted to be the recollections of a heartbroken parent, not the beginning one might have expected! At once sentimental and hard-boiled, the sentences are certainly as intimate as the title of the book has promised; indeed, they manifest a degree of intimacy greater than most readers may be ready to share. The contrast in feeling between "my tiny little girl" and "small red hole in your chest" is so shocking that for a moment we are tempted to put the book aside, as telling us more than we have any right to know. But Simenon appears so eager to tell the truth at any cost that we suppress this immediate, conventional response to his words and, however uneasily, read on. And in doing so we come to see that the passage isn't simply the cry of a grieving father but is, rather, the cunningly calculated opening passage of an ambitious work of art.

We perceive, in short, that despite the subject matter, Simenon's intention is an impersonal, aesthetic one: first of all, and above all, to fashion a story that will hold us spellbound. Glancing over the passage for a second time, we assume that this must be why he has chosen the old-fashioned epistolary form—to draw us into the heart of his story by making us participants in the ancient pleasure of reading other people's letters. And so tempting do we find this opportunity (forbidden to us in real life) that few of us may notice the oddity of the fact that in his very first letter Simenon is addressing a dead person, who cannot read what we are reading. Nor do we trouble to observe how certain necessary information is conveyed to us that would not have needed to be conveyed to Marie-Jo—for example, that Marc was "the one of your brothers who lives closest to Paris."

As the book proceeds, the epistolary form grows more and more diffuse and implausible, threatening from time to time to disappear altogether; now he is writing only to Marie-Jo, now only to Marc, and now he is writing to all four children simultaneously. There are passages, especially when he is recounting certain sexual adventures, that few fathers would be likely to burden their children with knowledge of. Though he claims again and again that the chief purpose of the book is to bring Marie-Jo back to life and in doing so to justify and give dignity to her struggle to achieve a place in the world, plainly it is also his purpose to justify and give dignity to the struggle that *he* has waged in the course of achieving a place for himself in the world—a struggle not vain, like hers, but phenomenally successful. It is he who is the hero of the book—a hero who in the traditional mode of all heroes in fiction passes from one perilous ordeal to the next. These ordeals happen to consist of bruising domestic encounters of a particularly sordid and disagreeable nature, but no matter; it is the incomparable narrative skill of the storyteller that lures us on and provides us with what we half long for and half fear: those blows in the face that are characteristic of a true simenon and that Simenon used to tell me long ago, during our walks and talks in Lakeville, were the primary purpose of all his writings.

Bernard Rudofsky

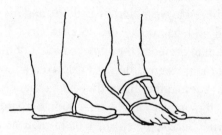

A PENALTY that one pays for living in any large city (and especially for living in New York, as the largest city in the country) is how hard one finds it to keep in touch with friends. The difficulty is compounded in the case of friends who are of a naturally fugitive disposition—friends who come and go without warning, vanishing without a trace for a year or so and then telephoning to suggest lunch next day at the usual place. To which the unhappy response is nearly always that one already has a luncheon engagement, and not only for tomorrow but for every other day of what is, after all, a particularly busy week (every week in New York being a particularly busy week). Moreover, the usual place is no longer quite so usual, it having also vanished without a trace some months earlier.

Again and again, this was a difficulty I confronted and was unable to resolve with my friend Bernard Rudofsky, a Vienna-born architect, designer, author, and tireless voyager to far places. Once every few years, we would happen to meet—collide would be a more accurate term—at a museum or art gallery or at the house of some friend that we had in common and we would embrace and bring our personal histories up to date and vow that henceforth we would be sure to keep in close touch, come hell or high water; and that would be the last of Bernard until the next unlooked-for stroke of good fortune brought us into collision.

I call Bernard a tireless voyager; he was also a tireless backer of lost causes. The fact is, Bernard had a genius for seeking out and championing notions that were absolutely certain to fail, and he continued to exploit this singular gift without interruption for half a century or more. The first time that I ever encountered him, he was curating an exhibit at the Museum of Modern Art that was intended as an all-out attack on the idiocy of twentieth-century dress. The Rudofsky thesis was that if one felt obliged to wear clothes at all (he and his wife always preferred going naked and habitually did so *chez eux*), they should have a natural relation to the body they covered and not merely conceal and/or falsify it. At the museum, Bernard displayed a few samples of such clothing, and as I remember them they had a vaguely Hollywood-Grecian look. Alas, they never caught on—poor Bernard had made the mistake of applying reason to an area of human activity that is nearly always deliberately, exuberantly unreasonable.

Nothing daunted, Bernard chose for his second crusade the equally difficult problem of shoes, arguing that they should follow the shape of the foot and that the closest approach to ideal footwear was sandals—as it happened, Rudofsky-designed sandals. As an extension and refinement of his plans for preserving the comfort and attractiveness of feet, Bernard argued in favor of having floors that went unevenly up and down. "The flat floor," he pontificated, "is the product of a craving on the part of our ancestors for something their primitive technology denied them. Since we can attain flatness with ease, it no longer deserves our respect." The Rudofsky floor of the future would not only be wavy but would also possess a variety of interesting textures, which our toes, being prehensile, would take a voluptuous pleasure in seizing. The foot-floor crusade failed as well, and the shoes that men and women wear today are every bit as preposterously at odds with their feet as the silliest shoes of a century ago, while our floors continue to be tiresomely level, smooth, and unvoluptuous. From the problem of floors it was but a hop, skip, and a jump to the problem of roads, which Bernard attacked in still another exhibit at the Museum of Modern Art. Being a highly sensible protest against the introduction into our countryside of multiple-laned expressways and interstate highways, it was bound to fall flat on its face.

"Why should we allow these great snakes and octopuses to stretch out in every direction, swallowing up our beautiful living landscape?" Bernard would ask, knowing full well that every red-blooded American car owner would reply at once, "Why should we not?" If somebody dared to argue that at least the superhighways were impressive feats of engineering virtuosity, Bernard would direct a withering glance at him out of his gray-green eyes and give the Gothic wishbone curve of his mustache a powerful tug, which for him in his gentleness evidently took the place of drawing a sword from its scabbard. "No, no! All those cloverleaves and double-decked crossovers are extremely simple," he would say. "What looks like ingenuity to the layman is merely a multiplication of unimaginative solutions. A stubborn child could do as much. Real ingenuity is often hard to detect. Take the ancients and the way they solved some of their problems. Heavy carts, with wide axles, had to stop at the outskirts of Pompeii, because only narrow-axled chariots could fit between the stepping stones at the street corners inside the city. Now, that is *real* ingenuity and that is how we ought to solve the traffic problem in our great cities. Stop all the private cars in the suburbs and permit only rapid transit within the city's boundaries!"

To Bernard's disappointment, if not to his surprise, America's great cities steadfastly refused to adopt the Pompeiian solution; superhighways proliferated across our hills and valleys and the number of cars inside our cities increased with every passing year. As an architect, Bernard enjoyed no better luck than he had enjoyed as a city planner and dress designer. In his youth, he had designed a couple of houses that achieved at least a temporary fame by being featured in architectural magazines and books; one was his own vacation cottage on the Mediterranean island of Ischia and the other was a very large house in Rio de Janeiro, where a number of walled gardens provided outdoor "rooms" as snug and livable as the indoor rooms that opened out into them. But Bernard had no intention of devoting his career to the creation of pretty lodgings for himself or for wealthy clients; like all backers of lost causes, he wished to help others, whether they wished to be helped or not.

Bernard deplored the sorry record of the architectural profession with respect to the design and construction of housing fit for the tens of millions of people in need of it throughout the world. He was a champion of what he dubbed "architecture without architects," citing as his ideal habitations the little whitewashed houses that climbed in higgledy-piggledy disarray up the steep hillsides of villages in the Greek islands and in the boot of Italy. The more he deplored something, the more eloquent he became. "In many places in the Mediterranean," he would say, with the urgency of an Old Testament prophet, "people whitewash the streets in front of their houses along with their houses, because the streets are their living rooms—they spend more time in them than they do indoors. And they keep the streets immaculately clean. But when they leave those cities and come to America, they forget the good manners of the culture they were brought up in. They start throwing refuse into our dark, ugly streets, making them all the darker and uglier, to say nothing of all the more unhealthy. Overnight they become 100 percent Americans, living in a squalor of their own invention. Shame on them! Shame on all of us!"

And off he would go to some unknown village in a remote corner of the planet and lie low there for a year or two, licking the wounds inflicted by his latest defeat and preparing a fresh assault upon the obdurate irrationality of the human race.

Nigel Nicolson

SOME YEARS AGO, my friend Nigel Nicolson boldly made public the secret—and scandalous—materials out of which the following sketch is composed. In doing so, he earned a reputation wholly at odds with what he had expected: that of being an authority on successful marriages. As one of his children said to him at the time, with laughter and affection, "Father, how funny! You of all people!"

The time of the sketch is 1920 and the place is England. In the depths of the Kentish countryside, a young woman is lying prone upon a patch of green bracken bright with little yellow and magenta wildflowers whose names she doesn't know. (This is curious and worth remarking as an initial mystery, because she is an expert gardener.) It is a perfect midsummer's afternoon. Behind her is a hazel wood, before her a wheat field. A breeze makes the ripe ears of wheat rustle like silk; there is no other sound save that of her pencil racing across the pages of a notebook. She has been, she writes, in a black temper all day, but the sunlight and the shadows of the ears of wheat dancing over her words as she sets them down have helped soothe her blackness. She mentions that her personality has yielded to that of Demeter, goddess of the fruitful soil. Nevertheless, she dares not obliterate herself entirely. She must go on writing, because for her it is the means of keeping mind and body whole. She is passionately in love with a woman, and the pain of guilt and the greater pain of remorse have prompted her to lie here facedown upon the earth, pouring out a confession.

The speed with which her pencil covers the cheap paper is a sign of how useful a therapy words are to her. It is also a sign that Clio, Muse of history, hovers as insistently upon the shimmering air as Demeter does. For in attempting to scrutinize her life for her soul's sake, the young woman is attempting the further feat of leaving behind an accurate report of that scrutiny. Though she writes in secret and though what she writes will remain a secret until her death, over forty years later, she pursues the agonizing truth almost as much for others as for herself. She counts on having readers in the future, to whom she offers the assurance that nothing she tells them will have been arranged for the purpose of improving it as art, much less for the purpose of protecting her reputation. ("I hate writing this, but I must, I must. When I began this I swore I would shirk nothing.") She sees herself as unquestionably a very strange person indeed, and yet she suspects that she may be less rare in her strangeness than the conventions of the time have led her and her family and friends to suppose. She feels what amounts to a duty to stand up and bear witness; at the very least she will serve as an example to all those who in later generations find themselves implicated in sexual and domestic misadventures as extreme and seemingly as insoluble as her own. Whoever her readers may prove to be—and she might not have liked us much in real life: she was a fearful snob—she will offer them from the grave Whitman's grand and consolatory "I am the man, I suffer'd, I was there." And the gender of that "I" will give her, in the grave, a rueful satisfaction; she had always longed to be a man.

It is an irony of which the young woman was herself well aware that if we had encountered her for the first time on that drowsy afternoon in Kent, we would have assumed that she was the most fortunate and least troubled of mortals. She was twenty-eight, tall, full-breasted, and good-looking in the horse-faced way that is a sign of breeding in England. She had a handsome, wellborn husband, who was beginning to make a name for himself as a diplomat. He was tenderhearted and witty and, like her, a gifted writer. They were the parents of two pretty and amiable little boys. She was the descendant of a family mentioned in the Domesday Book; in *Burke's Peerage* the family tree had long since come to be impenetrably pleached with dukes, earls, and lords. One of her ancestors had written the first English tragedy; another had helped to lose the battle of Saratoga. She had been brought up at Knole, an ancient, enchanting country house—one that was said to contain as many rooms as there are days in a year and that even in her childhood was the largest house in England remaining in private hands.

Her mother was celebrated for her beauty and vivacity and deserved to be celebrated for getting whatever she wanted; she was the illegitimate daughter of a Spanish dancer and a milord, and as a virgin in her early twenties was proposed to by no less a person than the president of the United States. Instead, she took care to marry her father's nephew and heir, which is to say her first cousin, and thus became a lady in her own right. Later, she accepted as an admirer a jolly fat man of immeasurable wealth, who left her a fortune upon his death. It was thanks to an allowance from the income of that fortune that the young woman by the wheat field could afford to live in a charming old house (remodeled by a world-famous architect, also to be numbered among her mother's admirers), there to write and garden and pour tea and be the very model of an imperturbable, countrified English aristocrat.

Now, everything in the preceding paragraphs is true, and it is not the truth. For the young woman, whose maiden name was Vita Sackville-West and who with reluctance consented in marriage to be known as Mrs. Harold Nicolson (and later, with greater reluctance, consented glaringly to be addressed as Lady Nicolson), had two aspects to her nature, and she was far from considering them of equal importance. A basilisk crouched in the country matron, heraldic, unbeautiful, with poison in its sting. On being reproached for having a Dr.-Jekyll-and-Mr.-Hyde personality, she at once agreed. "That is the whole crux of the matter," she wrote in the notebook, "and I see now that my whole curse has been a duality with which I was too weak and too self-indulgent to struggle." Not so, though it may have been necessary for her to insist on it for the time being—the repeated "whole" is significant—in order to proceed to the next stage in her confession. For it is obvious that she chose not to struggle against her duality; if she *had* struggled, she would surely have ended by embracing Mr. Hyde and abandoning Dr. Jekyll. Every word of the notebook lets us measure how much she preferred the harsh, aggressive, masculine Hyde in her to the conventionally nice and feminine Jekyll. Nor need we take seriously her reference to a curse—she was a romantic, to whom the notion of damnation on some high Faustian level was very attractive. In her imagination, she saw herself as a swashbuckling seventeenth-century swordsman-brigand of noble birth, who simultaneously abuses and protects women; and here she was in tender green Kent, a decorous young mother writing, so her family hoped, nothing more serious than poems. The anomaly of her divided selves fascinated her, and it was partly in order to be able to face both selves with candor that she set about filling her notebook. She called it an autobiography, but as such it would be merely a captivating, inadequate précis of a fraction of a life. Instead, it is an account of the one great love affair of her life, in which she dared to be as reckless and passionate and cruel and unprincipled as the fierce male Sackville in her was always urging her to be. It is as close to a cry from the heart as anybody writing in English in our time has come, and it is a cry that, once heard, is not likely ever to be forgotten.

The notebook, which contains perhaps twenty-five thousand words, was the occasion for—but only a portion of—a much longer book, called *Portrait of a Marriage*, written by Nigel Nicolson and published in 1973. Nigel is one of the two sons of Vita Sackville-West and Harold Nicolson; the other son is the art historian Ben Nicolson. Nigel has enjoyed a long career as an editor and publisher and has written several books, of which the most recent is *Journey to Dodge City*, an account, in the form of an exchange of letters between his son Adam and himself, of social conditions in the United States as they observed them in the course of separately crossing the country by car in 1986 (the father starting in Florida, the son in California, and meeting by prior arrangement in Dodge City, Kansas).

Long ago, Nigel and I became acquainted through friends in New York that we had in common—Dorothy and Daniel H. Silberberg. The Silberbergs lived in a big limestone-fronted house at 5 East Eighty-first Street, just off Fifth Avenue, and in a tile-roofed tawny stucco villa looking out over the Mediterranean in St. Tropez. They were often in England and therefore able to keep in close touch with the Nicolsons, living at Sissinghurst Castle, in Kent. Nigel, his wife Pippa, and their children (the eldest of whom was Dan's goddaughter) were to me images shining at an elusive distance, in the mirror of the Silberbergs' enviable transatlantic travels, but sometimes the Nicolsons were in New York and sometimes I shared a summer holiday with them at the Silberbergs' villa, which Dorothy had ingeniously fashioned out of two or three fishermen's houses on what were said to be the ruins of the port's ancient

Roman ramparts. On these holiday occasions, the Nicolsons seemed as conventional an upper-class English family as one could hope to encounter, and yet they were nothing of the kind. For how could Nigel, as the son of Vita Sackville-West and Harold Nicolson, have been a conventional husband?

It was characteristic of Nigel to have done nothing to prepare Pippa for the bizarre situation at Sissinghurst into which he had introduced her as a bride. A small, pretty woman, Pippa looked all the more diminutive next to Nigel, who had inherited his mother's height and rough-hewn good looks. She had been brought up in a state of sequestered Victorian unworldliness—a predictable consequence of her being a great-granddaughter of Alfred Lord Tennyson on one side of the family and of William Ewart Gladstone on the other—and she was radically unready for what she beheld at Sissinghurst: her mother-in-law and father-in-law carrying on openly in what was to her a wholly unnatural and reprehensible fashion: each in pursuit of lovers of their own sex.

Over the years, it became plain to their friends that Pippa and Nigel were unhappy in their marriage: he and his brother were more nearly their parents' children than they had supposed they were, or had wished to be. The Nicolsons were divorced; later, I heard that Pippa had married a well-known British builder and member of parliament, Sir Robert McIlwaine, but beyond that I heard nothing. Dorothy Silberberg died, and Dan, unwilling to visit the villa without her, sold it to a French family and retreated to the house on Eighty-first Street. There without complaint he awaited the day when he, too, as unobtrusively as possible, would slip away.

What of the sketch with which I began this chapter and those secret materials out of which Nigel created his book? The information the notebook contained had been almost as great a surprise to him as it would be, upon publication, to the world at large. In *Portrait*, he takes care to describe the circumstances under which he discovered the notebook, and it is just here that we are reminded of a well-plotted detective story. For upon his mother's death in 1962, he was obliged as her executor to go through all the papers she had stored up and filed away in her sitting room in the tower of Sissinghurst Castle, where the Nicolsons had lived since 1930. Nigel had entered his mother's sitting room only half a dozen times in thirty years; as a son, an executor, and a writer, he found much to occupy him there. From it was to emerge, thanks to a trifling accident, *Portrait*, which became an immediate best-seller. The accident was that of Nigel's having stumbled across a locked Gladstone bag in a little turret room off his mother's sitting room. (One thinks of the croquet box at Malahide castle; one thinks, too, of Miss Prism and *her* Gladstone bag.) He could tell that the bag held some-thing—his guess was a tiara. Finding no key, he cut the leather from around the lock of the bag and opened it. Inside was the notebook. In his introduction to *Portrait*, Nigel writes, "I had long known the barest outlines of the story (but not from her) and here was every detail of it, written with scarcely an erasure or correction at a moment when the wound was still fresh and painful."

Nicolson had plenty of time to ponder the question of whether to publish the notebook. He had no doubts as to his mother's intentions; there was ample internal evidence that she wished it to be published sooner or later. But other parties to the great affair were still alive in 1962. Harold Nicolson lived on until 1968, and Vita's lover, the sensual, irresistible Violet Trefusis, died only in 1972. By then, Nicolson was certain that the notebook should be published precisely as his mother had written it, accompanied by a text that would give enough background to render the often jumbled comings and goings in the notebook comprehensible to a contemporary audience. Moreover, as he writes: "To present the autobiography unexplained and without its sequel would do my parents less than justice, for it was written in the eighth year of a marriage that lasted forty-nine."

Portrait consists of five chapters—two devoted to the notebook and three to the background of the affair and its prolonged domestic sequel. And what an implausible marriage the Nicolsons prove to have had! (As virginal Pippa had discovered upon her arrival at Sissinghurst with her uncommunicative bridegroom.) For Vita, who had had at least one affair with a woman before she fell in love with Violet, went on to take many other lovers, including Virginia Woolf; and Harold, who had had male lovers before he married Vita, continued to have male lovers after their marriage. Harold appears not to have been very energetic with either sex; told his sons that the sexual side of a relationship between men and women was unlikely to last more than a year or so. He had a number of singular notions of this sort, for which the only evidence was his own life. Nigel and Ben grew up to observe their father and mother busying themselves with their separate love affairs; at the same time, they observed a devotion between their parents seemingly stronger and more nourishing than that between most of the conventionally married heterosexual couples they knew. It was puzzling. It made the boys long to ask questions that the parents would probably be disinclined to answer; the very rooms of Sissinghurst were designed, in a jumble of narrow halls and pinched stairways, so as to discourage an exchange of intimacies.

When the time came for the sons to marry, they found that their parents' good fortune in marriage was not to be theirs—". . . nature having endowed us," Nicolson writes in *Portrait*, "with a greater talent for friendship than for cohabitation, for fatherhood than for wedlock." This was to put discreetly what the Silberbergs and other friends of Nigel's would put more bluntly: "Nigel had no business marrying." For the parents' marriage could serve no one as a model; certainly it had little to do with the ancient Church of England vows that young Vita and Harold had uttered in the chapel at Knole, the Sackvilles' sprawling village of a house. The marriage was, in short, an inimitable freak. "My parents' love for each other survived all further threats to it," Nicolson states, "and made out of a nonmarriage a marriage that succeeded beyond their dreams." Mostly, Nicolson keeps at a distance from the scandalous revelations in his book; when his guard drops, as it does in the sentence just quoted, he betrays his personal uneasiness by becoming sentimental. The uncharacteristic women's-magazine prose makes one suspect that the marriage survived and prospered at a cost higher than Nicolson has yet been willing to admit. It may also measure the degree to which he feels responsible for the fact that his own marriage failed to survive and prosper.

I visited Nigel at Sissinghurst when *Portrait of a Marriage* was at the top of the British best-seller lists. Nigel took me round the castle, including in the tour his mother's sitting room and the little adjacent turret room in which the Gladstone bag had been found, and the famous gardens that his mother had designed, planted, tended, and written about and that are now among the leading tourist attractions in England. Afterward, I had dinner with Nigel and his children. We talked about the popularity of *Portrait* and, with increasing hilarity, about the fact that letters were now streaming in upon Sissinghurst from correspondents all over the world, begging Nigel to advise them about how to improve their marriages. Almost overnight, he had come to be seen as an ideal counselor on a subject that he was totally unfit to discuss. It was at that moment that his daughter exclaimed, "Father, how funny! You of all people!"

By way of reply, Nigel threw up his hands and stammered that life was indeed full of wonders: wonders of obtuseness, along with wonders of perception. Had his correspondents not read what he had been at such pains to say about his failure as a husband? As well as—he glanced round inquiringly at his children—his success, dared he say it in their presence, as a father? Upon which his children broke into the applause for which he had been waiting. In family life nothing fortunate is probable. That evening, in the candlelight at Sissinghurst, Nigel had much to be grateful for.

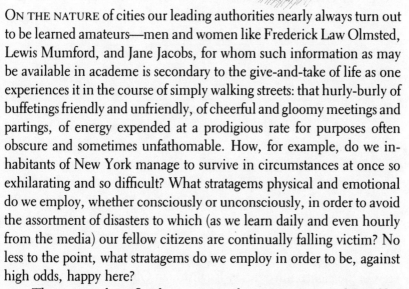

ON THE NATURE of cities our leading authorities nearly always turn out
to be learned amateurs—men and women like Frederick Law Olmsted,
Lewis Mumford, and Jane Jacobs, for whom such information as may
be available in academe is secondary to the give-and-take of life as one
experiences it in the course of simply walking streets: that hurly-burly of
buffetings friendly and unfriendly, of cheerful and gloomy meetings and
partings, of energy expended at a prodigious rate for purposes often
obscure and sometimes unfathomable. How, for example, do we inhabitants of New York manage to survive in circumstances at once so
exhilarating and so difficult? What stratagems physical and emotional
do we employ, whether consciously or unconsciously, in order to avoid
the assortment of disasters to which (as we learn daily and even hourly
from the media) our fellow citizens are continually falling victim? No
less to the point, what stratagems do we employ in order to be, against
high odds, happy here?

The person best fitted to answer these questions is himself a
seasoned New Yorker who for a large portion of his seventy-odd years
has been subjecting the city to a scrutiny as close as that to which
Thoreau—still another learned amateur—subjected Walden Pond and
its environs. His name is William H. Whyte, and his equivalent of
Thoreau's cabin is a narrow, high-stooped brownstone in the East

Nineties. The middle initial of Whyte's name stands for Hollingsworth, which has led to his being universally addressed by the affectionate diminutive of "Holly." When I first began hearing about Whyte, I was under the misapprehension that there were two separate and distinct Whytes—one named William and the other named Holly—and it was only as our acquaintanceship ripened into friendship that the single individual emerged. We have been friends and colleagues now for upward of forty years, and such is Holly's indubitable singularity that I marvel at my ever having supposed that there could be more than one of him. The Christmas merriment implicit in the name Holly is much added to by the fact that Holly's wife is named Jenny Bell; when we speak of Holly and Jenny Bell together, snow begins to fall in our minds.

Born in West Chester, Pennsylvania, educated at Princeton, and for many years a writer and editor at *Fortune*, in his comparative youth Whyte achieved a large measure of fame by writing a best-seller called *The Organization Man*—a pioneering study of American business executives. Over the past sixteen years or so, with the help of grants from one or another of several philanthropic foundations, Whyte has been at work in scores of different neighborhoods not only in this city but in other cities throughout the country and abroad, analyzing the way people use parks, plazas, streets, street furniture, sidewalks, and even curbstones and window ledges. He has earned a high place in the ranks of learned amateurs; indeed, he is not to be pigeonholed as this or that sort of professional only because no single profession can be said to contain him.

The fruit of Whyte's many years of labor was published a couple of years ago, in a book entitled *City*. Few books with a title so brief have succeeded in encompassing so much. The first thing to be said about the book is that it's a surprisingly sunny one. Much of the information that it imparts is so dire that one would expect the author to be a quintessential Gloomy Gus. Instead, Whyte appears to have embraced the point of view of the eighteenth-century Englishman Oliver Edwards, who said, "I have tried too in my time to be a philosopher; but I don't know how, cheerfulness was always breaking in." It is plain that Whyte prefers hard facts to philosophy, and the cheerfulness with which he adduces hard facts and draws hard conclusions from them often, and most welcomely, distills itself into wit; he even goes so far as to makes jokes, which unlike most New York City jokes do not amount to a species of gallows humor.

Whyte finds much to deplore in the mutilation of our contemporary urban fabric by blank-walled megastructures, by elevated walkways, by the rise of suburbia and its inhumanly vast shopping malls. He is well aware that the helter-skelter linear sprawl characteristic of so many contemporary American cities is a consequence of forces that are not specifically urban in nature. Chief among these forces is the automobile, which has come to dominate so many aspects of city planning but is by no means indispensable to cities; one could imagine with pleasure cities in which automobiles were banned and some form of subsidized rapid transit took their place. Automobiles tend to spin us away from the center, though in Whyte's view mankind is instinctively centripetal. He believes that a desire for concentration and not scatteration has been characteristic of city-dwellers since cities began; historically, they have always preferred the disorder of an overcrowded Middle Eastern bazaar to the clinical orderliness of the broad boulevards of Brasília. Indeed, to Whyte there can scarcely be such a thing as urban overcrowding; in most cases, he says, our streets suffer not from having too many people in them but too few.

It is Whyte's contention that we tamper at our peril with the age-old chaos of unpremeditated street activity. A street—any street—is, in effect, a room, and the more we live in it the more intensely roomlike it becomes and the more we ourselves become members of an unacknowledged (and not necessarily unquarrelsome) family. We may not know each other but we are far from being strangers. Napoleon is said to have called the Piazza San Marco, in Venice, the finest drawing room in Europe. By Whyte's reckoning, the plaza in front of the Seagram building, on Park Avenue between Fifty-first Street and Fifty-second Street, is the finest drawing room in New York, especially during the hot summer months, when at noontime picnickers from the neighboring office buildings are not above slipping off their shoes and stockings and wading barefoot in the large, shallow pools that occupy the plaza's outer corners.

Another favorite gathering place of New Yorkers is the clamorous, vendor-filled block of Lexington Avenue between Fifty-eighth Street and Fifty-ninth Street. Having sedulously kept count of pedestrian traffic on both sides of Lexington Avenue between the two side streets, Whyte has discovered that, contrary to what an armchair theorist might have predicted, New Yorkers *prefer* the busier east side of the avenue to the less busy west side; unreasonably, we go out of our way to join the family hubbub and so add to its size and incoherence.

Whyte is a tall man with a beaked nose, a lantern jaw, and the bent shoulders of the most sedentary of bookworms. He has the look of a professor who has spent his life in a library carrel several sizes too small for him, but this appearance is deceptive; in fact, he is an outdoorsman, a sort of urban Daniel Boone, who explores our streets and byways in all weathers and at all seasons of the year, accumulating data by means of still cameras, movie cameras, tape recorders, and pad and pencil. Over the years, he has acquainted himself with an extraordinary variety of street people and has become, in the eyes of his fellow citizens, a street person himself—an eccentric among a host of other eccentrics, including such star turns as Mr. Magoo, a plump, bespectacled man in his seventies, who takes it upon himself to direct traffic at busy intersections, especially on Fifth Avenue, and Tambourine Woman, who attracts the attention of passersby with vigorous shakings of a tambourine and who, in the course of the extended harangue that follows, confides that she was once the "little girlfriend" of Franklin Delano Roosevelt.

Again and again, Whyte is able to demonstrate that the people most exercised over the threatened death of the center of a city are the ones who unwittingly encourage that death. To merchants, street vendors are an illegal nuisance, whom the police are insufficiently eager to arrest; to Whyte, they are a harmless sign of urban vigor. As for the rest of us—we ordinary, peripatetic, anonymous New Yorkers—in our unself-conscious comings and goings he sees the richest embodiment of the benefits of the densely packed, vividly experienced street life of a great city. Unbeknownst to us, he has studied our least word and gesture and has discovered certain things about our conduct that most of us would be likely to deny on the grounds of their being totally unreasonable and therefore totally unlike us. After all, who knows us better than we know ourselves? The answer is that Whyte does, having monitored us with the help of time-lapse cameras and other precise instruments over many years; and what bizarre creatures we turn out to be! For example, how we encounter acquaintances on a busy street and chat with them follows a pattern that defies common sense; take our goodbyes, especially those that Whyte calls "failed goodbyes":

> Most goodbyes are brief: a fast "ciao," "take care," a wave, and they're off. But a number are protracted, particularly so when they are an extension of a failed goodbye . . . If people go through the motions of a goodbye and stop short at the point of consummation, a momentum is set up that can lead to progressively more emphatic goodbyes, up to the final resolving goodbye. It is fascinating to watch these three- and four-wave goodbyes and try to distinguish the real goodbye from the false ones. Don't be fooled by the glance at the watch. It is only premonitory. I have a wonderful film record of two men gripped in indecision in front of Saks Fifth Avenue. They just can't bring themselves to part. There are several rounds of goodbyes and looks at the watch, but it's not until a third party comes along that they finally break out of their impasse.

The question to which Whyte returns again and again is whether our center and the centers of other great American cities can hold. Having conscientiously marshaled all the evidence against the likelihood of their being able to do so, Whyte nevertheless dares to suggest that they will. His evidence in behalf of this suggestion is based upon an awesome mountain of paperwork—some of his statistics have already led to major improvements in the statutes that regulate the use of our light and air—but I suspect that far more important to Whyte than his paperwork is the intuition he has arrived at concerning the nature of the city's inhabitants. What he appears to find most admirable in us New Yorkers is our primordial, ineradicable animal bent for clustering. Plainly, he is confident of our ability to survive almost any amount of discomfort and even of danger so long as we can jam ourselves together in a strictly defined space. The rich as well as the poor are guided by this instinct. Whyte notes of Madison Avenue in the Sixties and Seventies that it is probably the finest specialty-shop street in the world; what does it consist of? The most commonplace of elements—a narrow thoroughfare whose basic module is the five-story brownstone, twenty feet wide, with ten brownstones to a block. Like Lexington Avenue, it has the advantage of being double-decked: shops and restaurants occupy the second floors of many of the brownstones as well as the ground floors.

Eagerly, customers climb the steep and narrow steps to the second floor, though if they were to find themselves at a two-story suburban shopping mall they would no doubt be looking about for an escalator.

With undisguised satisfaction, Whyte reports that many of the big companies that moved out of New York City into the quite distant suburbs in the fifties, sixties, and seventies are not as happy in the woods as they had counted on being. Employees find it lonely there among the chipmunks and woodchucks and are bored to encounter only one another in the company cafeterias, the company gymnasiums, the company grounds. The reasons that companies have given for moving out of New York are filled with what Whyte calls "self-serving pieties"; in 1976, Union Carbide, leaving an ideal location on Park Avenue at Forty-seventh Street, said that it was moving to new headquarters near Danbury, Connecticut, ninety miles to the north, largely for the sake of "the long-term quality-of-life needs of our headquarters employees."

The company had spent two years and a considerable sum of money conducting the study that led to this decision. Says Whyte:

> It's a wonder executives keep a straight face. Life-style needs of employees? Companies don't have to spend all that money researching them. They don't have to compare area A with area B and area C. All they have to do is look in the phone directory. Where does the boss live? That is where the company is going . . . During the height of the exodus I made a location study. I plotted the moves of all the major corporations that had moved from New York to the suburbs and beyond over the previous ten years. By checking old telephone directories, street maps, and registers of executives, I plotted the home locations of the chief executive officer and his fellow top executives at the time the decision was made to move. Then I plotted the location the company moved to. The correlation: of thirty-eight corporations, thirty-one moved to a place close to the top man's home. Average distance: about eight miles by road.

Today even the executives are lonely in their remote, well-groomed country kingdoms. Close as they may be to home and to their favorite golf courses, they miss the abrasive give-and-take of the street. Whyte has been amused to discover that some companies seek to outwit the torpid benignity of country living by making use of more and more consultants—strangers who will journey out to the sticks and stir up some degree of faux-urban excitement. In the course of his researches, he interviewed the CEO of an outlying corporation; gestering toward an empty visitors' parking lot, Whyte asked the CEO what the company did about visitors. "We hire them," said the CEO.

Thanks to Whyte, we dare to suppose that the center will hold, and not only because it is in our genes to wish it to do so. We who cherish the city are grateful to Whyte for providing us with a hundred—a thousand—formal arguments for doing so. How reassuring it is to be told that one has been acting wisely when one suspects oneself of having acted foolishly! Our own eccentric street person stands before us at a private dinner party (or before the city council, or before any "do-gooding" group that is willing to listen to him), and with seemingly unabatable zest harangues and bewitches his audience—his congregation—into seeing the city with his eyes. He is a Savonarola with a difference. He threatens us not with hellfire but with happiness. We who seek to preserve the urban fabric suffer many defeats, but Holly reminds us that we achieve a few victories as well. Is it not he, after all, who has caused new laws to come into existence, guaranteeing a certain measure of sunlight and air to our narrow side streets? The preacher in him prompts him to stride back and forth, the fist of one hand pounding into the palm of the other. Hear ye! Hear ye! And it is then that, for us as for Oliver Edwards, cheerfulness breaks in.

Al Hirschfeld

THE ARTIST Al Hirschfeld is the embodiment of a pleasing paradox. He is one of the most gifted caricaturists alive, as well as one of the most celebrated. His work, published regularly in the entertainment section of the Sunday *New York Times*, is admired by hundreds of thousands of people. His drawings and lithographs are so much in demand and fetch such high prices that the New York City art gallery specializing in Hirschfelds frequently purchases full pages in the *Times* (at no telling how many tens of thousands of dollars a page) to advertise his work. Books illustrated by him are passed among his followers like the sacred relics of some ancient cult. To be a star on Broadway is to have one's name in lights, yes, but it is also, and more significantly, to be drawn by Hirschfeld. And yet this master of caricature possesses none of what one assumes to be the normal attributes of the caricaturist.

Writing of Hirschfeld some years ago, the art historian Lloyd Goodrich said, "Caricature is usually considered a negative art. The word suggests hostility and malice. It implies distortion of the truth . . ." With a historian's guarded incredulity, Goodrich went on to point out that Hirschfeld's art is neither negative, nor hostile, nor malicious, nor a distortion of the truth. On the contrary, both as an artist and as a man, Hirschfeld is affirmative, friendly, good-hearted, and honest. These qualities are of no harm to a saint, but one would expect them to prove grave handicaps to a caricaturist, whose success depends upon his calling the world's attention to the visible physical oddities of whoever sits to his pencil.

How on earth does Hirschfeld contrive to catch a well-nigh perfect likeness of a subject without giving offense? Most of us are vain and few of us are beautiful; if Hirschfeld were to make a drawing of us, he would be sure to exaggerate the nose, the eyebrows, the paunch, or the skinny legs by which our friends find it easy to recognize us, often at an unflatteringly long distance. The features that we try to ignore when we glance into a mirror or see reflected by chance in a shop window are the very ones that Hirschfeld would seize upon and make a witty point of in black and white. As an old friend of Hirschfeld's, I was sure to be caricatured by him sooner or later; my turn came when an eleemosynary organization that I had helped to found wished to honor me on the occasion of my stepping down as chairman and rightly assumed that a likeness of me by Hirschfeld would prove a welcome keepsake. To my astonishment, it wasn't my beak of a nose but my chin that struck Hirschfeld as my most salient feature. In his drawing, I am depicted holding a glass of wine on what is evidently a party occasion; I had less difficulty recognizing the wine as characteristic than I did in recognizing that sharp axe-blade of chin.

If it is often hard for a private individual to accept the truth about his appearance, think how hard it must be for all those actors, actresses, singers, dancers, directors, playwrights, and producers who make up the world of the performing arts and among whom Hirschfeld has been strolling, Venus pencil in hand, for almost sixty years! Ought they not to tremble at his approach? One might expect so, but in practice they throw their arms around him and give him a big hug. And with reason, for Hirschfeld is not only kindly by nature, he is also mad about the theatre, and no one is more eager than he that it be seen at its best, even when that best is conveyed in comic terms. A Hirschfeld drawing in the Sunday *Times* of a musical that is scheduled to open during the week to come fills the viewer of the drawing with joyous anticipation. Whatever the eventual fate of the show, Hirschfeld will have given it a rousing send-off. He will also have been as busy as a cake of ice on a hot stove, for in order to have the drawing ready for publication before the opening of the show on Broadway, Hirschfeld ordinarily has to catch the show out of town. He makes his preliminary sketches in pencil, accompanied by notes scribbled in the dark of the theatre: "Broad stripes on dancer's pants; polka-dot tie."

If need be, Hirschfeld can fall back upon what amounts to a feat of magic. In order to remain inconspicuous during the turmoil of rehearsals and run-throughs, he long ago learned to make drawings inside his pocket, with a stub of pencil on tiny scraps of paper. The show may be in trouble out of town, but no hints of distress—a director's hot temper, an actress's tears—emerge from Hirschfeld's delectable inky squiggles in the *Times*. An artist who earns the love and trust of theatre people is the keeper of many secrets. Scandals that eventually make headlines are likely to have been long known to Hirschfeld; his response to any such headlines is a raising of his formidably profuse and snowy eyebrows, which silently conveys prior knowledge, inviolable discretion, and a hint that the follies of mankind are beyond cure.

Hirschfeld's professional association with the theatre began in the 1920s, through an encounter that seemed of little importance at the time. He was already a successful artist; indeed, there has never been a time when he wasn't a success, and if there is a dark night of the soul for most practitioners of the arts, for Hirschfeld it would appear that there has always been more than enough light to draw by. He was born in St. Louis in 1903, and his artistic talent was remarked on and encouraged from the moment his little fist could grasp a crayon. His energetic mother supported a family consisting of three sons and a husband who, adored by everyone, was totally disinclined to earn a living and who took a steady job for the first time in his life at the age of seventy-five. (History books give him credit for having coined the term "senior citizen.") In his nineties, getting ready to die, he summoned the family to the hospital. He appeared to be trying to make some sort of profound deathbed statement; the family drew near, and at last he spoke. "The nurses around here," he said, "should be playing professional football."

Mrs. Hirschfeld ran a neighborhood candy store that earned sufficient money for the family's needs. An art director to whom she showed some of the young Albert's drawings advised her that she should take the boy to New York City, where opportunities for artists were far more plentiful than they were in St. Louis. No sooner said than done; the brave and adventurous Mrs. Hirschfeld packed up and the family set off by train for the unknown metropolis. On arrival, they took a streetcar to the end of the line, which was Fort George Park, at 191st Street and Saint Nicholas Avenue. Carrying with them all their possessions, they walked from block to block, until they saw a vacancy sign on the second floor of a two-family frame house on 183rd Street. The rent proved to be six dollars a month and the happy family moved in at once. There was open farmland all round them—plenty of space for the father and boys to play baseball while the valorous Mrs. Hirschfeld went to work as a saleslady for Wertheimer's department store.

Hirschfeld remembers his childhood as idyllic. He drifted through school, taking occasional lessons in drawing and sculpture at the National Academy of Design, and at seventeen he got a job drawing advertisements for the Goldwyn Studios. (In those days, the movie industry was located mostly in New York.) Hirschfeld's pay was four dollars a week. Within a year, his fortunes skyrocketed; he was given a similar job at Warner Brothers, at a salary of seventy-five dollars a week, and at eighteen he was appointed art director of Selznick Pictures. Soon enough—after all, this was the Jazz Age, the Age of Flaming Youth—he was driving a Stutz Bearcat, frequenting fashionable speakeasies, and manifesting other characteristics of having hit the big time. (By then, his parents were living in a comfortable apartment at 177th Street and Saint Nicholas Avenue, where they were to remain for the next fifty-five years.)

One evening in the twenties, Hirschfeld attended a play that starred the French actor Sacha Guitry. In the course of the performance, he sketched a head of Guitry, which he showed to a friend of his, the press agent Richard Maney. Maney persuaded Hirschfeld to do the drawing over in ink on a fresh piece of paper, which Maney took to the drama desk of the Sunday *Herald Tribune*. To Hirschfeld's astonishment, the drawing was published the following week. A few days later, a telegram arrived from the *Times*, asking Hirschfeld to prepare a caricature of the Scottish vaudevillian Harry Lauder, who was making one of his innumerable farewell tours of the United States. Hirschfeld handed the finished drawing to an elderly attendant in the lobby of the *Times* building; the drawing ran in the Sunday edition, and a second telegram arrived, asking for a second caricature. Hirschfeld prepared many caricatures for the *Times* before meeting any member of the staff except the elderly attendant in the lobby. Over the years, he was content to draw for both the *Herald Tribune* and the *Times*; at last Lester Markel, editor of the Sunday *Times*, protested that he wanted Hirschfeld on an exclusive basis. "I'm not eccentric," Hirschfeld said. "If you pay me enough, I'll draw only for you." Occasional book and magazine illustrations aside, he has been doing so ever since.

The studio in which Hirschfeld works is on the fourth floor of a sturdy redbrick Victorian house on East Ninety-fifth Street in Manhattan. Set into the face of the building is the carved stone head of a man with an exceptionally long, horizontally flowing beard. Hirschfeld, who wears a moderately long, conventionally vertical beard, took the sculptured head for a good omen the moment he saw the house. He and his pretty, red-haired wife, the actress Dolly Haas, have lived there for almost forty years, among a fantastic assortment of mementos of Hirschfeld's many travels abroad. (In the 1920s, which were also his twenties, he spent long periods of time in Paris; in the early thirties, he spent a year in Bali, renting the house of his fellow caricaturist Miguel Covarrubias.)

The Hirschfelds' daughter Nina grew up on Ninety-fifth Street, teething on Polynesian masks and beating the odd Peruvian drum. When she was very young, her proud father took to concealing her name here and there in his drawings. At the request of the late Arthur Hays Sulzberger, publisher of the *Times*, he consented to note the number of times that one could hope to discover these "Ninas" in a given drawing (hidden in the upholstery of a couch, the fold of a dress) and the doting paternal practice continues. Most Hirschfeld fans and "Nina-seekers" go on thinking of Nina as a child; in fact, she is in her forties and is herself the parent of children.

When the Hirschfelds bought the house, they knew nobody in the block. Little by little through the years, they persuaded friends to buy houses in the vicinity; among their neighbors at one time or another have been Marlene Dietrich, Vincent Sardi, Alfred Drake, Viveca Lindfors, and Betty Comden—a kind of residential Broadway off Broadway. Other friends, including many who have long since died, remain present to the Hirschfelds in the form of their books, piled high upon library shelves. A number of these books are by Hirschfeld's close friend S. J. Perelman, with illustrations by Hirschfeld. Perelman, who died in 1979, was a famously gloomy character, as so many humorous writers throughout history have been. Hirschfeld's sunny disposition was at the opposite pole from Perelman's and that very opposition appears to have rendered them complementary. "Like yin and yang," Hirschfeld explained to me once. "Call me Yin, because that sounds so much more cheerful than Yang. Yin makes me think of grin, while yang makes me think of anger. Don't you agree?"

And of course I agreed, or pretended to agree—one never feels inclined (even the irascible Perelman cannot have felt inclined) to assume an adversarial stance with Hirschfeld; his benignity is invincible. One day, as if seeking to account for Perelman's dyspepsia on the grounds of the ill luck that often befell him, Hirschfeld showed me a copy of the first edition of Perelman's first book, *Dawn Ginsbergh's Revenge*. It was brought out in 1929, and its publisher neglected one important duty: nowhere in the book is there any mention of the author's name.

The house is without an elevator. Nimble in his late eighties, Hirschfeld hastens up to his studio, assuring me as I begin to lag behind that stairs are very good for one's health. A broad, deeply scarred drawing table dominates the studio; it appears to be of approximately the same age as the house, but to have suffered far harder use. Hirschfeld seats himself in an early twentieth-century barber's chair—the once celebrated name of Koken is spelled out in its florid nickel-plated footrest—and opens a bottle of Higgins India ink. He picks up a clotted Guillot crow-quill pen and tests it against a piece of stout illustrator's board. It is here that Hirschfeld turns his penciled sketches into finished drawings. North light floods in over him from a window that all but fills one wall of the room. He looks out into a green treetop and from there to the far-off skyline of the Bronx. He is a skillful raconteur and from time to time he likes to interrupt the scratch-scratch of his pen to tell a story. Plainly, he takes exceptional delight in words; not once but many times he has startled me with a phrase that Oscar Wilde himself might envy, as when he speaks of "the mere slime of amiability."

Many of his stories are about the actors and actresses whose likenesses are stacked in ranks all round the room. There they are in their hundreds, perhaps in their thousands, the harvest of decades: Lillian Gish, Katharine Cornell, Jane Cowl, Tallulah Bankhead, Ethel Barrymore, Bobby Clark, Leslie Howard, Ed Wynn, Mildred Natwick, Henry Fonda, Maureen Stapleton. There is Maurice Evans as Hamlet and Al Pacino as Richard the Third. There are likenesses of those who are themselves devoted collectors of Hirschfeld likenesses: Carol Channing, Mary Martin, Alexander Cohen. The artist sits at ease among his creations. He has the white hair of a patriarch, but his dark eyes are merry and his voice has the strength and timbre of a young man's. Being an artist, he has not found time to grow old. "I feel as I have always felt," he tells me. "No doubt when the moment comes I will collapse all at once, like Dr. Holmes' one-horse shay. Until then, here I am and the pen leaps into my hand." This quiet room at the top of the quiet house is where he wants to be, simultaneously at work and at play.

Harold Lloyd

REPORTERS TRADITIONALLY ignore (or affect to feel contempt for) a singular advantage of their calling—that of meeting their betters. To be sure, the professional posture that reporters assume implies that they *have* no betters: the people they interview, no matter how lofty the positions they have attained in the world, under the close scrutiny of the press are shown to be quite ordinary folk. To Browning's questions— "And did you once see Shelley plain? And did he stop and speak to you?"—the usual hard-nosed reporter would reply, "Yes, and he was a little blond fellow with a bad cold, who kept sneezing in my direction." In short, he would have seen Shelley plain but he would also claim to have seen *through* Shelley and to have found something distinctly second-rate about him.

As a reporter, I have always rejected this professional posture. When I am in the presence of my betters, it costs me no effort, as far as I can tell, to assert that they are indeed my betters. For example, I subscribe to the conventional view that the three greatest makers of movie comedies have been Charlie Chaplin, Buster Keaton, and Harold Lloyd, in that order. Thanks to my job as a member of the staff of *The New Yorker*, I was able to meet and talk with Keaton and Lloyd. I was grateful to be in their presence and my looking up to them had no discernibly adverse effect upon the accuracy of my dealings with them.

As for Chaplin, I met him only once, on a social occasion, and I have regretted ever since my not having been in a position to encounter him on a professional basis. The small talk of a social occasion is like a high glass wall, over which one climbs at one's peril; custom requires an exchange of piffling politenesses, the memory of which is all I retain of my visit with Chaplin.

It was Chaplin's long absence from this country, in combination with *The New Yorker*'s arduously maintained parochialism (we preferred our subjects to be here in town when we wrote about them), that prevented me from interviewing him. I met Lloyd twice; there was an interval of thirteen years between our meetings, but each of them took place under uncannily similar circumstances, in a suite high in the Sherry Netherland, over a couple of glasses of orangeade. (Lloyd was a lifelong teetotaler.) By the time of the second visit he was sixty-eight, but looked every bit as boyish as he had on the earlier occasion. His former tightly buttoned skinniness had given way to embonpoint, but he had plenty of hair, teeth, and bounce, and though he was a grandfather several times over, his repeated "Say!" and "Gosh!" were those of an impressionable youngster enjoying his first visit to a big town. In fact, Lloyd was flying to Paris and then on to Cannes, where a portmanteau movie composed of excerpts from eight of his most famous movies and entitled *Harold Lloyd's World of Comedy* was to be shown at the festival, *hors-concours*. When Lloyd leaned toward me and said confidentially, "A fellow can have lots of fun in Paris," I got the impression that he was thinking of a trip to the top of the Eiffel Tower.

At the time of my visit with him, Lloyd was widely thought to be the richest actor that had ever lived. (In the 1990s, Bob Hope is said to hold this distinction.) When I asked Lloyd—the impertinence of reporters!—how much he was worth, he replied modestly that he thought he might have around fifty million dollars, but since he is reputed to have earned some thirty thousand dollars a week during the twenties, when income taxes were low, and since he invested most of his early wealth in Los Angeles real estate, he must have been worth at least a couple of hundred million dollars as he sat there sipping his orangeade and saying, "Say!" He and his wife, Mildred Davis, who had once been his leading lady, lived in a house in Beverly Hills that cost a million dollars when it was built, back in 1926; it had twenty acres of grounds, intensively cultivated and populated in part by sixty-five Great Danes. I felt sure that Lloyd, who was known to be miserly, was keeping tabs on the increase in value of those twenty acres from one week to the next, if not from day to day. "When we moved out to Beverly Hills, it was open country," he said. "We looked straight across the valley to Valentino's place. Hollywood was a small town and we were all friends together— Mary and Doug and Charlie and Buster and Roscoe and the rest." (The first names belong, respectively, to the surnames Pickford, Fairbanks, Chaplin, Keaton, and Arbuckle.) I asked him about Keaton, who was rumored at the time to be in dire financial straits. I had heard that Chaplin, not ordinarily known for openhandedness, had given Keaton money, and I hoped to hear from Lloyd that he had done the same. "Poor Buster!" he said. "He was never very good at managing his affairs." I asked if he had been in touch with Keaton recently. "Gosh, no!" Lloyd exclaimed. "Not for a long time! Our paths just haven't crossed, you know how it is with old friends."

Lloyd estimated that he had made between three and four hundred movies, most of them two- or three-reelers. He slipped into making feature-length pictures of necessity, when two reels proved too brief a span for the development of a substantial situation. "*Grandma's Boy*, which we made in 1922, started as a two-reeler but grew into five reels," he said. "Situation comedy has to be built up step by step, with each gag seeming to spring naturally out of the one before it. Writing and making up gags haven't anything in common; every so often I'd hire a good writer, and he'd sit listening to my gagmen and me kicking an idea around, and after a while he'd give up in disgust, never having said a word. We used to build our gags literally from the ground up. When they started showing some of my movies on television, they had to crop the prints to make them fit, and at first they kept cutting off the bottoms, in order to keep my face intact, and I said, 'Gosh, you're ruining everything! Cut off the top of my head, but leave my feet. That's where the jokes are.'"

I mentioned that I could still recall, over the decades, a comedy in which he had played a college man who said to everyone he encountered, "Step right up and call me Speedy." (I saw the movie as a schoolboy, at the height of my infatuation with Lloyd's antics, and I imitated "Speedy" word for word for several months thereafter.) Lloyd looked pleased by my recollection. "I'll tell you why I think you remember that," he said. "Whenever I spoke those words—and since it was a silent picture, they were really only a subtitle on the screen—I'd dance a funny little jig. That jig was the visual counterpart of the words and made them stick in your mind. I hear that some of these young French directors are using sight gags the way I used them forty years ago. I'm eager to see their pictures. I don't have much French, but that's one of the good things about my kind of comedy—all you have to do is look."

Buster Keaton

WHEN, IN THE COURSE of my conversation with Harold Lloyd, I asked him whether he had seen Buster Keaton lately, my mildly disingenuous purpose was to discover whether Lloyd, as perhaps the richest actor on earth, had seen fit to lend any financial assistance to his down-and-out old friend. And when Lloyd replied that, no, he hadn't seen Buster, it signified to me that Lloyd's reputation for miserliness remained intact. I was sorry that this was the case, but I was not surprised. Long ago, I had learned that there is nothing to be done about misers; they are incurable and happy with their lot.

Like Lloyd, Keaton had been one of my heroes for as long as I had been going to the movies. It was my good luck as a reporter to have a talk with him in 1963—a moment at which, after a long interlude of domestic and professional mishaps, his star seemed about to rise again. We met in a local television studio, where a program was being taped that would include clips of a number of early Keaton movies. Keaton was sixty-eight, and although he appeared alert and in good spirits, he was physically used up; his small body, always so meagre, was now visibly but skin and bones. After a lifetime of too much alcohol and too many cigarettes, his voice was a hoarse croak, and he interrupted himself again and again with a cough that had the sound of something being torn apart inside him. The cough was terrifying to listen to, and must have been terrifying to experience, but each time, as the dreadful sound subsided, Keaton would thrust the fact of it away from us with an abrupt wave of his hand, as if to say, "No matter. There are worse things than a cough." Three years later, he was dead.

Keaton had an acrobat's disciplined grace of movement and a classic clown's face—chalk white, with sad, dark eyes, a permanently unsmiling mouth, and an air of blankness. And this blankness conveyed not stupidity but an innocence so pure that, asking nothing, fearing nothing, and hoping for nothing, it was beyond being violated; the toughs and rascals who might attempt to invade and besmirch it did so at their peril, because the innocence that the Keaton character embodied was not without resources of ingenuity. In the course of his movies, he was continuously hard-pressed, but by means of repeated feats of quick thinking and bodily agility he would end up victorious over his foes and yet (innocence having no room for pride) unexultant. The face we glimpsed in the last frames of the movie—a mask and yet not a mask—was the face that had greeted us at the start.

By contemporary reckoning, sixty-eight is not a great age, but Keaton plainly thought that it was and he marveled at his having been able to attain it. "Professionally, I'm about as old as they come," he said. "Older than Chevalier, Ed Wynn, Francis X. Bushman. I've been acting for sixty-four years. I was playing in Tony Pastor's Theatre, on East Fourteenth Street, before the twentieth century began." Buster's father and mother had what he described as the roughest knockabout low-comedy act in the history of vaudeville. Buster, who was born on the road, in Piqua, Kansas, joined the act after enduring a strenuous apprenticeship backstage in a bassinet. By the time he was five or six, his father was getting laughs by hurling him bodily through the scenery, and once in New Haven, when Buster was nine, his father pitched him all the way over the footlights and orchestra pit into the audience, by way of rebuking some Yale undergraduates for their reception of a saxophone solo by Buster's mother. "I hit two Yale boys broadside," Keaton said with satisfaction. "One of them got three ribs broken and the other lost two teeth. It didn't occur to my old man that I might get hurt. He knew me too well for that."

Keaton never heard of the supposed difficulty of the Oedipal relationship and would have expressed contempt for it if he had. As far as he was concerned, he and his father always got along splendidly. "I never took a lickin' from the old man offstage," he said. "If he was sore at me for something, he'd save up till we went on, then beat the tar out of me. Once in a while, I'd get back at him by hitting him extra hard with a shovel or broom handle. When I got started in Hollywood, I put him in my pictures. He's a Union general in *The General*. When I was making one scene, I shoved the old man off a flatcar onto the tracks. He didn't mind. If you're a low-comedy clown, that's what you expect."

The first movie that Keaton ever appeared in was a two-reeler called *The Butcher Boy*, which starred "Fatty" Arbuckle. It was shot in 1917, in a studio on East Forty-eighth Street, where the Buchanan apartment building now stands. He recalled that the studio had been slapped together out of an old livery stable and, because it lacked the requisite amount of artificial light, scenes could only be shot when the sun was shining. That was fine with Keaton, because whenever it rained a powerful odor of horse manure arose from the old livery-stable floor. "Draw a deep breath on a rainy day and it could knock you over," he said.

In 1922, after Fatty Arbuckle stood trial for having caused the death of a girl at a drunken party (in the end, he was acquitted), Will H. Hays, the newly appointed "czar" of the movie industry, ruled that Arbuckle could never make another movie and that the positives and negatives of all his films must be destroyed. A single print of *The Butcher Boy* survived only by the accident of its having been mislaid for several decades somewhere in Europe. In *The Butcher Boy*, Arbuckle throws a bag of flour at Keaton, and Keaton takes a terrible fall. "I didn't have to throw that fall," he said. "It was the real thing. Arbuckle caught me right smack in the face. He had a wonderful eye, Arbuckle did. Later, I took or threw an awful lot of pies. The art of pie-throwing depended on the pie. First, you had to make it with a double crust on the bottom, so you could get a good hold on it without your fingers going through. Then you made the filling of the pie out of flour and water, uncooked, so it would be sticky and stringy, and you topped it off with, say, blueberries and whipped cream, or maybe a nice meringue. I never threw a pie in any of my feature-length pictures. By then we thought pies were pretty silly."

The Keaton of those celebrated feature pictures wasn't simply a superb pantomimist. As James Agee wrote of him: "Keaton worked strictly for laughs, but his work came from so far inside a curious and original spirit that he achieved a great deal besides . . . He brought pure physical comedy to its greatest heights . . . With the humor, the craftsmanship, and the action there was often . . . a dreamlike beauty." As works of art, his pictures have a shapeliness all the more remarkable because they were made without a script.

"Two or three writers and I would start with an idea and then we'd work out a strong finish and let the middle take care of itself, as it always does," Keaton said. "Sometimes, we'd work out a gag in advance; other times, it would work itself out as we went along. In those days, we didn't use miniatures or process shots. The way a thing looked on the screen was the way you'd done it. In *Steamboat Bill, Jr.*, there's a windstorm that blows the whole front of a house over on top of me. I don't get killed, because there happens to be an open window in the part of the house that lands where I'm standing. We used six old Liberty airplane engines to make the wind, and it really blew. The window of the house was just big enough to give two inches' clearance on either side of me and above my head when the house came down. Two inches! Well, I drove a couple of tenpenny nails in the ground to mark the place where I had to stand, and I can tell you one thing—when the house started falling, I didn't *sway*."

Keaton wrote the story and continuity of *The General*, directed it, cut it, and, of course, played the leading role. It was shot in eighteen weeks, at a cost of $330,000. "I was pretty proud of it at the time," he said. "Right now, it's playing all over Europe, and they tell me people are laughing harder at it today than they did in 1927, when it came out." Keaton shuffled over to a television monitor to watch a clip of one of his early two-reelers being run off. In the picture, he is being chased by what looks like hundreds of frantic cops. They are about to capture him when an open touring car goes by and Keaton reaches out, grabs the brace supporting its canvas top, and is jerked into momentary safety. At that point, something astonishing happened in the television studio. On the screen was a mournful little man running lickety-split down the streets of a long-since-vanished Los Angeles; in the studio watching him was the same mournful little man, forty-two years older, and now, instead of being deadpan, the face was smiling.

Virgil Thomson

"THINGS ARE IN THE SADDLE and ride mankind." So Emerson was saying long ago, and throughout my lifetime I have found that, leaving aside wars, famines, and other disasters on a grand scale, his maxim holds equally well for events taking place on a small scale. As one might expect, I have in mind a number of just such small events, one of which—painfully vivid to me after twenty years—concerns a symposium that I was invited to conduct at the MacDowell Colony, in Peterborough, New Hampshire. The oldest and probably the best known of artists' colonies, the MacDowell was founded by the widow of the composer Edward MacDowell some eighty years ago, and has since provided a retreat, in individual studios scattered at a prudent distance from one another over hundreds of acres of pastures and pinewoods, for poets, dramatists, composers, artists, and the like. A total of many thousands of colonists have enjoyed the fruitful seclusion of the Mac-Dowell; among the more celebrated of them have been Edwin Arlington Robinson, Thornton Wilder (whose play *Our Town* was written at the MacDowell), Aaron Copland, and Milton Avery.

The topic that our symposium was intended to address had been chosen by the then president of the MacDowell, Russell Lynes, and had to do with the perennially vexing question of how best to fund the arts—whether with the help of public sources or private philanthropy, or without any help at all, letting the so-called creative person sink or swim according to the whim of the marketplace. The members of the symposium included of the poet Louise Bogan, the art historian Meyer Schapiro, and the composer Virgil Thomson, all familiar faces at the colony and all sure to hold strong opinions about the subject matter. Our platform was a grassy area within a grove of ancient pine trees; four folding chairs and a card table had been set up there, with a microphone resting in the center of the table. Our audience, numbering perhaps a hundred people, sat in a circle all round us.

The time was late August. A series of violent thunderstorms had passed through the area the night before, bringing lower than usual temperatures, and a strong wind was still blowing in gusts as the four of us took our places at the table. Still, the sun was shining, and I was in high spirits as I called the gathering to order. Acting upon some oldfangled notion of permitting women to speak first, I called upon Louise Bogan. A woman sad in face and sad in her personal history, she was an excellent poet and had served for many years as the poetry editor of *The New Yorker*. She was direct in speech but by no means direct in her fancy, and no sooner had she seized the microphone than some interior will-o'-the-wisp caused her to set off on a verbal ramble that had nothing whatever to do with the funding of the arts. As I was leaning forward to regain possession of the microphone, Virgil Thomson, a plump little man with an exceptionally high voice, piped up that he was feeling cold—would someone please fetch some blankets for him from a nearby studio? While blankets were being fetched, Louise wandered contentedly on, in a landscape of her own choosing. Meyer Schapiro sat staring at her, his handsome face a mask of polite inscrutability. When the blankets arrived, little Virgil got up and tucked himself adroitly into one of them, resembling as he sat down an uninhabited Indian tepee. Virgil had long been deaf and enjoyed the deaf person's privilege of speaking whenever he had a mind to. "What on earth is she saying *now?*" he asked, his birdy voice emerging from the top of the tepee. Gently, Schapiro wrested the microphone from Bogan and began to address our subject; at that moment, a particularly strong gust of wind rushed through the tops of the pines and whistled piercingly through the microphone, obliterating Schapiro's and Bogan's voices. Higher and more piercing even than the wind came Virgil's irritated tepee-cry: "I can't hear *any*thing!"

Humiliated and despairing, I watched as the symposium disintegrated. Grumbling, the audience got to its feet and began to shuffle away. Finding no other means of ending the nightmare, in a loud voice I announced that the symposium was abandoning its battle against adverse weather and that everyone was being invited to proceed to Hilltop—the MacDowell family farmhouse and now the residence of the local director of the colony—for cocktails and a hot supper. We would be arriving there an hour ahead of schedule, and if the food was not yet ready, the balm, the boon, the bliss of alcohol would be. In the snug, paneled living room at Hilltop, before a rosy fire, my colleagues and I drew what consolation we could from as much whisky as we were able to swallow. If ever there was an occasion on which things were in the saddle and rode mankind, it was that day at the MacDowell. And yet out of it came the beginning of my friendship with Virgil, which in memory soon came to outweigh the humiliation I had undergone.

Some years later, a glimpse of Virgil at seventy-five. With other friends, I have been invited to visit him in the lofty Victorian living room of his flat at the Chelsea Hotel, on West Twenty-third Street. I find him perched among the books, musical manuscripts, paintings, sculptures, and touch-for-luck mementos that make up the cherished protective debris of a lifetime. Round as an apple in both face and figure, he is bald save for a fringe of curly white hair that dawdles in monkish disarray over the back of his collar, and his eyes are large and merry, with formidably hooded lids. His voice, unchanged in timbre from the miserable day we shared at the MacDowell, is as high and urgent and droll as that of some improbable extinct bird—a three-way cross between an owl for wisdom, a rooster for bawdry, and a thrush for song. He talks at a rate faster than most people can think, and the drumfire of his recollections rattles and snaps with famous names and occasions. It seems that he has known everyone in the world for fifty years and has forgotten no one; he is a master at spinning assorted threads of names, dates, and places into a single cable of anecdote stout enough to hang a moon from—or, in a malicious mood, a man.

At the time of my visit, Virgil is approximately halfway through a royal progress of private and public birthday celebrations—dinner parties, concerts, university convocations, and television interviews—and it is plain that every moment of them gives him delight. The celebrations began several months ago and threaten to go on for years, and though some of the younger celebrants have dropped by the wayside from fatigue, the object of celebration remains undaunted; if anything, he is fresher now than he was at the start. On this particular evening at the Chelsea, he bounces off a sofa that for as long as it has borne his weight has seemed a throne, and offers refreshments to those of us who are about to attend with him a birthday-party musical performance at St. Peter's Episcopal Church, on nearby Twentieth Street. The performance will consist of *The Mother of Us All*, a pageantlike opera that has music by Virgil and text by Gertrude Stein. Virgil is wearing a gray tweed jacket and buff-colored socks, and the feat of simultaneously pulling the cork of a bottle of wine and passing a platter of turkey sandwiches heightens the intentness with which we listen to the enchanting torrent of his talk.

"Gertrude was twenty-two years older than I," Virgil says. "I made these sandwiches myself. That was a gap big enough for Gertrude and me to talk across. Anything less would have made for difficulties. Everyone in my family expects to live forever. We are *very* disappointed when things turn out otherwise. My mother lived to be ninety-two, and one of my grandfathers lived to a hundred. The other was killed in the Civil War—but for that, he might be with us still." One of the guests asks Virgil which of his birthdays is the earliest that he remembers. "I've a sister eleven years older than I," he replies, "and the curious thing is that I seem to remember her *constantly* having birthday parties when I was a little boy, but I have no recollection of *my* ever having one. The first birthday I felt strongly about was my twenty-fifth. I was living in Paris, in a *maison meublée* that was really a mild sort of whorehouse— very convenient for me, because the girls went out to work every night and I could work at the piano without annoying anyone. I remember having dinner by myself and then going back to the *maison* and writing a little piece—rather sad but very pretty—in honor of my birthday. I also remember people making lots of jokes about my getting to be thirty. I still had a baby face in those days, which led to my being thought to be even brighter than I was. A public fuss started being made over me when I was sixty-five and again at seventy. Heaven knows what somersaults I'll be expected to turn at eighty and eighty-five and ninety. Dear me, I must say I look forward to those birthdays! From everything I hear, the eighties can be very pleasant, though I'm none too confident about the nineties."

Virgil was an excellent prophet: many parties were indeed held for him in honor of his eightieth, eighty-fifth, and ninetieth birthdays. He was accurate, too, in his expectations for the decade of his eighties; he grew increasingly deaf, but his general health was excellent and he continued to be a lively party-giver and party-goer. As far as I could tell, he had always led an exceptionally happy life, or, rather, a life exceptionally free of major tragedies. I knew nothing about his financial situation, but he appeared to be (as they might say in his native Kansas City) "comfortably off." More than many of the homosexuals I have known, he gave the impression of being every bit as much at ease in his sexual relations as in his financial ones. I remember once at a dinner party in Chinatown that one of the guests, an Italian artist, arrived late and was making his way with some difficulty through the crowded room to our table. The artist was as young and tall and slender as Virgil was old and short and fat; catching sight of him, Virgil burst out appreciatively, "Well! *There's* a pretty boy!" The ardor in his voice was unmistakable. Long ago, Yeats wrote of Lady Gregory's white swans at Coole, "Their hearts have not grown old;/Wander where they will,/Passion and conquest wait upon them still." And so it was with Virgil.

As for the nineties, which Virgil had expressed a lack of confidence in: again, he was right to view them with foreboding, and not because of personal infirmities but because certain totally unexpected events— events on a mighty and dreadful scale—were in the saddle and were pitilessly riding mankind. AIDS struck down Virgil's companion of many years; subsequently, a young friend who had moved into the Chelsea flat to take care of Virgil was also stricken with the dread disease and died. On every side, a slaughter was taking place that Virgil could only observe and with the helplessness of a bystander be shocked and saddened by. Those invincible high spirits of his—that perky, peppery joie de vivre—seemed, under the circumstances, inappropriate almost to the point of being grotesque. One didn't so much outlive one's time as be outwitted by it; when he died, at ninety-two (the same age that his mother had attained), he was not unready for the grand caesura.

Theodore Besterman

OF SCHOLARS I have encountered over the years, none has filled me with greater awe than an English bibliophile named Theodore Deodatus Nathaniel Besterman. At the time of our first meeting, in the early 1960s, he was the director of the Institut et Musée Voltaire, which had been installed at Les Délices, Voltaire's old house in Geneva. A small, handsome, dark-eyed, piratical-looking man of fifty-seven, Besterman had come to New York to lay the groundwork for an international conference on the Enlightenment. He and I were brought together by Elinor Gimbel, a neighbor of the Gill family on East Seventy-eighth Street. Elinor and Mrs. Besterman, who was a member of a prominent New York family, had been at school together many years earlier. Elinor occupied a splendid old redbrick double-width town house that had belonged to a mistress of William H. Woodin's, secretary of the treasury under Franklin D. Roosevelt. Woodin, a saintly-looking old man with a white toupee and bee-stung lips, had died suddenly of a heart attack, and the only object of value that he had been in a position to set aside for his mistress was the house on Seventy-eighth Street. The mistress sold the house to Elinor, who lived there until her death in 1988.

The first thing I learned about Besterman was that he spoke with a flabbergasting velocity—so fast, indeed, that like his fellow Englishman

Sir Isaiah Berlin he seemed at first not to be speaking separate words at all but to be emitting a high-pitched, continuous hum, of the sort that makes a dog's ears twitch. Eventually, one got the hang of this hum and could break it down into sentences and into some of the words that made up the sentences, but by the time one had done so the topic of conversation introduced by the remarks that one had failed to take in was unrecapturable. A new topic, or several new topics, had been introduced; one went on nodding and smiling and hoping for the best.

The enterprise for which Besterman was then chiefly celebrated was the editing, in what finally amounted to well over a hundred volumes, of Voltaire's enormous correspondence. Being recognized as a genius while he was still a small child, Voltaire was in the fortunate position of having his letters saved from the moment he acquired the ability to write them. At the age of seven, he was corresponding with Ninon de l'Enclos; in his eighties, he was corresponding with Catherine the Great. Voltaire not only kept in constant touch with an extraordinarily diverse assortment of people (kings, popes, politicians, playwrights, scientists, manufacturers, farmers, and innumerable interesting women) but was extraordinarily prolific as well. An early edition of his correspondence contained approximately ten thousand letters; Besterman's edition contained close to twenty thousand. By comparison, several of Voltaire's epistolary runners-up appear to have suffered mild cases of writer's cramp. For example, Benjamin Franklin wrote about eight thousand letters and Horace Walpole about twelve thousand. The editions of the correspondence of Franklin and Walpole that were being prepared at about the same time that Besterman was working on his Voltaire correspondence were the products of substantial teams of scholars; Besterman, who had prodigious energy and little use for sleep, was a sort of one-man factory, geared to turn out ten volumes of Voltaire correspondence a year and able, by way of relaxation, to edit several volumes of Voltaire commentary a year, give occasional speeches on the great man, and preside over Les Délices. To make his edition of the Voltaire correspondence all the more prodigious, Besterman designed it, supervised its printing, and brought it out at his own expense. Reviewing a batch of volumes, a critic wrote in the *Times Literary Supplement*: "One is appalled by the magnitude of the task and full of admiration for Mr. Besterman's courageous and successful attack upon it. By any standard this edition is one of the most remarkable feats of scholarship of our lifetime and one which deserves the fullest and most genuine support."

A previous Besterman feat, in some ways even more remarkable than the correspondence, was his single-handed preparation of *A World Bibliography of Bibliographies*, in which he recorded and collated some eighty thousand bibliographies, under about twelve thousand headings and subheadings. The first edition of this formidable work came out in 1939–40; the third and final edition came out in 1955–56. "I was young when I tackled the bibliography," Besterman would say, with a rueful shake of his head. "In those days, I had a pretty fair memory and could pass several thousand volumes through my hands and be absolutely certain of the degree to which a given title page differed from the title page of another edition of the same book, which I mightn't have seen for months or years. I also had a good working knowledge of twelve or fifteen languages. That sort of job would be out of the question for me now." Still earlier in his career, the tireless Besterman wrote or edited books on half a dozen totally unrelated subjects; among these works are *Crystal-Gazing: A Study in the History, Distribution, Theory, and Practice of Scrying*, *The Mind of Annie Besant*, and *The Travelings and Sufferings of Father Jean de Brebouef among the Hurons of Canada*. He also founded and ran a private press in London, which was destroyed by bombing during the Second World War. "I bought my first book on Voltaire when I was ten," he would say, "but the record will demonstrate that I haven't been entirely obsessed with him."

Besterman's father came of a wealthy, cloth-manufacturing family in Yorkshire; his mother was of Polish-Jewish stock and a native of Cracow. Besterman's three given names all mean precisely the same thing—"gift of God," in Greek, Latin, and Hebrew, respectively. The names reflect not an unusually devout family background but, on the contrary, one unusually lacking in devotion. His father was a vehement atheist, who chose to make the naming of his infant son the occasion for a private dig at what he believed to be a nonexistent deity. An invalid as a child, Besterman was tutored at home and later became an extramural student at Oxford. He learned to type during his bedridden early years, balancing a typewriter on his midriff. He also grew accustomed to reading at least a book a day, often (in the case of detective novels) reading two or three. He and Mrs. Besterman moved into Les Délices in the 1950s, after he succeeded in negotiating a lease with the city fathers of Geneva. "I felt that all the Voltaire materials that I had accumulated—letters, manuscripts, books, paintings, a terra-cotta statue of Voltaire by Houdon—should find a home in what had been *his* home, so I made a gift of my Voltaireana to the city. Voltaire has always been a very lively ghost at Les Délices—one half expects to bump into him on the stairs or in the garden. We even shared with him certain housekeeping problems. Over two hundred years ago, Voltaire kept complaining to the authorities of a mysterious trickle of water that ran through a corner of the basement of the house. The trickle is still there, and, like Voltaire, I kept complaining about it, always, like Voltaire, in vain."

Over the years, Besterman and I enjoyed a correspondence that had a defect roughly equivalent to the one that I had experienced on first hearing him speak: he wrote a hand so exquisite in its calligraphy as to be almost totally illegible. Shapely lines of ink undulated in disciplined ranks across the page but without the conventional separation into words; one stared with pleasure at a work of art that, as an act of communication, resolutely failed to convey any information whatever, though one was certain that the information was there. I framed and hung on the wall of my office one or two of these works of art, hoping to enlist the assistance of my colleagues in their decipherment; all that I received were congratulations upon the elegance of my friend's penmanship.

I came to learn more about his private life as time passed. His mother, he said, had always hated him and he was ready to return the compliment. She was very rich and had promised to disown him. The Bestermans' marriage was evidently not a success and ended in divorce a few years after I met them. During the course of one of his visits to New York, Besterman confided to me that he was eager to marry again—had I any recommendations to make with respect to a young woman of intelligence, good looks, good manners, and good breeding? The requirements as he listed them gave off a chilling ring, as leaving little room for the spontaneity of an infatuation, whether appropriate or inappropriate. Nevertheless, I knew a few young women who would match his specifications and who I thought might be amused to meet the great savant. Silently assuming that there was little or no likelihood of their wishing to marry him, I introduced him to my young friends. He invited the first of them to have tea with him at the Grolier Club on a certain afternoon; within a few minutes of making her acquaintance, he proposed marriage to her and appeared (so she afterward told me) nonplussed by the alacrity with which she turned him down. The next day, he invited the second young woman to have tea with him at the Grolier; over the first cup of tea, he proposed marriage to *her* and received the same immediate and, to him, mysterious rejection. Disheartened, he retreated across the Atlantic.

Some time later, I heard that a young woman—no doubt intelligent, good-looking, with good manners, and of good family—had happened to wander one day into the Institut et Musée Voltaire. Catching sight of her, Besterman had invited her to tea, had instantly proposed marriage to her, and perhaps because she was a European and had a less romantic—certainly a more down-to-earth—notion of the nature of marriage than her American counterparts, she accepted his proposal. She appeared to like serving as the chatelaine of Les Délices, but Besterman's quarrels with the city fathers of Geneva eventually became too much for him. In his pessimistic (and possibly accurate) view, if one's family hadn't been in residence in Geneva since the time of John Calvin, one had no hope of penetrating its society. After a series of bitter quarrels, among the subjects of which the persistent unstopped and unstoppable trickle of water was but a symbol, the Bestermans gave up the Institut et Musée and retreated to London. There they rented a very grand flat at the top of a bank building in Pall Mall. The building had been designed by Edwin Lutyens and for a time Besterman took great pleasure in showing it off. Soon, though (for like many scholars he was of a highly contentious nature), there were reasons for him to find fault with those quarters as well. The Bestermans removed themselves to a cottage in the countryside. The last message I received from him before his death was a note that, after I had puzzled over it at length, appeared upon decoding to report that his mother had just died at a very great age and, true to her word, had left him not a penny; according to the terms of her will, her fortune was to go to a cat-and-dog hospital in London. "There are few satisfactions in life," he wrote, "greater than to be proven right in the bleak view that one has taken of other members of the human race." The language was that of Voltaire, but the message was pure Besterman. No cackle of humane Voltairean delight over the folly of taking sides in life—of seeing it as either dark or bright—accompanied the stylish words: very pretty they looked on the page, but prettiness is almost always, and especially in age, beside the point.

Ter Fuller

CROWNING A BLUFF in the hamlet of West Chop, on the island of Martha's Vineyard, is a sturdy, gray-shingled, high-gabled house that Charles Pelham Greenough, a lawyer in Boston, arranged to have built in 1890 as a summer retreat for himself and his numerous family. (The deed to the property stipulated that no pigs or chickens could be kept on the premises and that the house must cost a minimum of three thousand dollars. In fact, it cost five hundred dollars less than the minimum, but nobody appears to have raised any objections.) The house clings to its perch of rock and scanty grass above a narrow, inhospitable beach, which one reaches by means of a path and a rickety flight of wooden steps (in bare feet, the wise bather keeps an eye out for splinters). From the house, one looks west across the turbulent waters of Vineyard Sound to the island of Naushon, hereditary fiefdom of the Boston Forbeses (distant kin, if kin at all, of the late upstart Malcolm Forbes), and north to Woods Hole, at the crooked elbow of Cape Cod.

The house has withstood more than a century of fierce winter gales and summer storms; fire and ice have threatened it in vain. When I used to visit the house, it belonged to the eldest of Charles Greenough's seven children, Constance Greenough Fuller, widow of Samuel Fuller. Mrs. Fuller was a small, plump, plain-faced woman, whose raspy, baritone voice was a consequence of her having smoked pack after pack of

297

cigarettes daily throughout a long lifetime. When in extreme old age and with reluctance she stopped smoking, her voice rose a couple of octaves, becoming the voice of a coquette. And from photographs of her that I have seen, taken in her youth, I suspect that she was indeed a coquette. Which is to say that *my* Mrs. Fuller was but the last of the many women she had been. She was fourteen years older than her house and used to strike me as being equally indestructible. Having outlived her husband and her three sons, she presided, with the equanimity of a tyrant cherished and not feared, over a host of grandchildren and great-grandchildren.

Samuel Fuller had been a partner in one of the big stock-brokerage firms in New York City. A devoted graduate of Andover, over the years he made many substantial gifts to the school. By the time I came to know Mrs. Fuller, some years after her husband's death, she had given up her apartment in New York and had become a year-round resident of the Vineyard. From her place at one end of a long dining-room table, she would sit with her back to the fireplace and observe through the undraped windows opposite her the comings and goings of the big ferries—the *Uncatena* and the *Naushon*—that carried passengers and automobiles back and forth between Woods Hole and the Vineyard. According to a family story, in the early years of their marriage she and her husband had quarreled incessantly over the question of who should sit at the end of the table that offered the view of the ferries. Mrs. Fuller claimed the place by right of descent: that was where her father had sat. At last her husband achieved the next best thing; on the fireplace wall behind his wife Sam Fuller installed an enormous mirror, by means of which he, too, gained an excellent view of Vineyard Sound. From that moment on, the grounds of their quarreling shifted; competing to see which of them would be the first to catch sight of one or another of the ferries looming upon the horizon, each would accuse the other of speaking up too soon, before any vessel was in sight.

Everyone in and out of the family addressed Mrs. Fuller as "Ter," pronounced to rhyme with "where." The nickname was short for "Mater," and how she had happened to gain this formal Latin appellation was lost, as so many such things are, in the dim reaches of family lore. There was little about her that one was tempted to call motherly— indeed, one sensed that she possessed a certain gift for asperity, which one would do well to avoid evoking. In her presence, the utterance of fatuities by persons young or old was not to be encouraged. Still, there was no doubt that she loved children, especially in bulk. The sheer number of her descendants gave her pleasure: at the time of her death, the total was approaching twenty.

Nor did the generations of Ter's own copious family suffice to satisfy her dynastic cravings. Every year on her birthday, all the children in West Chop were gathered up and brought to the tennis club to have a mass photograph of them taken with Ter. Year after year, the sunlit pictures repeat themselves. Ter is seated in a chair at the center of a group of towheaded children; propped in her lap, in the place of honor, will be found the current "youngest" baby in the community. Glancing from one of these annual state photographs to the next, one watches as each "youngest" baby, having been plucked by the passage of time from Ter's lap, grows in size among his companions until at a certain age he disappears, having become too old to be included in her private army of the young. In some cases, however, we see him, or a close likeness of him, reappearing, and when this happens the odds are that we have stumbled upon a "youngest" who is the child of a "youngest" of a quarter of a century before. We recognize him because, given the exceptional persistence with which families return summer after summer and generation after generation to West Chop, certain facial characteristics—high cheekbones, a pointed chin—become as ready a source of identification as a West Chop family name.

Having acquired the agreeable habit of attending Ter's birthday parties every summer, I made sure to be among those present on the occasion of her ninetieth birthday. By then, Ter had taken to occupying two West Chop houses instead of one. In summer, she lived in the gray-shingled house that her father had built and during the rest of the year she lived in what was jovially known as "the Winter Palace"—a square, well-heated house that stood a couple of hundred yards inward from the shore, in the midst of a grove of oak trees that served to shield it from harsh winds and inclement weather. For the birthday weekend, many guests, myself among them, were put up in the Winter Palace, while Ter held court in the house on the bluff.

On the morning of her ninetieth birthday, I joined Ter for her habitual morning swim. Down the rickety wooden steps we trudged, Ter wearing her accustomed bright red cape over her bathing suit. (This cape was both a protection against chills and a signaling device; if she recognized the sailing craft of a friend, or if she believed that she had caught sight of a friend on the deck of one of the ferries, off would come the cape and it would be waved vigorously back and forth in a gesture of marine salute.) When we reached the pebbly beach at the foot of the bluff, we saw that a riptide was running, and I suggested as tactfully as I could that perhaps a quick dip at the edge of the beach would count as enough of a swim for both of us. Well, not at all! Ter was indignant. A swim was a *swim!* She cast off the cape and shuffled into the water. In a bathing suit, she cut a fairly bizarre figure, for with age it was as if all of her organs had been indiscriminately relocated at a point in the middle of her body, giving her the look, in profile, of having swallowed a very large medicine ball.

Following Ter into the sea, I discovered that the water was cold as well as rough. Reluctantly, I swam a few yards out from shore and then shouted back to her to be very careful—I could feel the riptide pulling me seaward, and a terrible thought had belatedly entered my mind: I was alone with Ter; if she were to be drowned on the morning of her ninetieth birthday, then I—an outsider from New York, and not even a member of the family!—would be held responsible for her death. "Stay by the shore, Ter!" I begged her. "This is far too dangerous for us!"

Ter plunged confidently into the water. Employing a breaststroke that must have been handed down in the Greenough family over several generations, she made her way toward me. "I'm a very slow swimmer," she said, her voice carrying easily to me over the ruffled surface of the water, "but a very strong one." And so she was; and so in good time we regained the shore and the birthday party went off as planned, hour after hour, with many a joyous toast and jubilant song.

Ter played tennis into her early nineties, golf into her middle nineties, and bridge every day of her life until the evening of the day she died. She had been slipping gradually out of life and making as little fuss as possible over the necessity of doing so. A favorite granddaughter and a nurse were in constant attendance upon her. Toward the end, the nurse attempted to get a reading of her blood pressure. Ter said, "You see, you shouldn't have bothered! I haven't any pressure left. Oh, dear! I never *meant* to be difficult." Then she turned to her granddaughter. "I'm really going to miss my family," she said. She had a poodle named Babu that everyone in the family except Ter considered a model of nastiness.

Now Ter worried that Babu would be looking around the house for her after she died. Her granddaughter attempted to comfort her by saying that she and Babu would be together in the afterlife. Ter had never expressed the slightest interest in life after death, but her granddaughter thought she detected a look of pleasure in her eyes at the thought of encountering Babu in heaven. Thereupon the granddaughter went too far. She added that Ter would soon be seeing *all* her dogs in heaven. The look of pleasure gave way to one of panic—that was plainly the last thing that Ter wanted, and so without another word she died.

Walker Evans

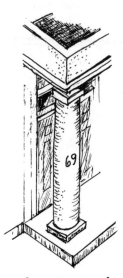

PEOPLE WHO KNEW Walker Evans only from those immaculate, unsentimental photographs of America in the thirties (especially the destitute countryside of the American South that he and the writer James Agee took as their subject in the book *Let Us Now Praise Famous Men*) assumed that he must be a leathery, hard-boiled, outdoors type of man, and in fact he was in every respect consummately unlike that imagined figure, being a shy, wry, dandiacal little man, with a love of dusky, book-filled interiors and a strong dislike for the rough side of life.

Walker had a nose as sharp as Falstaff's; on its upper reaches used to rest a pair of large, round spectacles, which served to heighten his usual expression of fastidious skepticism. He was as modest as his proper Protestant upbringing obliged him to pretend to be; nevertheless, he was under no misapprehension as to the value of the work that he had done. The sort of photography in which he pioneered—a photography bleak, abstinent, head-on, of the utmost clarity and seeming impersonality—was once considered shockingly inartistic. Among his unprecedented choices of subject matter were automobile graveyards, faded painted signs, Western ghost towns, serried factory windows, and rumpled tenement beds. Coolly keeping his distance, like his heroes Brady and Atget, he stared the assorted meannesses and failed promises of American life straight in the face, and they stared back.

In bits and pieces over the years of our friendship, I gathered certain small portions of Walker's biography, most of which remained by his decision unknown to me. (That he was bisexual never crossed my mind, as the fact of it never crossed his lips, but it appears that he and John Cheever were at one time lovers, and I see now that they had much in common. In their lifetimes, they both struck me as being, in an old-fashioned, simpleminded, Victorian fashion, mad about women, and indeed that impression remains true, whatever else may have been true: they *were* mad about women.) Born in St. Louis, Walker was the third generation in the Evans family to bear that name. In the course of his youth the family moved to Toledo, then to Kenilworth, Illinois, and finally to New York. His father was a successful copywriter for the well-known advertising agency of Lord and Thomas. He composed a once-celebrated advertisement for Aunt Jemima pancake mix showing a plump colored mammy in a kerchief; under the illustration was a caption reading—so Walker remembered with a shudder—"I'se in town, honey."

Walker attended two prep schools, Loomis and Andover, and passed a desultory year at Williams before deciding to go abroad and become a writer. In the 1920s, with the help of a small allowance from his father, he lived in Paris for a year. "I wanted so much to write that I couldn't write a word," he would say, with a sorry shake of his head. As for all the famous artists, writers, and dancers that everyone else who was in Paris at the time seemed to fall in with at every street corner, Walker failed to meet a single one. He knew Sylvia Beach, because he frequented her bookshop, Shakespeare and Company. Miss Beach was eager to introduce her young fellow American to James Joyce, who was often in and out of the shop and who might (or again might not) have spoken a kindly word to the neophyte, but at the very mention of the name of the great man Walker would blanch and flatten himself against the wall, uttering in an agony of timidity the then prevalent American slang word, "Nix!"

Walker's first published work was some photographic illustrations for a private edition of his friend Hart Crane's poem "The Bridge," published by the Black Sun Press in Paris in 1930. By that time, Walker had returned to this country and had pretty well given up his dream of becoming a poet or novelist; taking a trivial job on Wall Street, he settled down to photography. For long periods, he worked for *Time* and

Fortune, furnishing them with photographs that the editors may well have wondered why they were publishing, but, being in awe of his reputation, would have felt derelict in not publishing. His last formal job was teaching a course at the Yale School of Art and Architecture. "The catalogue listed the course as being about the aesthetics of photography," he would say. "How tiresome! Photography isn't a matter of taking pictures. It's a matter of having an eye."

Walker grew famous and—a phenomenon universally recognized but not yet clinically understood—with fame acquired the look of being somebody famous. For a time in his later years he wore a beard, which in my eyes caused him to resemble a latter-day Prospero, learned in feats of magic that were beyond my ken. Still, one of his feats of magic was, or so I surmised, easily seen through, at least by me. And because it turned out many years later that I was wrong in my surmise, it amounted to still another feat of magic on Walker's part to have pretended that I was right and so have caused me unconsciously to play the fool whenever, in reminiscing about him, I would recount the episode. On the opening day of an exhibition of his work in a local art gallery, I had noticed a close-up photograph of a portion of a pillar, which I guessed (and Walker, being present at the opening, was able to confirm my guess) framed the entrance to one of those grand stuccoed townhouses in the Belgravia section of London. The subject of the photograph was a number that had been painted by hand in bold black numerals on the face of the pillar: 69. It struck me that there was something infinitesimally "off" about the look of the number, and I accused Walker of having taken a photograph of a pillar bearing the number 96 and of having then adroitly flipped the negative in such a way as to make the number emerge in the finished print as 69. After a moment's hesitation, Walker confessed that he was indeed guilty of this schoolboy prank. "At my age!" he said, peering up owlishly over his round spectacles. "I should be ashamed." What I ought to have known is that there is no possible way to turn 96 into 69 in the fashion that I had suggested and that my accusation revealed far more about *my* belated schoolboy sexual prankishness than about Walker's.

Walker enjoyed drinking with friends at the Century Club. When S. J. Perelman was elected a member, I saw to it that a table of eight or ten convivial Centurions would be seated with him at the annual New Members' dinner. I was on Sid Perelman's right, Walker on his left, and during the course of the dinner I exchanged not a word with Sid, because an astonishing fact emerged, to wit, that he and Walker had been living in the city for several decades, had long admired each other's work, had scores of friends in common, and yet had never met. They found that they had much ground to cover that evening, and I felt a host's pride in being neglected for so excellent a reason.

One of Walker's close friends among Century members was Robert Beverly Hale, who for many years was a much-admired and much-loved teacher at the Art Students League. (It was Hale who set up the department of contemporary art at the Metropolitan Museum; he was succeeded by Henry Geldzahler, who in turn was succeeded by William Lieberman.) Walker had an aversion to travel; nevertheless, Bob Hale persuaded him to spend a weekend at the Hales' country place in Springs, Long Island. After a long evening of agreeable drinking and storytelling, nothing would do but that Walker should follow Hale out into the darkness of a field behind the house, to inspect a folly that Hale was engaged in building there—a wooden tower that, even allowing for its unfinished state, had the look of being distinctly ramshackle. Walker had an aversion to heights greater even than his aversion to travel, but alcohol had given him courage and when Hale invited him to enjoy the view from the top of the tower, he climbed a series of ladders behind Hale and stood on the swaying platform of two-by-fours at the top of the tower. Staring out into the moonless and starless night, Walker pronounced the view an admirable one; his only regret, he said, was that he had failed to bring his camera with him.

At breakfast late the next morning, Walker glanced out of a window of the house and asked Hale what the curious wooden structure in the backyard might be. "That's my folly," Hale said. "You climbed it last night." Walker began to tremble. "I climbed *that?*" he asked. Retrospectively, an expression of terror crossed his face. "Have some more coffee," Hale said. "We are on terra firma. Nothing awful is about to happen."

Man Ray

MAN RAY resided for many years in a large, two-story-high skylit studio on the rue Férou, in Paris, and it was there that I met him, immobilized by old age but in good spirits. "I'm all right," he proclaimed at once, "from the waist up"—and the mocking half-smile, half-leer that accompanied these words was plainly intended to convey that it wasn't only his legs that had failed him but that this other failure was also a matter of no great moment to him. Ray and his wife, Juliet, had established islands of coziness in the barren void of what Man Ray told me had once been a garage and then a sculptor's studio; I was made aware of its earlier purposes by the presence of exposed steel beams, exposed aluminum-foil insulation, and exposed plumbing. It may be that Man Ray wished it to look like a workplace, where various metals could be welded or hammered into shape, or it may be that he couldn't afford to turn it into a more nearly conventional domestic shelter. Plainly he was content with its oddity, as being appropriate to him—as, in effect, authenticating his own enviable oddity. Not that a personal authentication had ever been needed by him: whether in Paris, New York, or Hollywood (where he lived for a decade during and after the Second World War and where he met Juliet), he was acknowledged to be as nearly one of a kind as an Eskimo bookend.

If it is possible for an attic to be located at street level, then Man Ray on the rue Férou may be described as sitting enthroned in an attic full of precious objects, some of them made by him and others found and transformed by him—objects that, whatever their origins, bore the unmistakable stamp of his ingenuity and wit. Around the little god, his body mutilated by time but his mind whole and undismayed, were crowded the products of a long lifetime of incessant cranky invention, upon which his eyes, bright behind thick-lensed, dark-rimmed glasses, fell now with admiration. One saw there a replica of the flatiron with a row of steel tacks affixed to its smooth base that he had made as a present to Erik Satie and that has served ever since as a classic icon of the Dada aesthetic: by rendering a useful object unusable, one turned it into a work of art. Also on view in the studio were objects wrapped in burlap and tied with stout rope—toy specimens of the wrapped cliffsides and islands that Christo was later to earn his fame by. Like his friends Marcel Duchamp and Jean Cocteau, Man Ray was a tireless prankster, and if it had turned out that the world at large took his pranks seriously, so much the better for the world. Meanwhile, the mischievous maker of the pranks would have moved on to other experiments, which in the world of the arts (unlike the world of science) may give as much pleasure when they fail as when they succeed.

A number of Man Ray's successful experiments have entered history. One thinks, for example, of the Rayograph, a photograph taken without the instrumentality of a lens, by applying an object to a light-sensitive plate. The term amounts to a double play on words: it refers simultaneously to a ray of light and to its inventor's name, which was itself a shortened version—two monosyllables always used in tandem, as if they amounted to but a single name—of the cumbersomely octo-syllabic original. At the time of his birth, which took place in Phila-delphia in 1890, he had been given the name Emmanuel Radnowitz, which at an early age he decided was unsuited to the role in life that he had projected for himself. Indeed, nothing in his family background and in the years of his growing-up, which were passed mostly in the helter-skelter, first-generation Jewish ferment of Brooklyn, struck him as worthy of the talent and intelligence that he was aware of possessing and that he judged as coolly and with as little false modesty as if they belonged to a stranger.

Man Ray's friend Roland Penrose wrote of him during his lifetime that he had wished to be thought, like Adam, the first of his race. That

Adamic Man Ray may be said to have achieved birth when, in his late teens and early twenties, after erratic attendance at various art schools in Manhattan, he fell in with the circle of artists and photographers that Alfred Stieglitz had founded in cramped quarters at 291 Fifth Avenue. A year or so later, at the time of the celebrated Armory Show of 1913, Man Ray met Marcel Duchamp and they became fast friends. It was a friendship that lasted until Duchamp's sudden death from a heart attack in 1968, at the age of eighty. Duchamp, Man Ray, and their wives had just spent a happy evening together, over a dinner of pheasant and red wine, talking of old times. Man Ray himself would die several years later, at the age of eighty-six.

When, in 1921, after several years' residence in New York, Duchamp returned to France, he persuaded Man Ray to follow him. Through Duchamp, Man Ray had been observing the radical new Dadaist movement in Paris and had been eager to launch an equivalent movement in this country. With a mock authorization from Tristan Tzara, one of the founders of the movement, he and Duchamp had put out a single issue of a magazine called New York Dada. On its cover was a photograph of a bottle of perfume, bearing a likeness of a regal lady—actually Duchamp—and the name of the perfume, "Belle Haleine," where the name "Belle Hélène" might have been expected. (In translation, we are confronted with "beautiful breath" instead of "beautiful Helen." Dadaists placed much reliance upon the humor of puns and the power of free association; back of "Belle Haleine" lurks Offenbach's operetta La Belle Hélène, which tells the story of Helen of Troy. It was a characteristic Dada joke: Duchamp in drag equals Helen of Troy.) Thanks to the magazine and to word that had reached Paris of several paintings by Man Ray in a Dadaist vein, Man Ray found himself already highly regarded by the inner circle of Dadaists, including Tzara, Paul Eluard, Louis Aragon, and Jacques Rigaut.

Many years afterward, Man Ray was to claim that from the moment of his arrival in Paris he was kept so busy both as an artist (at the start, a darling of the Dadaists and later a darling of the Surrealists) and as a photographer (at the start, a photographer of fashion and later a photographer of fashionable people) that it was a full decade before he paid his first visit to the Louvre. He was himself one of the most prominent of the expatriate Americans living in Paris during the twenties and thirties, a group that included Virgil Thomson, Cole Porter, Gertrude Stein, Alice B. Toklas, Henry Miller, Ernest Hemingway, Josephine Baker, Gerald and Sara Murphy, Janet Flanner, and Natalie Barney. At the time, it was deemed a proof of the high place one had achieved in the world to be photographed by Man Ray. He took the photograph of Hemingway, shy and wearing a raggedy woolen sweater, that accompanied the publication of his first book, *In Our Time*. Joyce sat for him, with characteristic impatience, when *Ulysses* was about to be published. One of the Joyce photographs that became a favorite throughout the world showed him with his face turned away from the camera and his forehead resting upon his hand, as if deep in thought; in fact, Joyce was sheltering his eyes for a few moments from the glare of Man Ray's lights. Among a thousand or so other writers and artists that Man Ray photographed were Ezra Pound, T. S. Eliot, Brancusi, Aldous Huxley, Gertrude Stein, Sinclair Lewis, Picasso, and William Carlos Williams.

Man Ray was understandably content with *la vie parisienne*—a flat in town, a place in the country, a fast car, and a substantial income, to say nothing of a succession of mistresses who kept him company and who served him as models. The best known of these was a voluptuous young nightclub singer, Kiki of Montparnasse; she posed for perhaps the most celebrated of all Man Ray's photographs, *Le Violon d'Ingres*, in which we see painted on the back of a nude odalisque the curved sound holes of a violin case. In a sense, her body has been transformed into a convincing musical instrument; in another sense, we are invited to perceive that her body was already a convincing instrument, of delight if not primarily of music. To heighten the wit of the visual pun, the title of the photograph is an idiom that in French signifies "a favorite pastime."

Man Ray would certainly never have returned to the United States except for the outbreak of the Second World War. Landing in New York, of which he had few agreeable memories (the battle he had waged there in order to invent himself as Man Ray had left him, so he would say, with many scars), he set off at once for Hollywood. He had assumed that he would find in the citadel of the comparatively new art of the movies an exhilarating intellectual turmoil not unlike the one he had left behind in Paris; instead, he found a wilderness. Aside from the good fortune of his meeting and marrying Juliet—they shared a double wedding ceremony with Max Ernst and Dorothea Tanning—the years that Man Ray spent in California struck him as having gone largely to waste. His paintings and assemblages (the latter facetiously entitled *The Objects of My Affection*), when put on exhibition, were dismissed by ignorant critics as Johnny-come-lately imitations of the handiwork of those Surrealist artists among whom Man Ray himself had once been hailed as a pioneer. He made a few friends—the Al Lewins, Henry Miller, the Stravinskys, Bill Coply, the Jean Renoirs—but at last, and without reluctance, he and Juliet set out for Paris and the commencement, on the rue Férou, of a new stage of their lives.

By the time I met Man Ray, he had long been a figure to whom visitors to Paris came as they would to any generally acknowledged point of interest. Man Ray was aware of the role that he was expected to play as a *monument historique* and would throw himself into the role with considerable relish. To be old and chairbound and yet to be sought out and looked up to and listened to is by no means the worst fate in the world. How much there was to remember! The big black eyes in the round Kewpie-doll face would shine with pleasure as one anecdote plucked up out of memory would trip another and then another. When had he met the great couturier Paul Poiret and how had it happened—a favorite anecdote—that he had failed to take his picture? When had he met Cocteau, whose picture he took again and again, to that dandy's perennial delight? Man Ray's exceptionally acute memory had not failed with age—he was, as he had said, "all right from the waist up," and he recalled that it was the painter Francis Picabia who had given him an introduction to Cocteau. At once they had become friends, in spite of the fact that most of Man Ray's Dadaist colleagues despised Cocteau as a social butterfly.

As one of those innumerable visitors to the shrine on the rue Férou, I asked Man Ray about his well-known photograph of Proust's corpse, the eyes lying sunk into his skull, the chin and cheeks unshaven—never had a body looked more intensely (one might even say, Proust being Proust, more intently) dead—and he told me that it was Cocteau who had arranged for him to take it. The year was 1922, a short while after Man Ray and Cocteau had met. As Man Ray told the story, surely not for the first time and surely not for the last, his telephone rang one Sunday morning, and it was Cocteau babbling in a high, distressed voice, "*Venez toute de suite! Notre petit Marcel est mort!"* Man Ray picked up what he called his "old shoe" of a camera and made his way to Proust's apartment, to which Cocteau admitted him. The only available light came from a single electric light bulb of low wattage directly above Proust's bed. Had that made it difficult, I inquired, to take the picture? The little god in his attic looked at me with good-humored scorn. "Certainly not!" he exclaimed. "A corpse is the easiest thing in the world to photograph. The subject being motionless, I was able to set my camera for as long an exposure as I pleased. The results were, let me say, satisfactory."

Gerald and
Sara Murphy

F. Scott Fitzgerald's novel *Tender Is the Night* bears the dedication, "To Gerald and Sara: Many Fêtes." Reading it in 1934, the year that it was published—which happened also to be the year that I turned twenty—I was every bit as bewitched by the allusive reticence of those six dedicatory words as I was by the novel itself, the exquisite opening sentences of which I memorized after my first reading of them and which sometimes after all this while, waking at night in the dark (and content to be awake in the dark), I recite to myself for the pleasure they give me:

> On the pleasant shore of the French Riviera, about halfway between Marseilles and the Italian border, stands a large, proud, rose-colored hotel. Deferential palms cool its flushed facade, and before it stretches a short, dazzling beach . . . The hotel and its bright tan prayer rug of a beach were one.

A year or so after the novel was published, having come to New York City and begun my own career as a writer, I learned that Gerald and Sara's last name was Murphy and that they were the true-life figures upon whom Fitzgerald had based Dick and Nicole Diver, the chief characters in the book he had dedicated to them. Gerald as Dick is

312

introduced as "a fine man in a jockey cap and red-striped tights"; Sara-Nicole is described as a young woman lying under a roof of umbrellas and making out a list of things from a book open upon the sand. "Her bathing suit was pulled from her shoulders," Fitzgerald writes, "and her back, a ruddy, orange brown, set off by a string of creamy pearls, shone in the sun. Her face was hard and lovely and pitiful." Of the Murphys, I learned as well that they had a wide circle of friends, with whom, as Fitzgerald's dedication implied, they had indeed celebrated many fêtes. These friends included several major and minor figures in my personal pantheon, among them not only Scott Fitzgerald but Cole Porter, Philip Barry, Donald Ogden Stewart, Dorothy Parker, Ring Lardner, John Dos Passos . . . How glamorous those figures struck me as being—glamorous in the possession of their talent and in the possession of a grand worldly success as well!

Of course I wished to be in their presence, if not one of them. Admiration and envy linked me to them. I looked forward to the day when, if I too proved to have talent, I would earn their approbation and perhaps even their friendship—they would be to me, as they were to one another, Scott, Cole, Phil, Don, and the like. Set down in print, that aspiration has the look of a literary snobbery not necessarily to be forgiven on the grounds of youth; I can only assert that, at the time, it felt like worship, not snobbery—a worship so pure that I was content to remain at a distance from the pantheon until one of the gods emerged and indicated to me that I might approach.

Eager as I was to meet Fitzgerald, for example, I put off doing so on several occasions that would have been agreeable to me and, at worst, not painful to him. The place we would have met in was Asheville, North Carolina, where Fitzgerald's wife, Zelda, was confined in what was locally termed "a home for mentals." Having suffered severe financial losses during the depression, my wife's parents, Madelaine and Frank Barnard, had moved from New York to Asheville in the early 1930s. The city itself had fallen upon hard times; as a summer resort high in the Blue Ridge Mountains, it had enjoyed a real-estate boom that collapsed even before the stock-market crash of 1929. Its bonds were in default, a number of new civic buildings and schools remained unpaid-for, and on the outskirts of the city one encountered mile after mile of abandoned streets in unbuilt-upon subdivisions, where weeds and hardhack were forcing their way up out of cracks in the unused pavements and where the glass globes of the streetlights had long been smashed, their empty bulb sockets turned to rust.

In 1936, when I first began visiting my parents-in-law in Asheville, Madelaine Barnard was working in a small dress shop in downtown Asheville—the only fashionable dress shop in town, run by a friend of hers, Jean West. When Scott Fitzgerald came to Asheville to visit Zelda, he would stay at the Grove Park Inn, an immense, boulder-built fortress of a hotel rising as if out of the dawn of history on a mountainside overlooking the Asheville Golf Club. In the course of his stay in Asheville, Fitzgerald would drop in at Jean West's shop, seat himself on an Empire loveseat that filled the little space inside the show window, and chat with Madelaine Barnard. There were few people in Asheville that he felt inclined to see; his career was at its nadir (his books were selling in the secondhand bookshops in Asheville for ten cents apiece, when they sold at all), he had little money, he was drinking, and he felt permanently cut off from the friends with whom he had once been happy. Hemingway, then at the height of his fame, had written publicly of him as "poor Scott." It was a betrayal that he had not steeled his heart against; he was by no means eager to be pitied by anyone, least of all by Hemingway.

It happened that Madelaine Barnard, a pretty and exceptionally charming woman a few years older than Fitzgerald, came from the sort of background that Fitzgerald had long observed and envied—that of old money, at ease with itself and confident of itself even in adversity. She was descended from Dutch families in Brooklyn and upstate New York, her father had been a champion athlete at Yale, she had attended the Spence School in New York, had lived at the Dakota, and had "come out" at Sherry's, and her sister had married a Boston Coolidge (no mere farming Vermont Coolidge). Fitzgerald and she found that they had friends in common and, still better, recollections in common, of Rye and Great Neck, of Paris and Biarritz. Lady Astor's sister—one of the beauteous Langhornes of Virginia—had married a famous Princeton football player named "Lefty" Flynn. (Another sister married the artist Charles Dana Gibson.) The Flynns lived in Tryon, a few miles south of Asheville, and Mrs. Flynn was often in the shop, along with other friends of Madelaine; they did their best, those good-hearted women, to cheer Fitzgerald up in his time of troubles and he was grateful to them, though their efforts proved in vain.

In the course of their conversations, Madelaine Barnard spoke to Fitzgerald of her new son-in-law and of the start of his career at *The New Yorker* (the magazine had begun to buy some of my short stories in the fall of 1936, shortly after I graduated from Yale and got married. I was also selling short stories to the *Saturday Evening Post*, whose highest-paid writer Fitzgerald had once been). Fitzgerald courteously expressed an interest in meeting me, and my mother-in-law sought to bring us together on one or another of my visits to Asheville, which over the next couple of years I could easily have arranged to make coincide with one of Fitzgerald's. Not yet, I told her—in the words of the Latin Mass that Fitzgerald and I were both familiar with and that my Episcopalian mother-in-law neither knew nor, had she known them, would have felt any patience with: "*Domine non sum dignus.* Oh, Lord, I am not worthy."

Fitzgerald died in 1940. Two or three years later, his daughter, "Scottie," came to work as a reporter for *The New Yorker*. She was a small, fine-boned, good-looking young woman, exceptional in energy and in her sunny good nature—none of the series of misfortunes that had dogged her parents appeared to have cast the least shadow over her. In their youth, her parents had been among the most photographed of celebrities—their faces were almost as familiar to the public as the faces of movie stars—and it was curious to glimpse in Scottie portions of her parents' features: Scott in the blond hair and green eyes, Zelda in the bold mouth. Zelda was still living at the "home" in Asheville (many years later, she would die in agony there, in a fire that consumed the rickety frame structure) and from time to time she would mail to Scottie at the magazine drawings and watercolors that Scottie would hand on to me, hoping that I could persuade our art editor to take an interest in them. The pictures consisted of nonrepresentational diagonal slashes, triangles, and other geometric forms, in which one saw, or, given the circumstances, convinced oneself that one had seen, the expression of a violent, undischarged rage: in any event, works radically unsuited to *The New Yorker*.

Scottie was married to a man whom her father would have considered the ideal husband; for all I know, it may have been one of the reasons for her marrying him. He was tall and handsome, had money, and bore a distinguished name: Samuel Jackson Lanahan. He was also a Catholic, and to be a Catholic and at the same time to occupy a secure position in society was exceedingly rare in those days except in Baltimore, a city founded by Catholics. And it was Baltimore that Lanahan hailed from. (Scott Fitzgerald had felt a strong emotional bond with Baltimore. He and Zelda had lived just outside the city for a time, and Francis Scott Key, to whom Fitzgerald was distantly related and after whom he was proud to have been named, had practiced law in nearby Frederick.) During the Second World War, Lanahan served in the navy. With a knack for writing but with no professional experience, Scottie had succeeded in getting a job at *The New Yorker* in part because Harold Ross, its founder and editor, was impressed by her literary pedigree and in part because the draft instituted in the Second World War had plucked so many male members of the staff.

As the father of three, I was in a draft classification that was constantly being advised of the imminence of our being summoned into the armed forces; we would then be told that our entrance had been temporarily postponed. Had I been drafted, I would have been assigned to the Army Air Force's Office of Flying Safety, in Winston-Salem, North Carolina, where John Cheever, Max Shulman, and other writer-friends of mine were being kept only moderately busy composing the texts of training manuals. It wasn't a very heroic—indeed, it was quite a cozy—wartime activity, which left plenty of time to go on writing one's own short stories and novels. (Out of that particular air force program emerged James Gould Cozzens' *Guard of Honor*, one of the best novels of the Second World War.) Ironically, the factual pieces that I wrote for *The New Yorker* as a civilian—flying in bombers and fighter planes, coasting along the ocean floor in submarines, and other welcomely exhilarating adventures—entailed far greater risks than I was likely to have encountered in uniform in Winston-Salem.

Scottie doted on me as an "older" man—I was then in my late twenties and she was perhaps twenty-two. In an innocent fashion, she believed herself to be in love with me and went so far as to write a short story about her "crush" on me. The story, published in *The New Yorker*, was called "The Water Cooler," and the only action of its exceedingly skimpy plot consisted of two writers on the staff of a magazine, one male and the other female, meeting at a water cooler, where by accident the male writer happens to spill a Lily cup of water onto the dress of the female writer. Understandably, the story failed to create a scandal, or indeed to attract any attention whatever.

Through Scottie, I met a number of her father's friends—Jarvis Cromwell, Judge Betts—and also, in due course, the Murphys. They were giving a cocktail party one afternoon in an apartment they had taken in the immense neo-Renaissance apartment house at 131 East Sixty-sixth Street, designed at the turn of the century by Charles Platt. I knew by then, of course, that the Murphys had served as models for Dick and Nicole Diver, and from *Tender Is the Night* and other literary sources I had heard of that stylish domestic invention of theirs, the Villa America, perched high above the Mediterranean at Cap d'Antibes. The Murphys had a knack for transforming any space that they inhabited— even, it might be, a temporary hotel room—into something inimitably Murphyesque. Their apartment, with its great two-story-high studio living room, struck me as odd and amusing (the Divers were amusing at any cost), but also as something more than simply odd and amusing; some true emotion—an emotion beyond the desire to please—had gone into its creation.

In the hubbub of the party, Scottie introduced me to Sara and Gerald, and of that first meeting I recall feeling a certain negative shock: they seemed older, plumper, and less romantic-looking than I had expected them to be. Gerald had grown bald by then and Sara had grown fat. (My disappointment was based upon a miscalculation in respect to time: the Murphys were not, after all, the Divers of the 1920s, as in my imagination I had pictured them as being.) Quickly, with the ease of skilled hosts, they introduced me to other guests, who included that day two members of my pantheon of cherished writers—John Dos Passos and Archibald MacLeish. I caught a glimpse of Edmund Wilson as well, but I had met him some time earlier, at the *New Yorker* offices, and I was aware that it was just as well to avoid him at a party; his shyness caused him to be overbearing and garrulous, and he would speak on and on, in a penetrating, high-pitched voice, leaving his auditors with little to do but plan the least impolite means of escaping him.

The next time I met the Murphys was at a luncheon party at their ancient galleried house on the shore of the Hudson, at Snedens Landing. A suburb of New York City that seems infinitely removed not only from the city itself but from the twentieth century as well, Snedens (as it is commonly called) is just the sort of place that the Murphys were bound to have been drawn to. It consists of an all but invisible assortment of romantic houses clinging to a steep, thickly wooded cliffside on the west bank of the river. Gerald Murphy was fascinated by the minutiae of language, and he was delighted to be able to boast that, as far as he knew, Snedens was the only place in the United States capable of being spelled with equal correctness forward and backward. In his view, to live in a palindrome was better than to live in a palace. Their house, called Cheer Hall, looked out upon the site of a wharf that had been built in the eighteenth century by an early Sneden, who ran a ferry service across the Hudson at that point. Among its passengers on more than one occasion during the Revolution was General Washington, after whom a spring on the hillside at Snedens is named.

In 1870, a rich New York businessman named Henry Effington Lawrence bought a farm at Snedens, built a big mansion on a bluff above the Hudson, and began turning the property into an estate for the summer use of his family. One of his children, Mary, was two years old at the time; over the following three-quarters of a century, she devoted much of her life to the creation at Snedens of a community of artists, writers, architects, and actors, living in ramshackle Victorian cottages, barns, stables, greenhouses, and the like—structures that she bought, rebuilt from whatever likely or (more often) unlikely materials happened to present themselves, and then rented out to tenants whose tastes and temperaments were similar to her own. The community that she invented, at first glance so helter-skelter in layout, became over the years a coherent, highly individual work of art; to this day a visitor strolling the zigzag wooded lanes of Snedens senses that the stamp of a powerful personality has been placed upon its sequestered landscape.

Despite its seeming remoteness, Snedens is only a thirty minutes' drive from Broadway, making it an ideal hideaway for people in the theatre; among the residents of Snedens in the period during which the Murphys lived there were Katharine Cornell and her husband, Guthrie McClintic, Orson Welles, Burgess Meredith, Noël Coward, and Laurence Olivier. (Snedens is still a favorite dwelling place for actors. Bill Murray recently bought the Katharine Cornell house; other Snedens residents are William Hurt, Diane Keaton, and Al Pacino.) Many artists and writers also lived in Snedens, and on the occasion of my first visit to the Murphys I was in the company of my colleague at *The New Yorker*,

Maeve Brennan, whom the Murphys were—it is not too much to say— enraptured by.

Maeve was a tiny, fiery young Irishwoman, born in Dublin, who had come to this country after the Second World War, when her father, Robert Brennan, was appointed minister to the United States from the Irish Republic. (In the nomenclature of the State Department, "minister" was later raised to "ambassador.") Bent upon becoming a writer, Maeve had quickly made her way from Washington, D.C., to New York, where she secured a lowly job at the New York Public Library. A fellow Irishwoman, Carmel Snow, editor of *Harper's Bazaar*, befriended Maeve and invited her to join the editorial staff of that magazine. Along with writing, Maeve occasionally served as a model for *Bazaar* photographers, who admired her slanted eyes, high cheekbones, and tilted nose, to say nothing of her bizarre, topknotted hairdo and the extreme makeup that she chose to wear—a broad slash of red across her mouth, the thickest of mascara on her lashes. Having had a couple of short pieces accepted by *The New Yorker*, she was soon invited by William Shawn, then its managing editor, to join our staff. For a number of years she wrote a large portion of the book reviews that are published under the rubric "Briefly Noted." She also wrote many pieces for "Talk of the Town," ascribed to "Long-winded Lady," and short stories about the life that she and her family had known in Dublin. (Her father, a leader in the struggle for the independence of Ireland, had been captured by the British in the early twenties, imprisoned, and sentenced to death; his reprieve came only a few days before the date set for his execution. Awaiting death, he would look out from a barred window in Mountjoy Prison to see his wife in the street below, holding the infant Maeve high in her arms.)

Maeve had quickness of wit, a sharp tongue, and the gift of style; like the Murphys, she could bestow distinction upon the humblest objects—a painted biscuit tin, a table woven of straw—by the emphasis she gave them or by the unexpected uses to which she put them. Gerald Murphy was always eager to see other people succeed; he was determined that Maeve become the well-known writer she had it in her to be. If, as things turned out, her career was to be other (and far sadder) than what Gerald had hoped for her, it was not from any lack of effort on his part. He and Sara sheltered Maeve and sought to protect her against her demons, but it was as if Maeve—bitter, dazzling, talented, tenderhearted, intractable Maeve—were herself on the side of the demons, and so the demons won out against Gerald and all the rest of us who, well or badly, fought them in her behalf.

The day that Maeve brought me to the Murphys' house at Snedens, the victory of the demons was still far in the future. It was a bright autumn day and we were all in a holiday mood. Gerald greeted us at the open doorway of the house; as usual, he was turned out in a dapper fashion that stopped just short of self-mockery: one might say of him that he was simultaneously a dude and a parody of a dude. And how superbly he wore whatever he chose to put on his back! That day, he was wearing a short, striped apron of the kind that sommeliers in French restaurants customarily wear (where on earth would one go to buy such an apron? Only Gerald would know). Standing before his own exquisite painting of bar tools—a painting that he was later to give to Philip Barry's widow, Ellen, as a housewarming gift when she moved to Washington, and which is now on loan from her to the Dallas Art Museum—he mixed drinks for us in a frosted silver shaker and offered us hot hors d'oeuvres from a silver Georgian salver: which is a way of saying that, there before us stood Dick Diver in all his irresistible pleasingness.

That was the day on which we struck up, Gerald and I, a friendship that was to last until his death. It was a friendship in the shape of a triangle, with Sara and Gerald making up one angle, Maeve making up a second, and I a third. We had much to enjoy in our friendship aside from our shared affection and concern for Maeve, but it was the case that she was present among us even when she was absent. To utter an Irish bull, she was especially present to us when she was absent, for then we became preoccupied with the significance of her having slipped beyond our reach: *now* what awful thing had she contrived to have befall her? The weight of that question rested upon us even when we were at our merriest.

Although Gerald was a quarter of a century older than I, we found that we had much in common, beginning with our Irishness. My family had been in this country for several generations, while Gerald was the son of an immigrant, but the Gills had followed the usual narrow Irish tradition of continuously marrying with their own kind; up to my father's day, they were as intensely and parochially Irish in blood and custom as if they had just stepped off the boat. Having exceptional intelligence and exceptional energy (and a powerful mother determined to see that those attributes did not go to waste), my father emerged from the anonymity of the Connecticut farming community into which he had been born, gained his M.D. at Yale, undertook two or three years of further medical studies in Vienna and London, and became a highly successful physician and surgeon in Hartford, Connecticut. Gerald's father, Francis Patrick Murphy, was undoubtedly as intelligent and energetic as mine. In his teens, he became a clerk in a fashionable leather-goods shop in Boston called Mark Cross and within a few years became its owner. Boldly, he decided to move the shop to New York, where it proved an immediate success. Francis Patrick himself became a prominent citizen, known for his business acumen, his courtly manners, and his eloquence. I remember Gerald telling me that at a time when after-dinner speakers were much-admired figures in the social life of New York, his father was the most sought-after speaker on important occasions. In those days, audiences expected to hear memorized orations of long duration—an hour was a trifle—on assigned topics, but such was Francis Patrick's fame that he was able to impose three unprecedented conditions upon any speaking engagement that he consented to accept: he would be the last to speak; he would speak for only seven minutes; and, far from preparing a topic in advance, he would improvise a speech based on remarks that had been made by one of the earlier speakers. What self-assurance! Some would say, what arrogance! Yet it appears that no audience was ever disappointed in him.

Gerald attended Yale and although in later years he expressed contempt for those "bright college years," he was the proverbial "big man on campus," being elected in his senior year to the most prestigious of senior secret societies, Skull and Bones. Membership in that organization was one of the things Gerald and I had in common, and I was astonished to learn that he had disliked the experience. Trivial as undergraduate activities at any university may seem when measured against events in the outside world, the revelation implied a mystery. I told Gerald that he was the only person in the society who had ever said such a thing to me; why had he disliked it? Gerald smiled and made some evasive remark. On several later occasions, I pressed him to give me the reasons for his dislike, always in vain. Many years later, when my son Michael was elected to the society, Gerald teasingly promised that he would confide his reasons to Michael, but before Michael could approach him on the subject, Gerald died.

In Honoria Donnelly's touching biography of her parents, *Sara and Gerald*, published in 1982, she notes that Gerald would never speak of his Bones experience even to his closest friend, Archibald MacLeish, who was elected to the society a few years after him. Another close friend, Monty Woolley, who graduated from Yale in 1911, a year before Gerald, was of the opinion that some misadventure had befallen Gerald and one of his clubmates in Bones *after* graduation. Be that as it may, what Gerald appears to have chiefly disliked about Yale was its then prevalent philistinism, accompanied as it was by a preoccupation with sports and manly body contact (locker-room towel-snapping and the like). Gerald was exceedingly fastidious and the high-spirited horseplay that he may have been expected to participate in as an undergraduate would not have been to his taste. It was characteristic of Gerald to have befriended the shy and exquisite Cole Porter, of the class of '13. He saw to it that Porter was elected to the "right" fraternity (DKE, to which Gerald belonged) and to the socially correct secret society of Scroll and Key, which was second in prestige only to Bones.

In a book about Porter that I wrote the text for back in the early seventies, I included a reminiscence by Gerald of his first meeting with Cole. The tone of the reminiscence is characteristic of Gerald in its mingling of a repugnance to snobbery with an embrace of it:

> There was this barbarous custom of going around to the rooms of the sophomores and talking with them, to see which ones would be the right material for the fraternities. I remember going around and seeing several nights running, a sign on one boy's door saying "Back at 10 P.M. Gone to football song practice." Gordon Hamilton, the handsomest and most sophisticated boy in the class, was enormously irritated that *anyone* would have the gall to be out of his room on visiting night, and decided not to call on him at all. But one night I was passing his room and went in, just to say hello. There was a single electric light bulb in the center of the ceiling, wicker furniture, which was considered a bad sign at Yale in 1911, a piano with a box of caramels on it, and a little dark man with his hair parted in the middle and slicked back, and wearing a salmon pink tie and a checked suit, looking like a westerner dressed up for the East. He told me that he lived on an enormous apple farm in Indiana and

that he had a cousin called Desdemona and they both used to ride to market on the apple trucks. He said yes, he had submitted a song for the football team and that it has just been accepted. We had a long talk about music and composers—we were both crazy about Gilbert and Sullivan. I got the Glee Club [of which Gerald was a member] to take him in as a sophomore—something that was almost never done—so that he could sing a new song he had written which he performed on the tour that year. It was the hit of the show, a satire on the joys of owning an automobile. He came out front and sang it perfectly, without any sort of act, just folded his hands behind him and sang it in the simplest way, while the seniors and juniors on the stage behind him went "zoom, zoom, zoom."

In the years since Gerald's death, I have often discussed with friends and acquaintances of his the nature of his sexual life. Curiously enough, the Yale that Gerald despised for its masculine philistinism was influenced, to an extent that the hearty Dink Stovers of the time were totally unaware of, by a strong homosexual minority. At football games, the Yale Band played Cole Porter's stirring songs—"Bull Dog! Bull Dog! Bow-wow-wow!" and "Bingo! Bingo!" (in his undergraduate days, Cole Porter himself bounded up and down the sidelines as a cheerleader)—and the Yale Dramat was coached by Monty Woolley. The first musical the Dramat put on under Woolley's leadership had music by Cole and a libretto by T. Lawrason Riggs, later to become the Catholic chaplain at Yale. Cole, Woolley, and Riggs were all homosexuals, as was Cole's lifelong companion, Leonard Hanna, of the class of '13.

In the years immediately following their graduation from Yale, Gerald and Cole entered a world whose twin poles were New York and Paris—metropolises in which a considerable degree of sexual irregularity was observed without alarm by society and the arts. Cole, for example, was instantly taken up by Elizabeth Marbury, a leading theatrical agent in New York, who contrived to be a good friend of Governor Al Smith, most conventional of men, and the companion of Elsie De Wolfe. (Marbury and De Wolfe, who shared a house on Irving Place, were always referred to as "the bachelor girls.") Gerald's parents were strict disciplinarians, and Gerald, in awe of his father and disliking his devoutly Catholic mother, kept a wary distance from both of them. So did his elder brother and his sister Esther, who from the cradle was regarded by her intimates as a literary genius and who became one of the most prominent of that lesbian circle in Paris which included Gertrude Stein, Alice B. Toklas, Natalie Barney, and Janet Flanner. Esther planned for many years to write a biography of Louis XIV—"Talking with Esther," Ellen Barry has said, "you would think that she had just had breakfast with the Sun King"—and later she contemplated a biography of her friend Edith Wharton, but the two projects came to nothing. She earned a curious fame in Paris for her habit of relieving herself wherever she happened to be seated, on no matter what occasion, public or private; hostesses took care to lead her away from well-upholstered chairs. Gerald's sister-in-law, Noel Haskins Murphy, widow of his elder brother Frank, was also a lesbian, numbering among many lovers over a long lifetime Janet Flanner and Nancy Cunard.

There is no actual evidence that Gerald was a homosexual, or had homosexual experiences in his youth, but there *is* evidence that something caused him to take a forbidding view of sex, whether homosexual or heterosexual. It may have been his view of sex as somehow menacing to him that caused him to substitute for the ordinary rough-and-tumble of life a fabricated (and to many an off-putting) elegance of person and conduct—the same sort of elegance that other dandies (Whistler, Wilde, Beerbohm) adopted and found efficacious in keeping conventional amorous commotion at bay. The aesthete is a man standing at a calculated distance from his fellows; his posture silently instructs us "Touch me not."

A glimpse of Gerald's attitude toward sex, as related to me by Archibald MacLeish: having lunch one day at a New York club with Philip Barry and Gerald, MacLeish began with Barry a somewhat ribald discussion of the pleasures of lovemaking. The three men were then in their thirties and the topic was by no means an inappropriate one. To Archie's astonishment, Gerald threw up his hands and exclaimed, "Thank God all that is behind me!" After which, understandably, the conversation was quick to take a different turn.

Also exceptional was the length of time that Gerald courted Sara. Good-looking, intelligent, and affectionate, Sara was one of three daughters of Frank and Adeline Sherman Wiborg; her father, a Norwegian immigrant, had made a fortune in the manufacture of printing ink in Cincinnati and had come East to make good socially. (According to a turn-of-the-century custom satirized in the brilliant pen-and-ink drawings of Charles Dana Gibson, the self-made man invariably underwent the costly and exhausting quest to enter society not for his own sake but for that of an ambitious wife. In the Wiborgs' case, it was certainly true that Adeline Wiborg, a grandniece of the famous Civil War hero General William Tecumseh Sherman, was socially ambitious and that the vessels into which she poured her ambition were her three beautiful daughters.)

Wiborg had purchased eighty acres of land lying between the Atlantic Ocean and Hook Pond, in East Hampton, and had built a large and handsome mansion on the dunes there, along with a number of farm buildings to house help, horses, and cows. Gerald's family were members of the minor Irish "aristocracy" that had achieved a foothold in neighboring Southampton, but Gerald much preferred what was thought to be the artistic bohemianism of East Hampton, and from his undergraduate days in New Haven he was in and out of the Wiborgs' house as readily as if he were a member of the family. It was accepted that he and Sara loved each other, but it was apparently not accepted that this should lead to marriage. On the Murphys' side, the parents' objections were based on Gerald's assumed inability to earn a sufficient living to support a family; after graduating from Yale, he had gone to work for his father at Mark Cross, but plainly his heart wasn't in it. On the Wiborgs' side, the difficulty was far greater. Mrs. Wiborg had performed all the traditional social gestures that were supposed to prepare young women for a brilliant marriage—a coming-out party in New York, travel abroad, and presentation at the Court of St. James (Lady Diana Cooper wrote of them in her memoirs, "The Wiborg girls were the rage of London that summer")—but she was adamantly opposed to any of her daughters marrying; so possessive was she that one of her daughters never married and the other two married against her will. When Gerald finally asked for Sara's hand, Sara was thirty-one, which was many years beyond the usual age of marriage for women in her set; moreover, she was several years older than Gerald, which was also out of the ordinary. Significantly, she took care to conceal this disparity in their ages almost to her dying day.

Few passionate young men in Gerald's situation would have been content to pursue a chaste courtship year after year without protest, as he did, seemingly because he and Sara shared a common fear of their parents' wrath. When they finally married, they escaped at once to Europe, where their parents might visit them on occasion but where they could avoid that daily scrutiny and criticism that the parents thought it their duty to provide. Three children—Honoria, Patrick, and Baoth—were born within the next few years, with a speed that had the look of being a throwback to Gerald's Irish-Catholic origins but that is far likelier to have been a consequence of the fact that Sara was approaching what was then thought to be a dangerous age for childbearing. They were eager to have a family and they cherished the children with an exceptional fervor.

In Paris, the Murphys rented a spacious apartment on the quai des Grands-Augustins, with a romantic view up and down the Seine. In his usual compulsive fashion, Gerald undertook an immediate and intense apprenticeship as a painter. He also set about learning French on a level above that which he had attained at Hotchkiss and Yale. From his amusing, artful account of this experience, I perceived that I was meant to draw the conclusion that what almost anyone else would have regarded as bad luck was for Gerald the best of good luck. For the teacher he commissioned to give him private lessons was an elderly widow who had been married in her teens, some sixty years earlier, to an octogenarian guardian. This gentleman had been born at the court of Louis XVI, in the waning years of the eighteenth century, and it was the court language of that epoch in which Gerald, unbeknownst to him, was being instructed; when he spoke it to ordinary Parisians, they were struck dumb with bewilderment and consequently so was he. They could tell that he was speaking correct French, but as far as understanding him was concerned, he might have been speaking Choctaw. And so he discovered that an archaic correctness of language, like dandyism, like treating life as a fiction, could serve to establish a welcome distance between oneself and others; and it did so not only without giving offense but with a display of seemingly exceptional good manners.

This discovery became one of the secrets that Gerald took pleasure in keeping, some of which he carried to the grave. One sensed instantly upon meeting him that he had chosen to be a masked figure, and the adroit civility with which he conveyed to friends as well as to strangers that there was much behind the mask that was to remain permanently undisclosed was itself a mask, or, rather, an invisible, protective shield, set a fraction of an inch in front of the mask proper. In short, if there were secrets to be kept, there was also the unassailable secret of *why* the secrets were being kept. It is possible—it is even likely—that I exaggerate the degree of Gerald's maskedness; the greater part of his life was behind him by the time we met, and the scraps of information that I possessed had drifted my way more or less by chance, in many cases before our friendship began. I felt that it might strike Gerald as intrusive of me to seek to authenticate these scraps face to face, all the more so because I was professionally a reporter and might be suspected of pursuing a possible story. For Gerald and Sara had gained a measure of fame in literary circles by dint of their friendships with writers and artists; to their distaste, they had become figures to write about—had become, in the jargon of gossip columnists, legends. Toward the end of his life, Gerald allowed a trusted friend and Snedens neighbor, Calvin Tomkins, to write about Sara and him in an article in *The New Yorker*, later expanded into a delightful book called *Living Well Is the Best Revenge*, which became an unexpected best-seller. (The title, said to be translated from a Spanish proverb, is odder than it looks at first glance. It is certainly unlike the ever-precise Gerald in the ambiguity of "well," which can mean "in an admirable fashion" but also, and merely, "in a luxurious fashion." As for "revenge," the Murphys were too wise to suppose that it was possible for them to take revenge upon anyone or anything for the buffetings of fate that they had been so unready for and that, when the buffetings came, they bore so bravely.)

If Gerald chose to turn a crucial chapter of his life at Yale—his dislike of Skull and Bones—into a mystery and if the nature of his prolonged courtship also amounted to something of a mystery, still another mysterious chapter was that of his abandonment of a career as a painter. In the course of a few years during the period of their residence in Paris, he painted more than a dozen masterly oils. Gerald himself affected not to recollect the exact number (his uncertainty was surely a form of masking). At the time that an exhibition of the extant paintings was held at the Museum of Modern Art, in 1974, ten years after Gerald's death, William Rubin, then the curator of painting and sculpture at the museum, estimated the total number at perhaps fourteen, some of which had vanished without a trace. Though the paintings reflect the influence of other painters at work in Paris at the time, Léger and Braque among them, they are obviously the product of Gerald's own witty and fastidious intellect; depicting made things, in almost every case they take care to omit the makers of the things and they even omit—or pretend to omit—the maker of the painting as well.

An exception is the single self-portrait that Gerald is known to have completed. In the 1930s, with the coming of the depression and the death of Gerald's father, it appeared that Mark Cross, the shop that was the family's source of wealth, was threatened with financial failure; reluctantly, Gerald took on the task of saving it. Leaving for the States and uncertain of when, if ever, the family would be able to return, Gerald presented the self-portrait as a keepsake to his friend and employee Vladimir Orloff, skipper of the Murphys' schooner, the *Weatherbird* (named after a favorite song of Gerald's, as sung by Louis Armstrong). Many years later, Orloff was to claim that the painting had been lost in a fire, but Ellen Barry surmises that he sold it and that it will eventually turn up in some distinguished European collection. Mrs. Barry is convinced that at least one more Murphy painting remains rolled up and unidentified in the back room of an art gallery in Paris. One of the lost paintings, called *Boatdeck*, was eighteen feet high by twelve feet wide—a prodigious size at the time it was painted in 1923, though common enough today—and, thanks to its size, one would have thought it a hard picture to lose. Also on an exceptionally grand scale was the backdrop that Gerald painted that same year for a ballet, *Within the Quota*, presented in Paris by Les Ballets Suédois. Gerald wrote the libretto for the ballet and designed the costumes and setting; Cole Porter wrote the music, in a jazzy mode that to some extent—and by a few months—anticipated Gershwin's *Rhapsody in Blue*. The ballet was a great success in Paris and enjoyed an equal success in New York during the following year.

Like other friends of the Murphys', Ellen and Philip Barry never discussed with them the abrupt ending of Gerald's career as a painter. It was silently assumed that it came about in large part because of the domestic upheaval that followed the discovery that the Murphys' young son Patrick had contracted tuberculosis. From the moment of that discovery, the idyll that the Murphys had devoted themselves to achieving was shattered; the lives of every member of the family began to revolve around Patrick's illness. Year after year the gallant boy hung on, gradually losing ground; he was only a few months away from death when a totally unexpected disaster befell the Murphys—their other son, the sturdy, athletic Baoth, who was attending prep school in New England, underwent a double mastoid operation. An infection from the operation led to spinal meningitis, and within a few days Baoth was dead.

Mysteriously, Baoth died bearing the name of Wiborg and not Murphy, and again it was Gerald who was the author of the mystery. In the early seventies, I wrote to Archibald MacLeish, seeking an explanation. MacLeish had composed a poem in Baoth's memory, which he read at Baoth's funeral service at St. George's School. MacLeish replied:

> It *does* have every appearance of mystery—perhaps a tiny bundle left in a shoe box on the front porch. Actually, it is pure Gerald. Just before Sara's father (she was born Wiborg—ink—Cincinnati) died he let her know somehow how deeply it grieved him to have left no son—or, more precisely, to be about to leave no son. Gerald, therefore, made Mr. Wiborg a gift, as far as he could, of *his* . . . son, Baoth, who was already half-Scandinavian by name. Simple—and (really) wonderful as that! Thank you for telling me about the tree. [A tree had been planted as part of Baoth's memorial service. I had felt obliged to tell MacLeish that the tree had died.] Ogden Nash, whom I had not met, was there that day— old St. George's boy. I broke down reading the poem. He came over across the lawn in complete silence and took my hand.
>
> Thank you for asking the question of
>
> > yours,
> > Archie

Patrick was soon to follow Baoth. Each of the boys died shortly before his sixteenth birthday. The blasting of lives of such exceptional promise caused the Murphys and their friends to feel that fate had malignantly singled them out for punishment. What, then, had been their sin? That they had successfully pursued happiness in a world intended only to contain sorrow?

I have mentioned that it would have been unlike the Murphys to react to misfortune by seeking to take revenge upon it—it is the essence of tragic events that they leave us without any adequate means of responding to them; some of us utter a howl of anguish (Sara's way), others are reduced to numbness (Gerald's way). As the years passed, the Murphys came back slowly into the world, in a form that they themselves regarded as mutilated; such hopes as they entertained in respect to the future centered on Honoria's three children, who were in some sense (and yet with, oh, what a difference!) substitutes for the lost Patrick and Baoth. Those were the Murphys I came to know, and the shared field of energy in which they moved had a radiance that, I seemed to sense, had once been as natural to them as breathing and now cost them an effort, however courteously disguised. Which is to say that, in Yeats' phrase, the Murphys' circus animals were all on show, but these gorgeous creatures were made to caracole about as a gesture of the amiability owed to friends and not as a consequence of a spontaneous flow of invention.

The Murphys had never been rich and had never hesitated to dip into capital. After the Second World War, they consented reluctantly to the kind of fiscal prudence that their parents on both sides had constantly, tiresomely recommended to them in their youth. In East Hampton, they sold off much of the land that Sara had inherited; the big Wiborg house was thrown down in 1941 and a remnant of it transformed into a dwelling. (That remnant was turned over to Honoria and her family, who continue to own it to this day.)

A structure that had once served as a dairy barn on the Wiborg farm and that enjoyed a pleasing prospect of Hook Pond had been remodeled in the thirties by Gerald and his favorite team of architects, Hale Walker and Harold Heller. Gerald named it Swan House, after a swan (famous for its bad temper) that ruled the waters of the pond. On the far shore of the pond was a big white house of the Civil War period, called Somma Riva, which was said to be the first summer house ever built in East Hampton; it belonged then to the Murphys' close friends Ellen and Philip Barry. Gerald kept an ancient Venetian gondola on the pond, and among Ellen's family snapshots is one of Philip pretending to paddle it as it lies beached on the lawn at Swan House.

One of the innumerable houses that Gerald and Sara lived in for a time, but as always only for a time, Swan House was sold to Buffy Harkness, who later married the actor Robert Montgomery. After many years, the Montgomerys sold it to the theatrical producer Alfred de Liagre, and the de Liagre family has been in residence ever since. Thanks to Gerald, Swan House, clad in faded pink stucco, boasts today a full-grown *allée* of feathery ailanthus trees. Only he would have dared to grant ailanthuses—the weed tree of every scruffy backyard in

Manhattan—the dignity of an *allée*. Swan House evokes not the traditional sober mien of East Hampton (a village settled by seventeenth-century Connecticut Yankees) but an odd mixture of Mexico—a fleeting cultural infatuation of Gerald's—and the beach at La Garoupe, on the pagan Riviera, with Dick Diver sedulously raking the hot sand free of seaweed.

The last house that the Murphys occupied was a small A-frame structure that, save for their skill in transforming the commonplace, might have been mistaken for one of those innumerable cookie-cutter tract houses that have been insidiously usurping the fields and pastures of Long Island since the Second World War. Gerald's unerring eye had made sure that the house was sited with a modesty appropriate to its intentions; it was snugly—all but invisibly—tucked away in deep shrubbery on the dune adjacent to his daughter's house. From the living room, one looked out over the Atlantic, as once from the terrace of the Villa America one had looked out over the Mediterranean and as once, from the porches of Cheer Hall at Snedens, one had looked out over the Hudson. From the front door, the prospect was one that Honoria Donnelly describes as having been a favorite of her parents in old age: gazing back toward the village, they glimpsed a white church spire rising out of the tops of the great elms lining Main Street. The picture-postcard prettiness of the scene would have made it dear to Gerald: all his life he had sought out and found something of high value in the ordinary, the seemingly banal.

Gerald mentioned to me once that when he returned to New York in the Great Depression to take charge of Mark Cross, with a characteristic obsessional energy he undertook to walk every foot of Manhattan island. Starting at the South Ferry, weekend after weekend he walked the cat's cradle of streets in the financial district, and the lure of the obsession didn't falter until he had reached a point just north of what is now called Soho, where the numbered streets begin. "To my dismay, the island kept getting wider," he told me. "I had the uneasy feeling that I was losing ground instead of gaining it." In the course of that prolonged exploration of the city, it was the calculated anonymity of block after block of speculator-built cast-iron and brownstone fronts that Gerald was struck by and that kindled his imagination. How much there was to be said for not possessing an individual identity, for not bearing the burden of a proclaimed "personality"!

In East Hampton in Gerald's late years, the anonymous continued to seize his attention. A few descendants of the Shinnecock Indians who had occupied the eastern portion of Long Island before the arrival of the white man still lived in the Hamptons and made hand baskets, brooms, and other domestic utensils, fashioning them out of the local growth of willow, alder, and briarwood. Gerald made me a present of a stiff reddish-brown fibrous brush that he used for scraping vegetables; as far as he knew, it was identical to the brushes that the Shinnecocks had been making for the past two or three centuries. The simplicity and functional aptness of the brush and its lack of change over the centuries delighted him. He quoted Ortega y Gasset: "The things that could be more and are contented to be less!"

To the Murphys, simplicity was an indispensable ingredient even in the playing of a prank. I remember sharing an informal lunch with them on a day of blustering late-autumn wind and rain—was it my last lunch with them in the little house overlooking the Atlantic, with the light pressing like a gray scrim against the windows? A fire snapped and crackled on the stone hearth in the living room. Sara and I were seated on a sofa in front of a low, glass-topped coffee table, while Gerald assumed the role of butler, serving us a round of drinks and then what he called a "collation" (a term he may have recalled from his Catholic youth, as meaning a light monastic meal). He set a plate down before me with a brisk "Bon appétit!" When I began to fumble for the knife and fork on either side of the plate, Gerald and Sara grinned like mischievous children. With the ardor of ignorance (and probably of hunger as well: I had made the long drive out from New York that morning), I had fallen victim to a tiny conspiracy of theirs. For lo and behold! The knife and fork were of paper—they were photographs that Sara had neatly scissored out of an advertisement for silverware in some monthly household magazine and had then slipped under the glass tabletop. So great was their pleasure over having outwitted me that if I hadn't experienced a moment or two of authentic chagrin I would have felt obliged to manufacture it.

We die because we must, but also, little by little and perhaps unconsciously, because we wish to. Not for the world would Gerald— would most of us—admit at any age that we were eager to die, since such an admission might seem to imply to those who have loved us a rebuke for having failed to love us enough—a rebuke that we had no intention of uttering. I feel sure that Gerald wanted to die and was ready to die and that the time that it took him to do so was a form of courtesy—was an acting out of Dick Diver's gift of pleasingness. That fine man in a jockey cap and red-striped tights raking the sand at La Garoupe could make any group happy in spite of themselves. With something like the same intention, according to his daughter's account, Gerald managed to achieve a deathbed scene of old-fashioned gallantry, in which he humorously chaffed and teased the women busy at their weeping. Sara-Nicole, that young woman with her sunburned back and creamy pearls and lovely face, was less fortunate; her mind slipped away long before her stout heart permitted her to do so, and she survived Gerald by many years, dying in 1975, a few weeks before her ninety-second birthday.

Afterword

THE CARTOONIST Charles Addams died a year or so ago, with an absence of fuss so marked that it amounted to an example of his customary sardonic, unemphatic wit. His friends found themselves mingling dismay over the news of his death with a murmur of admiration for the seeming ease with which, even at that dread moment, he had contrived to be so entirely his own man. He was just seating himself in his car, parked outside his apartment building in New York City, when he suffered a massive heart attack; driven to a nearby hospital, he was pronounced dead within an hour. His valiant widow, Tee Miller, was quick to agree with his friends' view of his conduct and she added a further word of praise. In an obituary that appeared next day on the front page of the *New York Times*, she was quoted as saying that, since Charlie had enjoyed a lifelong passion for cars, the manner of his death struck her as a highly appropriate one.

Several weeks later, Tee invited a number of Charlie's friends to a gathering in his honor. Everyone said what a pleasing occasion it was: a true embodiment of Joyce's portmanteau pun, "funferall." Not that it was really a funeral, in spite of the fact that the man in whose name we had gathered had been obsessed with funerary practices. Wasn't it Charlie, after all, who had subscribed to morticians' magazines and gazed with admiration at illustrated advertisements of the tools of that necessary, repellent trade: cosmetics, embalming fluids, plastic bags for the tidy disposition of a corpse's internal organs? Wasn't it Charlie who persuaded Tee to marry him in a cemetery, with the happy couple wearing black? (The cemetery was, in fact, a portion of Tee's country place on Long Island, where several beloved dogs of hers lay buried.) Finally, wasn't it Charlie who rejoiced to draw in the pages of *The New Yorker* cartoons of coffins and gravestones and ghosts that even by a ghost's assumed low standards of fitness seemed notably unhealthy-looking?

No matter! If it wasn't a funeral, neither was it that currently popular successor to funerals, a memorial service. I grant that such services have certain obvious advantages over the barbaric, tearstained, filled-with-wailings funerals that I attended in my youth. One advantage is that they need not be held in a hurry, in the midst of a painful display of family grief; another advantage is that one need not be immersed in religious pieties that to many people nowadays seem as remote from reality as the Jabberwocky. Nevertheless, they are likely to be intentionally dismal events. Knowing that Charlie would have disliked with equal vehemence either a funeral or a memorial service, his widow decided to give a party instead, organized around a single strong principle: that it be a party that Charlie himself would have liked to attend.

The festivities—no other word will do—took place late one weekday afternoon, in the Celeste Bartos Forum at the New York Public Library. In recent years, the forum has been favored by artists and writers as an agreeable setting in which to bid farewell to dead colleagues. It is a marble-walled chamber with a domed skylight supported on a ring of cast-iron arches—a lilting Beaux Arts confection having far more to do with Paris at the turn of the twentieth century than with New York City in any century. The chamber puts one in mind of those drawings of spidery, glass-roofed European gallerias that Saul Steinberg used to draw forty-odd years ago, when he and Charlie and I were young contributors to *The New Yorker* and were just then becoming fast friends. The setting made it all the more appropriate that Saul should be one of the speakers during the course of the party. As he often does in age (and sometimes did even in youth), Saul's words that afternoon sounded a note of authority that the pope in Rome might well have envied. Because what Saul said was in praise of Charlie's high place as an artist, we had no reason to disagree with him.

The forum chamber had been arranged to resemble a French cabaret, with small tables and folding chairs scattered about and squat votive candles in glass containers burning upon rose-colored tablecloths. Two long, amply stocked bars had been set up in readily accessible corners of the room and were being well patronized. On an improvised wooden platform, a Dixieland band was strutting its stuff. Nor was anyone surprised that the occasion turned out to be one of almost continuous merriment, for merriment was the emotion that Charlie prompted in us as readily as certain other members of the *New Yorker* staff prompted gloom. (It is a notorious fact about people who are funny in print that they often emanate misery in person.) I was about to say that a benignity of spirit always "shone" out of Charlie, but in fact it didn't shine—rather, it smouldered there in the depths of his big, shapeless body and waited not impatiently to be provoked. Charlie's benignity of spirit was in the Bartos Forum that day, as old friends recounted tales of Charlie's adventures and misadventures, and it occurred to me then that for me, a professional writer, remembering the past is a sad-happy act that is also a duty. An ever-increasing army of the dead press all round me; in a sense, they are more importunate than the living, and I have no right to ignore them. Moreover, if one believes, with Wallace Stevens, that "words of the world are the life of the world," then one may also believe (or strive to believe) that words can serve to outwit death. At the least, it is a hypothesis worth testing. Then and there, I sat down at one of the little French cabaret tables and by the light of a votive candle, in a scribble that only I could read, set down the first sentence of this book.

Index

Abramovitz, Max, 152–54, 156
Addams, Barbara, 146
Addams, Charles, 146, 149, 159, 161, 181, 335–37
Agee, James, 286, 302
Alajalov, Constantin, 115
Albert, Prince Consort of England, 142
Aldrich, Chester Holmes, 89–90, 91
Alsop, Corinne, 16, 21
Alsop, Corinne Robinson, 16, 21
Alsop, John, 16, 21
Alsop, Joseph, Jr., 15–22
Alsop, Joseph, Sr., 16, 21
Alsop, Stewart, 16, 18
Ames, Amyas, 65
Anderson, Maxwell, 76, 197–204
Aragon, Louis, 308
Arbuckle, Roscoe "Fatty," 281, 285
Arlen, Michael, 223
Armstrong, Louis, 328
Arno, Peter, 115

Arnold, Matthew, 215
Astor, Nancy Langhorne, Lady, 314
Astor, Mrs. William Waldorf, 188
Atget, Eugène, 125, 302
Atkinson, Brooks, 202
Austen, Jane, 192
Austin, A. Everett, 86
Austin, Lyn, 211
Avedon, Richard, 127
Avery, Milton, 287

Bainbridge, John, 23
Baker, Alfred Pierce, 176
Baker, Josephine, 309
Balzac, Honoré de, 239
Bankhead, Tallulah, 133, 180, 188, 277
Barnard, Frank, 313
Barnard, Madelaine, 313–15
Barney, Natalie, 309, 324
Barry, Ellen Semple, 159, 161,

Barry, Ellen Semple, *continued*
176–78, 181, 320, 324, 328,
330
Barry, Philip, 159–66, 168, 172,
174, 175–81, 313, 324, 328,
330
Barrymore, Ethel, 35, 194, 277
Barrymore, John, 133
Basehart, Richard, 199–202
Baumgarten, Bernice, 199
Baxter, Anne, 113
Bazak, Oya, 184
Beach, Sylvia, 303
Becket, Thomas à, 141
Beckett, J. Campbell, 243
Beckett, Samuel, 183
Beebe, Lucius, 189
Beerbohm, Max, 324
Behan, Beatrice Salkeld, 133,135–
138
Behan, Brendan, 131–39
Behan, Brendan, Jr., 136–37, 138
Behrman, S. N., 199
Bemelmans, Ludwig, 28
Benchley, Robert, 115, 145, 146,
179, 180, 197
Berliawsky, Isaac, 62
Berliawsky, Minna, 62
Berlin, Isaiah, 293
Bernhardt, Sarah, 188
Bernstein, Leonard, 67
Besterman, Theodore Deodatus
Nathaniel, 292–96
Betjeman, John, 69–73, 141
Betts, Judge, 317
Bingham, Charles Tiffany, 188
Bingham, Hiram, 20, 188–89
Bingham, Jonathan, 20
Bodne, Ben, 114–19
Bodne, Mary, 114–19
Bogan, Louise, 288
Booth, Edwin, 26
Boule (Simenon's housekeeper),
241, 242, 245–46, 248

Bowen, Andrew, 225
Bowen, Emma Jane, 224–30
Bowen, Patrick, 225, 229–30
Brady, Mathew B., 302
Brancusi, Constantin, 309
Brandegee, Frank, 20
Brando, Marlon, 192
Brandt, Carl, 198–99
Braque, Georges, 327
Brassaï, 126
Brennan, Maeve, 319–20
Brennan, Robert, 319
Brewer, Joseph, 86
Browning, Robert, 216, 279
Buchwald, Art, 17–18
Buckley, William F., 47
Bulkeley, Bill, 16, 20
Bulkeley, Morgan, 20
Bulkeley, Morgan (grandson), 20
Bush, George, 174
Bush, Prescott, 174
Bushman, Francis X., 284

Calmann, John, 29
Calvin, John, 188, 296
Campbell, Alan, 145
Campbell, Joseph, 46–57
Carey, Pete, 16
Carnegie, Andrew, 161
Carrère, John Mervin, 90
Carter, Lady Violet Bonham, 65
Cartier-Bresson, Henri, 126
Caruso, Enrico, 227
Case, Frank, 117
Case, George, 211
Cather, Willa, 128, 147
Catherine the Great, Empress of
Russia, 293
Channing, Carol, 278
Chaplin, Charlie, 194, 243, 279–
280, 281
Charles, Prince of Wales, 140
Cheever, John, 303, 316

Chesterton, G. K., 141
Chevalier, Maurice, 284
Christo, 307
Church, Frederick, 39
Churchill, Winston, 49–50, 80, 188
Claire, Ina, 115, 194
Clark, Bobby, 277
Clurman, Harold, 199, 200–201
Cocteau, Jean, 310–11
Cohen, Alexander, 278
Cole, Bill, 16
Colette, 233
Colum, Padraic, 120–22
Comden, Betty, 276
Connelly, Marc, 146
Cooke, Alistair, 28
Coolidge, Calvin, 75
Cooper, Gary, 194
Cooper, Lady Diana, 325
Copland, Aaron, 287
Coply, Bill, 310
Corbett, Harvey Wiley, 152, 156
Cornell, Katharine, 200, 277, 318
Cory, William Johnson, 86
Costa-Gavras, 118
Covarrubias, Miguel, 276
Coward, Noël, 194, 217, 318
Cowl, Jane, 277
Cozzens, James Gould, 199, 316
Crane, Hart, 147, 303
Crane, Stephen, 170–71
Cromwell, Oliver, 163
Cromwell, Jarvis, 317
Cronkite, Walter, 51
Cunard, Nancy, 324
Cushing, Mrs. Harvey, 190

da Silva, Howard, 206, 207–8
Davison, F. Trubee, 175–76
Delano, Laura, 81
Delano, William Adams, 88–93, 156

de Liagre, Alfred, Jr., 181, 330
de Rezke, Jean, 227
Devonshire, Andrew R. B. Cavendish, 11th Duke of, 32
Devonshire, Deborah V. Freeman-Mitford, Duchess of, 32, 141–42
De Wint, Peter, 189
De Wolfe, Elsie, 190, 323
Dickens, Charles, 239
Diener, Joan, 205, 206, 208–10
Dietrich, Marlene, 276
Disney, Walt, 173
Donleavy, J. P., 132
Donne, John, 17, 147
Donnelly, Honoria Murphy, 322, 326, 330, 331
Dos Passos, John, 128, 147, 313, 317
Downey, Jim, 136, 138
Doyle, Larry, 189
Drake, Alfred, 276
Draper, Kay, 161
Dreiser, Theodore, 171
Duchamp, Marcel, 307, 308
Ducrot, Nicolas, 127, 129
DuFallo, Richard, 210
Duke, James B., 87
Dunn, Alan, 146
Dunn, Mary Petty, 146
Duveen, Joseph, 102

Eames, Ray, 187
Edel, Leon, 72–73
Edwards, Oliver, 266, 271
Eichelberger, Robert, 188
Eliot, T. S., 309
Elizabeth I, Queen of England, 198
Eluard, Paul, 308
Emerson, Ralph Waldo, 287
Emery, Ruth, 86
Ernst, Max, 310

Evans, Maurice, 277
Evans, Walker, 125, 127, 302–5

Fairbanks, Douglas, 133, 281
Fantin-Latour, Henri, 108
Farrar, John, 175–76
Faulkner, William, 118, 133, 147
Fields, W. C., 194
Firmian, Leopold, 183
Fish, Mrs. Stuyvesant, 27
Fitzgerald, F. Scott, 115, 147,
    166, 167–70, 172, 174, 177,
    179, 195, 312–16
Fitzgerald (Lanahan), Scottie,
    315–17
Fitzgerald, Zelda, 313–16
Flanner, Janet, 168, 309, 324
Flaubert, Gustave, 233
Flynn, Errol, 190, 194
Flynn, "Lefty," 314
Fonda, Henry, 277
Fontanne, Lynn, 194
Forbes, Malcolm, 297
Forrestal, James V., 180
Fouilhoux, André, 156
Franklin, Benjamin, 293
Freedman, Harold, 199, 201
Freud, Sigmund, 17, 49, 50, 78
Frick, Henry Clay, 37
Fuller, Buckminster, 86
Fuller, Constance Greenough
    "Ter," 297–301
Fuller, Samuel, 297, 298
Furness, Betty, 190

Gabel, Martin, 17–18
Gable, Clark, 194
Garbo, Greta, 194, 195
Garden, Mary, 227
Garfield, John, 194
Garland, Judy, 195
Gates, Artemus L., 175–76, 181

Gelderman, Carol, 99
Geldzahler, Henry, 305
Gershwin, George, 328
Getty, Ann, 212
Getty, Gordon, 212
Getty, J. Paul, 37
Gibbs, Wolcott, 173, 200
Gibson, Charles Dana, 314, 324–
    325
Gibson, Irene Langhorne, 314
Gide, André, 241
Gigli, Beniamino, 227
Gilbert, William, 215–16, 323
Gilkey, Stanley, 199
Gill, Eric, 141
Gill, Michael, 321–22
Gimbel, Elinor, 292
Gish, Lillian, 277
Gladstone, William Ewart, 261
Glimcher, Arnold, 61
Godard, Jean-Luc, 118
Goddard, Paulette, 194
Goodhue, Bertram Grosvenor, 152
Goodrich, Lloyd, 272
Grant, Cary, 189–90, 194–95, 200
Greene, Graham, 221
Greenough, Charles Pelham, 297
Gregory, Lady Augusta, 121, 291
Guinness, Alec, 133
Guinzberg, Tom, 65–66
Guitry, Sacha, 275

Hale, Robert Beverly, 305
Hamilton, Gordon, 322
Hammond, Percy, 197
Hanna, Leonard, 216, 323
Harding, Warren G., 75
Harkness, Buffy, 330
Harkness, Edward S., 167, 215
Harrison, Ellen Milton, 152, 158
Harrison, Wallace K., 151–58
Hart, Moss, 188, 217
Hastings, Thomas, 90

Haydon, Julie, 115
Hayes, Roland, 238
Hays, Will H., 285
Heller, Harold, 330
Hellman, Geoffrey, 23, 24, 26, 28, 36
Hellman, Lillian, 149
Hemingway, Ernest, 135, 147, 148, 167–68, 309, 314
Hepburn, Katharine, 179–80, 194
Hill, Oliver, 141
Hirschfeld, Al, 272–78
Hirschfeld, Dolly Haas, 276
Hirschfeld, Isaac, 274
Hirschfeld, Nina, 276
Hirschfeld, Rebecca Rothberg, 274–75
Hitchcock, Henry-Russell, 83–87
Hitler, Adolf, 49–50
Hoffmann, Donald, 112
Hofmann, Hans, 62
Homer, Winslow, 39, 128
Hood, Raymond, 152, 156, 157
Hoover, Herbert, 75
Hope, Bob, 280
Hopper, Hedda, 190
Horne (Sonnenberg's butler), 33
Houdon, Jean Antoine, 295
Howard, Leslie, 277
Howells, William Dean, 128
Hubbell, James, 187
Humes, Harold, 65–66
Hurt, William, 318
Huston, Anjelica, 198
Huston, John, 198
Huston, Walter, 198
Huxley, Aldous, 195, 222, 309

Ingersoll, Ralph, 242–43
Ives, Charles, 210–13
Ives, George, 210
Ives, Harmony Twitchell, 211

Jacobs, Jane, 265
James, Henry, 71, 72–73, 94, 128, 169, 239
James, Henry (nephew), 72–73
James, William, 18, 72
Joan of Arc, 76, 198
John, Augustus, 29, 35
Johnson, Philip, 84, 85, 113, 153
Johnston, John Taylor, 39–40, 41, 44
Jonson, Ben, 248
Joyce, James, 49, 50, 120, 121–122, 303, 309, 335
Jung, Carl Gustav, 49

Kaufmann, Edgar, Jr., 109–13
Kaufmann, Edgar, Sr., 110, 111–112
Keaton, Buster, 279, 281, 283–86
Keaton, Diane, 318
Kennedy, Joseph, 78
Kennedy, Roger, 19
Kennedy, Rose, 78
Kertész, André, 123–130
Kertész, Elizabeth, 126–27, 129–130
Key, Francis Scott, 168, 169, 316
Kiki of Montparnasse, 309
Kiley, Richard, 210
King, Martin Luther, Jr., 149
Kintner, Robert E., 18
Kirstein, Lincoln, 86
Kneeland, Yale, 94–97
Kneller, Godfrey, 189
Koolhaas, Rem, 157

Lanahan, Samuel Jackson, 315–16
Lanahan, Scottie Fitzgerald, 315–317
Lardner, Ring, 147, 179, 313
Larsen, Jonathan, 190
Larsen, Margot, 188

Larson, Brendan, 137
Lash, Joseph P., 76–77, 79, 80
Lauder, Harry, 275
Lawrence, D. H., 118, 133
Lawrence, Gertrude, 188
Lawrence, Henry Effington, 318
Lawrence, Jim, 244–45
Lawrence, Mary, 318
Le Corbusier, 153, 155
Lee, Ivy, 43
Léger, Fernand, 327
LeHand, Missy, 81
Lehman, Robert, 37
l'Enclos, Ninon de, 293
Leonard, Hugh, 184
Lewin, Al, 310
Lewis, S. Wilmarth, 176
Lewis, Sinclair, 173, 309
Lieberman, William, 305
Lind, Jenny, 229–30
Lindfors, Viveca, 276
Lindsay, Michael, 29, 32
Lindsay, Vachel, 175
Littlewood, Joan, 137
Lloyd, Harold, 279–82, 283
Lloyd, Mildred Davis, 280–81
Loeb, John L., 34
Lombard, Carole, 194
Louis II, Prince of Monaco, 235
Louis XIV, King of France, 324
Louis XVI, King of France, 326
Lovett, Robert, 174, 175–76, 177, 181
Lunt, Alfred, 194
Lutyens, Edwin, 296
Lynes, Russell, 287

MacArthur, Douglas, 188
McCarthy, Kevin, 199
McCarthy, Mary, 99–101, 102, 104, 107–8
McClain, John, 145
McClintic, Guthrie, 318

MacDowell, Edward, 287
McIlwaine, Robert, 261
McKim, Charles F., 35, 43, 89, 91, 92
MacLeish, Archibald, 174, 175–176, 317, 322, 324, 329
McManus, Jack, 163
Maeterlinck, Maurice, 233
Mailer, Norman, 118
Mali, Frances Johnston, 40, 42
Mali, Henry T., 39–45, 158
Mali, Katherine Lord Strauss, 43–44, 158
Maney, Richard, 199–200, 202, 275
Mann, Thomas, 49–50
Marbury, Elizabeth, 323
Marcus Aurelius, 159
Markel, Lester, 275–76
Marlowe, Christopher, 175
Marre, Albert, 205, 206, 209–10
Marshall, Benjamin, 103
Martin, George W., 96–97
Martin, Mary, 278
Martinon, Jean, 251
Masefield, John, 175
Maugham, W. Somerset, 221
Maxwell, William, 213
Melba, Nellie, 227
Mellon, Andrew W., 37
Mellon, Paul, 107
Mencken, H. L., 115
Meredith, Burgess, 318
Mielziner, Jo, 199–200, 203–4
Millay, Edna St. Vincent, 148
Miller, Henry, 309, 310
Miller, Kenneth Hayes, 62
Miller, Tee, 335–36
Mitford, Nancy, 141
Montgomery, Robert, 330
Moore, Archie, 67
Moore, Henry, 215
Morgan, Henry, 43
Morgan, J. Pierpont, 89, 91–92

Morrell, Lady Ottoline, 35
Mott, Lucretia Coffin, 43
Mount, Charles Merrill, 35–36
Moyers, Bill, 50–57
Mumford, Lewis, 265
Munnings, Alfred, 103
Murphy, Baoth, 326, 328–29, 330
Murphy, Esther, 323–24
Murphy, Francis Patrick, 321, 325–26, 328
Murphy, Frank, 324
Murphy, Gerald, 168, 174, 175–176, 178, 179, 309, 312–35
Murphy, Noel Haskins, 324
Murphy, Patrick, 326, 328–29, 330
Murphy, Sara Wiborg, 168, 178, 179, 309, 312–35
Murray, Bill, 318

Napoleon I, Emperor of France, 267
Nathan, George Jean, 115
Natwick, Mildred, 199, 277
Nevelson, Charles, 62
Nevelson, Louise, 58–63
Nevelson, Myron, 62
Nichols, Mike, 318
Nicolson, Adam, 260
Nicolson, Ben, 260, 263
Nicolson, Harold, 258–63
Nicolson, Nigel, 257–64
Nicolson, Pippa, 260–61, 262
Nimitz, Chester William, 188
Noguchi, Isamu, 86
Nollekens, Joseph, 29
Norris, Frank, 170–71

O'Connor, Frank, 137
O'Dwyer, Paul, 149
Oenslager, Donald, 181
Oestreicher, Gerard, 205–6, 209–210

Offenbach, Jacques, 205–10, 308
O'Hara, John, 167, 168, 170–76, 181
Oliver, Edith, 183
Olivier, Laurence, 318
Olmstead, Frederick Law, 265
Onassis, Jacqueline Kennedy, 67
O'Neill, Eugene, 147, 166–68, 170, 171, 174
O'Neill, James, 166–67
Ophuls, Max, 118
Orloff, Vladimir, 328
Ortega y Gasset. Josè, 322

Pacino, Al, 277, 318
Paley, Barbara Cushing "Babe," 192
Parker, Dorothy, 144–50, 179
Parker, Horatio, 212
Pendleton, Austin, 184
Penrose, Roland, 307
Perelman, S. J., 276–77, 304–5
Pevsner, Nikolaus, 85
Picasso, Pablo, 125, 309
Pickford, Mary, 194, 281
Picon, Molly, 205
Pirie, Robert, 28
Platt, Charles, 317
Plimpton, Francis T. P., 64–68
Plimpton, George, 64–68
Plimpton, Pauline Ames, 65
Plumb, John, 28
Plunkett, Horace, 71
Poiret, Paul, 310
Pope, Alexander, 29
Porter, Cole, 126, 216–17, 309, 313, 322–23, 328
Pound, Ezra, 309
Power, Tyrone, 194
Prince, Harold, 206
Proust, Marcel, 310–11

Quinn, Anthony, 206

Rainier III, Prince of Monaco, 235
Rand, Ayn, 56–57
Ray, Juliet Browner, 306, 309–10
Ray, Man, 306–11
Reagan, Ronald, 55, 57
Reinhardt, Max, 183, 185
Renoir, Jean, 310
Riddle, Theodate Pope, 83
Rigaut, Jacques, 308
Riggs, T. Lawrason, 216, 323
Robinson, Edwin Arlington, 287
Robinson, Henry Morton, 50
Rockefeller, Abby, 152
Rockefeller, John D., Jr., 152,
    156–57
Rockefeller, John D., Sr., 156
Rockefeller, Nelson A., 155–56
Rohmer, Eric, 118
Roosevelt, Anna, 81
Roosevelt, Eleanor, 16, 74–82
Roosevelt, Franklin Delano, 18,
    74, 77–82, 268, 292
Roosevelt, James, 78
Roosevelt, Sara Delano, 77
Roosevelt, Theodore, 78
Ross, Harold, 114, 174, 316
Rosse, Countess of, 140
Rothschild, Jacob, 140
Roubiliac, Louis-François, 29
Rousuck, Emmanuel Joseph "Jay,"
    98–108
Royce, Josiah, 18
Rubin, William, 327
Rudofsky, Bernard, 253–56
Rutherfurd, Lucy Mercer, 81
Ryskamp, Charles, 28–29, 36–37,
    106

Saarinen, Eero, 153
Sackville-West, Vita, 257–63

St. Gaudens, Augustus, 35, 36
Sardi, Vincent, 276
Sargent, John Singer, 29, 35, 36
Satie, Erik, 307
Sawyer, Diane, 318
Schapiro, Meyer, 288
Schmitt, Robert, 83–84, 86
Scott, Michael, 122
Scott, Randolph, 190
Scully, Vincent, 113
Sedgwick, Edie, 67
Segal, George, 206, 208
Semple, Lorenzo, 177, 178
Shakespeare, William, 94, 175,
    215–16, 248
Shawn, William, 133, 245, 319
Shelley, Percy Bysshe, 279
Shepherd, Sam, 183
Sherman, William Tecumseh, 325
Sherwood, Robert E., 146, 180
Shulman, Max, 316
Sickert, Walter Richard, 29
Silberberg, Daniel H., 260–61,
    263
Silberberg, Dorothy, 260–61, 263
Simenon, Denyse Ouimet, 241–
    242, 246, 247, 249–50
Simenon, Désiré, 232
Simenon, Georges, 231–52
Simenon, Henriette Brull, 232
Simenon, Johnny, 242, 247
Simenon, Marc, 240–42, 247,
    249, 251, 252
Simenon, Marie-Georges "Marie-
    Jo," 249, 250–52
Simenon, Mrs. Georges (first
    wife), 233, 234, 240–42, 246
Simenon, Pierre, 249
Sitwell, Sacheverell, 16
Skulnick, Menasha, 205, 206, 208
Smedley, William T., 59
Smith, Alfred E., 323
Snow, Carmel, 319
Sonnenberg, Benjamin, 23–38,

40, 43, 99, 101
Sonnenberg, Hilda, 33–35
Southern, Terry, 65
Spellacy, Thomas J., 75
Spofford, Charles, 153–54, 155
Stapleton, Maureen, 277
Starett, Goldwyn, 117
Steichen, Edward, 127
Stein, Gertrude, 290, 309, 324
Stein, Jean, 67
Steinberg, Saul, 336
Steloff, Frances, 120
Stendhal, 195
Sterne, Laurence, 29, 89
Stevens, Roger, 202
Stevens, Wallace, 12, 337
Stewart, Donald Ogden, 146, 175–
   176, 313
Stewart, Ellen, 182–86
Stieglitz, Alfred, 308
Stone, Edward Durrell, 156, 157
Stravinsky, Igor, 310
Strong, Roy, 142
Stuart, Gilbert, 36
Stubbs, George, 103
Styron, William, 65–66
Sullivan, Arthur, 215–16, 323
Sullivan, Louis, 56
Sully, Thomas, 29
Sulzberger, Arthur Hays, 276
Swanson, Gloria, 194
Swift, Jonathan, 121
Synge, John Millington, 121

Tagore, Rabindranath, 175
Tanning, Dorothea, 310
Taylor, Harold, 48
Temple, Shirley, 194
Tennyson, Alfred, Lord, 216, 261
Thaw, Harry K., 43
Thomas, Dylan, 137–38
Thomson, Virgil, 39, 86, 287–91
Thoreau, Henry David, 265

Thurber, James, 115, 133
Tissot, James Jacques Joseph, 29
Toklas, Alice B., 309, 324
Tomkins, Calvin, 327
Trefusis, Violet, 262
Truffaut, François, 118
Trumbauer, Horace, 87
Tucker, Helen Sonnenberg, 35
Twain, Mark, 42, 161, 211, 222
Twitchell, Joseph, 211
Tzara, Tristan, 308

Updike, John, 118

Valentino, Rudolph, 281
Vanderlip, Frank, 70
Verity, Simon, 140–43
Victoria, Queen of England, 142
Voltaire, 231, 292–96

Walker, Hale, 330
Walpole, Horace, 293
Walters, Henry, 91–92
Warner, Olin Levi, 204
Waugh, Alec, 220-23
Waugh, Evelyn, 18, 195, 220–22
Webb, Clifton, 217
Weill, Kurt, 198
Weir, J. Alden, 204
Welles, Orson, 318
Welty, Eudora, 18
Wescott, Glenway, 86
West, Jean, 314
West, Nathanael, 195, 222
West, Rebecca, 245
Wharton, Edith, 128, 147, 324
Wheeler, Monroe, 86
Whistler, James, 324
White, E. B., 114, 173
White, Katharine, 114
White, Stanford, 27, 33, 43, 89,

White, Stanford, *continued*
116
Whitehead, Robert, 199, 201–2, 207
Whitman, Walt, 128, 258
Whitney, John Hay "Jock," 177
Whitridge, Arnold, 214–19
Whitridge, Janetta, 216, 217–18
Whittredge, Worthington, 39
Whyte, Jenny Bell, 266
Whyte, William H., Jr., 265–71
Wiborg, Adeline Sherman, 324–325
Wiborg, Frank, 324–25, 329
Wilcox, Collin, 199, 201–3
Wilde, Oscar, 121, 277, 324
Wilder, Thornton, 50, 118, 133, 287
Williams, William Carlos, 309
Willys, Peggy, 29

Wilson, Edmund, 19, 245, 317
Wilson, Woodrow, 74–75
Winchell, Walter, 189
Wittstein, Ed, 208
Wolf, Henry, 127
Woodin, William H., 292
Woolf, Virginia, 262
Woolley, Monty, 216–17, 322, 323
Wright, Frank Lloyd, 56, 84, 143, 110–13, 244
Wright, Olgivanna, 111
Wynn, Ed, 277, 284

Yeats, William Butler, 80, 121, 125, 188, 291, 330

Zerbe, Jerome, 187–96, 145
Zola, Émile, 209